Feminist
Literary Theory

To my husband without whom this
book would not have been possible.

(p. 44)

Feminist
Literary Theory
A Reader

Edited by
Mary Eagleton

Basil Blackwell

First published 1986

Basil Blackwell Ltd
108 Cowley Road, Oxford OX4 1JF, UK

Basil Blackwell Inc.
432 Park Avenue South, Suite 1503,
New York, NY 10016, USA

British Library Cataloguing in Publication Data

Feminist literary theory : a reader.
  1. English literature—History and criticism
  2. Feminism and literature   3. Women critics
  I. Eagleton, Mary
  820.9'9287   PR65.W6

  ISBN 0-631-14804-3
  ISBN 0-631-14805-1 Pbk

Typeset by Pioneer Associates, Perthshire
Printed in Great Britain by Page Bros., Norwich

Contents

3   Gender and Genre

4   Towards Definitions of Feminist Writing

CONTENTS   vii

5   Do Women Write Differently?

Preface

In 1982 I became involved in writing two feminist literature courses for the English section of the college of higher education where I teach. Both courses were designed to introduce students not only to women writers but to the theoretical debates within feminist criticism. The idea for this reader sprang directly from the difficulties I faced in putting together those courses. As I sifted through book after book and article after article I became aware not only of the quantity of feminist literary criticism that has been published over the last 15 to 20 years but also of the absence of any introduction to feminist literary theory. The pedagogic problem confronting me was how to fill that gap, how to offer students some understanding of the theoretical context without involving them in endless hours searching through the back numbers of journals. Since then two surveys of the field have been produced — K. K. Ruthven's *Feminist Literary Studies: An Introduction* (1984) and Toril Moi's *Sexual/Textual Politics: Feminist Literary Theory* (1985). Collections of theoretical essays have also begun to appear — for example, *Making a Difference: Feminist Literary Criticism* (1985), edited by Gayle Greene and Coppélia Kahn, and *The New Feminist Criticism: Essays on Women, Literature and Theory* (1986), edited by Elaine Showalter. This book constitutes the first reader and its aim is to provide in a handy and accessible form key material in the development of a feminist literary theory. The introductions to the chapters set that material within current theoretical debates and suggest, without being too prescriptive, guidelines and interpretations.

I have in mind as my potential readers the women I teach now in higher education and those I have taught in the past in adult education and WEA classes. Students on MA courses in Women's Studies and women outside education who are interested in writing and recent theoretical developments will also find this book useful. My target audience may appear specific but I am aware that, in fact, it is very heterogeneous. It is not simply that women interested in feminist literature reveal the conflicting positions within feminism itself. What is equally evident in the courses that I teach is the profound gap between those women with a high level of feminist consciousness and a keen awareness of critical issues and those women for whom the whole situation is new, strange and intimidating. Thus the political spectrum I encounter in my teaching is wide. Within the same group demands for revolution are voiced alongside demands for increased parliamentary representation for women; the case for separatism is followed by a plea for the gentle conversion of men; women who aim to work in rape crisis talk over coffee to those who are applying for jobs in management.

Large sections of this wider audience have not taken part in theoretical debates. They see theory as either too difficult, or less immediate and enjoyable than reading fiction, or they reject theory altogether as a suspiciously 'male' way of relating to the world. Conversely, most theoreticians, when writing their books and articles, have clearly not had adult education students in mind. My intention in this reader is to intervene, to help in introducing a wider audience to theory and in alerting the theoreticians to the existence of that wider audience. I am motivated in this project by my belief that an engagement with theory is unavoidable; there is no non-theoretical space for women to inhabit. However abstract and intractable theory may seem at times, it is an essential aspect of our liberation.

I am indebted to Julia Mosse for her careful and constructive editorial work, to my students whose responses to some of this material helped to shape my own, to Liz Swainston for her secretarial skills, and to David Pierce for finding so well the balance between shrewd criticism and enthusiastic praise.

Acknowledgements

The editor and publishers acknowledge with thanks permission granted to reproduce in this volume the following material previously published elsewhere.

Excerpt from 'Paradoxes and Dilemmas, the Woman as Writer' in *Women in the Canadian Mosaic*, edited by Gwen Matheson, published by Peter Martin Associates, 1976. Permission to reproduce in this collection applied for. Excerpt from 'Naming the Fictions' by Elizabeth Baines, © Elizabeth Baines, reprinted by permission of the author. Excerpt from Introduction to *Virginia Woolf: Women and Writing* by Michèle Barrett, © Michèle Barrett, reprinted by permission of the publisher, The Women's Press, London. Excerpt from *Women's Oppression Today* by Michèle Barrett, published by Verso/New Left Books, reprinted by permission of the publisher. Excerpt from 'Feminism and the Definition of Cultural Politics' by Michèle Barrett in *Feminism, Culture and Politics*, edited by Rosalind Brunt and Caroline Rowan, published by Lawrence & Wishart Ltd, reprinted by permission. Excerpt from '"Spiritual Whoredom": An Essay on Female Prophets in the Seventeenth Century' by Christine Berg and Philippa Berry in *1642: Literature and Power in the Seventeenth Century*, edited by Francis Barker et al. (Sociology of Literature Conference Proceedings), published by the University of Essex and reprinted by permission. Excerpt from 'Black Woman Talk' by Black Woman Talk Collective reprinted from *Feminist Review*, No. 17, © Black Woman Talk Collective. Excerpts from 'The Laugh of the Medusa' by Hélène Cixous, 'Enslaved Enclave' by Catherine Clément, 'Variations on Common Themes' by the Editorial Collective of *Questions Féministes* and 'What Women's Eyes See' by Viviane Forrester, reprinted from *New French Feminisms: An Anthology*, edited by Elaine Marks and Isabelle de Courtivron (Amherst: University of Massachusetts Press, 1980), copyright © 1980 by the University of Massachusetts Press. Excerpt from '"This Novel Changes Lives": Are Women's Novels Feminist Novels?' by Rosalind Coward in *Feminist Review* No. 5 © Rosalind Coward, reprinted by permission. Excerpt from *Female Desire: Women's Sexuality Today* by Rosalind Coward, published by Grafton Books, a division of the Collins Publishing Group, reprinted by permission of the publisher. Excerpt from 'Representation vs. Communication' by Elizabeth Cowie, Claire Johnston, Cora Kaplan, Mary Kelly, Jacqueline

Rose and Marie Yates in *No Turning Back: Writings from the Women's Liberation Movement 1975—80*, published by The Women's Press, reprinted by permission. Excerpts from 'For the Etruscans: Sexual Difference and Artistic Production — The Debate over a Female Aesthetic' by Rachel Blau DuPlessis and Members of Workshop 9 and 'Language and Revolution' by Domna C. Stanton in *The Future of Difference*, edited by Hester Eisenstein and Alice Jardine, copyright © 1985 by Rutgers, the State University, copyright © 1980 by the Barnard College Women's Center. Excerpts from *Thinking About Women* by Mary Ellmann, published in the UK by Macmillan, London and Basingstoke and in the USA by Harcourt Brace Jovanovich, reprinted here by permission of the publishers. Excerpt from 'Women and Madness: The Critical Phallacy' by Shoshana Felman in *Diacritics*, Volume 5, No. 4 (1975), reprinted by permission of the publisher, Johns Hopkins University Press. Excerpt from *The Madwoman in the Attic: The Woman Writer and the Nineteenth-Century Literary Imagination* by Sandra M. Gilbert and Susan Gubar, published by Yale University Press, reprinted by permission. Excerpt from the Introduction to *Shakespeare's Sisters: Feminist Essays on Women Poets*, edited by Sandra M. Gilbert and Susan Gubar, published by Indiana University Press, reprinted by permission. Excerpt from *The Sexual Fix* by Stephen Heath, published in the UK by Macmillan, London and Basingstoke and in the USA by Shocken Books Inc., © 1982 Stephen Heath, reprinted by permission. Excerpt from *Fantasy: The Literature of Subversion* by Rosemary Jackson, published by Methuen & Co., reprinted by permission. Excerpts from 'The Buried Letter: Feminism and Romanticism in *Villette*' and 'The Difference of View' by Mary Jacobus, and 'Towards a Feminist Poetics' by Elaine Showalter (© Elaine Showalter) in *Women Writing and Writing About Women*, edited by Mary Jacobus, published by Croom Helm Limited and reprinted by permission of the publisher. Excerpt from 'Writing the Body: Toward an Understanding of L'Ecriture Féminine' by Ann Rosalind Jones in *Feminist Studies*, Volume 7, No. 2 (Summer 1981): 247—63, reprinted here by permission of the publisher, Feminist Studies, Inc., c/o Women's Studies Program, University of Maryland, College Park, MD 20742. Excerpt from 'Speaking/Writing/Feminism' by Cora Kaplan in *On Gender and Writing* edited by Michelene Wandor, published by Routledge and Kegan Paul PLC 1983, reprinted by permission of the publisher. Excerpt from the Introduction to Elizabeth Barrett Browning, *Aurora Leigh and Other Poems* by Cora Kaplan, published by The Women's Press, London, reprinted by permission of the author. Excerpt from the Introduction to *Daring to Dream* by Carol Farley Kessler, published by Routledge & Kegan Paul PLC 1984, reprinted by permission. Excerpt from 'Dancing Through the Minefield' by Annette Kolodny in *Feminist Studies*, Volume 6, No. 1 (Spring 1980), © Annette Kolodny, 1980; all rights reserved, reprinted by permission. Excerpt from 'Feminism and the Literary Critic' by Alison Light in *LTP: Journal of Literature, Teaching, Politics* reprinted by permission of the author. Excerpt from '"Returning to Manderley" — Romance Fiction, Female Sexuality and Class' by Alison Light in *Feminist Review*, 16 (1984), reprinted by permission of the author.

Excerpt from 'Writing Like a Woman: A Question of Politics' by Terry Lovell in *The Politics of Theory*, edited by Francis Barker et al. (Sociology of Literature Conference Proceedings), published by the University of Essex, reprinted by permission. Excerpt from 'New Directions for Black Feminist Criticism' by Deborah E. McDowell, copyright © 1980 by Deborah E. McDowell and *Black American Literature Forum*, reprinted by permission of the author and the publisher. Excerpt from 'Women's Writing: *Jane Eyre, Shirley, Villette, Aurora Leigh*' by Marxist-feminist Literature Collective in *1848: The Sociology of Literature* edited by Francis Barker et al. (Sociology of Literature Conference Proceedings), published by the University of Essex, reprinted by permission. Excerpt from *Women: The Longest Revolution* by Juliet Mitchell, published in the UK by Virago Press Ltd, copyright © 1984 by Juliet Mitchell and in the USA by Pantheon Books, a division of Random House, Inc., reprinted by permission. Excerpts from *Literary Women* by Ellen Moers, copyright © 1963, 1972, 1973, 1974, 1975, 1976, 1977 by Ellen Moers, reprinted by permission of the author and the publishers, W. H. Allen & Co PLC (UK) and Doubleday and Company, Inc., (USA). Excerpts from *Sexual/Textual Politics: Feminist Literary Theory* by Toril Moi, published by Methuen & Co, reprinted by permission. Excerpt from 'Sexual/Textual Politics' by Toril Moi in *The Politics of Theory*, edited by Francis Barker et al. (Sociology of Literature Conference Proceedings), published by the University of Essex, reprinted by permission. Excerpt from 'Is There a Female Voice?' by Joyce Carol Oates in *Women and Literature Volume I, Gender and Literary Voice*, edited by Janet Todd, reprinted by permission of Holmes & Meier Publishers, Inc., New York, NY, copyright © 1980. Excerpt from 'Emily Brontë in the Hands of Male Critics' by Carol Ohmann in *College English*, Volume 32, No. 8, May 1971, copyright © 1986 by the National Council of Teachers of English, reprinted by permission of the publisher and the author. Excerpts from *Silences* by Tillie Olsen, copyright © Tillie Olsen 1965, 1972, 1978, reprinted by permission of the publishers, Virago Press Ltd (UK) and Delacorte Press/Seymour Lawrence (USA). Excerpt from 'Women and Creativity: The Demise of the Dancing Dog' by Cynthia Ozick in *Woman in Sexist Society: Studies in Power and Powerlessness*, edited by Vivian Gornick and Barbara K. Moran, © 1971 by Basic Books, Inc., Publishers, reprinted by permission of the publisher. Excerpt from 'Women Read the Romance: The Interaction of Text and Context' by Janice A. Radway, in *Feminist Studies*, Volume 9, No. 1 (1983): 53—78, reprinted by permission of the publisher, Feminist Studies Inc., c/o Women's Studies Program, University of Maryland, College Park, MD 20742. Excerpt from 'American Feminist Literary Criticism: A Bibliographical Introduction' by Cheri Register in *Feminist Literary Criticism: Explorations in Theory*, edited by Josephine Donovan, published by the University Press of Kentucky, copyright © 1975 by The University Press of Kentucky, reprinted by permission. Excerpt from 'Compulsory Heterosexuality and Lesbian Existence' by Adrienne Rich, copyright © 1980 by Adrienne Rich in *The Signs Reader: Women, Gender and Scholarship*, edited by Elizabeth Abel and Emily K. Abel, published by University of Chicago Press 1983, copyright © 1983 by University of Chicago Press. Excerpts from 'When We Dead Awaken: Writing as Re-Vision' from *On Lies, Secrets, and Silence: Selected Prose 1966–1978* by Adrienne Rich, reprinted by permission of the author and the publisher, W. W. Norton & Company, Inc., copyright © 1979 by W. W. Norton & Company Inc. Excerpt from *Feminist Literary Studies: an introduction* by K. K. Ruthven, published by Cambridge University Press, reprinted by permission of the publisher. Excerpt from *A Literature of Their Own: British Women Novelists from Brontë to Lessing* by Elaine Showalter, copyright © 1977 by Princeton University Press; excerpt pp. 10–16 reprinted by permission of Princeton University Press. Excerpt from 'Toward a Black Feminist Criticism' by Barbara Smith in *Conditions Two*, Volume 1, No. 2, October 1977, © Barbara Smith, reprinted by permission of the author. Excerpt from 'Mass Market Romance: Pornography for Women Is Different' by Ann Barr Snitow in *Radical History Review*, No. 20, Spring/Summer 1979, reprinted by permission. Excerpt from 'French Feminism in an International Frame' by Gayatri Chakravorty Spivak in *Yale French Studies*, 62 (1981), reprinted by permission of author and publisher. Excerpts from *In Search of Our Mothers' Gardens* by Alice Walker, published by The Women's Press (UK) and Harcourt Brace Jovanovich (USA) reprinted by permission of the author and publisher. Excerpt from 'The Impact of Feminism on the Theatre' by Michelene Wandor in *Feminist Review*, No. 18, reprinted by permission of the author. Excerpt from *The Rise of the Novel* by Ian Watt, published by Chatto & Windus, The Hogarth Press, reprinted by permission of the author and publisher. Excerpt from *Mirror Writing: An Autobiography* by Elizabeth Wilson, published by Virago Press Ltd, 1982, copyright © Elizabeth Wilson 1982, reprinted by permission. Excerpts from *A Room of One's Own*, and 'Professions for Women' in *The Death of a Moth and Other Essays* by Virginia Woolf, published by Chatto & Windus, The Hogarth Press (UK) and Harcourt Brace Jovanovich (USA), reprinted by permission of the author's literary estate and the publishers. Excerpt from 'What Has Never Been: An Overview of Lesbian Feminist Literary Criticism' by Bonnie Zimmerman in *Feminist Studies*, Volume 7, No. 3 (Fall 1981): 451–75, reprinted by permission of the publisher, Feminist Studies Inc., c/o Women's Studies Program, University of Maryland, College Park, MD 20742.

1

Finding a Female Tradition

INTRODUCTION

Breaking the Silence

It is the women's movement, part of the other movements of our time for a fully human life, that has brought this forum into being; kindling a renewed, in most instances a first-time, interest in the writings and writers of our sex.

Linked with the old, resurrected classics on women, this movement in three years has accumulated a vast new mass of testimony, of new comprehensions as to what it is to be female. Inequities, restrictions, penalties, denials, leechings have been painstakingly and painfully documented; damaging differences in circumstances and treatment from that of males attested to; and limitations, harms, a sense of wrong, voiced.[1]

Tillie Olsen's essay, from which this quotation comes, was first published in 1972 and, later, became part of a volume entitled *Silences*. Both the date and the title are significant. English and American feminist critics in the 1970s were preoccupied with the idea that women writers had been silenced, by and large excluded from literary history. Olsen's quotation exemplifies the key interests of many feminist critics at that time — the desire to rediscover the lost work of women writers, while providing a context that would be supportive of contemporary women writers, and the wish to manifest 'what it is to be female', to declare the experience and perceptions that have been unheard. Aware that critical attention concentrated mostly on male writers, these critics demanded a status and recognition for women authors. But the aim was not simply to fit women into the male-dominated tradition; they also wanted to write the history of a tradition *among* women themselves. The extracts from Ellen Moers and Elaine Showalter, building on the earlier work of Virginia Woolf, reveal the affinity which women writers have felt for each other, the interest — sometimes encouraging, sometimes anxiously competitive — that they have taken in each other's work, the way the writing of one might prepare the ground for another, the problems all faced, and still face, in handling the institutions of literary production. The expansion of feminist literary criticism and, particularly in America, of courses about women's writing, and the establishment of feminist publishing houses or feminist lists within existing houses introduced to readers an extensive new area of work: a teacher could no longer use the 'lack of material' argument to explain the absence of women writers from a course.

Showalter offers two cautionary notes. Firstly, she questions Moers's use of the term 'movement', which rather suggests a steady and continuous development in women's writing, and mentions the 'holes and hiatuses', the absences, gaps and disruptions which have broken that history. Though no writer ever enjoys continuous critical acclaim, Showalter agrees with Germaine Greer that women writers tend to disappear more easily from literary history, leaving their sisters bereft and struggling to reconstruct the lost tradition. Secondly, Showalter considers that the notion of a 'female imagination' can confirm the belief in 'a deep, basic, and inevitable difference between male and female ways of perceiving the world'. Such 'essentialist' or 'biologistic' beliefs imply that there is something intrinsic in the experience of being female and thus render gender biological rather than cultural; they tend to privilege gender at the expense of class or race; and they can too easily become ahistorical and apolitical, presuming an unproblematic unity among women across culture, class and history.

At the same time, it is necessary to stress that the search for women writers has constituted an important political challenge. To ask the questions — Where are the women writers? What has aided or inhibited their writing? How has criticism responded to their work? — introduces into literary criticism the determinant of gender and exposes literary tradition as a construct. The popular idea that 'talent will out', that 'great' writers will spontaneously and inevitably reveal their quality is shown to be false. To the questioning from Marxist criticism about the class bias of the literary tradition are added feminist queries about its androcentricity. What are proposed by mainstream criticism as impartial and objective academic judgements now look, to feminists, value-laden and ideologically suspect.

Who Belongs to the Female Tradition?

Feminists researching the female tradition constantly emphasize both the amount and the variety of material to be uncovered — as Olsen says, 'a vast new mass of testimony'. Ironically, however, the contents of books purporting to deal with this extensive tradition often display a very narrow and homogeneous literary production, chiefly that of white, middle-class, heterosexual (or presented as heterosexual) women, living in England and America during the nineteenth and twentieth centuries. This description would apply to many of the critical works produced in America in the late 1960s and throughout the 1970s, books which are considered founding texts in feminist literary criticism: Mary Ellmann's *Thinking About Women* (1968), Patricia Meyer Spacks's *The Female Imagination* (1975), Ellen Moers's *Literary Women* (1976), Elaine Showalter's *A Literature of Their Own: British Women Novelists from Brontë to Lessing* (1977). Lesbians, both black and white, and heterosexual women of colour criticize white heterosexual feminists for creating a literary history which is almost as selective and ideologically bound as the male tradition. Sexism is challenged in the white, heterosexual work but heterosexism or homophobia or racism or ethnocentricity may not be. All the faults of male critics with respect to women's writing generally are reproduced by some feminist critics with respect to lesbian or black writing. There is the failure to recognize difference, the presumption that what is said about white, heterosexual women's writing will count for all women. Thus critical texts often establish an unconscious and unarticulated complicity between author and reader that the world is white and heterosexual. Black critics, for example, complain that the female stereotypes which so preoccupy white feminists — the Southern belle, or the Angel in the House, or the submissive wife — simply do not apply to them, though they are offered in the criticism as the dominant stereotypes and as widely relevant.[2] Where writing from a different position does exist its place is usually marginal — the odd paragraph, the single essay.

Bonnie Zimmerman, Adrienne Rich and Alice Walker have had to seek out their own traditions, looking for names, for a history, for foremothers. In so doing they dispute the dominant literary values and expose the heterosexism and racism both within and without the women's movement. Rich's emphasis on the *political* importance of lesbianism and on heterosexuality as an institution challengingly moves the debate beyond the level of liberal pluralism. Lesbianism exists not as 'sexual preference' or an 'alternative life style' or as the choice of a minority group but as a fundamental critique of the dominant order and as an organizing principle for women. It is notable, though, that the determinant of class in women's writing continues to be largely ignored. The same critics who are taken to task for their lack of awareness about heterosexism or racism can be accused very often also of a class blindness; dozens of nineteenth-century women novelists are discussed with little more than a passing reference to their class positions. Equally, critics studying the work of lesbians or women of colour frequently write as if class does not exist, as if sexual orientation and colour are the only factors to be considered. Among American critics, Tillie Olsen emerges as an early honourable exception, her lifetime involvement in working-class politics generating a strong class consciousness. In England, the Marxist-feminist Literature Collective has attempted to marry class and gender in an understanding of women's writing, an approach which several members of the collective have developed further in their subsequent individual work.[3]

New Wine in Old Bottles?

Michèle Barrett alerts us to another danger in creating a female tradition, namely that feminists may continue to employ aesthetic concepts that are compromised and intrinsically linked with the very social order they wish to undermine. To talk of the female tradition of writing can reinforce the canonical view, which looks upon literary history as a continuum of significant names. Rather than disrupting the individualistic values by which the mainstream canon has been created, feminist critics sometimes merely replace a male First Eleven with a female one: so you study Aphra Behn instead of Dryden, Edith Wharton instead of Henry James, Dorothy Wordsworth instead of William. The very approach which has always seemed to find the majority of women writers lacking is transposed, uncritically, to a separate female tradition, and the humanist ethic which supports that approach is often accepted as basically valid, merely in need of extending its franchise.

The hierarchical nature of the mainstream canon and the tendency in conventional criticism to rank writers as 'great', 'good', or 'mediocre' has also proved awkward for feminist literary criticism. Eager to establish women writers and sensitive to dismissive criticism, feminists have often overcompensated; 'good' or 'mediocre' does not exist; all women writers are 'great'. For feminist publishing companies every reprinted book is a forgotten 'classic', guaranteed to rival *War and Peace*. Yet, although reluctant to rank our own writers, feminists have become embroiled, according to Michèle Barrett, in a fruitless competition with the male tradition. Such criticism argues either that women have not reached the standard of men because they have not been allowed to, or, alternatively, that they have reached the standard of male writers but their work has not been valued. In either case it is the male-dominated tradition which is taken as the reference point for women's writing.

Though we may dismiss the crude ranking of authors — a feminist Top Ten — and the futility of competing with the male tradition, this does not solve the problem of aesthetic value. Why do we find certain works more pleasurable, relevant, important than others? Barrett would say that the first need is to define the 'we'. Aesthetic value is not universal, or eternal; it does not reside within the text. Rather, it is culturally and historically specific, produced in the act of reading. In one sense feminists instinctively realize this. We recognize that the books we hold dear are not always prized by the literary establishment; hence these books cannot have an intrinsic quality to be perceived by *every* reader. On the other hand, the wish to establish a female tradition alongside and 'as good as' the male tradition can lead to idealist claims that underplay the materialist analysis of literature and ignore difference. Theoretically, a materialist politics should offer a real possibility for women who are non-white or lesbian or working class or any combination of the three. If the critic believes that race, sexual orientation and class are important constituents of writing, then a criticism which recognizes difference and represents more than a small privileged group of women becomes possible.

The French Perspective

The last three extracts in this chapter speak from a very different position. They all derive from recent developments in French feminist theory that have attempted to relate ideas from philosophy, linguistics and psycho-analysis. One of the presumptions of the Anglo-American criticism is that there definitely is a female tradition, buried like hidden treasure in literary history — Showalter refers to it as like the lost continent of Atlantis, rising from the sea — and that the task of the feminist critic is to dig it out, brush it down and exhibit it. The French perspective, as the Viviane Forrester passage indicates, contends that we cannot know what women are. The feminine is that which has been repressed and women's vision — in Forrester's case with regard to film — is only evident in 'what you don't see', what is absent. While Anglo-American critics are looking for women in history, French women writers, Elaine Marks tells us, are:

> looking for women in the unconscious, which is to say in their own language. "Cherchez la femme" might be one of their implied mottos; where repression is, she is.[4]

Thus, although we may uncover a whole list of forgotten novels by women or films with female directors, feminists of this school are unwilling to see that as necessarily a female tradition. They want to put the series of questions that Shoshana Felman asks. Are these novelists and directors speaking as women or are they 'speaking the language of men'? Can they be said to be speaking as women simply because they are born female? To bring the point painfully close to home, is Margaret Thatcher speaking as a woman or is she merely the ventriloquist's dummy for the male voice?

Felman's questions raise a further issue echoed by Gayatri Chakravorty Spivak's work. The problem is not only who is speaking and how is she speaking but to whom is she speaking and on behalf of whom is she speaking. Spivak stresses a double focus:

> not merely who am I? but who is the other woman? How am I naming her? How does she name me?

Such questioning offers interesting insights into the problems of constructing a female tradition. The possibility for some feminists to speak, without awareness, from a highly privileged position must result, in part, from not asking the question, 'Who am I?'; the neglect of the non-white, or working-class, or lesbian perspective must relate to the failure to ask, 'To whom am I speaking?'; and the tendency to universalize, to make claims on behalf of all women, must mean that Felman's anxiety about women as 'the silent and subordinate object' that is 'spoken for', has not been fully heeded. Spivak extends the context of this argument further beyond our own countries to the women of the Third World. How are the academic First World feminist and the illiterate Indian woman to speak together with understanding, without patronage, without exploitation, with a full recognition of both community and diversity? Spivak does not reject out of hand the historical approach or the textual analysis of the Anglo-American critics; indeed, it is partly for her lack of attention to these aspects that she criticizes Julia Kristeva. But it is to French feminist theory and to a politics of desire and women's sexual pleasure that Spivak chiefly looks for her answers — and that is an approach I shall consider more fully in the final chapter.

NOTES

1 Tillie Olsen, *Silences* (New York, Dell, 1978), p. 23.
2 See Deborah E. McDowell, 'New Directions for Black Feminist Criticism', in *Black American Literature Forum 14*, 1980. Also Andrea B. Rushing, 'Images of Black Women in Modern African Poetry: An Overview' in Roseann P. Bell, Bettye J. Parker, Beverly Guy-Sheftall, *Sturdy Black Bridges: Visions of Black Women in Literature* (New York, Anchor/Doubleday, 1979). Also Alice Walker, 'A Letter of the Times, or Should this Sado-Masochism Be Saved?' in *You Can't Keep A Good Woman Down* (New York, Harcourt Brace Jovanovich, 1982).
3 An extract from the Marxist-feminist Literature Collective, outlining its approach, is to be found in Ch. 4, p. 194. Examples of the work of three of the Collective's members — Cora Kaplan, Mary Jacobus and Michèle Barrett — are also included elsewhere in this book.
4 Elaine Marks, 'Women and Literature in France', in *Signs: Journal of Women in Culture and Society*, vol. 3, no. 4 (1978), p. 836.

VIRGINIA WOOLF
A Room of One's Own

And with Mrs. Behn we turn a very important corner on the road. We leave behind, shut up in their parks among their folios, those solitary great ladies who wrote without audience or criticism, for their own delight alone. We come to town and rub shoulders with ordinary people in the streets. Mrs. Behn was a middle-class woman with all the plebeian virtues of humour, vitality and courage; a woman forced by the death of her husband and some unfortunate adventures of her own to make her living by her wits. She had to work on equal terms with men. She made, by working very hard, enough to live on. The importance of that fact outweighs anything that she actually wrote, even the splendid 'A Thousand Martyrs I have made,' or 'Love in Fantastic Triumph sat,' for here begins the freedom of the mind, or rather the possibility that in the course of time the mind will be free to write what it likes. For now that Aphra Behn had done it, girls could go to their parents and say, You need not give me an allowance; I can make money by my pen. Of course the answer for many years to come was, Yes, by living the life of Aphra Behn! Death would be better! and the door was slammed faster than ever. That profoundly interesting subject, the value that men set upon women's chastity and its effect upon their education, here suggests itself for discussion, and might provide an interesting book if any student at Girton or Newnham cared to go into the matter. Lady Dudley, sitting in diamonds among the midges of a Scottish moor, might serve for frontispiece. Lord Dudley, *The Times* said when Lady Dudley died the other day, 'a man of cultivated taste and many accomplishments, was benevolent and bountiful, but whimsically despotic. He insisted upon his wife's wearing full dress, even at the remotest shooting-lodge in the Highlands; he loaded her with gorgeous jewels,' and so on, 'he gave her everything — always excepting any measure of responsibility.' Then Lord Dudley had a stroke and she nursed him and ruled his estates with supreme competence for ever after. That whimsical despotism was in the nineteenth century too.

But to return. Aphra Behn proved that money could be made by writing at the sacrifice, perhaps, of certain agreeable qualities; and so by degrees writing became not merely a sign of folly and a distracted mind, but was of practical importance. A husband might die, or some disaster overtake the family. Hundreds of women began as the eighteenth century drew on to add to their pin money, or to come to the rescue of their families by making translations or writing the innumerable bad novels which have ceased to be recorded even in text-books, but are to be picked up in the fourpenny boxes in the Charing Cross Road. The extreme activity of mind which showed itself in the later eighteenth century among women — the talking, and the meeting, the writing of essays on Shakespeare, the translating of the classics — was founded on the solid fact that women could make money by writing. Money dignifies what is frivolous if unpaid for. It might still be well to sneer at 'blue stockings with an itch for scribbling,' but it could not be denied that they could put money in their purses. Thus, towards the end of the eighteenth century a change came about which, if I were rewriting history, I should describe more fully and think of greater importance than the Crusades or the Wars of the Roses. The middle-class woman began to write. For if *Pride and Prejudice* matters, and *Middlemarch* and *Villette* and *Wuthering Heights* matter, then it matters far more than I can prove in an hour's discourse that women generally, and not merely the lonely aristocrat shut up in her country house among her folios and her flatterers, took to writing. Without those forerunners, Jane Austen and the Brontës and George Eliot could no more have written than Shakespeare could have written without Marlowe, or Marlowe without Chaucer, or Chaucer without those forgotten poets who paved the ways and tamed the natural savagery of the tongue. For masterpieces are not single and solitary births; they are the outcome of many years of thinking in common, of thinking by the body of the people, so that the experience of the mass is behind the single voice. Jane Austen should have laid a wreath upon the grave of Fanny Burney, and George Eliot done homage to the robust shade of Eliza Carter — the valiant old woman who tied a bell to her bedstead in order that she might wake early and learn Greek. All women together ought to let flowers fall upon the tomb of Aphra Behn which is, most scandalously but rather appropriately, in Westminster Abbey, for it was she who earned them the right to speak their minds. It is she — shady and amorous as she was — who makes it not quite fantastic for me to say to you tonight: Earn five hundred a year by your wits.

ELLEN MOERS
Literary Women

We dwell with satisfaction upon the poet's difference from her predecessors, especially her immediate predecessors: we endeavor to find something that can be isolated in order to be enjoyed. Whereas if we approach a poet without this prejudice we shall often find that not only the best, but the most individual parts of her work may be those in which the dead poets, her ancestors, assert their immortality most vigorously.

— T. S. Eliot

I

To be a woman writer long meant, may still mean, belonging to a literary movement apart from but hardly subordinate to the mainstream: an undercurrent, rapid and powerful. The word 'movement' gives an inaccurate idea of an association often remote and indirect. To use the word George Sand imposed, and speak of a 'solidarity' of women, would also be misleading, for writing women have never felt much of a sentimental loyalty to their own kind — quite the contrary. The harshest criticism of trashy books by lady writers came from women writers themselves; sometimes, as in the case of Elizabeth Rigby's famous review of *Jane Eyre*, they denounced books that were not trashy at all. George Eliot's 'Silly Novels by Lady

Novelists' of 1856 is the classic of the genre, as well as one of the funniest pieces of serious criticism ever written; but long before, in 1789, there was Mary Wollstonecraft's swift dispatch of one of the worst specimens of female pap that she encountered as a reviewer with the line, 'Pray Miss, write no more!'

Not loyalty but confidence was the resource that women writers drew from the possession of their own tradition. And it was a confidence that until very recently could come from no other source. Male writers have always been able to study their craft in university or coffeehouse, group themselves into movements or coteries, search out predecessors for guidance or patronage, collaborate or fight with their contemporaries. But women through most of the nineteenth century were barred from the universities, isolated in their own homes, chaperoned in travel, painfully restricted in friendship. The personal give-and-take of the literary life was closed to them. Without it, they studied with a special closeness the works written by their own sex, and developed a sense of easy, almost rude familiarity with the women who wrote them.

When fame at last propelled Charlotte Brontë to London and gave her the opportunity to meet her greatest male contemporaries, she exhibited an awkwardness and timidity in literary society that have become legendary — except in one encounter, that with Harriet Martineau, to whom she sent a brusquely confident note soliciting a meeting. 'I could not help feeling a strong wish to see you,' she wrote; '. . . It would grieve me to lose this chance of seeing one whose works have so often made her the subject of my thoughts.' And George Eliot could write in her first letter to Harriet Beecher Stowe, though they had not and would not ever meet, that she knew her as a woman as well as a writer, for she had years before taken the liberty, rude but comprehensible, of reading Mrs. Stowe's intimate correspondence with another woman. Later Stowe and George Eliot would correspond about the source of Casaubon in *Middlemarch*; their letters provide a tragicomedy of mutual misunderstanding about each other's married life, but they also reveal that there is a human component to literature which a woman writer can more easily discuss with another woman writer, even across an ocean, than she can with the literary man next door.

Emily Dickinson's literary solitude was breached by the incorporeal presence of women writers she knew exclusively but intimately from reading their works and everything she could find about their lives. Jack Capps calls it an 'intimate kinship,' and the phrase is excellent, because it suggests a family relationship which can be either hostile or loving, competitive or supportive, but is always available. Through the closed doors and narrow windows that so often shut on the literary woman's life seeped a whole family of literary relationships for her to exploit: patterns to be followed, deficiencies to be made up, abuses to correct, achievements in works by other women to surpass. What was supplied for the nourishment of male literary production by simple acquaintance was replaced for women writers by the reading of each other's work, reading for intimate reverberation, for what Gertrude Stein called 'a sounding board.'

Take Jane Austen on the one hand, and her contemporaries Wordsworth, Coleridge, and Southey on the other. Wordsworth went to Bristol to meet Coleridge; both were Cambridge men, and they had university friends in common. At Bristol, Wordsworth found Coleridge rooming with an Oxford undergraduate named Southey: they were planning to emigrate to America. Instead, Wordsworth and Coleridge drew close together, settled near each other in the Lake District, and collaborated on a volume which made history, called *Lyrical Ballads*. Meanwhile Jane Austen, almost exactly the same age and from a similar social milieu (had she been a man, she would probably have gone to university), stayed home with her mother at Steventon, Bath, and Chawton. She visited a brother's family now and then, wrote letters to sister and nieces, and read Sarah Harriet Burney, Mrs. Jane West, Anna Maria Porter, Mrs. Anne Grant, Elisabeth Hamilton, Laetitia Matilda Hawkins, Helen Maria Williams, and the rest of the women writers of her day.

'I think I may boast myself to be, with all possible vanity,' she once said, 'the most unlearned and uninformed female who ever dared to be an authoress.' Scholars have industriously scraped together evidence that softens if it does not essentially alter this self-portrait; for Austen of course knew something of the major English writers from Shakespeare to Johnson and read the best poetry of her day. But scholarship has averted its refined and weary eyes from the female fiction that Austen's letters inform us was her daily sustenance in the years that she became one of the greatest writers in the language. Who wants to associate the great Jane Austen, companion of Shakespeare, with someone named Mary Brunton? Who wants to read or indeed can find a copy of *Self-Control* (1810) by that lady, which Austen was nervous about reading while revising *Sense and Sensibility* for publication and starting *Mansfield Park*, nervous because she was 'always half afraid of finding a clever novel *too clever* — and of finding my own story and my own people all forestalled.' She did, however, read and reread the Brunton book, and said (jokingly), 'I will redeem my credit . . . by writing a close imitation of "Self-Control" . . . I will improve upon it.'

It can be argued that Jane Austen achieved the classical perfection of her fiction because there was a mass of women's novels, excellent, fair, and wretched, for her to study and improve upon. Mary Brunton and the rest of the ladies were her own kind; she was at ease with them. They were her undergraduate fellows in the novel, her literary roommates and incorporeal collaborators, as someone like Walter Scott could never be. Austen's comment on Scott, when she learned he had turned to the then woman-dominated field of fiction, was wickedly female but also half-serious. 'Walter Scott has no business to write novels, especially good ones. — It is not fair. — He has Fame and Profit enough as a Poet, and should not be taking the bread out of other people's mouths. — I do not like him, & do not mean to like Waverley if I can help it — but fear I must.' The fact is that Austen studied Maria Edgeworth more attentively than Scott, and Fanny Burney more than Richardson; and she came closer to meeting Mme de Staël than she did to meeting any of the literary men of her age.

In the case of some women writers, Austen preeminent among them, women's literature has been their major tradition; in the case of others — and I think quality has nothing to do with the difference — it has mattered hardly at all: here Emily Brontë's name comes to mind. In the case of most women writers, women's traditions have been fringe benefits superadded upon the literary associations of period, nation, and class that they shared with their male contemporaries.

In spite of the advent of coeducation, which by rights should have ended this phenomenon, twentieth-century women appear to benefit still from their membership in the wide-spreading family of women writers. Willa Cather, exceptionally well trained to literature in the educational, and journalistic institutions of a man's world, found her literary mentor in Sarah Orne Jewett; in that relationship sex easily canceled out the distance between Nebraska and Maine. Even wider incongruities appear in the productive pairings of Jean Rhys and Charlotte Brontë, Carson McCullers and Isak Dinesen, Nathalie Sarraute and Ivy Compton-Burnett. And the last provided, in her first novel, *Dolores*, the oddest exhibit that women's literature has to offer: a groping retrieval of what could be made modern in Austen and Gaskell, necessary to Compton-Burnett's development of her own apparently idiosyncratic fictional manner.

ELAINE SHOWALTER
A Literature of Their Own

As the works of dozens of women writers have been rescued from what E. P. Thompson calls 'the enormous condescension of posterity,'[16] and considered in relation to each other, the lost continent of the female tradition has risen like Atlantis from the sea of English literature. It is now becoming clear that, contrary to Mill's theory, women have had a literature of their own all along. The woman novelist, according to Vineta Colby, was 'really neither single nor anomalous,' but she was also more than a 'register and a spokesman for her age.'[17] She was part of a tradition that had its origins before her age, and has carried on through our own.

Many literary historians have begun to reinterpret and revise the study of women writers. Ellen Moers sees women's literature as an international movement, 'apart from, but hardly subordinate to the mainstream: an undercurrent, rapid and powerful. This "movement" began in the late eighteenth century, was multinational, and produced some of the greatest literary works of two centuries, as well as most of the lucrative pot-boilers.'[18] Patricia Meyer Spacks, in *The Female Imagination*, finds that 'for readily discernible historical reasons women have characteristically concerned themselves with matters more or less peripheral to male concerns, or at least slightly skewed from them. The differences between traditional female preoccupations and roles and male ones make a difference in female writing.'[19] Many other critics are beginning to agree that when we look at women writers collectively we can see an imaginative continuum, the recurrence of certain patterns, themes, problems, and images from generation to generation.

This book is an effort to describe the female literary tradition in the English novel from the generation of the Brontës to the present day, and to show how the development of this tradition is similar to the development of any literary subculture. Women have generally been regarded as 'sociological chameleons,' taking on the class, lifestyle, and culture of their male relatives. It can, however, be argued that women themselves have constituted a subculture within the framework of a larger society, and have been unified by values, conventions, experiences, and behaviors impinging on each individual. It is important to see the female literary tradition in these broad terms, in relation to the wider evolution of women's self-awareness and to the ways in which any minority group finds its direction of self-expression relative to a dominant society, because we cannot show a pattern of deliberate progress and accumulation. It is true, as Ellen Moers writes, that 'women studied with a special closeness the works written by their own sex';[20] in terms of influences, borrowings, and affinities, the tradition is strongly marked. But it is also full of holes and hiatuses, because of what Germaine Greer calls the 'phenomenon of the transience of female literary fame'; 'almost uninterruptedly since the Interregnum, a small group of women have enjoyed dazzling literary prestige during their own lifetimes, only to vanish without trace from the records of posterity.'[21] Thus each generation of women writers has found itself, in a sense, without a history, forced to rediscover the past anew, forging again and again the consciousness of their sex. Given this perpetual disruption, and also the self-hatred that has alienated women writers from a sense of collective identity, it does not seem possible to speak of a 'movement.'

I am also uncomfortable with the notion of a 'female imagination.' The theory of a female sensibility revealing itself in an imagery and form specific to women always runs dangerously close to reiterating the familiar stereotypes. It also suggests permanence, a deep, basic, and inevitable difference between male and female ways of perceiving the world. I think that, instead, the female literary tradition comes from the still-evolving relationships between women writers and their society. Moreover, the 'female imagination' cannot be treated by literary historians as a romantic or Freudian abstraction. It is the product of a delicate network of influences operating in time, and it must be analyzed as it expresses itself, in language and in a fixed arrangement of words on a page, a form that itself is subject to a network of influences and conventions, including the operations of the marketplace. In this investigation of the English novel, I am intentionally looking, not at an innate sexual attitude, but at the ways in which the self-awareness of the woman writer has translated itself into a literary form in a specific place and time-span, how this self-awareness has changed and developed, and where it might lead.

I am therefore concerned with the professional writer who wants pay and publication, not with the diarist or letter-writer. This emphasis has required careful consideration of the novelists, as well as the novels, chosen for discussion. When we turn from the overview of the literary tradition to look at the individuals who composed it, a different but interrelated set of motives, drives, and sources becomes prominent. I have needed to ask why women began to write for money and how they negotiated the activity of writing within their families. What was their professional self-image? How was their work received, and what effects did criticism have upon them? What were their experiences as women, and how were these reflected in books? What was their understanding of womanhood? What were their relationships to other women, to men, and to their readers? How did changes in women's status affect their lives and careers? And how did the vocation of writing itself change the women who committed themselves to it? In looking at literary subcultures, such as black, Jewish, Canadian, Anglo-Indian, or even American, we can see that they all go through three major phases. First, there is a prolonged phase of *imitation* of the prevailing modes of the dominant tradition, and *internalization* of its standards of art and its views on social roles. Second, there is a phase of *protest* against these standards and values, and *advocacy* of minority rights and values, including a demand for autonomy. Finally, there is a phase of *self-discovery*, a turning inward freed from some of the dependency of opposition, a search for identity.[22] An appropriate terminology for women writers is to call these stages, *Feminine, Feminist,* and *Female*. These are obviously not rigid categories, distinctly separable in time, to which individual writers can be assigned with perfect assurance. The phases overlap; there are feminist elements in feminine writing, and vice versa. One might also find all three phases in the career of a single novelist. Nonetheless, it seems useful to point to periods of crisis when a shift of literary values occurred. In this book I identify the Feminine phase as the period from the appearance of the male pseudonym in the 1840s to the death of George Eliot in 1880, the Feminist phase as 1880 to 1920, or the winning of the vote; and the Female phase as 1920 to the present, but entering a new stage of self-awareness about 1960.

It is important to understand the female subculture not only as what Cynthia Ozick calls 'custodial'[23] — a set of opinions, prejudices, tastes, and values prescribed for a subordinate group to perpetuate its subordination — but also as a thriving and positive entity. Most discussions of women as a subculture have come from historians describing Jacksonian America, but they apply equally well to the situation of early Victorian England. According to Nancy Cott, 'we can view women's group consciousness as a subculture uniquely divided against itself by ties to the dominant culture. While the ties to the dominant culture are the informing and restricting ones, they provoke within the subculture certain strengths as well as weaknesses, enduring values as well as accommodations.'[24] The middle-class ideology of the proper sphere of womanhood, which developed in post-industrial England and America, prescribed a woman who would be a Perfect Lady, an Angel in the House, contentedly submissive to men, but strong in her inner purity and religiosity, queen in her own realm of the Home.[25] Many observers have pointed out that the first professional activities of Victorian women, as social reformers, nurses, governesses, and novelists, either were based in the home or were extensions of the feminine role as teacher, helper, and mother of mankind. In describing the American situation, two historians have seen a subculture emerging from the doctrine of sexual spheres:

> By "subculture" we mean simply "a habit of living" . . . of a minority group which is self-consciously distinct from the dominant activities, expectations, and values of a society. Historians have seen female church groups, reform associations, and philanthropic activity as expressions of this subculture in actual behavior, while a large and rich body of writing by and for women articulated the subculture impulses on the ideational level. Both behavior and thought point to child-rearing, religious activity, education, home life, associationism, and female communality as components of women's subculture. Female friendships, strikingly intimate and deep in this period, formed the actual bonds.[26]

For women in England, the female subculture came first through a shared and increasingly secretive and ritualized physical experience. Puberty, menstruation, sexual initiation, pregnancy, childbirth, and menopause — the entire female sexual life cycle — constituted a habit of living that had to be concealed. Although these episodes could not be openly discussed or acknowledged, they were accompanied by elaborate rituals and lore, by external codes of fashion and etiquette, and by intense feelings of female solidarity.[27] Women writers were united by their roles as daughters, wives, and mothers; by the internalized doctrines of evangelicalism, with its suspicion of the imagination and its emphasis on duty; and by legal and economic constraints on their mobility. Sometimes they were united in a more immediate way, around a political cause. On the whole these are the implied unities of culture, rather than the active unities of consciousness.

From the beginning, however, women novelists' awareness of each other and of their female audience showed a kind of covert solidarity that sometimes amounted to a genteel conspiracy. Advocating sisterhood, Sarah Ellis, one of the most conservative writers of the first Victorian generation, asked: 'What should we think of a community of slaves, who betrayed each other's interests? of a little band of shipwrecked mariners upon a friendless shore who were false to each other? of the inhabitants of a defenceless nation, who would not unite together in earnestness and good faith against a common enemy?'[28] Mrs. Ellis felt the binding force of the minority experience for women strongly enough to hint, in the prefaces to her widely read treatises on English womanhood, that her female audience would both read the messages between her lines and refrain from betraying what they deciphered. As another conservative novelist, Dinah Mulock Craik, wrote, 'The intricacies of female nature are incomprehensible except to a woman; and any biographer of real womanly feeling, if ever she discovered, would never dream of publishing them.'[29] Few English women writers openly advocated the use of fiction as revenge against a patriarchal society (as did the American novelist Fanny Fern, for example), but many confessed to sentiments of 'maternal feeling, sisterly affection, *esprit de corps*'[30] for their readers. Thus the clergyman's daughter, going to Mudie's for her three-decker novel by another clergyman's daughter, participated in a cultural exchange that had a special personal significance.

NOTES

16 *The Making of the English Working Class*, New York, 1973, p. 12.
17 Vineta Colby, *The Singular Anomaly: Women Novelists of the Nineteenth Century*, New York, 1970, p. 11.
18 'Women's Lit: Profession and Tradition,' *Columbia Forum* 1 (Fall 1972): 27.
19 Spacks, p. 7.
20 Moers, 'Women's Lit.' 28.
21 'Flying Pigs and Double Standards,' *Times Literary Supplement*, (July 26, 1974): 784.
22 For helpful studies of literary subcultures, see Robert A. Bone, *The Negro Novel in America*, New York, 1958; and Northrop Frye, 'Conclusion to *A Literary History of Canada*,' in *The Stubborn Structure: Essays on Criticism and Society*, Ithaca, 1970, pp. 278—312.
23 'Women and Creativity,' p. 442.
24 Nancy F. Cott, introduction to *Root of Bitterness*, New York, 1972, pp. 3—4.
25 For the best discussions of the Victorian feminine ideal, see Françoise Basch, 'Contemporary Ideologies,' in *Relative Creatures*, pp. 3—15; Walter E. Houghton, *The Victorian Frame of Mind*, New Haven, 1957, pp. 341—343; and Alexander Welsh's theory of the Angel in the House in *The City of Dickens*, London, 1971, pp. 164—195.
26 Christine Stansell and Johnny Faragher, 'Women and Their Families on the Overland Trail, 1842—1867,' *Feminist Studies* 11 (1975): 152—153. For an overview of recent historical scholarship on the 'two cultures,' see Barbara Sicherman, 'Review: American History.' *Signs: Journal of Women in Culture and Society* 1 (Winter 1975): 470—484.
27 For a sociological account of patterns of behavior for Victorian women, see Leonore Davidoff, *The Best Circles: Society, Etiquette and the Season*, London, 1973, esp. pp. 48—58, 85—100.
28 Sarah Ellis, *The Daughters of England*, New York, 1844, ch. ix, p. 90.
29 Dinah M. Craik, 'Literary Ghouls,' *Studies from Life*, New York, n.d., p. 13.
30 Letter of October 6, 1851, in *Letters of E. Jewsbury to Jane Welsh Carlyle*, ed. Mrs. Alex Ireland, London, 1892, p. 426. For Fanny Fern, see Ann Douglas Wood, 'The "Scribbling Women" and Fanny Fern: Why Women Wrote,' *American Quarterly* XXIII (Spring 1971): 1—24.

BONNIE ZIMMERMAN
'What Has Never Been: An Overview of Lesbian Feminist Literary Criticism', *Feminist Studies*

One way in which this unique world view takes shape is as a 'critical consciousness about heterosexist assumptions.'[5] Heterosexism is the set of values and structures that assumes heterosexuality to be the only natural form of sexual and emotional expression, '*the* perceptual screen provided by our [patriarchal] cultural conditioning.'[6] Heterosexist assumptions abound in literary texts, such as feminist literary anthologies, that purport to be open-minded about lesbianism. When authors' biographies make special note of husbands, male mentors, and male companions, even when that author was primarily female-identified, but fail to mention the female companions of prominent lesbian writers — that is heterosexism. When anthologists ignore historically significant lesbian writers such as Renée Vivien and Radclyffe Hall — that is heterosexism. When anthologies include only the heterosexual or nonsexual works of a writer like Katherine Philips or Adrienne Rich who is celebrated for her lesbian or homo-emotional poetry — that is heterosexism. When a topically organized anthology includes sections on wives, mothers, sex objects, young girls, aging women, and liberated women, but not lesbians — that is heterosexism. Heterosexism in feminist anthologies — like the sexism of androcentric collections — serves to obliterate lesbian existence and maintain the lie that women have searched for emotional and sexual fulfillment only through men — or not at all.

Lesbians have also expressed concern that the absence of lesbian material in women's studies journals such as *Feminist Studies, Women's Studies*, and *Women and Literature* indicates heterosexism either by omission or by design. Only in 1979 did lesbian-focused articles appear in *Signs* and *Frontiers*. Most lesbian criticism first appeared in alternative, non-establishment lesbian journals, particularly *Sinister Wisdom* and *Conditions*, which are unfamiliar to many feminist scholars. For example, *Signs'* first review article on literary criticism by Elaine Showalter (1975) makes no mention of lesbianism as a theme or potential critical perspective, not even to point out its absence. Annette Kolodny, in the second review article in *Signs* (1976), does call Jane Rule's *Lesbian Images* 'a novelist's challenge to the academy and its accompanying critical community,' and further criticizes the homophobia in then-current biographies, calling for 'candor and sensitivity' in future work.[7] However, neither this nor subsequent review articles familiarize the reader with 'underground' sources of lesbian criticism, some of which had appeared by this time, nor do they explicate lesbianism as a literary theme or critical perspective. Ironically, more articles on lesbian literature have appeared in traditional literary journals than in the women's studies press, just as for years only male critics felt free to mention lesbianism. Possibly, feminist critics continue to feel that they will be identified as 'dykes,' thus invalidating their work.

The perceptual screen of heterosexism is also evident in most of the acclaimed works of feminist literary criticism. None of the current collections of essays — such as *The Authority of Experience* or *Shakespeare's Sisters* — includes even a token article from a lesbian perspective. Ellen Moers' *Literary Women*, germinal work as it is, is homophobic as well as heterosexist. Lesbians, she points out, appear as monsters, grotesques, and freaks in works by Carson McCullers, Djuna Barnes (her reading of *Nightwood* is at the very least questionable), and Diane Arbus, but she seems to concur in this identification rather than call it into question or explain its historical context. Although her so-called defense of unmarried women writers against the 'charge' of lesbianism does criticize the way in which this word has been used as a slur, she neither condemns such antilesbianism nor entertains the possibility that some women writers were, in fact, lesbians. Her chapter on 'Loving Heroinism' is virtually textbook heterosexism, assuming as it does that women writers only articulate love for men.[8] Perceptual blinders also mar *The Female Imagination* by Patricia Meyer Spacks which never uses the word 'lesbian' (except in the index) or 'lover' to describe either the 'sexual ambiguity' of the bond between Jane and Helen in *Jane Eyre*, nor Margaret Anderson's relationship with a 'beloved older woman.' Furthermore, Spacks claims that Gertrude Stein, 'whose life lack[ed] real attachments' (a surprise to Alice B. Toklas), also 'denied whatever is special to women' (which lesbianism is not?).[9] This latter judgment is particularly ominous because heterosexuals often have difficulty accepting that a lesbian, especially a role-playing 'butch,' is in fact a woman. More care is demonstrated by Elaine Showalter who, in *A Literature of Their Own*, uncovers the attitudes toward lesbianism held by nineteenth-century writers Eliza Lynn Linton and Mrs. Humphrey Ward. However, she does not integrate lesbian issues into her discussion of the crucial generation of early twentieth-century writers (Virginia Woolf, Vita Sackville-West, Dorothy Richardson, and Rosamond Lehmann among others; Radclyffe Hall is mentioned, but not *The Well of Loneliness*), all of whom wrote about sexual love between women. Her well-taken point that modern British novelists avoid lesbianism might have been balanced, however, by a mention of Maureen Duffy, Sybille Bedford, or Fay Weldon.[10] Finally, Sandra Gilbert and Susan Gubar's *The Madwoman in the Attic* does not even index lesbianism; the lone reference made in the text is to the possibility that 'Goblin Market' describes 'a covertly (if ambiguously) lesbian world.' The authors' tendency to interpret all pairs of female characters as aspects of the self sometimes serves to mask a relationship that a lesbian reader might interpret as bonding or love between women.[11]

Lesbian critics, who as feminists owe much to these critical texts, have had to turn to other resources, first to develop a lesbian canon, and then to establish a lesbian critical perspective. Barbara Grier who, as Gene Damon, reviewed books for the pioneering lesbian journal *The Ladder*, laid the groundwork for this canon with her incomparable, but largely unknown *The Lesbian in Literature: A Bibliography.*[12] Equally obscure was Jeanette Foster's *Sex Variant Women in Literature*, self-published in 1956 after having been rejected by a university press because of its subject matter. An exhaustive chronological account of every reference to love between women from Sappho and Ruth to the fiction of the fifties, *Sex Variant Women* has proven to be an invaluable starting point for lesbian readers and scholars. Out of print almost immediately after its publication and lost to all but a few intrepid souls, it was finally reprinted by Diana Press in 1975.[13] A further resource and gathering point for lesbian critics was the special issue on lesbian writing and publishing in *Margins*, a review of small press publications, which appeared in 1975, the first issue of a literary journal devoted entirely to lesbian writing. In 1976, its editor, Beth Hodges, produced a second special issue, this time in *Sinister Wisdom.*[14] Along with the growing visibility and solidarity of lesbians within the academic profession, and the increased availability of lesbian literature from feminist and mass-market presses, these two journal issues propelled lesbian feminist literary criticism to the surface.[15]

The literary resources available to lesbian critics form only part of the story, for lesbian criticism is equally rooted in political ideology. Although not all lesbian critics are activists, most have been strongly influenced by the politics of lesbian feminism. These politics travel the continuum from civil rights advocacy to separatism; however, most, if not all, lesbian feminists assume that lesbianism is a healthy lifestyle chosen by women in virtually all eras and all cultures, and thus strive to eliminate the stigma historically attached to lesbianism. One way to remove this stigma is to associate lesbianism with positive and desirable attributes, to divert women's attention away from male values and toward an exclusively female communitas. Thus, the influential Radicalesbians' essay, 'The Woman-Identified Woman,' argues that lesbian feminism assumes 'the primacy of women relating to women, of women creating a new consciousness of and with each other. . . . We see ourselves as prime, find our centers inside of ourselves.'[16] Many lesbian writers and critics have also been influenced profoundly by the politics of separatism which provides a critique of heterosexuality as a political institution rather than a personal choice, 'because relationships between men and women are essentially political, they involve power and dominance.'[17] As we shall see, the notion of 'woman-identification,' that is, the primacy of women bonding with women emotionally and politically, as well as the premises of separatism, that lesbians have a unique and critical place at the margins of patriarchal society, are central to much current lesbian literary criticism.

[. . .]

One of the first tasks of this emerging lesbian criticism has been to provide lesbians with a tradition, even if a retrospective one. Jane Rule, whose *Lesbian Images* appeared about the same time as *Literary Women*, first attempted to establish this tradition.[33] Although her text is problematic, relying overly much on biographical evidence and derivative interpretations and including some questionable writers (such as Dorothy Baker) while omitting others, *Lesbian Images* was a milestone in lesbian criticism. Its importance is partially suggested by the fact that it took five years for another complete book — Faderman's — to appear on lesbian literature. In a review of *Lesbian Images*, I questioned the existence of a lesbian 'great tradition' in literature, but now I think I was wrong.[34] Along with Rule, Dolores Klaich in *Woman Plus Woman* and Louise Bernikow in the introduction to *The World Split Open* have explored the possibility of a lesbian tradition,[35] and recent critics such as Faderman and Cook in particular have begun to define that tradition, who belongs to it, and what links the writers who can be identified as lesbians. Cook's review of lesbian literature and culture in the early twentieth century proposes 'to analyze the literature and attitudes out of which the present lesbian feminist works have emerged, and to examine the continued denials and invalidation of the lesbian experience.'[36] Focusing on the recognized lesbian networks in France and England that included Virginia Woolf, Vita Sackville-West, Ethel Smythe, Gertrude Stein, Radclyffe Hall, Natalie Barney, and Romaine Brooks, Cook provides an important outline of a lesbian cultural tradition and an insightful analysis of the distortions and denials of homophobic scholars, critics, and biographers.

Faderman's *Surpassing the Love of Men*, like her earlier critical articles, ranges more widely through a literary tradition of romantic love between women (whether or not one calls that 'lesbian') from the sixteenth to the twentieth centuries. Her thesis is that passionate love between women was labeled neither abnormal nor undesirable — probably because women were perceived to be asexual — until the sexologists led by Krafft-Ebing and Havelock Ellis 'morbidified' female friendship around 1900.

Although she does not always clarify the dialectic between idealization and condemnation that is suggested in her text, Faderman's basic theory is quite convincing. Most readers, like myself, will be amazed at the wealth of information about women's same-sex love that Faderman has uncovered. She rescues from heterosexual obscurity Mary Wollstonecraft, Mary Wortley Montagu, Anna Seward, Sarah Orne Jewett, Edith Somerville, 'Michael Field,' and many others, including the Scottish schoolmistresses whose lesbian libel suit inspired Lillian Hellman's *The Children's Hour*. Faderman has also written on the theme of same-sex love and romantic friendship in poems and letters of Emily Dickinson; in novels by Henry James, Oliver Wendell Holmes, and Henry Wadsworth Longfellow; and in popular magazine fiction of the early twentieth century.[37]

Faderman is preeminent among those critics who are attempting to establish a lesbian tradition by rereading writers of the past previously assumed to be heterosexual or 'spinsters.' As songwriter Holly Near expresses it: 'Lady poet of great acclaim/I have been misreading you/I never knew your poems were meant for me.'[38] It is in this area of lesbian scholarship that the most controversy — and some of the most exciting work — occurs. Was Mary Wollstonecraft's passionate love for Fanny Blood, recorded in *Mary, A Fiction*, lesbian? Does Henry James dissect a lesbian relationship in *The Bostonians*? Did Emily Dickinson address many of her love poems to a woman, not a man? How did Virginia Woolf's relationships with Vita Sackville-West and Ethel Smythe affect her literary vision? Not only are some lesbian critics increasingly naming such women and relationships 'lesbian,' they are also suggesting that criticism cannot fail to take into account the influence of sexual and emotional orientation on literary expression.

In the establishment of a self-conscious literary tradition, certain writers have become focal points both for critics and for lesbians in general, who affirm and celebrate their identity by 'naming names,' establishing a sense of historical continuity and community through the knowledge that incontrovertibly great women were also lesbians. Foremost among these heroes (or 'heras') are the women who created the first self-identified lesbian feminist community in Paris during the early years of the twentieth century. With Natalie Barney at its hub, this circle included such notable writers as Colette, Djuna Barnes, Radclyffe Hall, Renée Vivien, and, peripherally, Gertrude Stein. Contemporary lesbians — literary critics, historians, and layreaders — have been drawn to their mythic and mythmaking presence, seeing in them a vision of lesbian society and culture that may have existed only once before — on the original island of Lesbos.[39] More interest, however, has been paid to their lives so far than to their art. Barnes's portraits of decadent, tormented lesbians and homosexuals in *Nightwood* and silly, salacious ones in *The Ladies Almanack* often prove troublesome to lesbian readers and critics.[40] However, Elaine Marks's perceptive study of French lesbian writers traces a tradition and how it has changed, modified by circumstance and by feminism, from the Sappho of Renée Vivien to the amazons of Monique Wittig.[41]

NOTES

5   Elly Bulkin, '"Kissing Against the Light": A Look at Lesbian Poetry,' *Radical Teacher* 10 (December 1978): 8. This article was reprinted in *College English* and *Women's Studies Newsletter*, an expanded version is available from the Lesbian-Feminist Study Clearinghouse, Women's Studies Program, University of Pittsburgh, Pittsburgh, Pennsylvania 15260.

6   Julia Penelope [Stanley], 'The Articulation of Bias: Hoof in Mouth Disease,' paper presented at the 1979 convention of the National Council of Teachers of English, San Francisco, November 1979, pp. 4—5. On the same panel, I presented a paper on 'Heterosexism in Literary Anthologies,' which develops some of the points of this paragraph.

7   Annette Kolodny, 'Literary Criticism: Review Essay,' *Signs* 2, no. 2 (Winter 1976): 416, 419.

8   Ellen Moers, *Literary Women: The Great Writers* (Garden City, N.Y.: Doubleday & Co., 1976), pp. 108—9, 145.

9   Patricia Meyer Spacks, *The Female Imagination* (New York: Avon Books, 1975), pp. 89, 214, 363.

10 Elaine Showalter, *A Literature of Their Own: British Women Novelists From Brontë to Lessing* (Princeton: Princeton University Press, 1977), pp. 178, 229, 316.

11 Sandra M. Gilbert and Susan Gubar, *The Madwoman in the Attic: The Woman Writer and the Nineteenth Century Literary Imagination* (New Haven: Yale University Press, 1979), p. 567. Regarding another issue — their analysis of Emily Dickinson's poem no. 1722 — Nadean Bishop says, 'It is hard to fathom how Sandra Gilbert and Susan Gubar could take this erotic representation of lesbian love-making to be an "image of the chaste moon goddess Diana," who does not have hand or tender tongue or inspire incredulity.' See Nadean Bishop, 'Renunciation in the Bridal Poems of Emily Dickinson,' paper presented at the National Women's Studies Association, Bloomington, Indiana, 16—20 May 1980. One other major critical study, Judith Fetterley's *The Resisting Reader: a*

Feminist Approach to American Fiction (Bloomington: Indiana University Press, 1978), is uniquely sensitive to lesbianism in its interpretation of *The Bostonians*.

12 Gene Damon, Jan Watson, and Robin Jordan, *The Lesbian in Literature: A Bibliography* (1967; reprinted, Reno, Nev.: Naiad Press, 1975).

13 Jeannette Foster, *Sex Variant Women in Literature* (1956; reprinted, Baltimore: Diana Press, 1975). See also, Karla Jay, 'The X-Rated Bibliographer: A Spy in the House of Sex,' in *Lavender Culture*, ed. Karla Jay and Allen Young (New York: Harcourt Brace Jovanovich, 1978), pp. 257—61.

14 Beth Hodges, ed., Special Issue on Lesbian Writing and Publishing, *Margins* 23 (August 1975). Beth Hodges, ed., Special Issue on Lesbian Literature and Publishing, *Sinister Wisdom* 2 (Fall 1976).

15 In addition, networks of lesbian critics, teachers, and scholars were established through panels at the Modern Language Association's annual conventions and at the Lesbian Writer's Conference in Chicago, which began in 1974 and continued for several years. Currently, networking continues through conferences, journals, and other institutionalized outlets. The Lesbian-Feminist Study Clearinghouse reprints articles, bibliographies, and syllabi pertinent to lesbian studies. See note 5 for the address. The Lesbian Herstory Archives collects all material documenting lesbian lives past or present; their address is P.O. Box 1258, New York, New York 10001. *Matrices*, 'A Lesbian-Feminist Research Newsletter,' is a network of information about research projects, reference materials, calls for papers, bibliographies, and so forth. There are several regional editors; the managing editor is Bobby Lacy, 4000 Randolph, Lincoln, Nebraska 68510.

16 Radicalesbians, 'The Woman-Identified Woman,' in *Radical Feminism*, ed. Anne Koedt, Ellen Levine, and Anita Rapone (New York: Quadrangle, 1973). This article is extensively reprinted in women's studies anthologies.

17 Charlotte Bunch, 'Lesbians in Revolt,' in *Lesbianism and the Women's Movement*, ed. Nancy Myron and Charlotte Bunch (Baltimore: Diana Press, 1975), p. 30.

[. . .]

33 Jane Rule, *Lesbian Images* (Garden City, N.Y.: Doubleday & Co., 1975).

34 Bonnie Zimmerman, 'The New Tradition,' *Sinister Wisdom* 2 (Fall 1976): 34—41.

35 Dolores Klaich, *Woman Plus Woman: Attitudes Toward Lesbianism* (New York: William Morrow, 1974); Louise Bernikow, *The World Split Open: Four Centuries of Women Poets in England and America, 1552—1950* (New York: Vintage Books, 1974).

36 Cook, 'Women Alone Stir My Imagination,' p. 720.

37 See Lillian Faderman's articles: 'The Morbidification of Love Between Women by Nineteenth-Century Sexologists,' *Journal of Homosexuality* 4, no. 1 (Fall 1978): 73—90; 'Emily Dickinson's Letters to Sue Gilbert,' *Massachusetts Review* 18, no. 2 (Summer 1977): 197—225; 'Emily Dickinson's Homoerotic Poetry,' *Higginson Journal* 18 (1978): 19—27; 'Female Same-Sex Relationships in Novels by Longfellow, Holmes, and James,' *New England Quarterly* 60, no. 3 (September 1978): 309—32; and 'Lesbian Magazine Fiction in the Early Twentieth Century,' *Journal of Popular Culture* 11, no. 4 (Spring 1978: 800—17.

38 Holly Near, 'Imagine My Surprise,' on *Imagine My Surprise!* (Redwood Records, 1978).

39   See Klaich, chap. 6. Also, see Bertha Harris, 'The More Profound Nationality of
     their Lesbianism: Lesbian Society in Paris in the 1920s,' *Amazon Expedition*
     (New York: Times Change Press, 1973), pp. 77—88; and Gayle Rubin's
     Introduction to Renée Vivien's: *A Woman Appeared to Me*, trans. Jeanette
     Foster (Reno, Nev.: Naiad Press, 1976).
40   For example, see Lanser, 'Speaking in Tongues.'
41   Marks, 'Lesbian Intertextuality,' in *Homosexualities and French Literature*, ed.
     George Stambolian and Elaine Marks (Ithaca, N.Y.: Cornell University Press,
     1979), pp. 353—77.

ADRIENNE RICH
'Compulsory Heterosexuality and Lesbian Existence'

I

Biologically men have only one innate orientation — a sexual one that draws
them to women — while women have two innate orientations, sexual toward
men and reproductive toward their young.[1]

. . . I was a woman terribly vulnerable, critical, using femaleness as a sort of
standard or yardstick to measure and discard men. Yes — something like that.
I was an Anna who invited defeat from men without ever being conscious of it.
(But I am conscious of it. And being conscious of it means I shall leave it all
behind me and become — but what?) I was stuck fast in an emotion common
to women of our time, that can turn them bitter, or Lesbian, or solitary. Yes,
that Anna during that time was . . .

[Another blank line across the page:][2]

The bias of compulsory heterosexuality, through which lesbian experience is
perceived on a scale ranging from deviant to abhorrent, or simply rendered
invisible, could be illustrated from many other texts than the two just
preceding. The assumption made by Rossi, that women are 'innately sexually
oriented' toward men, or by Lessing, that the lesbian choice is simply an
acting-out of bitterness toward men, are by no means theirs alone; they are
widely current in literature and in the social sciences.

I am concerned here with two other matters as well: first, how and why
women's choice of women as passionate comrades, life partners, co-workers,
lovers, tribe, has been crushed, invalidated, forced into hiding and disguise;
and second, the virtual or total neglect of lesbian existence in a wide range of
writings, including feminist scholarship. Obviously there is a connection
here. I believe that much feminist theory and criticism is stranded on this
shoal.

My organizing impulse is the belief that it is not enough for feminist
thought that specifically lesbian texts exist. Any theory or cultural/political
creation that treats lesbian existence as a marginal or less 'natural'
phenomenon, as mere 'sexual preference,' or as the mirror image of either
heterosexual or male homosexual relations, is profoundly weakened thereby,

whatever its other contributions. Feminist theory can no longer afford merely to voice a toleration of 'lesbianism' as an 'alternative life-style,' or make token allusion to lesbians. A feminist critique of compulsory heterosexual orientation for women is long overdue. In this exploratory paper, I shall try to show why.

I will begin by way of examples, briefly discussing four books that have appeared in the last few years, written from different viewpoints and political orientations, but all presenting themselves, and favorably reviewed, as feminist.[3] All take as a basic assumption that the social relations of the sexes are disordered and extremely problematic, if not disabling, for women; all seek paths toward change. I have learned more from some of these books than from others; but on this I am clear: each one might have been more accurate, more powerful, more truly a force for change, had the author felt impelled to deal with lesbian existence as a reality, and as a source of knowledge and power available to women; or with the institution of heterosexuality itself as a beachhead of male dominance.[4] In none of them is the question ever raised, whether in a different context, or other things being equal, women would *choose* heterosexual coupling and marriage; hetero-sexuality is presumed as a 'sexual preference' of 'most women,' either implicitly or explicitly. In none of these books, which concern themselves with mothering, sex roles, relationships, and societal prescriptions for women, is compulsory heterosexuality ever examined as an institution powerfully affecting all these; or the idea of 'preference' or 'innate orientation' even indirectly questioned.

[. . .]

III

I have chosen to use the term *lesbian existence* and *lesbian continuum* because the word *lesbianism* has a clinical and limiting ring. *Lesbian existence* suggests both the fact of the historical presence of lesbians and our continuing creation of the meaning of that existence. I mean the term *lesbian continuum* to include a range — through each woman's life and throughout history — of woman-identified experience; not simply the fact that a woman has had or consciously desired genital sexual experience with another woman. If we expand it to embrace many more forms of primary intensity between and among women, including the sharing of a rich inner life, the bonding against male tyranny, the giving and receiving of practical and political support; if we can also hear in it such associations as *marriage resistance* and the 'haggard' behavior identified by Mary Daly (obsolete meanings: 'intractable,' 'willful,' 'wanton,' and 'unchaste' . . . 'a woman reluctant to yield to wooing')[45] — we begin to grasp breadths of female history and psychology which have lain out of reach as a consequence of limited, mostly clinical, definitions of 'lesbianism.'

Lesbian existence comprises both the breaking of a taboo and the rejection of a compulsory way of life. It is also a direct or indirect attack on male right of access to women. But it is more than these, although we may first begin to perceive it as a form of nay-saying to patriarchy, an act of resistance. It has of course included role playing, self-hatred, breakdown, alcoholism, suicide, and intrawoman violence; we romanticize at our peril what it means to love and act against the grain, and under heavy penalties; and lesbian existence has been lived (unlike, say, Jewish or Catholic existence) without access to any knowledge of a tradition, a continuity, a social underpinning. The destruction of records and memorabilia and letters documenting the realities of lesbian existence must be taken very seriously as a means of keeping heterosexuality compulsory for women, since what has been kept from our knowledge is joy, sensuality, courage, and community, as well as guilt, self-betrayal, and pain.[46]

Lesbians have historically been deprived of a political existence through 'inclusion' as female versions of male homosexuality. To equate lesbian existence with male homosexuality because each is stigmatized is to deny and erase female reality once again. To separate those women stigmatized as 'homosexual' or 'gay' from the complex continuum of female resistance to enslavement, and attach them to a male pattern, is to falsify our history. Part of the history of lesbian existence is, obviously, to be found where lesbians, lacking a coherent female community, have shared a kind of social life and common cause with homosexual men. But this has to be seen against the differences: women's lack of economic and cultural privilege relative to men; qualitative differences in female and male relationships, for example, the prevalence of anonymous sex and the justification of pederasty among male homosexuals, the pronounced ageism in male homosexual standards of sexual attractiveness, etc. In defining and describing lesbian existence I would hope to move toward a dissociation of lesbian from male homosexual values and allegiances. I perceive the lesbian experience as being, like motherhood, a profoundly *female* experience, with particular oppressions, meanings, and potentialities we cannot comprehend as long as we simply bracket it with other sexually stigmatized existences. Just as the term 'parenting' serves to conceal the particular and significant reality of being a parent who is actually a mother, the term 'gay' serves the purpose of blurring the very outlines we need to discern, which are of crucial value for feminism and for the freedom of women as a group.

As the term 'lesbian' has been held to limiting, clinical associations in its patriarchal definition, female friendship and comradeship have been set apart from the erotic, thus limiting the erotic itself. But as we deepen and broaden the range of what we define as lesbian existence, as we delineate a lesbian continuum, we begin to discover the erotic in female terms: as that which is unconfined to any single part of the body or solely to the body itself, as an energy not only diffuse but, as Audre Lorde has described it, omnipresent in 'the sharing of joy, whether physical, emotional, psychic,' and in the sharing of work; as the empowering joy which 'makes us less willing to accept powerlessness, or those other supplied states of being which are not native to me, such as resignation, despair, self-effacement, depression, self-denial.'[47] In another context, writing of women and work, I quoted the autobiographical passage in which the poet H. D. described how her friend Bryher supported her in persisting with the visionary experience which was to shape her mature work:

> . . . I knew that this experience, this writing-on-the-wall before me, could not be shared with anyone except the girl who stood so bravely there beside me. This girl had said without hesitation, "Go on." It was she really who had the detachment and integrity of the Pythoness of Delphi. But it was I, battered and dissociated . . . who was seeing the pictures, and who was reading the writing or granted the inner vision. Or perhaps, in some sense, we were "seeing" it together, for without her, admittedly, I could not have gone on. . . .[48]

If we consider the possibility that all women — from the infant suckling her mother's breast, to the grown woman experiencing orgasmic sensations while suckling her own child, perhaps recalling her mother's milk-smell in her own; to two women, like Virginia Woolf's Chloe and Olivia, who share a laboratory;[49] to the woman dying at ninety, touched and handled by women — exist on a lesbian continuum, we can see ourselves as moving in and out of this continuum, whether we identify ourselves as lesbian or not. It allows us to connect aspects of woman-identification as diverse as the impudent, intimate girl-friendships of eight- or nine-year olds and the banding together of those women of the twelfth and fifteenth centuries known as Beguines who 'shared houses, rented to one another, bequeathed houses to their room-mates . . . in cheap subdivided houses in the artisans' area of town,' who 'practiced Christian virtue on their own, dressing and living simply and not associating with men,' who earned their livings as spinners, bakers, nurses, or ran schools for young girls, and who managed — until the Church forced them to disperse — to live independent both of marriage and of conventual restrictions.[50] It allows us to connect these women with the more celebrated 'Lesbians' of the women's school around Sappho of the seventh century B.C.; with the secret sororities and economic networks reported among African women; and with the Chinese marriage resistance sisterhoods — communities of women who refused marriage, or who if married often refused to consummate their marriages and soon left their husbands — the only women in China who were not footbound and who, Agnes Smedley tells us, welcomed the births of daughters and organized successful women's strikes in the silk mills.[51] It allows us to connect and compare disparate individual instances of marriage resistance: for example, the type of autonomy claimed by Emily Dickinson, a nineteenth-century white woman genius, with the strategies available to Zora Neale Hurston, a twentieth-century black woman genius. Dickinson never married, had tenuous intellectual friendships with men, lived self-convented in her genteel father's house, and wrote a lifetime of passionate letters to her sister-in-law Sue Gilbert and a smaller group of such letters to her friend Kate Scott Anthon. Hurston married twice but soon left each husband, scrambled her way from Florida to Harlem to Columbia University to Haiti and finally back to Florida, moved in and out of white patronage and poverty, professional success, and failure; her survival relationships were all with women, beginning with her mother. Both of these women in their vastly different circumstances were marriage resisters, committed to their own work and selfhood, and were later characterized as 'apolitical.' Both were drawn to men of intellectual quality; for both of them women provided the on-going fascination and sustenance of life.

NOTES

I want to mention, for this 1983 reprinting, some texts which have appeared since the writing of this article. Documentation on male violence against women has been accumulating. *Aegis, Magazine on Ending Violence against Women*, continues to be an important resource. Single copy is $3.25 from Feminist Alliance against Rape, P.O. Box 21033, Washington, D.C. 20009. See also Louise Armstrong, *Kiss Daddy Goodnight* (New York: Pocket Books, 1976); Sandra Butler, *Conspiracy of Silence: The Trauma of Incest* (San Francisco: New Glide Publications, 1978); F. Delacoste and F. Newman, eds., *Fight Back! Feminist Resistance to Male Violence* (Minneapolis: Cleis Press, 1981); Judy Freespirit, *Daddy's Girl: An Incest Survivor's Story* (Langlois, Oreg., Diaspora Distribution, 1982); Judith Herman, *Father-Daughter Incest* (Cambridge, Mass.: Harvard University Press, 1981); T. McNaron and Y. Morgan, eds., *Voices in the Night: Women Speaking about Incest* (Minneapolis: Cleis Press, 1982); Florence Rush, *The Best-Kept Secret* (New York: McGraw-Hill Book Co., 1980); Diana Russell, *Rape in Marriage* (New York: Macmillan Publishing Co., 1982); and Betsy Warrior's richly informative, multipurpose compilation of essays, statistics, listings, and facts, the *Battered Women's Directory* (formerly titled *Working on Wife Abuse*; 8th ed. [1982], obtainable at $9.50 from Directory, Betsy Warrior, 46 Pleasant St., Cambridge, MA 02139). See also Wini Breines and Linda Gordon, 'The New Scholarship on Family Violence,' *Signs: Journal of Women in Culture and Society* 8, no. 3 (Spring 1983): 490–531. For more recent literature which depicts woman-bonding and woman-identification as a basis for female survival, see, among others, Gloria Anzaldúa and Cherríe Moraga, eds., *This Bridge Called My Back: Writings by Radical Women of Color* (Watertown, Mass.: Persephone Press, 1981); Juanita Ramos and Mirtha Quintinales, eds., *Compañeras: Antología Lesbiana Latina, Latina Lesbian Anthology* (tentatively from Kitchen Table/Women of Color Press, 1984); J. R. Roberts, *Black Lesbians: An Annotated Bibliography* (Tallahassee, Fla.: Naiad Press, 1981); Barbara Smith, ed., *Home Girls: A Black Feminist Anthology* (Kitchen Table/Women of Color Press, 1983). For accounts of contemporary Jewish lesbian existence, see E. T. Beck, ed., *Nice Jewish Girls: A Lesbian Anthology* (Watertown, Mass.: Persephone Press, 1982). See also Elly Bulkin, ed., *Lesbian Fiction: An Anthology* (Watertown, Mass.: Perspehone Press, 1981). The earliest formulation that I know of heterosexuality as institution was in the lesbian-feminist paper the *Furies*, founded in 1971. For a collection of articles from that paper, see Nancy Myron and Charlotte Bunch, eds., *Lesbianism and the Women's Movement* (Oakland, Calif.: Diana Press, 1975; distributed by Crossing Press, Trumansburg, N.Y. 14886). EDITOR'S NOTE: This is a revised and updated version of the note that appeared in the Summer 1980 issue of *Signs: Journal of Women in Culture and Society*.

1   Alice Rossi, 'Children and Work in the Lives of Women' (paper delivered at the University of Arizona, Tucson, February 1976).
2   Doris Lessing, *The Golden Notebook* (New York: Bantam Books [1962] 1977), p. 480.

3   Nancy Chodorow, *The Reproduction of Mothering* (Berkeley: University of
    California Press, 1978); Dorothy Dinnerstein, *The Mermaid and the Minotaur:
    Sexual Arrangements and the Human Malaise* (New York: Harper & Row,
    1976); Barbara Ehrenreich and Deirdre English, *For Her Own Good: 150
    Years of the Experts' Advice to Women* (Garden City, N.Y.: Doubleday & Co.,
    Anchor Press, 1978); Jean Baker Miller, *Toward a New Psychology of Women*
    (Boston: Beacon Press, 1976).

4   I could have chosen many other serious and influential recent books, including
    anthologies, which would illustrate the same point: e.g., *Our Bodies, Ourselves*,
    the Boston Women's Health Collective's best-seller (New York: Simon &
    Schuster, 1976), which devotes a separate (and inadequate) chapter to lesbians,
    but whose message is that heterosexuality is most women's life preference;
    Berenice Carroll, ed., *Liberating Women's History: Theoretical and Critical
    Essays* (Urbana: University of Illinois Press, 1976), which does not include
    even a token essay on the lesbian presence in history, though an essay by Linda
    Gordon, Persis Hunt, et al. notes the use by male historians of 'sexual deviance'
    as a category to discredit and dismiss Anna Howard Shaw, Jane Addams, and
    other feminists ('Historical Phallacies: Sexism in American Historical Writing');
    and Renate Bridenthal and Claudia Koonz, eds., *Becoming Visible: Women in
    European History* (Boston: Houghton Mifflin Co., 1977), which contains three
    mentions of male homosexuality but no materials that I have been able to locate
    on lesbians. Gerda Lerner, ed., *The Female Experience: An American
    Documentary* (Indianapolis: Bobbs-Merrill Co., 1977), contains an abridgment
    of two lesbian/feminist position papers from the contemporary movement but
    no other documentation of lesbian existence. Lerner does note in her preface,
    however, how the charge of deviance has been used to fragment women and
    discourage women's resistance. Linda Gordon, in *Woman's Body, Woman's
    Right: A Social History of Birth Control in America* (New York: Viking Press,
    Grossman, 1976), notes accurately that: 'It is not that feminism has produced
    more lesbians. There have always been many lesbians, despite high levels of
    repression; and most lesbians experience their sexual preference as innate . . .'
    (p. 410).

[. . .]

45 Daly, *Gyn/Ecology*, p. 15.
46 'In a hostile world in which women are not supposed to survive except in
    relation with and in service to men, entire communities of women were simply
    erased. History tends to bury what it seeks to reject' (Blanche W. Cook,
    '"Women Alone Stir My Imagination": Lesbianism and the Cultural Tradition,'
    Signs: Journal of Women in Culture and Society 4, no. 4 [Summer 1979]:
    719–20). The Lesbian Herstory Archives in New York City is one attempt to
    preserve contemporary documents on lesbian existence — a project of enormous
    value and meaning, still pitted against the continuing censorship and obliteration
    of relationships, networks, communities, in other archives and elsewhere in the
    culture.
47 Audre Lorde, *Uses of the Erotic: The Erotic as Power*, Out & Out Books
    Pamphlet no. 3 (New York: Out & Out Books [476 2d Street, Brooklyn, New
    York 11215], 1979).
48 Adrienne Rich, 'Conditions for Work: The Common World of Women,' in *On
    Lies, Secrets, and Silence* (p. 209); H. D., *Tribute to Freud* (Oxford: Carcanet
    Press, 1971), pp. 50–54.

49 Woolf, *A Room of One's Own*, p. 126.
50 Gracia Clark, 'The Beguines: A Mediaeval Women's Community,' *Quest: A Feminist Quarterly* 1, no. 4 (1975): 73—80.
51 See Denise Paulmé, ed., *Women of Tropical Africa* (Berkeley: University of California Press, 1963), pp. 7, 266—67. Some of these sororities are described as 'a kind of defensive syndicate against the male element' — their aims being 'to offer concerted resistance to an oppressive patriarchate,' 'independence in relation to one's husband and with regard to motherhood, mutual aid, satisfaction of personal revenge.' See also Audre Lorde, 'Scratching the Surface: Some Notes on Barriers to Women and Loving,' *Black Scholar* 9, no. 7 (1978): 31—35; Marjorie Topley, 'Marriage Resistance in Rural Kwangtung,' in *Women in Chinese Society*, ed. M. Wolf and R. Witke (Stanford, Calif.: Stanford University Press, 1978), pp. 67—89; Agnes Smedley, *Portraits of Chinese Women in Revolution*, ed. J. MacKinnon and S. MacKinnon (Old Westbury, N.Y.: Feminist Press, 1976), pp. 103—10.

ALICE WALKER
'Saving the Life That Is Your Own:
The Importance of Models in the Artist's Life',
In Search of Our Mothers' Gardens

I have often been asked why, in my own life and work, I have felt such a desperate need to know and assimilate the experiences of earlier black women writers, most of them unheard of by you and by me, until quite recently. Why I felt a need to study them and to teach them.

I don't recall the exact moment I set out to explore the works of black women, mainly those in the past, and certainly, in the beginning, I had no desire to teach them. Teaching being for me, at that time, less rewarding than star-gazing on a frigid night. *My discovery of them* — most of them out of print, abandoned, discredited, maligned, nearly lost — came about, as many things of value do, almost by accident. As it turned out — and this should not have surprised me — I found I was in need of something that only one of them could provide.

Mindful that throughout my four years at a prestigious black and then a prestigious white college I had heard not one word about early black women writers, one of my first tasks was simply to determine whether they had existed. After this, I could breathe easier, with more assurance about the profession I myself had chosen.

But the incident that started my search began several years ago: I sat down at my desk one day, in a room of my own, with key and lock, and began preparations for a story about voodoo, a subject that had always fascinated me. Many of the elements of this story I had gathered from a story that my mother several times told me. She had gone, during the Depression, into town to apply for some government surplus food at the local commissary, and had been turned down, in a particularly humiliating way, by the white woman in charge.

My mother always told this story with a most curious expression on her face. She automatically raised her head higher than ever — it was always high — and there was a look of righteousness, a kind of holy *heat* coming from her eyes. She said she had lived to see this same white woman grow old and senile and so badly crippled she had to get about on *two* sticks.

To her, this was clearly the working of God, who, as in the old spiritual, '. . . may not come when you want him, but he's right on time!' To me, hearing the story for about the 50th time, something else was discernible: the possibilities of the story, for fiction.

What, I asked myself, would have happened, if, after the crippled old lady died, it was discovered that someone, my mother perhaps (who would have been mortified at the thought, Christian lady that she is), had voodooed her?

Then, my thoughts sweeping me away into the world of hexes and conjures of centuries past, I wondered how a larger story could be created out of my mother's story; one that would be true to the magnitude of her humiliation and grief, and to the white woman's lack of sensitivity and compassion.

My third quandary was: How could I find out all I needed to know in order to write a story that used *authentic* black witchcraft?

Which brings me back, almost, to the day I became really interested in black women writers. I say 'almost' because one other thing, from my childhood, made the choice of black magic a logical and irresistible one for my story. Aside from my mother's several stories about rootdoctors she had heard of or known, there was the story I had often heard about my crazy Walker aunt.

Many years ago, when my aunt was a meek and obedient girl growing up in a strict, conventionally religious house in the rural South, she had suddenly thrown off her meekness and had run away from home, escorted by a rogue of a man permanently attached elsewhere.

When she was returned home by her father she was declared quite 'mad.' In the backwoods South at the turn of the century, 'madness' of this sort was cured, not by psychiatry, but by powders and by spells. (One may see Scott Joplin's *Treemonisha* to ascertain the role voodoo played among black people of that period.) My aunt's 'madness' was treated by the community conjurer, who promised, and delivered, the desired results. His 'treatment' was a bag of white powder, bought for fifty cents, and sprinkled on the ground around her house, with some of it sewed, I believe, into the bodice of her nightgown.

So when I sat down to write my story about voodoo, my crazy Walker aunt was definitely on my mind.

But she had experienced her temporary craziness so long ago that her story had all the excitement of a might-have-been. I needed, instead of family memories, some hard facts about the *craft* of voodoo, as practiced by Southern blacks in the 19th century. (It never once, fortunately, occurred to me that voodoo was not worthy of the interest I had in it, or was too ridiculous to seriously study.)

I began reading all I could find on the subject of 'The Negro and His Folkways and Superstitions.' There were Botkin and Puckett and others, all

white, most racist. How was I to believe anything they wrote, since at least
one of them, Puckett, was capable of wondering, in his book, if 'The Negro'
had a large enough brain? Who needed *him*, the racist turkey!

Well, I thought, where are the *black* collectors of folklore? Where is the
black anthropologist? Where is the *black* person who took the time to travel
the backroads of the South and collect the information I need: how to cure
heart trouble, treat dropsy, hex somebody to death, lock bowels, cause joints
to swell, eyes to fall out, and so on. Where was this black person?

And that is when I first saw, in a *footnote* to the white voices of authority,
the name of Zora Neale Hurston.

Folklorist, novelist, anthropologist, serious student of voodoo, also all
around black woman, with guts enough to take a slide rule and measure
random black heads in Harlem; not to prove their inferiority, but to prove
that whatever their size, shape, or present condition of servitude, those
heads contained all the intelligence anyone could use to get through this
world.

Zora Hurston, who went to Barnard to learn how to study what she really
wanted to learn: the ways of her own people, and what ancient rituals,
customs and beliefs had made them unique.

Zora, of the sandy-colored hair and the daredevil eyes, a girl who escaped
poverty and parental neglect by hard work and a sharp eye for the main
chance.

Zora, who left the South only to return to look at it again. Who went to
rootdoctors from Florida to Louisiana and said, 'Here I am. I want to learn
your trade.'

Zora, who had collected all the black folklore I could ever use.

That Zora.

And having found *that* Zora (like a golden key to a storehouse of varied
treasure), I was hooked.

What I had discovered, of course, was a model. A model, who, as it
happened, provided more than voodoo for my story, more than one of the
greatest novels America had produced — though, being America, it did not
realize this. She had provided, as if she knew someday I would come along
wandering in the wilderness, a nearly complete record of her life. And
though her life sprouted an occasional wart, I am eternally grateful for that
life, warts and all.

It is not irrelevant, nor is it bragging (except perhaps to gloat a little on the
happy relatedness of Zora, my mother, and me), to mention here that the
story I wrote, called 'The Revenge of Hannah Kemhuff,' based on my
mother's experiences during the Depression, and on Zora Hurston's folklore
collection of the 1920s, and on my own response to both out of a
contemporary existence, was immediately published and later selected, by a
reputable collector of short stories, as one of the *Best Short Stories of 1974.*

I mention it because this story might never have been written, because the
very bases of its structure, authentic black folklore, viewed from a black
perspective, might have been lost.

Had it been lost, my mother's story would have had no historical underpinning, none I could trust, anyway. I would not have written the story, which I enjoyed writing as much as I've enjoyed writing anything in my life, had I not known that Zora had already done a thorough job of preparing the ground over which I was then moving.

In that story I gathered up the historical and psychological threads of the life my ancestors lived, and in the writing of it I felt joy and strength and my own continuity. I had that wonderful feeling writers get sometimes, not very often, of being *with* a great many people, ancient spirits, all very happy to see me consulting and acknowledging them, and eager to let me know, through the joy of their presence, that indeed, I am not alone.

To take Toni Morrison's statement further, if that is possible, in my own work I write not only what I want to read — understanding fully and indelibly that if I don't do it no one else is so vitally interested, or capable of doing it to my satisfaction — I write all the things I *should have read.*

Consulting, as belatedly discovered models, those writers — most of whom, not surprisingly, are women, who understood that their experience as ordinary human beings was also valuable, and in danger of being misrepresented, distorted, or lost:

Zora Hurston — novelist, essayist, anthropologist, autobiographer.

Jean Toomer — novelist, poet, philosopher, visionary, a man who cared what women felt.

Colette — whose crinkly hair enhances her French, part-black face: novelist, playwright, dancer, essayist, newspaper woman, lover of women, men, small dogs. Fortunate not to have been born in America.

Anaïs Nin, recorder of everything, no matter how minute.

Tillie Olsen, a writer of such generosity and honesty, she literally saves lives . . .

It is, in the end, the saving of lives that we writers are about. Whether we are 'minority' writers or 'majority.' It is simply in our power to do this.

We do it because we care. We care that Vincent Van Gogh mutilated his ear. We care that behind a pile of manure in the yard he destroyed his life. We care that Scott Joplin's music *lives!* We care because we know this: *The life we save is our own.*

ALICE WALKER
title essay, *In Search of Our Mothers' Gardens*

What did it mean for a black woman to be an artist in our grandmothers' time? In our great-grandmothers' day? It is a question with an answer cruel enough to stop the blood.

Did you have a genius of a great-great-grandmother who died under some ignorant and depraved white overseer's lash? Or was she required to bake biscuits for a lazy backwater tramp, when she cried out in her soul to paint watercolors of sunsets, or the rain falling on the green and peaceful pasturelands? Or was her body broken and forced to bear children (who were more often than not sold away from her) — eight, ten, fifteen, twenty children — when her one joy was the thought of modeling heroic figures of rebellion, in stone or clay?

How was the creativity of the black woman kept alive, year after year and century after century, when for most of the years black people have been in America, it was a punishable crime for a black person to read or write? And the freedom to paint, to sculpt, to expand the mind with action did not exist. Consider, if you can bear to imagine it, what might have been the result if singing, too, had been forbidden by law. Listen to the voices of Bessie Smith, Billie Holliday, Nine Simone, Roberta Flack, and Aretha Franklin, among others, and imagine those voices muzzled for life. Then you may begin to comprehend the lives of our 'crazy,' 'Sainted' mothers and grandmothers. The agony of the lives of women who might have been Poets, Novelists, Essayists, and Short-Story Writers (over a period of centuries), who died with their real gifts stifled within them.

And, if this were the end of the story, we would have cause to cry out in my paraphrase of Okot p'Bitek's great poem:

> O, my clanswomen
> Let us all cry together!
> Come,
> Let us mourn the death of our mother,
> The death of a Queen
> The ash that was produced
> By a great fire!
> O, this homestead is utterly dead
> Close the gates
> With *lacari* thorns,
> For our mother
> The creator of the Stool is lost!
> And all the young women
> Have perished in the wilderness!

But this is not the end of the story, for all the young women — our mothers and grandmothers, *ourselves* — have not perished in the wilderness. And if we ask ourselves why, and search for and find the answer, we will know beyond all efforts to erase it from our minds, just exactly who, and of what, we black American women are.

One example, perhaps the most pathetic, most misunderstood one, can provide a backdrop for our mothers' work: Phillis Wheatley, a slave in the 1700s.

Virginia Woolf, in her book *A Room of One's Own*, wrote that in order for a woman to write fiction she must have two things, certainly: a room of her own (with key and lock) and enough money to support herself.

What then are we to make of Phillis Wheatley, a slave, who owned not even herself? This sickly, frail black girl who required a servant of her own at times — her health was so precarious — and who, had she been white, would have been easily considered the intellectual superior of all the women and most of the men in the society of her day.

Virginia Woolf wrote further, speaking of course not of our Phillis, that 'any woman born with a great gift in the sixteenth century [insert 'eighteenth century,' insert 'black woman,' insert 'born or made a slave'] would certainly have gone crazed, shot herself, or ended her days in some lonely cottage outside the village, half witch, half wizard [insert 'Saint'], feared and mocked at. For it needs little skill and psychology to be sure that a highly gifted girl who had tried to use her gift for poetry would have been so thwarted and hindered by contrary instincts [add 'chains, guns, the lash, the ownership of one's body by someone else, submission to an alien religion'], that she must have lost her health and sanity to a certainty.'

The key words, as they relate to Phillis, are 'contrary instincts.' For when we read the poetry of Phillis Wheatley — as when we read the novels of Nella Larsen or the oddly false-sounding autobiography of that freest of all black women writers, Zora Hurston — evidence of 'contrary instincts' is everywhere. Her loyalties were completely divided, as was, without question, her mind.

But how could this be otherwise? Captured at seven, a slave of wealthy, doting whites, who instilled in her the 'savagery' of the Africa they 'rescued' her from . . . one wonders if she was even able to remember her homeland as she had known it, or as it really was.

Yet, because she did try to use her gift for poetry in a world that made her a slave, she was 'so thwarted and hindered by . . . contrary instincts, that she . . . lost her health. . . .' In the last years of her brief life, burdened not only with the need to express her gift but also with a penniless, friendless 'freedom' and several small children for whom she was forced to do strenuous work to feed, she lost her health, certainly. Suffering from malnutrition and neglect and who knows what mental agonies, Phillis Wheatley died.

So torn by 'contrary instincts' was black, kidnapped, enslaved Phillis that her description of 'the Goddess' — as she poetically called the Liberty she did not have — is ironically, cruelly humorous. And, in fact, has held Phillis up to ridicule for more than a century. It is usually read prior to hanging Phillis's memory as that of a fool. She wrote:

> The Goddess comes, she moves divinely fair,
> Olive and laurel binds her *golden* hair.
> Wherever shines this native of the skies,
> Unnumber'd charms and recent graces rise. [My italics]

It is obvious that Phillis, the slave, combed the 'Goddess's' hair every morning; prior, perhaps, to bringing in the milk, or fixing her mistress's lunch. She took her imagery from the one thing she saw elevated above all others.

With the benefit of hindsight we ask, 'How could she?'

But at last, Phillis, we understand. No more snickering when your stiff, struggling, ambivalent lines are forced on us. We know now that you were not an idiot or a traitor; only a sickly little black girl, snatched from your home and country and made a slave; a woman who still struggled to sing the song that was your gift, although in a land of barbarians who praised you for your bewildered tongue. It is not so much what you sang, as that you kept alive, in so many of our ancestors, *the notion of song.*

MICHELE BARRETT
Women's Oppression Today

Although Woolf's account is more systematic than most, we still await a substantial account of *consumption* and reception of texts from the point of view of the ideology of gender (or from any other point of view, one could add). There has been a failure to develop a theory of reading. This is largely, I suspect, because any such analysis would have to confront directly one of the most difficult problems of a materialist aesthetics: the problem of value. Virginia Woolf, it might be noted, simply ignored this problem. Although challenging much of what constituted 'the canon' of great literature of her period, she slides quite unremorsefully into the worst kind of aesthetic league-tabling in much of her criticism. Preoccupation with the question of value ('quality', 'standards') has been detrimental for feminist criticism and appears to have been posed as a choice between two limited options. On the one hand, we have the view exemplified by Virginia Woolf: that women have not reached the achievements of male writers, but that this is to be attributed to the constraints historically inherent in the conditions in which their work was produced and consumed. On the other hand, there is the view that women *have* achieved equally in respect of aesthetic value and we only think otherwise because of the warped and prejudiced response of a predominantly male, and sexist, critical and academic establishment.

This debate is fruitless (although admittedly seductive) in that it reproduces the assumption that aesthetic judgment is independent of social and historical context. Simply to pose the question at this level is to deny what we do already know: that not only are refined details of aesthetic ranking highly culturally specific, but that there is not even any consensus across classes, let alone across cultures, as to which cultural products can legitimately be subjected to such judgments. I am not contending that these observations obviate the problem of aesthetic value, since I believe it to be an urgent task of feminist criticism to take it on in the context of the female literary tradition, but merely that it should not be posed in simplistic terms.

VIVIANE FORRESTER
'What Women's Eyes See', New French Feminisms

We don't know what women's vision is. What do women's eyes see? How do they carve, invent, decipher the world? I don't know. I know my own vision, the vision of one woman, but the world seen through the eyes of others? I only know what men's eyes see.

So what do men's eyes see? A crippled world, mutilated, deprived of women's vision. In fact men share our malaise, suffer from the same tragedy: the absence of women particularly in the field of cinema.

If we were responsible for this absence, couldn't they complain about it? 'After all,' they would say, 'we have communicated our images, our vision to you; you are withholding yours. That is why we present a castrated universe, a life whose essential answers are unknown to us. We make films, we attempt to say, to translate, to destroy, to know, to invent, and you condemn us to a monologue that confines us to stale repetition, an isolation such that we are becoming petrified in endless narcissism. We have only fathers. We see only through our own fantasms, our malaise, the tricks we play on you, our renunciations (this network of conventions which replaces you and propagates itself dangerously at every level of our work) and the vacuum created by your absence and the dolls who fill it and whom we have fabricated. And we do not know how you see us. You do not look at us, etc.'

We don't hear such complaints and for obvious reasons. Because this blindness to women's vision, which in fact prohibits any global vision of the world, any vision of the human species, has been fashioned by men for our mutual impoverishment.

How can male directors today not beg women to pick up the camera, to open up unknown areas to them, to liberate them from their redundant vision which is deeply deformed by this lack? Women's vision is what is lacking and this lack not only creates a vacuum but it perverts, alters, annuls every statement. Women's vision is what you don't see; it is withdrawn, concealed. The images, the pictures, the frames, the movements, the rhythms, the abrupt new shots of which we have been deprived, these are the prisoners of women's vision, of a confined vision.

The quality of this vision is not the point — in the hierarchical sense — it is not better (how absurd to speak of a 'better' vision), it is not more efficient, more immediate (certain women will assert that it is, but that's *not* the point); but it is lacking. And this deficiency is suicidal.

Women are going to seize (they are beginning to do so) what they should have acquired naturally at the same time as men did, what men after this bad start should have eventually begged women to undertake: the practice of film making. Women will have to defend themselves against an accumulation of clichés, of sacred routines which men delight in or reject and which will frequently trap women as well. They will need a great deal of concentration and above all of precision. They will have to see, to look, to look at themselves unaffectedly, with a natural gaze that is so difficult to maintain; they will have to dare to see not only their own fantasms, but also, instead of an old catalogue, fresh, new images of a weary world. Why will they be more apt to rid themselves of whatever obstructs men's vision? Because women are the secret to be discovered, they are the fissures. They are the source where no one has been.

Translated by Isabelle de Courtivron

SHOSHANA FELMAN
'Women and Madness: The Critical Phallacy', *Diacritics*

A question could be raised: if 'the woman' is precisely the Other of any conceivable Western theoretical locus of speech, how can the woman as such be speaking in this book? Who is speaking here, and who is asserting the otherness of the woman? If, as Luce Irigaray suggests, the woman's silence, or the repression of her capacity to speak, are constitutive of philosophy and of theoretical discourse as such, from what theoretical locus is Luce Irigaray herself speaking in order to develop her own theoretical discourse about the woman's exclusion? Is she speaking the language of men, or the silence of women? Is she speaking *as* a woman, or *in place of* the (silent) woman, *for* the woman, *in the name of* the woman? Is it enough to *be* a woman in order to *speak* as a woman? Is 'speaking as a woman' a fact determined by some biological *condition* or by a strategic, theoretical *position*, by anatomy[1] or by culture? What if 'speaking as a woman' were not a simple 'natural' fact, could not be taken for granted? With the increasing number of women and men alike who are currently choosing to share in the rising fortune of female misfortune, it has become all too easy to be a speaker '*for* women.' But what does 'speaking *for* women' imply? What is 'to speak *in the name of* the woman'? What, in a general manner, does 'speech in the name of' mean? Is it not a precise repetition of the oppressive gesture of *representation*, by means of which, throughout the history of logos, man has reduced the woman to the status of a silent and subordinate object, to something inherently *spoken for*? To 'speak in the name of,' to 'speak *for*,' could thus mean, once again, to appropriate and to silence. This important theoretical question about the status of its own discourse and its own 'representation' of women, with which any feminist thought has to cope, is not thought out by Luce Irigaray, and thus remains the blind spot of her critical undertaking.

NOTE

1   Freud has thus pronounced his famous verdict on women: 'Anatomy is destiny.' But this is precisely the focus of the feminist contestation.

GAYATRI CHAKRAVORTY SPIVAK
'French Feminism in an International Frame', *Yale French Studies*

A young Sudanese woman in the Faculty of Sociology at a Saudi Arabian University said to me, surprisingly: 'I have written a structural functionalist dissertation on female circumcision in the Sudan.' I was ready to forgive the sexist term 'female circumcision.' We have learned to say 'clitoridectomy' because others more acute than we have pointed out our mistake.

But Structural Functionalism? Where 'integration' is 'social control [which] defines and *enforces* . . . a degree of *solidarity*'? Where 'interaction, seen from the side of the economy,' is defined as 'consist[ing] of the supply of income and wealth applied to purposes strengthening the persistence of cultural patterns?'[1] Structural functionalism takes a 'disinterested' stance on society as functioning structure. Its implicit interest is to applaud a system — in this case sexual — because it functions. A description such as the one below makes it difficult to credit that this young Sudanese woman had taken such an approach to clitoridectomy:

> In Egypt it is only the clitoris which is amputated, and usually not completely. But in the Sudan, the operation consists in the complete removal of all the external genital organs. They cut off the clitoris, the two major outer lips (*labia majora*) and the two minor inner lips (*labia minora*). Then the wound is repaired. The outer opening of the vagina is the only portion left intact, not however without having ensured that, during the process of repairing, some narrowing of the opening is carried out with a few extra stitches. The result is that on the marriage night it is necessary to widen the external opening by slitting one or both ends with a sharp scalpel or razor so that the male organ can be introduced.[2]

In my Sudanese colleague's research I found an allegory of my own ideological victimage:

The 'choice' of English Honors by an upper-class young woman in the Calcutta of the fifties was itself highly overdetermined. Becoming a professor of English in the U.S. fitted in with the 'brain drain.' In due course, a commitment to feminism was the best of a collection of accessible scenarios. The morphology of a feminist theoretical practice came clear through Jacques Derrida's critique of phallocentrism and Luce Irigaray's reading of Freud. (The stumbling 'choice' of French avant-garde criticism by an undistinguished Ivy League Ph.D. working in the Midwest is itself not without ideology-critical interest.) Predictably, I began by identifying the 'female academic' and feminism as such. Gradually I found that there was indeed an area of feminist scholarship in the U.S. that was called 'International Feminism:' the arena usually defined as feminism in England, France, West Germany, Italy, and that part of the Third World most easily accessible to American interests: Latin America. When one attempted to think of so-called Third World women in a broader scope, one found oneself caught, as my Sudanese colleague was caught and held by Structural Functionalism, in a web of information retrieval inspired at best by: 'what can I do *for* them?'

I sensed obscurely that this articulation was part of the problem. I re-articulated the question: What is the constituency of an international feminism? The following fragmentary and anecdotal pages approach the question. The complicity of a few French texts in that attempt could be part both of the problem — the 'West' out to 'know' the 'East' determining a 'westernized Easterner's' symptomatic attempt to 'know her own world'; or of something like a solution, — reversing and displacing (if only by juxtaposing 'some French texts' and a 'certain Calcutta') the ironclad opposition of West and East. As soon as I write this, it seems a hopelessly idealistic restatement of the problem. I am not in a position of choice in this dilemma.

To begin with, an obstinate childhood memory.

I am walking alone in my grandfather's estate on the Bihar-Bengal border one winter afternoon in 1949. Two ancient washerwomen are washing clothes in the river, beating the clothes on the stones. One accuses the other of poaching on her part of the river. I can still hear the cracked derisive voice of the one accused: 'You fool! Is this your river? The river belongs to the Company!' — the East India Company, from whom India passed to England by the Act for the Better Government of India (1858); England had transferred its charge to an Indian Governor-General in 1947. India would become an independent republic in 1950. For these withered women, the land as soil and water to be used rather than a map to be learned still belonged, as it did one hundred and nineteen years before that date, to the East India Company.

I was precocious enough to know that the remark was incorrect. It has taken me thirty-one years and the experience of confronting a nearly inarticulable question to apprehend that their facts were wrong but the fact was right. The Company does still own the land.

I should not consequently patronize and romanticize these women, nor yet entertain a nostalgia for being as they are. The academic feminist must learn to learn from them, to speak to them, to suspect that their access to the political and sexual scene is not merely to be *corrected* by our superior theory and enlightened compassion. Is our insistence upon the especial beauty of the old necessarily to be preferred to a careless acknowledgment of the mutability of sexuality? What of the fact that my distance from those two was, however micrologically you defined class, class-determined and determining?

How, then, can one learn from and speak to the millions of illiterate rural and urban Indian women who live 'in the pores of' capitalism, inaccessible to the capitalist dynamics that allow us our shared channels of communication, the definition of common enemies? The pioneering books that bring First World feminists news from the Third World are written by privileged informants and can only be deciphered by a trained readership. The distance between 'the informant's world,' her 'own sense of the world she writes about,' and that of the non-specialist feminist is so great that, paradoxically, *pace* the subtleties of reader-response theories, here the distinctions might easily be missed.

This is not the tired nationalist claim that only a native can know the scene. The point that I am trying to make is that, in order to learn enough about Third World women and to develop a different readership, the immense heterogeneity of the field must be appreciated, and the First World feminist must learn to stop feeling privileged *as a woman*.

[. . .]

As soon as one steps out of the classroom, if indeed a 'teacher' ever fully can, the dangers rather than the benefits of academic feminism, French or otherwise, become more insistent. Institutional changes against sexism here or in France may mean nothing or, indirectly, further harm for women in the Third World.[44] This discontinuity ought to be recognized and worked at. Otherwise, the focus remains defined by the investigator as subject. To bring us back to my initial concerns, let me insist that here, the difference between 'French' and 'Anglo-American' feminism is superficial. However unfeasible and inefficient it may sound, I see no way to avoid insisting that there has to be a simultaneous other focus: not merely who am I? but who is the other woman? How am I naming her? How does she name me? Is this part of the problematic I discuss? Indeed, it is the absence of such unfeasible but crucial questions that makes the 'colonized woman' as 'subject' see the investigators as sweet and sympathetic creatures from another planet who are free to come and go; or, depending on her own socialization in the colonizing cultures, see 'feminism' as having a vanguardist class fix, the liberties it fights for as luxuries, finally identifiable with 'free sex' of one kind or another. Wrong, of course. My point has been that there is something equally wrong in our most sophisticated research, our most benevolent impulses.

NOTES

1   Bert F. Hoselitz, 'Development and the Theory of Social Systems,' in M. Stanley, ed., *Social Development* (New York: Basic Books, 1972), pp. 44, 45. I am grateful to Professor Michael Ryan for drawing my attention to this article.
2   Nawal El Saadawi, *The Hidden Face of Eve: Women in the Arab World* (London: Zed Press, 1980), p. 5.

[. . .]

44   To take the simplest possible American examples, even such innocent triumphs as the hiring of more tenured women or adding feminist sessions at a Convention might lead, since most U.S. universities have dubious investments, and most Convention hotels use Third World female labor in a most oppressive way, to the increasing proletarianization of the women of the less developed countries.

2

Women and Literary Production

INTRODUCTION

Problems for the Woman Writer

Why are women under-represented as published writers? The extracts by Virginia Woolf, Tillie Olsen and Adrienne Rich point not to a maliciously planned conspiracy by top male publishers to keep women out of print, but to a complex combination of material and ideological factors that inhibit the potential woman writer. The catalogue of material problems is long — inequalities in the educational system, lack of privacy, the burdens of child-bearing and rearing, domestic obligations — but equally decisive are the restrictions of family and social expectations. Even when women writers solve the material problems that prevent their writing, an anxiety about their chosen role and how they are perceived continues to surface. For many women writers what cannot be easily overcome is an awareness of an oppressive male presence constraining their work; Woolf's irritation about the unsympathetic male reader and Rich's consciousness of following a line of male poets testify to that. Woolf herself illustrates how deeply entrenched is the problem. Despite her strong belief that 'it is fatal for anyone who writes to think of their sex', despite her privileged position of economic independence and a room of her own, despite her high level of conciousness, she still has to admit, in 'Professions for Women', that she has 'many ghosts to fight, many prejudices to overcome'.

Repeatedly, the woman writer finds herself at a point of tension, aware that her writing both challenges the conventional view of what is appropriate for women and encroaches on what some see as a male preserve. If the woman writer writes about women, she risks the label of 'partiality', 'narrowness', 'a woman's book'. If she tries to write about her own deepest responses, particularly sexual, she feels anxious about revealing 'the truth about my own experiences as a body' (Woolf), or about 'experiencing myself as a woman' (Rich). Indeed the very act of writing is seen as expressing a conflict between 'traditional female functions' and 'the subversive function of the imagination' (Rich). Sandra Gilbert and Susan Gubar go even further. With what must be among the most memorable opening sentences in literary criticism — 'Is a pen a metaphorical penis?' — they trace that literary history which sees writing as essentially 'male', a kind of extension of the male generative act, and which confers on the male writer authority, the right to create, control, and possess. Thus 'phallic' criticism will find the woman writer compromised, unfeminine and presumptuous.[1] In trying to negotiate such criticism, Gilbert and Gubar believe the woman writer is involved in a complex balancing act between apparent conformity to certain patriarchal literary norms and a trenchant critique of those same standards. The figure of the madwoman is an aspect of that critique, expressing the unacceptable, the authorial rage and desire and antagonism.

Mary Jacobus and Toril Moi have taken issue with Gilbert and Gubar's thesis. Jacobus feels that in Gilbert and Gubar's work women writers become 'exceptionally articulate victims of a patriarchally engendered plot'.[2] Moi asks a related question:

> How did women manage to write at all given the relentless patriarchal indoctrination which surrounded them from the moment they were born?[3]

Jacobus believes that Gilbert and Gubar's analysis, preoccupied as it is with plot and author, 'immobilises the play of meaning in the text',[4] while Moi indicates the need to understand 'the contradictory, fragmentary nature of patriarchal ideology'.[5] For both Jacobus and Moi, Gilbert and Gubar's book is uneasily situated between a view of the literary establishment as comprehensively antagonistic to women writers and the historical evidence that many women did actually write.

The problem for the woman writer lies not only in the production of writing; an equally fraught area is its reception. What Gilbert and Gubar call the 'anxiety of authorship' has been created and maintained in part through the practices of reviewing and literary criticism. Adrienne Rich comments at the end of her extract on the false and polarized definitions which link women with selflessness and altruism and men with a driving egotism that produces art. In an entirely circular way, according to this definition, art is male and men are the 'natural' creators of art. Thus, if women do attempt to write, they are seen simply as bringing to the major body of established male texts the 'feminine' qualities they are supposed to represent in life generally. Elaine Showalter, in her analysis of Victorian periodical reviews, demonstrates the construction of a literary criticism based on the traditional stereotypes of male and female attributes:

> If we break down the categories that are the staple of Victorian periodical reviewing, we find that women writers were acknowledged to possess sentiment, refinement, tact, observation, domestic expertise, high moral tone, and knowledge of female character; and thought to lack originality, intellectual training, abstract intelligence, humor, self-control, and knowledge of male character. Male writers had most of the desirable qualities: power, breadth, distinctness, clarity, learning, abstract intelligence, shrewdness, experience, humor, knowledge of everyone's character, and open-mindedness.[6]

Margaret Atwood's research reveals that this practice of ascribing rigidly structured concepts of male and female to styles of writing — what she terms the 'Quiller-Couch Syndrome' — is still alive and well in twentieth-century reviewing.

The Position of the Black Woman Writer

For the black woman writer, Barbara Smith suggests, problems of literary production are compounded by racism. Black writing by both women and men in the States exists as a 'discrete subcategory of American literature', and reviewing and literary criticism again play their parts in reinforcing certain values and ignoring or discrediting others. It is salutary to read Woolf's 'Judith Shakespeare' story alongside Alice Walker's rewriting of it to appreciate how the creativity of the black woman has been thwarted and how, generally, the white woman has failed to notice the injustice.[7] Towards the end of the Judith Shakespeare extract Woolf makes one of her very characteristic rapid developments of an idea, moving within a few lines from the silence of women, to the desire of men to mark, name and possess, to the imperialist claim for the control of land and other people. Set against Woolf's dubious contention that a white *woman* would not wish to so dominate and refashion a black woman is Walker's story of the black poet, Phillis Wheatley, sold into slavery, combing the white mistress's hair and, tragically, finding in the white woman her imagery for godliness. For Woolf, the black woman enters the argument not as a potential writer — she is white — but as a victim of imperialism. Despite all we know of women's involvement in anti-slavery, anti-racist, anti-apartheid movements it is misleading of Woolf to suggest that the white woman has not been complicit in the oppression of the black. How are we to interpret that phrase, 'even a very fine negress'? What are the attributes of 'a very fine negress'; are we supposed to recognize her difference from 'a less fine negress'; does the word 'even' suggest that the white woman would be tempted to co-opt certain 'superior' black women but not others? Moreover, what does the word 'advantages' mean; is Woolf congratulating the white woman on her lack of racism, taking quiet pleasure in her 'virtue'? Woolf, who is so acute on issues of gender, so sophisticated in her awareness, exhibits here an unconscious racism in what can be described as hardly more than a liberal gesture against the era of high imperialism.

When the non-white woman does gain some access to literary production it is usually, the Black Woman Talk Collective indicates, as a small, token subordinate group. Furthermore, the Collective asks why even that presence should be dominated by the work of Afro-American women. Who, indeed, constitute 'black women' in literary production? The Black Woman Talk Collective makes clear that its members and prime area of concern are 'women of Asian and African descent living in Britain'. Recent work on feminism and racism has debated, though not from a literary perspective, the value of a deconstructive approach, disentangling the meanings of the terms 'black' and 'white', rather than accepting the polarized categories.[8]

The point is contentious. There is the fear that in rejecting the black/white distinction we may also lose sight of 'the political, social and ideological force of racism in our society'.[9] Other feminists suggest the need to work on two fronts, at once deconstructive *and* oppositional. Gayatri Chakravorty Spivak, for instance, writes of feminism's joint programme:

> *against* sexism, where women unite as a biologically oppressed caste; and *for* feminism, where human beings train to prepare for a transformation of consciousness.[10]

Presumably, a similar double programme is possible for the black woman, both against racism and for a new understanding of the categories 'black' and 'white'. Hitherto in black feminist criticism it is the oppositional role that has been uppermost. The difference of black women, the immediacy of struggle is repeatedly and necessarily emphasized. Spivak would not negate that need but would insist that it becomes part of a twin perspective.

Possibilities for the Woman Writer

Most of the work on gender and literary production has looked at the *problems* of female literary production. The marked difference in the number of male and female writers and the prevalence, particularly in the early 1970s, of the debate about gaining access have both prompted such an approach. But it is equally important to turn the question on its head, as Terry Lovell does, and ask, not what has inhibited women's writing, but what has made it possible. Rejecting Gilbert and Gubar's assertion that literary production in Western culture is firmly associated with the male, Lovell suggests that it is, on the contrary, 'gender ambiguous'. The emphatic claims of the male writers whom Gilbert and Gubar quote, speaking so conclusively of the masculine nature of literary production, reveal to Lovell, not a confident and consolidated tradition, but a deep insecurity about femininity and how it might relate to writing. Though Lovell dismisses Lacanian psychoanalytical theory, her argument here seems in line with Julia Kristeva's concept of the 'semiotic'. Terry Eagleton characterizes the semiotic as 'a pattern or play of forces which we can detect inside language', a description which certainly corresponds with Lovell's interpretation.[11]

Lovell remarks on the popular 'feminine' image of creative writing, on the involvement of female students in the study of languages and literature, and on the development of the novel, as all indicating the gender ambiguity of literary production — an ambiguity which women can exploit. But not all literary forms have been as accessible to women as the novel. The theatre is not associated in the popular imagination with 'manliness', and, as students of drama, women are well represented. Yet there are far fewer women playwrights than women novelists. A survey of plays in performance between September 1982 and September 1983 revealed that women constituted 108.5 of the total number of playwrights whereas men constituted 915.5.[12] Similarly, to take up Lovell's fourth point, theatrical production is public rather than domestic and the key roles in the public arena remain firmly in the hands of men. The same survey shows that during the period in question 103 men held the position of artistic director against 14 women, 54 men were resident associate directors against 11 women, and 220 men were acting as freelance directors against 70 women. None of this discounts Lovell's thesis; it merely stresses that gender and literary production do not interrelate in a uniform or consistent way and a consideration of literary form is but one of the many variables that needs to be taken into account.

The Relation of Women to Male Literary Production

Three aspects, in particular, feature in the debates concerning women's relation to the literary production of men: firstly, the place of women as the unacknowledged support of the male writer, the power behind the throne; secondly, the feminist challenge to the notion of 'writer'; and thirdly, the place of 'woman' as sign in male writing.

The Power Behind the Throne. Feminists believe that the contribution of women, as research assistants, secretaries, or supportive wives, to the literary production of men has been, largely, unrecognized. A perfunctory dedication — 'To my wife without whom this book would not have been possible' — is the most acknowledgement that literary wives can expect for the domestic labour that often has, indeed, facilitated the book. Some effort has been made in feminist criticism to discover the lives of these hidden women — Dorothy Wordsworth, or Alice James, or Zelda Fitzgerald, or Jane Carlyle. At times the involvement goes beyond domestic labour or clerical work. Elizabeth Hardwick notices in certain literary wives a level of emotional and intellectual commitment to the man's writing that amounts almost to collaboration. For instance, she remarks that the Countess Tolstoy, 'worried and copied and thought about *his* books with an energy that would have put George Sand to shame'.[13] Tillie Olsen makes an even greater claim and reassesses the hidden women as lost literary talents, *their* imaginative potential becoming channelled into the writing of their husbands, brothers or fathers. The women leave behind only letters or diaries or journals as an indication of their creativity:

> How much is revealed of the differing circumstances and fate of their own *as-great* capacities, in the diaries (and lives) of those female bloodkin of great writers: Dorothy Wordsworth, Alice James, Aunt Mary Moody Emerson. (Editor's italics)[14]

Challenging the Notion of 'Writer'. Adrienne Rich, in her initial paragraph, is aware of how the woman writer can bathe in the reflected glory of the male writer. The woman writer is the 'special woman', one of the few chosen to join the select group of male writers. As such, she is in danger of being incorporated, a token, removed from her sisters in less prestigious forms of labour. What is present, but not fully developed, in Rich's argument is a critique of the notion of 'writer' in our culture. She recognizes the privilege of writing, the elitist division between the writer and the housewife, and the glamour and cachet value in 'being a writer', but she stops short of a full-scale deconstructive analysis. She questions the authority of the writer in terms of his/her social position, but not the authority of the writer as the source of meaning, the inspired originator of insights and truths. Thus, her way forward is not through 'the death of the author', as Roland Barthes would have it, but through the author placing at the service of all women her special talent and perceptions.

'Woman' as Sign. Virginia Woolf in *A Room of One's Own* has commented on the contradictory position of women in history, charged with symbolic significance while materially deprived:

> Imaginatively she is of the highest importance; practically she is completely insignificant. She pervades poetry from cover to cover; she is all but absent from history. She dominates the lives of kings and conquerors in fiction; in fact she was the slave of any boy whose parents forced a ring upon her finger. Some of the most inspired words, some of the most profound thoughts in literature fall from her lips; in real life she could hardly read, could hardly spell, and was the property of her husband.[15]

A similar contradiction exists within literary production. Women have difficulty in gaining access to literary production as writers, but as the characters, images, myths or symbols in writing they are richly present. The difference is between 'women', active, productive, historical beings, and 'woman' as a sign, a construct created in culture. 'Woman' as a sign is central in the writing of men; in fact, as Virginia Woolf discovers in the British Museum, seemingly every male writer is anxious to make his contribution to the category 'woman':

> Sex and its nature might well attract doctors and biologists; but what was surprising and difficult of explanation was the fact that sex — woman, that is to say — also attracts agreeable essayists, light-fingered novelists, young men who have taken the M.A. degree; men who have taken no degree; men who have no qualification save that they are not women.[16]

For Cynthia Ozick, 'woman' appears in the writing of men as the Muse — 'She *is* the Muse' — the idealized inspiration for the male writer. On the other hand, Mary Ellmann explores the construction of 'woman' as a 'vicious influence upon writing by men'. She is a literary Eve who leads astray the male writer, a literary Delilah who destroys his creative power. What is reproduced here is one of the basic dichotomies in the patriarchal understanding of 'woman'; she is both virgin and whore.

NOTES

1 The term 'phallic' criticism is taken from Mary Ellmann, *Thinking About Women* (New York, Harcourt Brace Jovanovich, 1968), Ch. 2.
2 Mary Jacobus, 'Review of *The Madwoman in the Attic: The Woman Writer and the Nineteenth-Century Literary Imagination*', in *Signs: Journal of Women in Culture and Society*, vol. 6, no. 3 (1981), p. 522.

3   Toril Moi, *Sexual/Textual Politics: Feminist Literary Theory* (London, Methuen, 1985), p. 64.

4   Jacobus, 'Review of *The Madwoman in the Attic*', p. 518.

5   Moi, *Sexual/Textual Politics*, p. 64.

6   Elaine Showalter, *A Literature of Their Own: British Women Novelists from Brontë to Lessing* (London, Virago, 1978), p. 90.

7   The extract from Alice Walker I refer to here is to be found in Ch. 1, p. 31.

8   See, for instance, Floya Anthias and Nira Yuval-Davis, 'Contextualizing feminism — gender, ethnic and class divisions', in *Feminist Review*, 15 (1983).

9   Michèle Barrett and Mary McIntosh, 'Ethnocentricism and Socialist-Feminist Theory', in *Feminist Review*, 20 (1985). This article directly responds to that of Anthias and Yuval-Davis.

10   Gayatri Chakravorty Spivak, 'French Feminism in an International Frame', in *Yale French Studies*, 62 (1981), p. 170. See also Moi, pp. 12—13.

11   Terry Eagleton, *Literary Theory: An Introduction* (Oxford, Blackwell, 1983), p. 188. The passage from which this quotation comes is included in Ch. 5, p. 213. I am grateful to Julia Mosse for pointing out this connection.

12   Sue Dunderdale, 'The Status of Women in the British Theatre', in *Drama*, 152, (1984).

13   Elizabeth Hardwick, *Seduction and Betrayal: Women and Literature* (New York, Vintage Books/Random House, 1975), p. 156.

14   Tillie Olsen, *Silences* (New York, Dell, 1978), p. 17.

15   Virginia Woolf, *A Room of One's Own* (New York, Harcourt Brace Jovanovich, 1963), pp. 45—6.

16   Ibid., p. 27.

VIRGINIA WOOLF
A Room of One's Own

Let me imagine, since facts are so hard to come by, what would have happened had Shakespeare had a wonderfully gifted sister, called Judith, let us say. Shakespeare himself went, very probably — his mother was an heiress — to the grammar school, where he may have learnt Latin — Ovid, Virgil and Horace — and the elements of grammar and logic. He was, it is well known, a wild boy who poached rabbits, perhaps shot a deer, and had, rather sooner than he should have done, to marry a woman in the neighbourhood, who bore him a child rather quicker than was right. That escapade sent him to seek his fortune in London. He had, it seemed, a taste for the theatre; he began by holding horses at the stage door. Very soon he got work in the theatre, became a successful actor, and lived at the hub of the universe, meeting everybody, knowing everybody, practising his art on the boards, exercising his wits in the streets, and even getting access to the palace of the queen. Meanwhile his extraordinarily gifted sister, let us suppose, remained at home. She was as adventurous, as imaginative, as agog to see the world as he was. But she was not sent to school. She had no chance of learning grammar and logic, let alone of reading Horace and Virgil. She picked up a book now and then, one of her brother's perhaps, and read a few pages. But then her parents came in and told her to mend the stockings or mind the stew and not moon about with books and papers. They would have spoken sharply but kindly, for they were substantial people who knew the conditions of life for a woman and loved their daughter — indeed, more likely than not she was the apple of her father's eye. Perhaps she scribbled some pages up in an apple loft on the sly, but was careful to hide them or set fire to them. Soon, however, before she was out of her teens, she was to be betrothed to the son of a neighbouring wool-stapler. She cried out that marriage was hateful to her, and for that she was severely beaten by her father. Then he ceased to scold her. He begged her instead not to hurt him, not to shame him in this matter of her marriage. He would give her a chain of beads or a fine petticoat, he said; and there were tears in his eyes. How could she disobey him? How could she break his heart? The force of her own gift alone drove her to it. She made up a small parcel of her belongings, let herself down by a rope one summer's night and took the road to London. She was not seventeen. The birds that sang in the hedge were not more musical than she was. She had the quickest fancy, a gift like her brother's, for the tune of words. Like him, she had a taste for the theatre. She stood at the stage door; she wanted to act, she said. Men laughed in her face. The manager — a fat, loose-lipped man — guffawed. He bellowed something about poodles dancing and women acting — no woman, he said, could possibly be an actress. He hinted — you can imagine what. She could get no training in her craft. Could she even seek her dinner in a tavern or roam the streets at midnight? Yet her genius was for fiction and lusted to feed abundantly upon the lives of men and women and the study of their ways. At last — for she was very young, oddly like Shakespeare the poet in her face, with the same grey eyes and rounded brows — at last Nick Greene the actor-manager took pity on her; she found herself with child by that gentleman and so — who shall measure the heat and violence of the poet's heart when caught and tangled in a woman's body? — killed herself one winter's night and lies buried at some cross-roads where the omnibuses now stop outside the Elephant and Castle.

That, more or less, is how the story would run, I think, if a woman in Shakespeare's day had had Shakespeare's genius. But for my part, I agree with the deceased bishop, if such he was — it is unthinkable that any woman in Shakespeare's day should have had Shakespeare's genius. For genius like Shakespeare's is not born among labouring, uneducated, servile people. It was not born in England among the Saxons and the Britons. It is not born today among the working classes. How, then, could it have been born among women whose work began, according to Professor Trevelyan, almost before they were out of the nursery, who were forced to it by their parents and held to it by all the power of law and custom? Yet genius of a sort must have existed among women as it must have existed among the working classes. Now and again an Emily Brontë or a Robert Burns blazes out and proves its presence. But certainly it never got itself on to paper. When, however, one reads of a witch being ducked, of a woman possessed by devils, of a wise woman selling herbs, or even of a very remarkable man who had a mother, then I think we are on the track of a lost novelist, a suppressed poet, of some mute and inglorious Jane Austen, some Emily Brontë who dashed her brains out on the moor or mopped and mowed about the highways crazed with the torture that her gift had put her to. Indeed, I would venture to guess that Anon, who wrote so many poems without signing them, was often a woman. It was a woman Edward Fitzgerald, I think, suggested who made the ballads and the folk-songs, crooning them to her children, beguiling her spinning with them, or the length of the winter's night.

This may be true or it may be false — who can say? — but what is true in it, so it seemed to me, reviewing the story of Shakespeare's sister as I had made it, is that any woman born with a great gift in the sixteenth century would certainly have gone crazed, shot herself, or ended her days in some lonely cottage outside the village, half witch, half wizard, feared and mocked at. For it needs little skill in psychology to be sure that a highly gifted girl who had tried to use her gift for poetry would have been so thwarted and hindered by other people, so tortured and pulled asunder by her own contrary instincts, that she must have lost her health and sanity to a certainty. No girl could have walked to London and stood at a stage door and forced her way into the presence of actor-managers without doing herself a violence and suffering an anguish which may have been irrational — for chastity may be a fetish invented by certain societies for unknown reasons — but were none the less inevitable. Chastity had then, it has even now, a religious importance in a woman's life, and has so wrapped itself round with nerves and instincts that to cut it free and bring it to the light of day demands courage of the rarest. To have lived a free life in London in the sixteenth century would have meant for a woman who was poet and playwright a nervous stress and dilemma which might well have killed her. Had she survived, whatever she had written would have been twisted and deformed, issuing from a strained and morbid imagination. And undoubtedly, I thought, looking at the shelf where there are no plays by women, her work would have gone unsigned. That refuge she would have sought certainly. It was the relic of the sense of chastity that dictated anonymity to women even so late as the nineteenth century. Currer Bell, George Eliot, George Sand, all the victims of inner strife as their writings prove, sought ineffectively to veil themselves by using the name of a man. Thus they did homage to the convention, which if not implanted by the other sex was liberally encouraged by them (the chief glory of a woman is not to be talked of, said Pericles, himself a much-talked-of man), that publicity in women is detestable. Anonymity runs in their blood. The desire to be veiled still possesses them. They are not even now as concerned about the health of their fame as men are, and, speaking generally, will pass a tombstone or a signpost without feeling an irresistible desire to cut their names on it, as Alf, Bert or Chas. must do in obedience to their instinct, which murmurs if it sees a fine woman go by, or even a dog, Ce chien est à moi. And, of course, it may not be a dog, I thought, remembering Parliament Square, the Sieges Allee and other avenues; it may be a piece of land or a man with curly black hair. It is one of the great advantages of being a woman that one can pass even a very fine negress without wishing to make an Englishwoman of her.

[. . .]

But for women, I thought, looking at the empty shelves, these difficulties were infinitely more formidable. In the first place, to have a room of her own, let alone a quiet room or a sound-proof room, was out of the question, unless her parents were exceptionally rich or very noble, even up to the beginning of the nineteenth century. Since her pin money, which depended on the good will of her father, was only enough to keep her clothed, she was debarred from such alleviations as came even to Keats or Tennyson or Carlyle, all poor men, from a walking tour, a little journey to France, from the separate lodging which, even if it were miserable enough, sheltered them from the claims and tyrannies of their families. Such material difficulties were formidable; but much worse were the immaterial. The indifference of the world which Keats and Flaubert and other men of genius have found so hard to bear was in her case not indifference but hostility. The world did not say to her as it said to them, Write if you choose; it makes no difference to me. The world said with a guffaw, Write? What's the good of your writing? Here the psychologists of Newnham and Girton might come to our help, I thought, looking again at the blank spaces on the shelves. For surely it is time that the effect of discouragement upon the mind of the artist should be measured, as I have seen a dairy company measure the effect of ordinary milk and Grade A milk upon the body of the rat. They set two rats in cages side by side, and of the two one was furtive, timid and small, and the other was glossy, bold and big. Now what food do we feed women as artists upon? I asked, remembering, I suppose, that dinner of prunes and custard. To answer that question I had only to open the evening paper and to read that Lord Birkenhead is of opinion — but really I am not going to trouble to copy out Lord Birkenhead's opinion upon the writing of women. What Dean Inge says I will leave in peace. The Harley Street specialist may be allowed to rouse the echoes of Harley Street with his vociferations without raising a hair on my head. I will quote, however, Mr. Oscar Browning, because Mr. Oscar Browning was a great figure in Cambridge at one time, and used to examine the students at Girton and Newnham. Mr. Oscar Browning was wont to declare 'that the impression left on his mind, after looking over any set of examination papers, was that, irrespective of the marks he might give, the best woman was intellectually the inferior of the worst man.' After saying that Mr. Browning went back to his rooms — and it is this sequel that endears him and makes him a human figure of some bulk and majesty — he went back to his rooms and found a stable-boy lying on the sofa — 'a mere skeleton, his cheeks were cavernous and sallow, his teeth were black, and he did not appear to have the full use of his limbs. . . . "That's Arthur" [said Mr. Browning]. "He's a dear boy really and most high-minded."' The two pictures always seem to me to complete each other. And happily in this age of biography the two pictures often do complete each other, so that we are able to interpret the opinions of great men not only by what they say, but by what they do.

But though this is possible now, such opinions coming from the lips of important people must have been formidable enough even fifty years ago. Let us suppose that a father from the highest motives did not wish his daughter to leave home and become writer, painter or scholar. 'See what Mr. Oscar Browning says,' he would say; and there was not only Mr. Oscar Browning; there was the *Saturday Review*; there was Mr. Greg — the 'essentials of a woman's being,' said Mr. Greg emphatically, 'are that *they are supported by, and they minister to, men*' — there was an enormous body of masculine opinion to the effect that nothing could be expected of women intellectually. Even if her father did not read out loud these opinions, any girl could read them for herself; and the reading, even in the nineteenth century, must have lowered her vitality, and told profoundly upon her work. There would always have been that assertion — you cannot do this, you are incapable of doing that — to protest against, to overcome. Probably for a novelist this germ is no longer of much effect; for there have been women novelists of merit. But for painters it must still have some sting in it; and for musicians, I imagine, is even now active and poisonous in the extreme. The woman composer stands where the actress stood in the time of Shakespeare. Nick Greene, I thought, remembering the story I had made about Shakespeare's sister, said that a woman acting put him in mind of a dog dancing. Johnson repeated the phrase two hundred years later of women preaching. And here, I said, opening a book about music, we have the very words used again in this year of grace, 1928, of women who try to write music. 'Of Mlle. Germaine Tailleferre one can only repeat Dr. Johnson's dictum concerning a woman preacher, transposed into terms of music. "Sir, a woman's composing is like a dog's walking on his hind legs. It is not done well, but you are surprised to find it done at all."'[2] So accurately does history repeat itself.

NOTE

2   *A Survey of Contemporary Music*, Cecil Gray, p. 246.

VIRGINIA WOOLF
'Professions for Women', *Women and Writing*

What could be easier than to write articles and to buy Persian cats with the profits? But wait a moment. Articles have to be about something. Mine, I seem to remember, was about a novel by a famous man. And while I was writing this review, I discovered that if I were going to review books I should need to do battle with a certain phantom. And the phantom was a woman, and when I came to know her better I called her after the heroine of a famous poem, The Angel in the House. It was she who used to come between me and my paper when I was writing reviews. It was she who bothered me and wasted my time and so tormented me that at last I killed her. You who come of a younger and happier generation may not have heard of her — you may not know what I mean by the Angel in the House. I will describe her as shortly as I can. She was intensely sympathetic. She was immensely charming. She was utterly unselfish. She excelled in the difficult arts of family life. She sacrificed herself daily. If there was chicken, she took the leg; if there was a draught she sat in it — in short she was so constituted that she never had a mind or a wish of her own, but preferred to sympathize always with the minds and wishes of others. Above all — I need not say it — she was pure. Her purity was supposed to be her chief beauty — her blushes, her great grace. In those days — the last of Queen Victoria — every house had its Angel. And when I came to write I encountered her with the very first words. The shadow of her wings fell on my page; I heard the rustling of her skirts in the room. Directly, that is to say, I took my pen in my hand to review that novel by a famous man, she slipped behind me and whispered: 'My dear, you are a young woman. You are writing about a book that has been written by a man. Be sympathetic; be tender; flatter; deceive; use all the arts and wiles of our sex. Never let anybody guess that you have a mind of your own. Above all, be pure.' And she made as if to guide my pen. I now record the one act for which I take some credit to myself, though the credit rightly belongs to some excellent ancestors of mine who left me a certain sum of money — shall we say five hundred pounds a year? — so that it was not necessary for me to depend solely on charm for my living. I turned upon her and caught her by the throat. I did my best to kill her. My excuse, if

I were to be had up in a court of law, would be that I acted in self-defence. Had I not killed her she would have killed me. She would have plucked the heart out of my writing. For, as I found, directly I put pen to paper, you cannot review even a novel without having a mind of your own, without expressing what you think to be the truth about human relations, morality, sex. And all these questions, according to the Angel of the House, cannot be dealt with freely and openly by women; they must charm, they must conciliate, they must — to put it bluntly — tell lies if they are to succeed. Thus, whenever I felt the shadow of her wing or the radiance of her halo upon my page, I took up the inkpot and flung it at her. She died hard. Her fictitious nature was of great assistance to her. It is far harder to kill a phantom than a reality. She was always creeping back when I thought I had despatched her. Though I flatter myself that I killed her in the end, the struggle was severe; it took much time that had better have been spent upon learning Greek grammar; or in roaming the world in search of adventures. But it was a real experience; it was an experience that was found to befall all women writers at that time. Killing the Angel in the House was part of the occupation of a woman writer.

[. . .]

I want you to figure to yourselves a girl sitting with a pen in her hand, which for minutes, and indeed for hours, she never dips into the inkpot. The image that comes to my mind when I think of this girl is the image of a fisherman lying sunk in dreams on the verge of a deep lake with a rod held out over the water. She was letting her imagination sweep unchecked round every rock and cranny of the world that lies submerged in the depths of our unconscious being. Now came the experience, the experience that I believe to be far commoner with women writers than with men. The line raced through the girl's fingers. Her imagination had rushed away. It had sought the pools, the depths, the dark places where the largest fish slumber. And then there was a smash. There was an explosion. There was foam and confusion. The imagination had dashed itself against something hard. The girl was roused from her dream. She was indeed in a state of the most acute and difficult distress. To speak without figure she had thought of something, something about the body, about the passions which it was unfitting for her as a woman to say. Men, her reason told her, would be shocked. The consciousness of what men will say of a woman who speaks the truth about her passions had roused her from her artist's state of unconsciousness. She could write no more. The trance was over. Her imagination could work no longer. This I believe to be a very common experience with women writers — they are impeded by the extreme conventionality of the other sex. For though men sensibly allow themselves great freedom in these respects, I doubt that they realize or can control the extreme severity with which they condemn such freedom in women.

These then were two very genuine experiences of my own. These were two of the adventures of my professional life. The first — killing the Angel in the

House — I think I solved. She died. But the second, telling the truth about my own experiences as a body, I do not think I solved. I doubt that any woman has solved it yet. The obstacles against her are still immensely powerful — and yet they are very difficult to define. Outwardly, what is simpler than to write books? Outwardly, what obstacles are there for a woman rather than for a man? Inwardly, I think, the case is very different; she has still many ghosts to fight, many prejudices to overcome. Indeed it will be a long time still, I think, before a woman can sit down to write a book without finding a phantom to be slain, a rock to be dashed against. And if this is so in literature, the freest of all professions for women, how is it in the new professions which you are now for the first time entering?

TILLIE OLSEN
Silences

Work first:

> Within our bodies we bore the race. Through us it was shaped, fed and clothed. . . . Labour more toilsome and unending than that of man was ours. . . . No work was too hard, no labour too strenuous to exclude us.[1]

True for most women in most of the world still.

Unclean; taboo. The Devil's Gateway. The three steps behind; the girl babies drowned in the river; the baby strapped to the back. Buried alive with the lord, burned alive on the funeral pyre, burned as witch at the stake. Stoned to death for adultery. Beaten, raped. Bartered. Bought and sold. Concubinage, prostitution, white slavery. The hunt, the sexual prey, 'I am a lost creature, O the poor Clarissa.' Purdah, the veil of Islam, domestic confinement. Illiterate. Denied vision. Excluded, excluded, excluded from council, ritual, activity, learning, language, when there was neither biological nor economic reason to be excluded.

Religion, when all believed. In sorrow shalt thou bring forth children. May thy wife's womb never cease from bearing. Neither was the man created for the woman but the woman for the man. Let the woman learn in silence and in all subjection. Contrary to biological birth fact: Adam's rib. The Jewish male morning prayer: thank God I was not born a woman. Silence in holy places, seated apart, or not permitted entrance at all; castration of boys because women too profane to sing in church.

And for the comparative handful of women born into the privileged class; being, not doing; man does, woman is; to you the world says work, to us it says seem. God is thy law, thou mine. Isolated. Cabin'd, cribb'd, confin'd; the private sphere. Bound feet: corseted, cosseted, bedecked; denied one's body. Powerlessness. Fear of rape, male strength. Fear of aging. Subject to. Fear of expressing capacities. Soft attractive graces; the mirror to magnify man. Marriage as property arrangement. The vices of slaves:[2] dissembling, flattering, manipulating, appeasing.

Bolstering. Vicarious living, infantilization, trivialization. Parasitism, individualism, madness. Shut up, you're only a girl. O Elizabeth, why couldn't you have been born a boy? For twentieth-century woman: roles, discontinuities, part-self, part-time; conflict; imposed 'guilt'; 'a man can give full energy to his profession, a woman cannot.'

> How is it that women have not made a fraction of the intellectual, scientific, or artistic-cultural contributions that men have made?

Only in the context of this punitive difference in circumstance, in history, between the sexes; this past, hidden or evident, that (though objectively obsolete — yes, even the toil and the compulsory childbearing obsolete) *continues so terribly, so determiningly to live on, only in this context can the question be answered or my subject here today — the women writer in our century: one out of twelve — be understood.*

How much it takes to become a writer. Bent (far more common than we assume), circumstances, time, development of craft — but beyond that: how much conviction as to the importance of what one has to say, one's right to say it. And the will, the measureless store of belief in oneself to be able to come to, cleave to, find the form for one's own life comprehensions. Difficult for any male not born into a class that breeds such confidence. Almost impossible for a girl, a woman.

The leeching of belief, of will, the damaging of capacity begin so early. Sparse indeed is the literature on the way of denial to small girl children of the development of their endowment as born human: active, vigorous bodies; exercise of the power to do, to make, to investigate, to invent, to conquer obstacles, to resist violations of the self; to think, create, choose; to attain community, confidence in self. Little has been written on the harms of instilling constant concern with appearance; the need to please, to support; the training in acceptance, deferring. Little has been added in our century to George Eliot's *The Mill on the Floss* on the effect of the differing treatment — 'climate of expectation' — for boys and for girls.

But it is there if one knows how to read for it, and indelibly there in the resulting damage. One — out of twelve.

In the vulnerable girl years, unlike their sisters in the previous century, women writers go to college.[3] The kind of experience it may be for them is stunningly documented in Elaine Showalter's pioneering "Women and the Literary Curriculum."[4] Freshman texts in which women have little place, if at all; language itself, all achievement, anything to do with the human in male terms — *Man in Crises, The Individual and His World.* Three hundred thirteen male writers taught; seventeen women writers: That classic of adolescent rebellion, *A Portrait of the Artist as a Young Man*; and sagas (male) of the quest for identity (but then Erikson, the father of the concept, propounds that identity concerns girls only insofar as making themselves into attractive beings for the right kind of man).[5] Most, *not all*, of the predominantly male literature studied, written by men whose understandings are not universal, but restrictively male (as Mary Ellmann, Kate Millett, and

Dolores Schmidt have pointed out); in our time more and more surface, hostile, one-dimensional in portraying women.

In a writer's young years, susceptibility to the vision and style of the great is extreme. Add the aspiration-denying implication, consciously felt or not (although reinforced daily by one's professors and reading) that (as Virginia Woolf noted years ago) women writers, women's experience, and literature written by women are by definition minor. (Mailer will not grant even the minor: 'the one thing a writer has to have is balls.') No wonder that Showalter observes:

> Women [students] are estranged from their own experience and unable to perceive its shape and authenticity, in part because they do not see it mirrored and given resonance in literature. . . . They are expected to identify with masculine experience, which is presented as the human one, and have no faith in the validity of their own perceptions and experiences, rarely seeing them confirmed in literature, or accepted in criticism . . . [They] notoriously lack the happy confidence, the exuberant sense of the value of their individual observations which enables young men to risk making fools of themselves for the sake of an idea.

Harms difficult to work through. Nevertheless, some young women (others are already lost) maintain their ardent intention to write — fed indeed by the very glories of some of this literature that puts them down.

But other invisible worms are finding out the bed of crimson joy.[6] Self-doubt; seriousness, also questioned by the hours agonizing over appearance; concentration shredded into attracting, being attractive; the absorbing real need and love for working with words felt as hypocritical self-delusion ('I'm not truly dedicated'), for what seems (and is) esteemed is being attractive to men. High aim, and accomplishment toward it, discounted by the prevalent attitude that, as girls will probably marry (attitudes not applied to boys who will probably marry), writing is no more than an attainment of a dowry to be spent later according to the needs and circumstances within the true vocation: husband and family. The growing acceptance that going on will threaten other needs, to love and be loved; ('a woman has to sacrifice all claims to femininity and family to be a writer').[7]

And the agony — peculiarly mid-century, escaped by their sisters of pre-Freudian, pre-Jungian times — that 'creation and femininity are incompatible.'[8] Anaïs Nin's words.

> The aggressive act of creation; the guilt for creating. I did not want to rival man; to steal man's creation, his thunder. I must protect them, not outshine them.[9]

The acceptance — against one's experienced reality — of the sexist notion that the act of creation is not as inherently natural to a woman as to a man, but rooted instead in unnatural aggression, rivalry, envy, or thwarted sexuality.

And in all the usual college teaching — the English, history, psychology, sociology courses — little to help that young woman understand the source or nature of this inexplicable draining self-doubt, loss of aspiration, of confidence.

It is all there in the extreme in Plath's *Bell Jar* — that (inadequate)[10] portrait of the artist as young woman (significantly, one of the few that we have) — from the precarious sense of vocation to the paralyzing conviction that (in a sense different from what she wrote years later)

> Perfection is terrible. It cannot have children.
> It tamps the womb.

And indeed, in our century as in the last, until very recently almost all distinguished achievement has come from childless women: Willa Cather, Ellen Glasgow, Gertrude Stein, Edith Wharton, Virginia Woolf, Elizabeth Bowen, Katherine Mansfield, Isak Dinesen, Katherine Anne Porter, Dorothy Richardson, Henry Handel Richardson, Susan Glaspell, Dorothy Parker, Lillian Hellman, Eudora Welty, Djuna Barnes, Anaïs Nin, Ivy Compton-Burnett, Zora Neale Hurston, Elizabeth Madox Roberts, Christina Stead, Carson McCullers, Flannery O'Connor, Jean Stafford, May Sarton, Josephine Herbst, Jessamyn West, Janet Frame, Lillian Smith, Iris Murdoch, Joyce Carol Oates, Hannah Green, Lorraine Hansberry.

Most never questioned, or at least accepted (a few sanctified) this different condition for achievement, not imposed on men writers. Few asked the fundamental human equality question regarding it that Elizabeth Mann Borghese, Thomas Mann's daughter, asked when she was eighteen and sent to a psychiatrist for help in getting over an unhappy love affair (revealing also a working ambition to become a great musician although 'women cannot be great musicians'). 'You must choose between your art and fulfillment as a woman,' the analyst told her, 'between music and family life.' 'Why?' she asked. 'Why must I choose? No one said to Toscanini or to Bach or my father that they must choose between their art and personal, family life; fulfillment as a man. . . . Injustice everywhere.' Not where it is free choice. But where it is forced because of the circumstances for the sex into which one is born — a choice men of the same class do not have to make in order to do their work — that is not choice, that is a coercive working of sexist oppression.[11]

NOTES

1 Olive Schreiner. *Women and Labour.*
2 Elizabeth Barrett Browning's phrase; other phrases throughout from the Bible, John Milton, Richardson's *Clarissa*, Matthew Arnold, Elizabeth Cady Stanton, Virginia Woolf, Viola Klein, Mountain Wolf Woman.
3 True almost without exception among the writers who are women in *Twentieth Century Authors* and *Contemporary Authors*.
4 *College English*, May 1971. A year later (October 1972), *College English* published an extensive report, "Freshman Textbooks," by Jean Mullens. In the 112 most used texts, she found 92.47 percent (5,795) of the selections were by men; 7.53 percent (472) by women (One Out of Twelve). Mullens deepened Showalter's insights as to the subtly undermining effect on freshman students

of the texts' contents and language, as well as the minuscule proportion of women writers.

5   In keeping with his 1950s—60s thesis of a distinctly female 'biological, evolutionary need to fulfil self through serving others.'

6   O Rose thou art sick./The invisible worm,
     That flies in the night/In the howling storm:

     Has found out thy bed/Of crimson joy:
     And his dark secret love/Does thy life destroy.
     William Blake

7   Plath. A letter when a graduate student.

8   *The Diary of Anaïs Nin*, Vol. III, 1939—1944.

9   A statement that would have baffled Austen, the Brontës, Mrs Gaskell, Eliot, Stowe, Alcott, etc. The strictures were felt by them in other ways.

10   Inadequate, for the writer-being ('muteness is sickness for me') is not portrayed. By contrast, how present she is in Plath's own *Letters Home*.

11   'Them lady poets must not marry, pal,' is how John Berryman, poet (himself oft married) expressed it. The old patriarchal injunction: 'Woman, this is man's realm. If you insist on invading it, unsex yourself — and expect the road to be made difficult.' Furthermore, this very unmarriedness and childlessness has been used to discredit women as unfulfilled, inadequate, somehow abnormal.

ADRIENNE RICH
'When We Dead Awaken: Writing as Re-Vision',
On Lies, Secrets, and Silence

I have hesitated to do what I am going to do now, which is to use myself as an illustration. For one thing, it's a lot easier and less dangerous to talk about other women writers. But there is something else. Like Virginia Woolf, I am aware of the women who are not with us here because they are washing the dishes and looking after the children. Nearly fifty years after she spoke, the fact remains largely unchanged. And I am thinking also of women whom she left out of the picture altogether — women who are washing other people's dishes and caring for other people's children, not to mention women who went on the streets last night in order to feed their children. We seem to be special women here, we have liked to think of ourselves as special, and we have known that men would tolerate, even romanticize us as special, as long as our words and actions didn't threaten their privilege of tolerating or rejecting us and our work according to *their* ideas of what a special woman ought to be. An important insight of the radical women's movement has been how divisive and how ultimately destructive is this myth of the special woman, who is also the token woman. Every one of us here in this room has had great luck — we are teachers, writers, academicians; our own gifts could not have been enough, for we all know women whose gifts are buried or aborted. Our struggles can have meaning and our privileges — however precarious under patriarchy — can

be justified only if they can help to change the lives of women whose gifts —
and whose very being — continue to be thwarted and silenced.

[. . .]

I know that my style was formed first by male poets: by the men I was
reading as an undergraduate — Frost, Dylan Thomas, Donne, Auden,
MacNiece, Stevens, Yeats. What I chiefly learned from them was craft.[5] But
poems are like dreams: in them you put what you don't know you know.
Looking back at poems I wrote before I was twenty-one, I'm startled because
beneath the conscious craft are glimpses of the split I even then experienced
between the girl who wrote poems, who defined herself in writing poems,
and the girl who was to define herself by her relationships with men. 'Aunt
Jennifer's Tigers' (1951), written while I was a student, looks with deliberate
detachment at this split.[6]

> Aunt Jennifer's tigers stride across a screen,
> Bright topaz denizens of a world of green.
> They do not fear the men beneath the tree;
> They pace in sleek chivalric certainty.
>
> Aunt Jennifer's fingers fluttering through her wool
> Find even the ivory needle hard to pull.
> The massive weight of Uncle's wedding band
> Sits heavily upon Aunt Jennifer's hand.
>
> When Aunt is dead, her terrified hands will lie
> Still ringed with ordeals she was mastered by.
> The tigers in the panel that she made
> Will go on striding, proud and unafraid.

In writing this poem, composed and apparently cool as it is, I thought I was
creating a portrait of an imaginary woman. But this woman suffers from the
opposition of her imagination, worked out in tapestry, and her life-style,
'ringed with ordeals she was mastered by.' It was important to me that Aunt
Jennifer was a person as distinct from myself as possible — distanced by the
formalism of the poem, by its objective, observant tone — even by putting
the woman in a different generation.

In those years formalism was part of the strategy — like asbestos gloves,
it allowed me to handle materials I couldn't pick up bare-handed. A later
strategy was to use the persona of a man, as I did in 'The Loser' (1958):

> *A man thinks of the woman he once loved: first, after her wedding, and then*
> *nearly a decade later.*
>
> I
> I kissed you, bride and lost, and went
> home from that bourgeois sacrament,
> your cheek still tasting cold upon
> my lips that gave you benison
> with all the swagger that they knew —
> as losers somehow learn to do.

Your wedding made my eyes ache; soon
the world would be worse off for one
more golden apple dropped to ground
without the least protesting sound,
and you would windfall lie, and we
forget your shimmer on the tree.

Beauty is always wasted: if
not Mignon's song sung to the deaf,
at all events to the unmoved.
A face like yours cannot be loved
long or seriously enough.
Almost, we seem to hold it off.

II
Well, you are tougher than I thought.
Now when the wash with ice hangs taut
this morning of St. Valentine,
I see you strip the squeaking line,
your body weighed against the load,
and all my groans can do no good.

Because you are still beautiful,
though squared and stiffened by the pull
of what nine windy years have done.
You have three daughters, lost a son.
I see all your intelligence
flung into that unwearied stance.

My envy is of no avail.
I turn my head and wish him well
who chafed your beauty into use
and lives forever in a house
lit by the friction of your mind.
You stagger in against the wind.

I finished college, published my first book by a fluke, as it seemed to me, and broke off a love affair. I took a job, lived alone, went on writing, fell in love. I was young, full of energy, and the book seemed to mean that others agreed I was a poet. Because I was also determined to prove that as a woman poet I could also have what was then defined as a 'full' woman's life, I plunged in my early twenties into marriage and had three children before I was thirty. There was nothing overt in the environment to warn me: these were the fifties, and in reaction to the earlier wave of feminism, middle-class women were making careers of domestic perfection, working to send their husbands through professional schools, then retiring to raise large families. People were moving out to the suburbs, technology was going to be the answer to everything, even sex; the family was in its glory. Life was extremely private; women were isolated from each other by the loyalties of marriage. I have a sense that women didn't talk to each other much in the fifties — not about their secret emptinesses, their frustrations. I went on trying to write; my second book and first child appeared in the same month.

But by the time that book came out I was already dissatisfied with those poems, which seemed to me mere exercises for poems I hadn't written. The book was praised, however, for its 'gracefulness'; I had a marriage and a child. If there were doubts, if there were periods of null depression or active despairing, these could only mean that I was ungrateful, insatiable, perhaps a monster.

About the time my third child was born, I felt that I had either to consider myself a failed woman and a failed poet, or to try to find some synthesis by which to understand what was happening to me. What frightened me most was the sense of drift, of being pulled along on a current which called itself my destiny, but in which I seemed to be losing touch with whoever I had been, with the girl who had experienced her own will and energy almost ecstatically at times, walking round a city or riding a train at night or typing in a student room. In a poem about my grandmother I wrote (of myself): 'A young girl, thought sleeping, is certified dead' ('Halfway'). I was writing very little, partly from fatigue, that female fatigue of suppressed anger and loss of contact with my own being; partly from the discontinuity of female life with its attention to small chores, errands, work that others constantly undo, small children's constant needs. What I did write was unconvincing to me; my anger and frustration were hard to acknowledge in or out of poems because in fact I cared a great deal about my husband and my children. Trying to look back and understand that time I have tried to analyze the real nature of the conflict. Most, if not all, human lives are full of fantasy — passive day-dreaming which need not be acted on. But to write poetry or fiction, or even to think well, is not to fantasize, or to put fantasies on paper. For a poem to coalesce, for a character or an action to take shape, there has to be an imaginative transformation of reality which is in no way passive. And a certain freedom of the mind is needed — freedom to press on, to enter the currents of your thought like a glider pilot, knowing that your motion can be sustained, that the buoyancy of your attention will not be suddenly snatched away. Moreover, if the imagination is to transcend and transform experience it has to question, to challenge, to conceive of alternatives, perhaps to the very life you are living at that moment. You have to be free to play around with the notion that day might be night, love might be hate; nothing can be too sacred for the imagination to turn into its opposite or to call experimentally by another name. For writing is re-naming. Now, to be maternally with small children all day in the old way, to be with a man in the old way of marriage, requires a holding-back, a putting-aside of that imaginative activity, and demands instead a kind of conservatism. I want to make it clear that I am *not* saying that in order to write well, or think well, it is necessary to become unavailable to others, or to become a devouring ego. This has been the myth of the masculine artist and thinker; and I do not accept it. But to be a female human being trying to fulfill traditional female functions in a traditional way *is* in direct conflict with the subversive function of the imagination. The word traditional is important here. There must be ways, and we will be finding out more and more about them, in which the energy of creation and the energy of relation can be united. But in those years I always felt the conflict as a failure of love in myself. I had thought I was choosing a full life: the life available to most men, in which sexuality, work, and parenthood could coexist. But I felt, at twenty-nine, guilt toward the people closest to me, and guilty toward my own being.

I wanted, then, more than anything, the one thing of which there was never enough: time to think, time to write. The fifties and early sixties were years of rapid revelations: the sit-ins and marches in the South, the Bay of Pigs, the early antiwar movement, raised large questions — questions for which the masculine world of the academy around me seemed to have expert and fluent answers. But I needed to think for myself — about pacifism and dissent and violence, about poetry and society, and about my own relationship to all these things. For about ten years I was reading in fierce snatches, scribbling in notebooks, writing poetry in fragments; I was looking desperately for clues, because if there were no clues then I thought I might be insane. I wrote in a notebook about this time:

> Paralyzed by the sense that there exists a mesh of relationships — e.g., between my anger at the children, my sensual life, pacifism, sex (I mean sex in its broadest significance, not merely sexual desire) — an interconnectedness which, if I could see it, make it valid, would give me back myself, make it possible to function lucidly and passionately. Yet I grope in and out among these dark webs.

I think I began at this point to feel that politics was not something 'out there' but something 'in here' and of the essence of my condition.

In the late fifties I was able to write, for the first time, directly about experiencing myself as a woman. The poem was jotted in fragments during children's naps, brief hours in a library, or at 3·00 a.m. after rising with a wakeful child. I despaired of doing any continuous work at this time. Yet I began to feel that my fragments and scraps had a common consciousness and a common theme, one which I would have been very unwilling to put on paper at an earlier time because I had been taught that poetry should be 'universal,' which meant, of course, nonfemale. Until then I had tried very much *not* to identify myself as a female poet. Over two years I wrote a ten-part poem called 'Snapshots of a Daughter-in-Law' (1958—1960), in a longer looser mode than I'd ever trusted myself with before. It was an extraordinary relief to write that poem. It strikes me now as too literary, too dependent on allusion; I hadn't found the courage yet to do without authorities, or even to use the pronoun 'I' — the woman in the poem is always 'she.' One section of it, No. 2, concerns a woman who thinks she is going mad; she is haunted by voices telling her to resist and rebel, voices which she can hear but not obey.

> 2.
> Banging the coffee-pot into the sink
> she hears the angels chiding, and looks out
> past the raked gardens to the sloppy sky.
> Only a week since They said: *Have no patience.*

The next time it was: *Be insatiable.*
Then: *Save yourself; others you cannot save.*
Sometimes she's let the tapstream scald her arm,
a match burn to her thumbnail,

or held her hand above the kettle's snout
right in the woolly steam. They are probably angels,
since nothing hurts her anymore, except
each morning's grit blowing into her eyes.

The poem 'Orion,' written five years later, is a poem of reconnection with
a part of myself I had felt I was losing — the active principle, the energetic
imagination, the 'half-brother' whom I projected, as I had for many years,
into the constellation Orion. It's no accident that the words 'cold and
egotistical' appear in this poem, and are applied to myself.

Far back when I went zig-zagging
through tamarack pastures
you were my genius, you
my cast-iron Viking, my helmed
lion-heart king in prison.
Years later now you're young

my fierce half-brother, staring
down from that simplified west
your breast open, your belt dragged down
by an oldfashioned thing, a sword
the last bravado you won't give over
though it weighs you down as you stride

and the stars in it are dim
and maybe have stopped burning.
But you burn, and I know it;
as I throw back my head to take you in
an old transfusion happens again:
divine astronomy is nothing to it.

Indoors I bruise and blunder,
break faith, leave ill enough
alone, a dead child born in the dark.
Night cracks up over the chimney,
pieces of time, frozen geodes
come showering down in the grate.

A man reaches behind my eyes
and finds them empty
a woman's head turns away
from my head in the mirror
children are dying my death
and eating crumbs of my life.

Pity is not your forte.
Calmly you ache up there
pinned aloft in your crow's nest,

> my speechless pirate!
> You take it all for granted
> and when I look you back
>
> it's with a starlike eye
> shooting its cold and egotistical spear
> where it can do least damage.
> Breathe deep! No hurt, no pardon
> out here in the cold with you
> you with your back to the wall.

The choice still seemed to be between 'love' — womanly, maternal love, altruistic love — a love defined and ruled by the weight of an entire culture; and egotism — a force directed by men into creation, achievement, ambition, often at the expense of others, but justifiably so. For weren't they men, and wasn't that their destiny as womanly, selfless love was ours? We know now that the alternatives are false ones — that the word 'love' is itself in need of re-vision.

NOTES

5 A. R., 1978: Yet I spent months, at sixteen, memorizing and writing imitations of Millay's sonnets; and in notebooks of that period I find what are obviously attempts to imitate Dickinson's metrics and verbal compression. I knew H. D. only through anthologized lyrics; her epic poetry was not then available to me.
6 A. R., 1978: Texts of poetry quoted herein can be found in A. R. *Poems Selected and New: 1950—1974* (New York: Norton, 1975).

SANDRA M. GILBERT and SUSAN GUBAR
The Madwoman in the Attic

And the lady of the house was seen only as she appeared in each room, according to the nature of the lord of the room. None saw the whole of her, none but herself. For the light which she was was both her mirror and her body. None could tell the whole of her, none but herself.

— Laura Riding

Alas! A woman that attempts the pen
Such an intruder on the rights of men,
Such a presumptuous Creature is esteem'd
The fault can by no vertue be redeem'd.

— Anne Finch, Countess of Winchilsea

As to all that nonsense Henry and Larry talked about, the necessity of 'I am God' in order to create (I suppose they mean 'I am God. I am not a woman'). . . . this 'I am God,' which makes creation an act of solitude and pride, this image of God alone making sky, earth, sea, it is this image which has confused woman.

— Anaïs Nin

Is a pen a metaphorical penis? Gerard Manley Hopkins seems to have thought so. In a letter to his friend R. W. Dixon in 1886 he confided a crucial feature of his theory of poetry. The artist's 'most essential quality,' he declared, is 'masterly execution, which is a kind of male gift, and especially marks off men from women, the begetting of one's thought on paper, on verse, or whatever the matter is.' In addition, he noted that 'on better consideration it strikes me that the mastery I speak of is not so much in the mind as a puberty in the life of that quality. The male quality is the creative gift.'[1] Male sexuality, in other words, is not just analogically but actually the essence of literary power. The poet's pen is in some sense (even more than figuratively) a penis.

Eccentric and obscure though he was, Hopkins was articulating a concept central to that Victorian culture of which he was in this case a representative male citizen. But of course the patriarchal notion that the writer 'fathers' his text just as God fathered the world is and has been all-pervasive in Western literary civilization, so much so that, as Edward Said has shown, the metaphor is built into the very word, *author*, with which writer, deity, and *pater familias* are identified. Said's miniature meditation on the word *authority* is worth quoting in full because it summarizes so much that is relevant here:

> *Authority* suggests to me a constellation of linked meanings: not only, as the OED tells us, 'a power to enforce obedience,' or 'a derived or delegated power,' or 'a power to influence action,' or 'a power to inspire belief,' or 'a person whose opinion is accepted'; not only those, but a connection as well with *author* — that is, a person who originates or gives existence to something, a begetter, beginner, father, or ancestor, a person also who sets forth written statements. There is still another cluster of meanings: *author* is tied to the past participle *auctus* of the verb *augere*; therefore *auctor*, according to Eric Partridge, is literally an increaser and thus a founder. *Auctoritas* is production, invention, cause, in addition to meaning a right of possession. Finally, it means continuance, or a causing to continue. Taken together these meanings are all grounded in the following notions: (1) that of the power of an individual to initiate, institute, establish — in short, to begin; (2) that this power and its product are an increase over what had been there previously; (3) that the individual wielding this power controls its issue and what is derived therefrom; (4) that authority maintains the continuity of its course.[2]

In conclusion, Said, who is discussing 'The Novel as Beginning Intention,' remarks that 'All four of these [last] abstractions can be used to describe the way in which narrative fiction asserts itself psychologically and aesthetically through the technical efforts of the novelist.' But they can also, of course, be used to describe both the author and the authority of any literary text, a point Hopkins's sexual/aesthetic theory seems to have been designed to elaborate. Indeed, Said himself later observes that a convention of most literary texts is 'that the unity or integrity of the text is maintained by a series of genealogical connections: author — text, beginning-middle-end, text — meaning, reader — interpretation, and so on. *Underneath all these is the imagery of succession, of paternity, or hierarchy*' (italics ours).[3]

There is a sense in which the very notion of paternity is itself, as Stephen Dedalus puts it in *Ulysses*, a 'legal fiction,'[4] a story requiring imagination if not faith. A man cannot verify his fatherhood by either sense or reason, after all; that his child is *his* is in a sense a tale he tells himself to explain the infant's existence. Obviously, the anxiety implicit in such storytelling urgently needs not only the reassurances of male superiority that patriarchal misogyny implies, but also such compensatory fictions of the Word as those embodied in the genealogical imagery Said describes. Thus it is possible to trace the history of this compensatory, sometimes frankly stated and sometimes submerged imagery that elaborates upon what Stephen Dedalus calls the 'mystical estate' of paternity[5] through the works of many literary theoreticians besides Hopkins and Said. Defining poetry as a mirror held up to nature, the mimetic aesthetic that begins with Aristotle and descends through Sidney, Shakespeare, and Johnson implies that the poet, like a lesser God, has made or engendered an alternative, mirror-universe in which he actually seems to enclose or trap shadows of reality. Similarly, Coleridge's Romantic concept of the human 'imagination or esemplastic power' is of a virile, generative force which echoes 'the eternal act of creation in the infinite I AM,' while Ruskin's phallic-sounding 'Penetrative Imagination' is a 'possession-taking faculty' and a 'piercing . . . mind's tongue' that seizes, cuts down, and gets at the root of experience in order 'to throw up what new shoots it will.'[6] In all these aesthetics the poet, like God the Father, is a paternalistic ruler of the fictive world he has created. Shelley called him a 'legislator.' Keats noted, speaking of writers, that 'the antients [*sic*] were Emperors of vast Provinces' though 'each of the moderns' is merely an 'Elector of Hanover.'[7]

In medieval philosophy, the network of connections among sexual, literary, and theological metaphors is equally complex: God the Father both engenders the cosmos and, as Ernst Robert Curtius notes, writes the Book of Nature: both tropes describe a single act of creation.[8] In addition, the Heavenly Author's ultimate eschatological power is made manifest when, as the *Liber Scriptus* of the traditional requiem mass indicates, He writes the Book of Judgment. More recently, male artists like the Earl of Rochester in the seventeenth century and Auguste Renoir in the nineteenth, have frankly defined aesthetics based on male sexual delight. 'I . . . never Rhym'd, but for my Pintle's [penis's] sake,' declares Rochester's witty Timon,[9] and (according to the painter Bridget Riley) Renoir 'is supposed to have said that he painted his paintings with his prick.'[10] Clearly, both these artists believe, with Norman O. Brown, that 'the penis is the head of the body,' and they might both agree, too, with John Irwin's suggestion that the relationship 'of the masculine self with the feminine-masculine work is also an autoerotic act . . . a kind of creative onanism in which through the use of the phallic pen on the "pure space" of the virgin page . . . the self is continually spent and wasted. . . .'[11] No doubt it is for all these reasons, moreover, that poets have traditionally used a vocabulary derived from the patriarchal 'family romance' to describe their relations with each other. As Harold Bloom has pointed out, 'from the sons of Homer to the sons of Ben Jonson, poetic influence [has] been described as a filial relationship,' a relationship of '*sonship*.' The fierce struggle at the heart of literary history, says Bloom, is a 'battle between strong equals, father and son as mighty opposites, Laius and Oedipus at the crossroads.'[12]

Though many of these writers use the metaphor of literary paternity in different ways and for different purposes, all seem overwhelmingly to agree that a literary text is not only speech quite literally embodied, but also power mysteriously made manifest, made flesh. In patriarchal Western culture, therefore, the text's author is a father, a progenitor, a procreator, an aesthetic patriarch whose pen is an instrument of generative power like his penis. More, his pen's power, like his penis's power, is not just the ability to generate life but the power to create a posterity to which he lays claim, as, in Said's paraphrase of Partridge, 'an increaser and-thus a founder.' In this respect, the pen is truly mightier than its phallic counterpart the sword, and in patriarchy more resonantly sexual. Not only does the writer respond to his muse's quasi-sexual excitation with an outpouring of the aesthetic energy Hopkins called 'the fine delight that fathers thought' — a delight poured seminally from pen to page — but as the author of an enduring text the writer engages the attention of the future in exactly the same way that a king (or father) 'owns' the homage of the present. No sword-wielding general could rule so long or possess so vast a kingdom.

Finally, that such a notion of 'ownership' or possession is embedded in the metaphor of paternity leads to yet another implication of this complex metaphor. For if the author/father is owner of his text and his reader's attention, he is also, of course, owner/possessor of the subjects of his text, that is to say of those figures, scenes, and events — those brain children — he has both incarnated in black and white and 'bound' in cloth or leather. Thus, because he is an *author*, a 'man of letters' is simultaneously, like his divine counterpart, a father, a master or ruler, and an owner: the spiritual type of a patriarch, as we understand that term in Western society.

Where does such an implicitly or explicitly patriarchal theory of literature leave literary women? If the pen is a metaphorical penis, with what organ can females generate texts? The question may seem frivolous, but as our epigraph from Anaïs Nin indicates, both the patriarchal etiology that defines a solitary Father God as the only creator of all things, and the male metaphors of literary creation that depend upon such an etiology, have long 'confused' literary women, readers and writers alike. For what if such a profoundly masculine cosmic Author is the sole legitimate model for all earthly authors? Or worse, what if the male generative power is not just the only legitimate power but the only power there is? That literary theoreticians from Aristotle to Hopkins seemed to believe that this was so no doubt prevented many women from ever 'attempting the pen' — to use Anne Finch's phrase — and caused enormous anxiety in generations of those women who were 'presumptuous' enough to dare such an attempt. Jane Austen's Anne Elliot understates the case when she decorously observes, toward the end of *Persuasion*, that 'men have had every advantage of us in telling their story. Education has been theirs in so much higher a degree; the pen has been in their hands' (II, chap. 11).[13] For, as Anne Finch's complaint suggests, the pen has been defined as not just accidentally but essentially a male 'tool,' and therefore not only inappropriate but actually alien to women. Lacking Austen's demure irony, Finch's passionate protest goes almost as far toward the center of the metaphor of literary paternity as Hopkins's letter to Canon Dixon. Not only is 'a woman that attempts the pen' an intrusive and 'presumptuous Creature,' she is absolutely unredeemable: no virtue can outweigh the 'fault' of her presumption because she has grotesquely crossed boundaries dictated by Nature:

> They tell us, we mistake our sex and way;
> Good breeding, fassion, dancing, dressing, play
> Are the accomplishments we shou'd desire;
> To write, or read, or think, or to enquire
> Wou'd cloud our beauty, and exaust our time,
> And interrupt the conquests of our prime;
> Whilst the dull mannage, of a servile house
> Is held by some, our outmost art and use.[14]

Because they are by definition male activities, this passage implies, writing, reading, and thinking are not only alien but also inimical to 'female' characteristics. One hundred years later, in a famous letter to Charlotte Brontë, Robert Southey rephrased the same notion: 'Literature is not the business of a woman's life, and it cannot be.'[15] It cannot be, the metaphor of literary paternity implies, because it is physiologically as well as sociologically impossible. If male sexuality is integrally associated with the assertive presence of literary power, female sexuality is associated with the absence of such power, with the idea — expressed by the nineteenth-century thinker Otto Weininger — that 'woman has no share in ontological reality.' As we shall see, a further implication of the paternity/creativity metaphor is the notion (implicit both in Weininger and in Southey's letter) that women exist only to be acted on by men, both as literary and as sensual objects. Again one of Anne Finch's poems explores the assumptions submerged in so many literary theories. Addressing three male poets, she exclaims:

> Happy you three! happy the Race of Men!
> Born to inform or to correct the Pen
> To proffitts pleasures freedom and command
> Whilst we beside you but as Cyphers stand
> T' increase your Numbers and to swell th' account
> Of your delights which from our charms amount
> And sadly are by this distinction taught
> That since the Fall (by our seducement wrought)
> Our is the greater losse as ours the greater fault.[16]

Since Eve's daughters have fallen so much lower than Adam's sons, this passage says, *all* females are 'Cyphers' — nullities, vacancies — existing merely and punningly to increase male 'Numbers' (either poems or persons) by pleasuring either men's bodies or their minds, their penises or their pens.

In that case, however, devoid of what Richard Chase once called 'the masculine *élan*,' and implicitly rejecting even the slavish consolations of her 'femininity,' a literary woman is doubly a 'Cypher,' for she is really a 'eunuch,' to use the striking figure Germaine Greer applied to all women in patriarchal society. Thus Anthony Burgess recently declared that Jane Austen's novels fail because her writing 'lacks a strong male thrust,' and William Gass lamented that literary women 'lack that blood congested genital drive which energizes every great style.'[17] The assumptions that underlie their statements were articulated more than a century ago by the nineteenth-century editor-critic Rufus Griswold. Introducing an anthology entitled *The Female Poets of America*, Griswold outlined a theory of literary sex roles which builds upon, and clarifies, these grim implications of the metaphor of literary paternity.

> It is less easy to be assured of the genuineness of literary ability in women than in men. The moral nature of women, in its finest and richest development, partakes of some of the qualities of genius; it assumes, at least, the similitude of that which in men is the characteristic or accompaniment of the highest grade of mental inspiration. We are in danger, therefore, of mistaking for the efflorescent energy of creative intelligence, that which is only the exuberance of personal 'feelings unemployed.' . . . The most exquisite susceptibility of the spirit, and the capacity to mirror in dazzling variety the effects which circumstances or surrounding minds work upon it, may be accompanied by *no power to originate, nor even, in any proper sense, to reproduce.* [Italics ours][18]

Since Griswold has actually compiled a collection of poems by women, he plainly does not believe that all women lack reproductive or generative literary power all the time. His gender-definitions imply, however, that when such creative energy appears in a woman it may be anomalous, freakish, because as a 'male' characteristic it is essentially 'unfeminine.'

The converse of these explicit and implicit definitions of 'femininity' may also be true for those who develop literary theories based upon the 'mystical estate' of fatherhood: if a woman lacks generative literary power, then a man who loses or abuses such power becomes like a eunuch — or like a woman. When the imprisoned Marquis de Sade was denied 'any use of pencil, ink, pen, and paper,' declares Roland Barthes, he was figuratively emasculated, for 'the scriptural sperm' could flow no longer, and 'without exercise, without a pen, Sade [became] *bloated*, [became] a eunuch.' Similarly, when Hopkins wanted to explain to R. W. Dixon the aesthetic consequences of a *lack* of male mastery, he seized upon an explanation which developed the implicit parallel between women and eunuchs, declaring that 'if the life' is not 'conveyed into the work and . . . displayed there . . . the product is one of those *hens' eggs* that are good to eat and look just like live ones but never hatch' (italics ours).[19] And when, late in his life, he tried to define his own sense of sterility, his thickening writer's block, he described himself (in the sonnet 'The Fine Delight That Fathers Thought') both as a eunuch and *as a woman*, specifically a woman deserted by male power: 'the widow of an insight lost,' surviving in a diminished 'winter world' that entirely lacks 'the roll, the rise, the carol, the creation' of male generative power, whose 'strong/Spur' is phallically 'live and lancing like the blow pipe flame.' And once again some lines from one of Anne Finch's plaintive protests against male literary hegemony seem to support Hopkins's image of the powerless and sterile woman artist. Remarking in the conclusion of her 'Introduction' to her *Poems* that women are 'to be dull/Expected and dessigned' she does not repudiate such expectations, but on the contrary admonishes herself, with bitter irony, to *be* dull:

> Be caution'd then my Muse, and still retir'd;
> Nor be dispis'd, aiming to be admir'd;
> Conscious of wants, still with contracted wing,
> To some few friends, and to thy sorrows sing;
> For groves of Lawrell, thou wert never meant;
> Be dark enough thy shades, and be thou there content.[20]

Cut off from generative energy, in a dark and wintry world, Finch seems to be defining herself here not only as a 'Cypher' but as 'the widow of an insight lost.'

NOTES

Epigraphs. 'In the End,' in *Chelsea* 35:96; 'The Introduction,' in *The Poems of Anne Countess of Winchilsea*, ed. Myra Reynolds (Chicago: University of Chicago Press, 1903), pp. 4—5; *The Diary of Anaïs Nin. Vol. Two, 1934—1939*, ed. Gunther Stuhlmann (New York: The Swallow Press and Harcourt, Brace, 1967), p. 233.

1   *The Correspondence of Gerard Manley Hopkins and Richard Watson Dixon*, ed. C. C. Abbott (London: Oxford University Press, 1935), p. 133.

2   Edward W. Said, *Beginnings: Intention and Method* (New York: Basic Books, 1975), p. 83.

3   Ibid., p. 162. For an analogous use of such imagery of paternity, see Gayatri Chakravorty Spivak's 'Translator's Preface' to Jacques Derrida, *Of Grammatology* (Baltimore: Johns Hopkins University Press, 1976), p. xi: 'to use one of Derrida's structural metaphors, [a preface is] the son or seed . . . caused or engendered by the father (text or meaning).' Also see her discussion of Nietzsche where she considers the 'masculine style of possession' in terms of 'the stylus, the stiletto, the spurs,' p. xxxvi.

4   James Joyce, *Ulysses* (New York: Modern Library, 1934), p. 205.

5   Ibid. The whole of this extraordinarily relevant passage develops this notion further: 'Fatherhood, in the sense of conscious begetting, is unknown to man,' Stephen notes. 'It is a mystical estate, an apostolic succession, from only begetter to only begotten. On that mystery and not on the madonna which the cunning Italian intellect flung to the mob of Europe the church is founded and founded irremovably because founded, like the world, macro- and microcosm, upon the void. Upon incertitude, upon unlikelihood. *Amor matris*, subjective and objective genitive, may be the only true thing in life. Paternity may be a legal fiction' (pp. 204—5).

6   Coleridge, *Biographia Literaria*, chapter 13. John Ruskin, *Modern Painters*, vol. 2, *The Works of John Ruskin*, ed. E. T. Cook and Alexander Wedderburn (London: George Allen, 1903), pp. 250—51. Although Virginia Woolf noted in *A Room of One's Own* that Coleridge thought 'a great mind is androgynous' she added dryly that 'Coleridge certainly did not mean . . . that it is a mind that has any special sympathy with women' (*A Room of One's Own* [New York:

70 WOMEN AND LITERARY PRODUCTION

Harcourt Brace, 1929], p. 102). Certainly the imaginative power Coleridge describes does not sound 'man-womanly' in Woolf's sense.

7 Shelley, 'A Defense of Poetry.' Keats to John Hamilton Reynolds, 3 February 1818; *The Selected Letters of John Keats*, ed. Lionel Trilling (New York: Doubleday, 1956), p. 121.

8 See E. R. Curtius, *European Literature and the Latin Middle Ages* (New York: Harper Torchbooks, 1963), pp. 305, 306. For further commentary on both Curtius's 'The Symbolism of the Book' and the 'Book of Nature' metaphor itself, see Derrida, *Of Grammatology*, pp. 15 — 17.

9 'Timon, A Satyr,' in *Poems by John Wilmot Earl of Rochester*, ed. Vivian de Sola Pinto (London: Routledge and Kegan Paul, 1953), p. 99.

10 Bridget Riley, 'The Hermaphrodite,' *Art and Sexual Politics*, ed. Thomas B. Hass and Elizabeth C. Baker (London: Collier Books, 1973), p. 82. Riley comments that she herself would 'interpret this remark as expressing his attitude to his work as a celebration of life.'

11 Norman O. Brown, *Love's Body* (New York: Vintage Books, 1968), p. 134.; John T. Irwin, *Doubling and Incest. Repetition and Revenge* (Baltimore: Johns Hopkins University Press, 1975), p. 163. Irwin also speaks of 'the phallic generative power of the creative imagination' (p. 159).

12 Harold Bloom, *The Anxiety of Influence* (New York: Oxford University Press, 1973), pp. 11, 26.

13 All references to *Persuasion* are to volume and chapter of the text edited by R. W. Chapman, reprinted with an introduction by David Daiches (New York: Norton, 1958).

14 Anne Finch, *Poems of Anne Countess of Winchilsea*, pp. 4—5.

15 Southey to Charlotte Brontë, March 1837. Quoted in Winifred Gérin, *Charlotte Brontë: The Evolution of Genius* (Oxford: Oxford University Press, 1967), p. 110.

16 Finch, *Poems of Anne Countess of Winchilsea*, p. 100. Otto Weininger, *Sex and Character* (London: Heinemann, 1906), p. 286. This sentence is part of an extraordinary passage in which Weininger asserts that 'women have no existence and no essence; they are not, they are nothing,' this because 'woman has no relation to the idea . . . she is neither moral nor anti-moral,' but 'all existence is moral and logical existence.'

17 Richard Chase speaks of the 'masculine *élan*' throughout 'The Brontës, or Myth Domesticated,' in *Forms of Modern Fiction*, ed. William V. O'Connor (Minneapolis: University of Minnesota Press, 1948), pp. 102—13. For a discussion of the 'female eunuch' see Germaine Greer, *The Female Eunuch* (New York: McGraw Hill, 1970). See also Anthony Burgess, 'The Book Is Not For Reading,' *New York Times Book Review*, 4 December 1966, pp. 1, 74, and William Gass, on Norman Mailer's *Genius and Lust, New York Times Book Review*, 24 October 1976, p. 2. In this connection, finally, it is interesting (and depressing) to consider that Virginia Woolf evidently defined *herself* as 'a eunuch.' (See Noel Annan, 'Virginia Woolf Fever,' *New York Review*, 20 April 1978, p. 22.)

18 Rufus Griswold, Preface to *The Female Poets of America* (Philadelphia: Carey & Hart, 1849), p. 8.

19 Roland Barthes, *Sade/Fourier/Loyola*, trans. Richard Miller (New York: Hill & Wang, 1976), p. 182; Hopkins, *Correspondence*, p. 133.

20 Finch, *Poems of Anne Countess of Winchilsea*, p. 5.

CAROL OHMANN
'Emily Brontë in the Hands of Male Critics',
College English

The pseudonyms all the Brontës chose for their joint volumes of poems and for their novels were, Charlotte reported, deliberately selected to admit of ambiguous interpretation. They did not wish to choose names avowedly masculine; they would not call themselves, for example, Charles, Edward, and Alfred. On the other hand, as Charlotte wrote afterwards, 'We did not like to declare ourselves women, because — without at that time suspecting that our mode of writing and thinking was not what is called "feminine" — we had a vague impression that authoresses are liable to be looked on with prejudice; we had noticed how critics sometimes use for their chastisement the weapon of personality, and for their reward, a flattery, which is not true praise.'[2]

Contemporary reviews of *Wuthering Heights*, all five found in Emily Brontë's writing desk and others as well, referred to Ellis Bell as 'he.' 'He' had written a book which, give or take certain differences of emphasis, was declared to be powerful and original. Although an occasional review acknowledged that it was a story of love, its essential subject was taken to be a representation of cruelty, brutality, violence, of human depravity or wickedness in its most extreme forms. Its lack of moral statement or purpose was taken to be either puzzling or censurable. It was awkwardly constructed. But, even so, in spite of the degree to which the reviewers were, variously, displeased, inclined to melancholy, shocked, pained, anguished, disgusted, and sickened, a number of them allowed the novel to be the work of a promising, possibly a great, new writer.

Most of the reviewers simply assumed without comment that the writer's sex was masculine. Two American reviewers did more: they made much of the novelist's sex and found plain evidence of it in the novel itself. Percy Edwin Whipple, in *The North American Review*, found in *Jane Eyre* the signatures of both a male and a female mind.[3] He supposed that two persons had written it, a brother and a sister. To the sister, he attributed certain 'feminine peculiarities': 'elaborate descriptions of dress'; 'the minutiae of the sick-chamber'; and 'various superficial refinements of feeling in regard to the external relations of the sex.' He went on to assert, 'It is true that the noblest and best representations of female character have been produced by men; but there are niceties of thought and emotion in a woman's mind which no man can delineate, but which often escape unawares from a female writer' (356).

From the brother, Whipple derived the novel's clarity and firmness of style, all its charm, and its scenes of profanity, violence, and passion. These scenes, he was virtually certain, were written by the same hand that wrote *Wuthering Heights*. Turning to *Wuthering Heights*, Whipple concentrated on the novel's presentation of Heathcliff, whom he found quintessentially bestial, brutal, indeed monstrous. He did allot a few lines to Heathcliff in love, but without mentioning Catherine. He scored the author of *Wuthering Heights* for 'coarseness' and for being a 'spendthrift of malice and profanity' (358).

George Washington Peck, in *The American Review*, did not overtly theorize on the sex of the author of *Wuthering Heights*. He assumed it to be masculine, then elaborated on the assumption in a rush of comparisons. The novel's language might be that of a Yorkshire farmer or a boatman or of frequenters of 'bar-rooms and steamboat saloons.'[4] He cautioned young ladies against imitating it, lest American social assemblies come to resemble certain scenes in Tammany Hall. The novel's author Peck likened to a 'rough sailor [with] a powerful imagination' (573). He is like a friend of whom one is fond and yet by whom one is continually embarrassed. He is not a gentleman. He would embarrass you with his *gaucheries* whether you were walking down Broadway with him or across the fields of Staten Island or dropping into a shop or store anywhere. Among his eccentricities or faults is a disposition to believe that he understands women. But he does *not* understand them. *He* cannot see *them* as *they* are. He can only see them as he is, and then, just slightly, refine them.

There are not so many reviews of the second edition of *Wuthering Heights*. But there are enough, I think, to show that once the work of Ellis Bell was identified as the work of a woman, critical responses to it changed. Where the novel had been called again and again 'original' in 1847 and 1848, the review in the *Athenaeum* in 1850 began by firmly placing it in a familiar class, and that class was not in the central line of literature. The review in the *Athenaeum* began by categorizing *Wuthering Heights* as a work of 'female genius and female authorship.'[5] The reviewer was really not surprised to learn that *Jane Eyre* and its 'sister-novels' were all written by women. The nature of the novels themselves, together with 'instinct or divination,' had already led the reviewer to that conclusion, which was now simply confirmed by Charlotte Brontë's 'Biographical Notice.' The review quotes a great deal from the 'Notice': Charlotte's description of the isolation of Haworth, her discovery of Emily's poems, the silence that greeted their publication in *Poems by Currer, Ellis, and Acton Bell*, and the deaths of both Emily and Anne. It is on Emily Brontë's *life* that the review spends most of its 2,000 words. References to *Wuthering Heights* are late and few, and then it is grouped not only with *Jane Eyre* but also with *Agnes Grey*. All three are 'characteristic tales' — characteristic of the Bell, that is to say the Brontë, sisters, and, more generally, of tales women write. A single sentence is given to *Wuthering Heights* alone: 'To those whose experience of men and manners is neither extensive nor various, the construction of a self-consistent monster is easier than the delineation of an imperfect or inconsistent reality. . . .' The review ends there, repeating still another time its classification of the novel. *Wuthering Heights*, with its 'Biographical Notice,' is a 'more than usually interesting contribution to the history of female authorship in England.'

I don't mean to suggest that this is the first time a reviewer for the *Athenaeum* was ever condescending; the particular terms of the condescension are my point. Emily Brontë the novelist is reduced to Emily

Brontë the person, whose fiction in turn is seen to be limited by the experiential limitation of the life. *Wuthering Heights* is an addition to the 'history of female authorship in England.'

There are other consequences that attend the knowledge or the presumption that Ellis Bell is not a man but a woman. Sydney Dobell published a long essay titled 'Currer Bell' in the *Palladium* three months before he could have known on Charlotte's authority that her sister had written *Wuthering Heights*. But he already 'knew' from the intrinsic nature of *Jane Eyre, Wuthering Heights, Agnes Grey*, and *The Tenant of Wildfell Hall* that they were written by women; indeed, he thought them written by the same woman.[6] Approaching *Wuthering Heights* with that conviction, he stressed the youthfulness of its author. And he likened her to a little bird fluttering its wings against the bars of its cage, only to sink at the last exhausted. Later, when it had more practice writing novels, it would fly freely into the heavens. Dobell stressed also the 'involuntary art' of the novel. (Whipple, you may remember, had said that female authors sometimes wrote well 'unawares.') Finally, Dobell saw the novel primarily as a love story, and for the first time made the heroine Catherine the major focus of interest, but only insofar as she was in love. With Heathcliff, Dobell contended, the 'authoress' was less successful.

It is clear, I hope, in these instances (and the same can be argued of other contemporary responses) that there is a considerable correlation between what readers assume or know the sex of the writer to be and what they actually see, or neglect to see, in 'his' or her work. *Wuthering Heights* is one book to Percy Edwin Whipple and George Washington Peck, who quarrel strenuously with its 'morals' and its taste, but another to the reviewer for the *Athenaeum*, who puts it calmly in its place and discourses on the life of the clergyman's daughter who wrote it. And Peck's rough sailor is born anew as Dobell's piteous birds with wings too young to fly.

NOTES

2　'Biographical Notice of Ellis and Acton Bell,' *Wuthering Heights: An Authoritative Text with Essays in Criticism*, ed. William M. Sale, Jr. (New York: W. W. Norton, 1963), p. 4. All quotations from *Wuthering Heights* are taken also from this edition.

3　'Novels of the Season,' *The North American Review*, LXVII (1848), 353. K. J. Fielding identifies the reviewer in 'The Brontës and "The North American Review": A Critic's Strange Guesses,' *Brontë Society Transactions*, XIII (1957), 14–18.

4　'Wuthering Heights,' *The American Review*, NS I (1848), 573. Additional reviews of the first edition consulted are the following: *The Athenaeum*, Dec. 25, 1847, 1324–25; *The Atlas*, XXIII (1848), 59; *Britannia*, Jan. 15, 1848; *Douglas Jerrold's Weekly Newspaper*, Jan. 15, 1848; *The Examiner*, Jan. 8, 1848, 21–22; *Godey's Magazine and Lady's Book*, XXXVII (1848), 57; *Graham's Magazine*, XXXIII (1848), 60; *Literary World*, III (1848), 243; *The New Monthly Magazine and Humourist*, LXXXII (1848), 140; *The Quarterly Review*, LXXXIV (1848), 153–185; *The Spectator*, XX (1847), 1217; *Tait's Edinburgh Magazine*, XV

(1848), 138—140; *The Union Magazine*, June, 1848, 287; and an unidentified review quoted in full by Charles Simpson in *Emily Brontë* (London: Country Life, 1929). I am indebted for references to reviews of *Wuthering Heights* both to Melvin R. Watson, '*Wuthering Heights* and the Critics,' *Trollopian*, III (1949), 243—263 and to Jane Gray Nelson, 'First American Reviews of the Works of Charlotte, Emily, and Anne Brontë,' *BST*, XIV (1964), 39—44. Nelson lists one review that I have not so far seen: *Peterson's Magazine*, June, 1848.

5   *The Athenaeum*, Dec. 28, 1850. All quotations are from pp. 1368—69.

6   'Currer Bell,' *Palladium*, I (1850). Reprinted in *Life and Letters of Sydney Dobell*, ed. E. Jolly (London, 1878), I, 163—186 and in *BST*, V (1918), 210—236. Additional reviews of the second edition consulted are the following: *The Eclectic Review*, XCIII (1851), 222—227; *The Examiner*, Dec. 21, 1850, 815; *The Leader*, Dec. 28, 1850, 953; *The North American Review*, LXXXV (1857), 293—329. The last review, later than the others, appeared in response to Mrs. Gaskell's *Life of Charlotte Brontë*. It implies an apology for the first *North American* review of *Wuthering Heights*. Knowing the lives of the Brontës, the 1857 reviewer finds *Wuthering Heights* peculiar, but he also finds the novel easy to dismiss — its peculiarity or strangeness mirrors the 'distorted fancy' of the writer's life, lived in isolation and deprivation. The novel lies outside normal human experience; it would be inappropriate to bring moral judgment to bear on it. Virtually the same attitude is taken by the reviewer in *The Eclectic Review*. The review in *The Leader*, by G. H. Lewes, is probably the best of the contemporary ones. Still, it would not be difficult to trace in it the operation of sexual prejudice, although the argument would, I think, take more space than I have allotted to any single review here. Charlotte Brontë was quite alert to Lewes's bias, as she revealed in a letter to him dated Nov. 1, 1849. Allan R. Brick gives excerpts from the *Leader* review and comments revealingly on Charlotte Brontë's attitude toward it and toward other early reviews in 'Lewes's Review of *Wuthering Heights*,' *NCF*, XIV (1960), 355—359.

MARGARET ATWOOD
'Paradoxes and Dilemmas, the Woman as Writer',
Women in the Canadian Mosaic

Reviewing and the Absence of an Adequate Critical Vocabulary

Cynthia Ozack, in the American magazine *Ms.*, says, 'For many years, I had noticed that no book of poetry by a woman was ever reviewed without reference to the poet's sex. The curious thing was that, in the two decades of my scrutiny, there were *no* exceptions whatever. It did not matter whether the reviewer was a man or a woman; in every case, the question of the 'feminine sensibility' of the poet was at the center of the reviewers' response. The maleness of male poets, on the other hand, hardly ever seemed to matter.'

Things aren't this bad in Canada, possibly because we were never thoroughly indoctrinated with the Holy Gospel according to the distorters of Freud. Many reviewers manage to get through a review without displaying the kind of bias Ozick is talking about. But that it does occur was demonstrated to me by a project I was involved with at York University in 1971—72.

One of my student groups was attempting to study what we called 'sexual bias in reviewing,' by which we meant not unfavourable reviews, but points being added or subtracted by the reviewer on the basis of the author's sex and supposedly associated characteristics rather than on the basis of the work itself. Our study fell into two parts: (i) a survey of writers, half male, half female, conducted by letter: had they ever experienced sexual bias directed against them in a review?; (ii) the reading of a large number of reviews from a wide range of periodicals and newspapers.

The results of the writers' survey were perhaps predictable. Of the men, none answered Yes, a quarter Maybe, and three-quarters No. Of women, half were Yeses, a quarter Maybes and a quarter Nos. The women replying Yes often wrote long, detailed letters, giving instances and discussing their own attitudes. All the men's letters were short.

This proved only that women were more likely to *feel* they had been discriminated against on the basis of sex. When we got round to the reviews, we discovered they were sometimes justified. Here are the kinds of things we found.

i) *Assignment of Reviews.* Several of our letter-writers discussed the mechanics of review assignment. Some felt books by women tended to be passed over by book-page editors assigning books for review; others that books by women tended to get assigned to women reviewers. When we started toting up reviews we found that most books in this society are written by men, and so are most reviews. Disproportionately often, books by women were assigned to women reviewers, indicating that books by women fell in the minds of those dishing out the reviews into a special 'female' category. Likewise, women reviewers tended to be reviewing books by women rather than books by men (though because of the preponderance of male reviewers, there were quite a few male-written reviews of books by women).

ii) *The Quiller-Couch Syndrome.* This phrase refers to the turn-of-the-century essay by Quiller-Couch, defining 'masculine' and 'feminine' styles in writing. The 'masculine' style is, of course, bold, forceful, clear, vigorous, etc.; the 'feminine' style is vague, weak, tremulous, pastel, etc. In the list of pairs you can include 'objective' and 'subjective,' 'universal' or 'accurate depiction of society' versus 'confessional,' 'personal,' or even 'narcissistic' and 'neurotic.' It's roughly seventy years since Quiller-Couch's essay, but the 'masculine' group of adjectives is still much more likely to be applied to the work of male writers; female writers are much more likely to get hit with some version of 'the feminine style' or 'feminine sensibility,' whether their work merits it or not.

iii) *The Lady Painter Syndrome, or She Writes Like a Man.* This is a pattern in which good equals male, bad equals female. I call it the Lady Painter Syndrome because of a conversation I had about female painters with a male painter in 1960. 'When she's good,' he said, 'we call her a painter; when she's bad, we call her a lady painter.' 'She writes like a man' is part of the same pattern; it's usually used by a male reviewer who is impressed by a female writer. It's meant as a compliment. See also 'She thinks like a man,' which means the author thinks, unlike most women, who are held to be incapable of objective thought (their province is 'feeling'). Adjectives which often have similar connotations are ones such as 'strong,' 'gutsy,' 'hard,' 'mean,' etc. A hard-hitting piece of writing by a man is liable to be thought of as merely realistic; an equivalent piece by a woman is much more likely to be labelled 'cruel' or 'tough.' The assumption is that women are by nature soft, weak and not very talented, and that if a woman writer happens to be a good writer, she should be deprived of her identity as a female and provided with higher (male) status. Thus the woman writer has, in the minds of such reviewers, two choices. She can be bad but female, a carrier of the 'feminine sensibility' virus; or she can be 'good' in male-adjective terms, but sexless. Badness seems to be ascribed then to a surplus of female hormones, whereas badness in a male writer is usually ascribed to nothing but badness (though a 'bad' male writer is sometimes held, by adjectives implying sterility or impotence, to be deficient in maleness). 'Maleness' is exemplified by the 'good' male writer; 'femaleness,' since it is seen by such reviewers as a handicap or deficiency, is held to be transcended or discarded by the 'good' female one. In other words, there is no critical vocabulary for expressing the concept 'good/female.' Work by a male writer is often spoken of by critics admiring it as having 'balls'; have you ever heard anyone speak admiringly of work by a woman as having 'tits'?

Possible antidotes: Development of a 'good/female' vocabulary (wow, has that ever got womb . . .'); or, preferably, the development of a vocabulary that can treat structures made of words as though they are exactly that, not biological entities possessed of sexual organs.

iv) *Domesticity.* One of our writers noted a (usually male) habit of concentrating on domestic themes in the work of a female writer, ignoring any other topic she might have dealt with, then patronizing her for an excessive interest in domestic themes. We found several instances of reviewers identifying an author as a 'housewife' and consequently dismissing anything she has produced (since, in our society, a 'housewife' is viewed as a relatively brainless and talentless creature). We even found one instance in which the author was called a 'housewife' and put down for writing like one when in fact she was no such thing.

For such reviewers, when a man writes about things like doing the dishes, it's realism; when a woman does, it's an unfortunate feminine genetic limitation.

v) *Sexual Compliment/Put-down.* This syndrome can be summed up as follows:

She: 'How do you like my (design for an airplane/mathematical formula/ medical miracle)?'
He: 'You sure have a nice ass.'

In reviewing it usually takes the form of commenting on the cute picture of the (female) author on the cover, coupled with dismissal of her as a writer.

BARBARA SMITH
'Toward a Black Feminist Criticism', *Conditions: Two*

The role that criticism plays in making a body of literature recognizable and real hardly needs to be explained here. The necessity for non-hostile and perceptive analysis of works written by persons outside the 'mainstream' of white/male cultural rule has been proven by the Black cultural resurgence of the 1960s and '70s and by the even more recent growth of feminist literary scholarship. For books to be real and remembered they have to be talked about. For books to be understood they must be examined in such a way that the basic intentions of the writers are at least considered. Because of racism Black literature has usually been viewed as a discrete subcategory of American literature and there have been Black critics of Black literature who did much to keep it alive long before it caught the attention of whites. Before the advent of specifically feminist criticism in this decade, books by white women, on the other hand, were not clearly perceived as the cultural manifestation of an oppressed people. It took the surfacing of the second wave of the North American feminist movement to expose the fact that these works contain a stunningly accurate record of the impact of patriarchal values and practice upon the lives of women and more significantly that literature by women provides essential insights into female experience.

In speaking about the current situation of Black women writers, it is important to remember that the existence of a feminist movement was an essential pre-condition to the growth of feminist literature, criticism and women's studies, which focused at the beginning almost entirely upon invesigations of literature. The fact that a parallel Black feminist movement has been much slower in evolving cannot help but have impact upon the situation of Black women writers and artists and explains in part why during this very same period we have been so ignored.

There is no political movement to give power or support to those who want to examine Black women's experience through studying our history, literature and culture. There is no political presence that demands a minimal level of consciousness and respect from those who write or talk about our lives. Finally, there is not a developed body of Black feminist political theory whose assumptions could be used in the study of Black women's art. When

Black women's books are dealt with at all, it is usually in the context of Black literature which largely ignores the implications of sexual politics. When white women look at Black women's works they are of course ill-equipped to deal with the subtleties of racial politics. A Black feminist approach to literature that embodies the realization that the politics of sex as well as the politics of race and class are crucially interlocking factors in the works of Black women writers is an absolute necessity. Until a Black feminist criticism exists we will not even know what these writers mean. The citations from a variety of critics which follow prove that without a Black feminist critical perspective not only are books by Black women misunderstood, they are destroyed in the process.

Jerry H. Bryant, the *Nation's* white male reviewer of Alice Walker's *In Love & Trouble: Stories of Black Women*, wrote in 1973:

> The subtitle of the collection, 'Stories of Black Women,' is probably an attempt by the publisher to exploit not only black subjects but feminine ones. There is nothing feminist about these stories, however.[2]

Blackness and feminism are to his mind mutually exclusive and peripheral to the act of writing fiction. Bryant of course does not consider that Walker might have titled the work herself, nor did he apparently read the book which unequivocally reveals the author's feminist consciousness.

In *The Negro Novel in America*, a book that Black critics recognize as one of the worst examples of white racist pseudo-scholarship, Robert Bone cavalierly dismisses Ann Petry's classic, *The Street*. He perceives it to be '. . . a superficial social analysis' of how slums victimize their Black inhabitants.[3] He further objects that:

> It is an attempt to interpret slum life in terms of *Negro* experience, when a larger frame of reference is required. As Alain Locke has observed, '*Knock on Any Door* is superior to *The Street* because it designates class and environment, rather than mere race and environment, as its antagonist.'[4]

Neither Robert Bone nor Alain Locke, the Black male critic he cites, can recognize that *The Street* is one of the best delineations in literature of how sex, race, *and* class interact to oppress Black women.

In her review of Toni Morrison's *Sula* for the *New York Times Book Review* in 1973, putative feminist Sara Blackburn makes similarly racist comments. She writes:

> . . . Toni Morrison is far too talented to remain only a marvelous recorder of the black side of provincial American life. If she is to maintain the large and serious audience she deserves, she is going to have to address a riskier contemporary reality than this beautiful but nevertheless distanced novel. *And if she does this, it seems to me that she might easily transcend that early and unintentionally limiting classification 'black women writer' and take her place among the most serious, important and talented American novelists now working.*[5] [Italics mine.]

Recognizing Morrison's exquisite gift, Blackburn unashamedly asserts that Morrison is 'too talented' to deal with mere Black folk, particularly those double nonentities, Black women. In order to be accepted as 'serious,' 'important,' 'talented,' and 'American,' she must obviously focus her efforts upon chronicling the doings of white men.

The mishandling of Black women writers by whites is paralleled more often by their not being handled at all, particularly in feminist criticism. Although Elaine Showalter in her review essay on literary criticism for *Signs* states that: 'The best work being produced today [in feminist criticism] is exacting and cosmopolitan,' her essay is neither.[6] If it were, she would not have failed to mention a single Black or Third-World woman writer, whether 'major' or 'minor' to cite her questionable categories. That she also does not even hint that lesbian writers of any color exist renders her purported overview virtually meaningless. Showalter obviously thinks that the identities of being Black and female are mutually exclusive as this statement illustrates.

> Furthermore, there are other literary subcultures (black American novelists, for example) whose history offers a precedent for feminist scholarship to use.[7]

The idea of critics like Showalter *using* Black literature is chilling, a case of barely disguised cultural imperialism. The final insult is that she footnotes the preceding remark by pointing readers to works on Black literature by white males Robert Bone and Roger Rosenblatt!

Two recent works by white women, Ellen Moers' *Literary Women: The Great Writers* and Patricia Meyer Spacks' *The Female Imagination* evidence the same racist flaw.[8] Moers includes the names of four Black and one Puertorriqueña writer in her seventy pages of bibliographical notes and does not deal at all with Third-World women in the body of her book. Spacks refers to a comparison between Negroes (sic) and women in Mary Ellmann's *Thinking About Women* under the index entry, 'blacks, women and.' *'Black Boy* (Wright)' is the preceding entry. Nothing follows. Again there is absolutely no recognition that Black and female identity ever co-exist, specifically in a group of Black women writers. Perhaps one can assume that these women do not know who Black women writers are, that they have had little opportunity like most Americans to learn about them. Perhaps. Their ignorance seems suspiciously selective, however, particularly in the light of the dozens of truly obscure white women writers they are able to unearth. Spacks was herself employed at Wellesley College at the same time that Alice Walker was there teaching one of the first courses on Black women writers in the country.

I am not trying to encourage racist criticism of Black women writers like that of Sara Blackburn, to cite only one example. As a beginning I would at least like to see in print white women's acknowledgement of the contradictions of who and what are being left out of their research and writing.[9]

Black male critics can also *act* as if they do not know that Black women writers exist and are, of course, hampered by an inability to comprehend Black women's experience in sexual as well as racial terms. Unfortunately there are also those who are as virulently sexist in their treatment of Black women writers as their white male counterparts. Darwin Turner's discussion of Zora Neale Hurston in his *In a Minor Chord: Three Afro-American Writers and Their Search for Identity* is a frightening example of the near assassination of a great Black woman writer.[10] His descriptions of her and her work as 'artful,' 'coy,' 'irrational,' 'superficial,' and 'shallow' bear no relationship to the actual quality of her achievements. Turner is completely insensitive to the sexual political dynamics of Hurston's life and writing.

In a recent interview the notoriously misogynist writer, Ishmael Reed, comments in this way upon the low sales of his newest novel:

> . . . but the book only sold 8000 copies. I don't mind giving out the figure: 8000. Maybe if I was one of those young *female* Afro-American writers that are so hot now, I'd sell more. You know, fill my books with ghetto women who can *do no wrong.* . . . But come on, I think I could have sold 8000 copies by myself.[11]

The politics of the situation of Black women are glaringly illuminated by this statement. Neither Reed nor his white male interviewer has the slightest compunction about attacking Black women in print. They need not fear widespread public denunciation since Reed's statement is in perfect agreement with the values of a society that hates Black people, women and Black women. Finally the two of them feel free to base their actions on the premise that Black women are powerless to alter either their political or cultural oppression.

In her introduction to 'A Bibliography of Works Written by American Black Women' Ora Williams quotes some of the reactions of her colleagues toward her efforts to do research on Black women. She writes:

> Others have reacted negatively with such statements as, 'I really don't think you are going to find very much written.' 'Have "they" written anything that is any good?' and, 'I wouldn't go overboard with this woman's lib thing.' When discussions touched on the possibility of teaching a course in which emphasis would be on the literature by Black women, one response was, 'Ha, ha. That will certainly be the most nothing course ever offered!'[12]

A remark by Alice Walker capsulizes what all the preceding examples indicate about the position of Black women writers and the reasons for the damaging criticism about them. She responds to her interviewer's question, 'Why do you think that the black woman writer has been so ignored in America? Does she have even more difficulty than the black male writer, who perhaps has just begun to gain recognition?' Walker replies:

> There are two reasons why the black woman writer is not taken as seriously as the black male writer. One is that she's a woman. Critics seem unusually ill-equipped to intelligently discuss and analyze the works of black women. Generally, they do not even make the attempt; they prefer, rather, to talk about the lives of black women writers, not about what they write. And, since black women writers are not — it would seem — very likeable — until recently they were the least willing worshippers of male supremacy — comments about them tend to be cruel.[13]

NOTES

2 Jerry H. Bryant, 'The Outskirts of a New City,' in the *Nation*, 12 November 1973, p. 502.
3 Robert Bone, *The Negro Novel in America* (Yale University Press, New Haven: orig. c. 1958), p. 180.
4 *Ibid.* (*Knock on Any Door* is a novel by Black writer, Willard Motley.)
5 Sara Blackburn, 'You Still Can't Go Home Again,' in the *New York Times Book Review*, 30 December 1973, p. 3.
6 Elaine Showalter, 'Review Essay: Literary Criticism,' *Signs*, Vol. 1, no. 2 (Winter, 1975), p. 460.
7 *Ibid.*, p. 445.
8 Ellen Moers, *Literary Women: The Great Writers* (Anchor Books, Garden City, New York: 1977, orig. c. 1976).
Patricia Meyer Spacks, *The Female Imagination* (Avon Books, New York: 1976).
9 An article by Nancy Hoffman, 'White Women, Black Women: Inventing an Adequate Pedagogy,' in *Women's Studies Newsletter*, Vol. 5, nos. 1 & 2 (Spring, 1977), pp. 21−24, gives valuable insights into how white women can approach the writing of Black women.
10 Darwin T. Turner, *In a Minor Chord: Three Afro-American Writers and Their Search for Identity* (Southern Illinois University Press, Carbondale and Edwardsville: c. 1971).
11 John Domini, 'Roots and Racism: An Interview With Ishmael Reed,' in *The Boston Phoenix*, 5 April 1977, p. 20.
12 Ora Williams, 'A Bibliography of Works Written by American Black Women,' in *College Language Association Journal*, March 1972, p. 355. There is an expanded book-length version of this bibliography: *American Black Women in the Arts and Social Sciences: A Bibliographic Survey* (The Scarecrow Press, Inc., Metuchen, N.J.: 1973).
13 John O'Brien, ed., *Interviews With Black Writers* (Liveright, New York: c. 1973), p. 201.

BLACK WOMAN TALK COLLECTIVE
'Black Woman Talk', *Feminist Review*

Black Woman Talk is a collective of women of Asian and African descent living in Britain. As Black women we feel that the publishing industry has ignored and silenced the views and ideas of Black women living in Britain. It is important for us therefore to restore the lines of communication which have been historically destroyed and to re-establish the links between our scattered and isolated communities.

As Black women we experience oppression due to our sex, race, class and sexual orientation. This is reflected in every area of our lives and the publishing industry is no exception. It is a very powerful medium for communication and it reflects the racism and sexism of this society. The amount of work published for, by and about Black women is totally negligible and Black women's voices have gone unheard. Instead racist and sexist stereotypes have been perpetuated and until now been unchallenged.

More recently, it appears that there is a growing awareness amongst some of the established mainstream and feminist publishers of the need to make Black voices heard. Unfortunately, their enthusiasm to publish works by Black women, particularly from America, seems to stem from their recognition that such books have a lucrative market, rather than any genuine commitment to making publishing accessible to Black women writers in Britain. Afro-American women seem to be the vogue for feminist publishers such as the Women's Press. Such publishers are not only reluctant to hear the voices of Black women in Britain but there is little concern about including Black women in the publishing industry in a way which gives them any decision-making powers at all levels.

Black Woman Talk began as a small group of unemployed women who came together to form a workers' publishing co-operative. We feel there is an urgent need to see more publications available by Black women living in Britain to express our experiences and history. Our own varied experiences in working in Black organizations as well as our varied involvement in creative work such as writing, visual arts, theatre and music places us in contact with Black women who are writing and/or doing visual work. We are all writers and artists who want to see more Black women get access to publishing and the various skills involved in this field.

Black Woman Talk aims to provide a means by which women of Asian and African descent can publish their work, and through the publication of short stories, poetry, political writings, photo-essays, calendars reflect the wide variety of written and visual works produced by us. We would like to encourage more Black women to write and record their life experiences and to provide a greater knowledge and understanding of the lives and history of Black women in the wider community. We would also like to make alternative materials available for use in schools, libraries and other public information centres.

We will shortly be asking for manuscripts by Black women and as we grow we shall provide employment in a co-operative situation where Black women work with and for other Black women, thus sharing the skills and knowledge we gain, and providing encouragement and advice to other Black women. We would like to extend to cover typesetting and printing in the long term, which would give us greater self-determination and more skills to share.

The existence of *Black Woman Talk* is testimony to the strength of Black Women organizing to create our own means of communication. The international movement of Black women organizing in this way is illustrated by the existence of our sister press in America, Kitchen Table; Women of Color Press, and Kali Press; Third World Women Press in Delhi.

TERRY LOVELL
'Writing Like a Woman: A Question of Politics',
The Politics of Theory

Literary Production and Gender

The penetration of capital, and the transformation of literature into a commodity, has been limited to the stages of printing and publishing, and distribution. The first stage of literary production has been untouched either by technological transformation or by the division of labour. Unlike other forms of intellectual work, novel writing has not become institutionalised within the University. In terms of masculine/feminine poles of ideology, novel-writing is deeply ambivalent, like all categories of so-called 'creative writing'. It is paid work, work for breadwinners; and despite recurrent male complaints of female competition, it is dominated by men. Richard Altick estimates that the proportion of female to male novelists remained at about 20%, from 1800–1935.[1] Yet novel-writing is frequently seen as 'feminine' rather than 'masculine'. Even male writers can be found who make this association. John Fowles links all kinds of creativity with femininity. However, this does not mean that he considers it fit work for women. 'There are', he tells us, 'Adam-women and Eve-men; singularly few of the world's great progressive artists and thinkers, have not belonged to the latter category'.[2]

John Fowles' views are of course his own. But I believe he articulates the gender ambiguity of literary production in our culture. However, a recent massive contribution to feminist literary theory has argued the opposite case. Sandra Gilbert and Susan Gubar claim that

In patriarchal Western culture . . . the text's author is a father, a progenitor, an aesthetic patriarch whose pen is an instrument of generative power like his penis.

They back up their claim with quotations from literary men and women:

The artist's most essential quality is masterly execution, which is a kind of male gift, and especially marks off men from women . . . (Gerard Manley Hopkins, 1886)

Literature is not the business of a woman's life, and it cannot be . . . (Robert Southey, 1837)

Jane Austen's novels fail because her writing lacks a strong male thrust. (Anthony Burgess)

Literary women lack that blood congested genital drive which energises every great style. (William Gass)[3]

These quotations fail to establish Gilbert and Gubar's claim — in fact they cast doubt upon it. Where femininity and masculinity are strongly marked in culture and ideology, they do not have to be stridently claimed. The writers she quotes protest too much. Their over-insistence paradoxically confirms the gender-ambiguity of 'creative writing' in Western culture, rather than establishing its masculine credentials.

Perhaps this is a further reason for the greater interest which feminism as opposed to socialism has displayed for literature. Literary production has been a contested area vis-à-vis gender in a way in which it has not been for class. I want to argue that this gender ambiguity has made it easier for women and for feminists to breach literary production, but that this has created particular problems for feminist literary theory.

First, though, it is necessary to substantiate my claim that literary production *is* gender ambiguous.

i.   I would hazard a guess that there is no strong association among the population at large, of creative writing with 'manliness' — quite the opposite in fact.

ii.   The study of literature and languages, through the school system and at university, is heavily dominated by female students.

iii.   Women gained access to novel-writing and to other forms of literary work at a time when they were excluded from virtually all other (middle-class) professions except governessing. It was, moreover, the only paid occupation in which they could hope to achieve independence and financial parity with men.[4]

iv.   Novel writing is a form of domestic production. Here, home and workplace have never been separated. It is an individual and personalised form of production.

v.   Fictional worlds have been largely restricted to the sphere which is conventionally and ideologically assigned to women, or for which women are assumed to have a special responsibility — that of personal relations.

. . . the development of the novel has been closely bound up with the social and political position of women . . . there is a fundamental continuity which firmly places them in a private domestic world where emotions and personal relationships are at once the focus of moral value and the core of women's experience. In the novel women are 'prisoners' of feeling and of private life.[5]

Naturally, male writers have struggled against this taint of feminine identification. Hence the sentiments quoted above. They have often done so by denigrating their female colleagues. Women, urged to write, if they must, like ladies, were despised as inferior when they did, attacked as 'unfeminine' when, like Charlotte Brontë, they did not.[6] Certain genres have been marked off as 'lesser' forms, and ceded to women (e.g. romantic fiction). Others have been developed and colonised as vehicles of strident masculinity (the Hemingway-Miller-Mailer school attacked by Kate Millett[7]). More recently, structuralist theory applied to literature has offered a new offensive in the field of literary criticism. Showalter argues that 'The new sciences of the text . . . have offered literary critics the opportunity to demonstrate that the work they do is as manly and aggressive as nuclear physics — not intuitive, expressive, feminine'.[8] Where structuralism is allied to Lacanian psycho-analytic theory, the bid to masculinise is strongest. Variants of this approach have consigned the feminine *per se* to absence, silence, incoherence, even madness. Several feminists have attempted to construct theories of feminine identity and a feminist aesthetic upon this marginal territory ceded by a phallocentric theory of language. I believe this to be a mistaken strategy, for it abandons territory which can and ought to be defended against masculine imperialism; coherence, rationality, articulateness.

NOTES

1 Richard Altick, *The English Common Reader* (Chicago, University of Chicago Press, 1957).
2 John Fowles, *The Aristos* (London, Triad Granada, 1981), p. 157.
3 Sandra M. Gilbert and Susan Gubar, *The Madwoman in the Attic: The Woman Writer and the Nineteenth-Century Literary Imagination* (New Haven, Yale University Press, 1979).
4 Elaine Showalter, *A Literature of Their Own: British Women Novelists From Brontë to Lessing* (London, Virago, 1979).
5 Patricia Stubbs, *Women and Fiction: Feminism and the Novel, 1880–1920* (London, Methuen, 1979), p. x.
6 Showalter, *A Literature of Their Own.*
7 Kate Millett, *Sexual Politics* (London, Virago, 1977).
8 Elaine Showalter, 'Towards a Feminist Poetics', *Women Writing and Writing about Women,* edited by Mary Jacobus (London, Croom Helm, 1979).

CYNTHIA OZICK
'Women and Creativity: The Demise of the Dancing Dog',
Woman in Sexist Society

Consider, in this vein, the habits of reviewers. I think I can say in good conscience that I have never repeat, *never* read a review of a novel or, especially, of a collection of poetry by a woman which did not include somewhere in its columns a gratuitous allusion to the writer's sex and its supposed effects. The Ovarian Theory of Literature is the property of all society, not merely of freshmen and poor Ph.D. lackeys: you will find it in all the best periodicals, even the most highbrow. For example: a few years ago a critic in *The New York Review of Books* considered five novels, three of which were by women. And so his review begins: 'Women novelists, we have learned to assume, like to keep their focus narrow.' And from this touchstone — with no ground other than the 'we have learned to assume' — falls his praise and his censure. The touchstone, of course, is properly qualified, as such touchstones always are, by reverent asides concerning the breadth of George Eliot and the grasp of Jane Austen. Ah, indispensable George and Jane! They have come into the world, one concludes, only to serve as exceptions to the strictures of reviewers; and they *are* exceptions. Genius always is; it is how genius is defined. But if the exception is to be dragged into every routine review of novelists and poets who are women, then the rule must drop equally on all. Let every new poet, male and female, be reviewed in the shadow of Emily Dickinson and Coleridge. Let every unknown novelist, male and female, be reviewed in the blaze of *Anna*

Karenina and *Wuthering Heights*. If this seems like nonsense, then reviewers must take merit as their point of concentration, not the flap of skirts, not the glibbest of literary canards.

Still, the canards are, in their way, great fun, being as flexible and fragile as other toys. A collection of canards is bound to be a gaggle of contradictions. When, for instance, my bright engineering student identified Flannery O'Connor as 'sentimental,' she was squarely in one-half of a diluvial, though bifurcated, tradition. Within that tradition there are two hoary veins of woman. One: she is sentimental, imprecise, irrational, overemotional, impatient, unperseveringly flighty, whimsical, impulsive, unreliable, unmechanical, not given to practicality, perilously vague, and so on. In this view she is always contrasted with man, who is, on the other hand, unsentimental, exact, rational, controlled, patient, hard-headed, mechanically gifted, a meeter of payrolls, firm of purpose, wary of impulse, anything but a dreamer. Description One accounts for why throughout her history she has been a leader neither of empires nor of trades nor of armies. But it is also declared that, her nature having failed her in the practical world, she cannot succeed in the world of invention either: she is unequipped, for example, for poetry, in that (here is Description Two) she is above all pragmatic, sensible and unsentimental, unvisionary, unadventurous, empirical, conservative, down-to-earth, unspontaneous, perseveringly patient and thus good at the minutiae of mechanical and manipulative tasks, and essentially unimaginative. In short, she will wander too much or she will wander not at all. She is either too emotional or she is not emotional enough. She is either too spontaneous or she is not spontaneous enough. She is either too sensitive (that is why she cannot be president of General Motors) or she is not sensitive enough (that is why she will never write *King Lear*).

But none of this is to imply that woman is damned, and damned from every direction. Not at all. The fact is that woman *qua* woman is more often celebrated. If she cannot hear the Muse, says Robert Graves, what does it matter? She *is* the Muse. *Man Does, Woman Is* is the title of Graves' most recent collection of poetry. If we are expected to conclude from this that woman is an It rather than a Thou (to use Martin Buber's categories), why deplore it? The Parthenon too is beautiful, passive, inspiring. Who would long to *build* it, if one can *be* it?

MARY ELLMANN
Thinking About Women

I do not mean to underestimate this conviction on the part of many writers that they live among strangers and aliens. On the contrary, I am alienated in turn by the habitual identification of this complex and all-encompassing enmity with the relatively narrow circumstance of sexuality. It is through this identification that phallic criticism regularly and rapidly shifts from writing by women, which can be dismissed as innocuous, to their vicious influence upon writing by men. It is clear that sexual conflict has become the specific focus, literal as well as metaphoric, of a general and amorphous sense of intellectual conflict. A simple instance is this last novel of Philip Roth's, *When She Was Good*, in which a pimple of a young woman is created only to be squeezed, interminably, to death — a small self-gratification which none of us would deny each other, but still prefer not to witness. And yet this tiny tumor, this Emma Bovary in galoshes, is supposed to define the Morality of the Middle West. Nothing much must stand for everything.

But the metaphoric focus is ordinarily more interesting. The capacity to write, even as it is held more and more precariously, is made synonymous with sexual capacity, whereupon the woman becomes the enemy of both. She appears as the risk that the writer has to take, or the appetite, at once sluggish and gargantuan, which must be roused and then satisfied in order to prove that the writer is capable of giving satisfaction of any kind. So she is all that offers stubborn and brute resistance to achievement even as she is its only route. Her range is limitless, all internal obstacle as well as external impediment, all that within the writer himself may prevent his accomplishing his aim — weakness, dullness, caution, fear, dishonesty, triviality.

At the crudest level of this metaphoric struggle, the writer finds his professional and sexual activities incompatible, on the grounds of the distribution of resources. This anxiety seems distinctly modern. The association of the two faculties, intellectual and sexual, is ancient, but the expressed inability to reconcile them is recent. Blake, for example, celebrated 'the lineaments of gratified desire,' and seemed to sense no contradiction between them and artistic gratification. In fact, he considered sexual intercourse, rather like having breakfast or a walk in the garden, an essential prelude to composition. Hemingway, instead, found a young writer to warn against making love during periods of composition: the best ideas would be lost in bed. An intense frugality has set in, a determination not to squander vital spirits. Goods produced or released by the self, like semen and words, become oddly equivalent and interdependent. The Samson law. the consumption or removal of one product, particularly by a woman, must inevitably diminish another. Naturally then, the minds which so balance the books of themselves frequently remark upon the materiality of women. The impression is deflected from their own sense of possessing a warehouse of scarce, conglomerate materials, all subtracting strength from each other, and all consequently in need of vigilant supervision. A loss of all one's buttons will inevitably mean a strain on one's supply of safety pins. A fear of insufficiency develops, a terror of running out. All sexual difficulties have therefore shifted in fiction from women to men, from feminine barrenness to masculine impotence or sterility or utter indifference. The women are uniformly and insatiably greedy (again, of course, in fiction) for conception. The men cannot afford to give them, indiscriminately, all the children they demand. The expenditure could only mean their going, as writers, into debtors' prison.

3

Gender and Genre

INTRODUCTION

Women and the Novel

Any discussion of gender and literary form is dominated by the need to explain women's special relationship with the novel. Most work in this area springs from the sociology of literature or from cultural history. It examines the changes in class structure and in the position of women, and demonstrates a particular interest in the emergence of a leisured female middle class, from whose ranks came not only the women novelists but an extensive female readership. As Ellen Moers discusses, novel-writing played an important role in the development of professions for women. The woman novelist could write in the privacy of her own home; indeed, many biographies of nineteenth-century women novelists point to the domesticity of the writing arrangements — frequently at a sitting-room or dining-room table. Unlike writing for the theatre there was no need for an unseemly involvement in public life. All negotiations with the publisher could be by letter or even conducted by a father or husband.

The novel's lack of status and tradition, the belief that it demanded less intellectual rigour than other forms of writing, opened up possibilities for women. At its most disparaging, as Ken Ruthven's extract indicates, novels could be viewed dismissively as the best that women were capable of: men study classics; women amuse themselves with novels. In a more opportunist way, women might recognize that 'the novel alone was young enough to be soft in (their) hands',[1] that here was a form without a long history of male authorities. Because the novel's genesis lay partly in forms of writing familiar to women — the diary, the journal, letters — the form could seem more accessible and approachable than a poetry dependent on Greek and Latin allusions. In its content, also, the novel was often considered — and still is — an appropriate form for women. Tolstoy may have written novels that range over half of Europe but it was equally possible, as Jane Austen proves, to write novels that go no further than Bath. What happens in the family, in the neighbouring Big House, in the next street or town, has been the staple diet of the novel, and it is the very world that women know so well. For Virginia Woolf, the marking of the nuances of inter-personal relations constitutes women's distinct contribution; the 'training in the observation of character, in the analysis of emotion' becomes an education for novel writing. G. H. Lewes's comment in the Ruthven extract illustrates how some critics have interpreted these attributes as confirmation of women's 'natural' character, which conveniently finds expression in the new literary form. Far more fruitful than Lewes's biologistic stance is to relate the development of the novel and the emergence of the woman novelist to what Terry Eagleton calls the 'feminization of discourse'. He writes:

> In a contradictory movement, "feminine" values relegated by the sexual division of labour to the private realm are now returning to transvaluate the ruling ideologies themselves. The feminization of discourse prolongs the fetishizing of women at the same time as it lends them a more authoritative voice.[2]

One location for this reintegration of feminine values has been the novel. It has frequently concerned itself with the ideological confrontation between masculine and feminine values and has offered as resolution the 'feminizing' of the aggressive, ego-centred hero by the gentle, conciliatory qualities of the heroine: Dombey reformed by his endlessly suffering Florence, or the ruthless manufacturers, Robert Moore in *Shirley* or John Thornton in *North and South*, made more amenable and socially responsible by the intervention of caring women.

Juliet Mitchell turns to psychology rather than sociology in her exploration of the novel. Using the psychoanalytical approach of the French theorist Jaques Lacan, she sees the development of the novel, not as an account of a given reality, but as a way of forming a history, a way of describing what a woman's life means under capitalism: in the novel women 'create themselves as a category: women'. The woman writer, Mitchell suggests, must both 'be feminine and . . . refuse femininity'; she creates a woman's world within her novels while, at the same time, rejecting that world by the very act of becoming a novelist, by taking up the pen, Gilbert and Gubar's 'metaphorical penis'.[3] Mitchell sees no alternative for the woman writer. She has to work within the dominant order, what is termed the 'symbolic', for to be outside the dominant order is to be mad or dead. But, equally, she must disrupt that symbolic order with a new symbolism.

Subverting the Forms

Mitchell's comments are suggestive of a critical approach which is very common in the gender/genre debate, namely the interest in how the woman writer can *subvert* the male-dominated forms. This is not necessarily a conscious aim by the author but is generated by the ideological conflict that is taking place in the text. Rosemary Jackson speaks of Mary Shelley's writing as fantasizing 'a violent attack on the symbolic order' and as part of a tradition of women Gothic writers whose writings '*subvert* patriarchal society' (my italics). The non-realist narrative forms, which question linear narrative, are thought by Jackson to be an important aspect of that attack on the symbolic order. She sees in Mary Shelley's work no strong narrative line but fragmentary and circular forms which, by leaving the work open and

indeterminate, reject an authoritative and definitive resolution. Claims that
periods of utopian writing by women parallel periods of feminist agitation,
as well as the recent noticeable increase in science-fiction writing by women,
would support Jackson's view that non-realist forms can help women writers
to disturb what is commonly perceived as 'real', 'natural', or 'inevitable'.
Utopian writing — and often science-fiction — offers a vision of a future
society with a social order and values critically at odds with the present. The
fact that it is not realistic, nor practically possible, is precisely the point; the
utopia shows us ways of thinking and relating that our society disregards or
discredits.

Women's subversive appropriation of the public male voice has been
viewed differently in relation to different literary forms. Christine Berg and
Philippa Berry consider that the voice of the seventeenth-century women
prophets is undermining because it sustains 'a multiplicity of various levels
of speech and meaning' and because it relinquishes 'the "I" as the subjective
centre of speech'. Using an argument similar to Jackson's, they contend that
the refusal of the women prophets to offer a single, constant, rational
meaning makes them difficult to assimilate, and thus the spasmodic,
irrational, irresolute nature of that voice becomes its quality rather than its
failing. Moreover, the voice of the women prophets is androgynous. As
women speaking the word of God, they refuse to accept sexual difference
and encroach on the most sacred areas of male language. Michelene Wandor
believes that what is threatening in the woman playwright is that she has
the 'control of a multiple set of voices', not simply her own, and that this
control is publicly exhibited on the stage. Gilbert and Gubar feel that it is the
assertive 'I' of the lyric that is challenging. Yet Cora Kaplan suggests that it
is not the lyric but the epic which is the real 'venture into a male stronghold'.

Women-Centred Novels

There is a suggestion throughout this line of argument that women writers,
in subverting male-dominated forms, can better express what women are
and what women want. It seems ironic, then, that the contemporary women-
centred novels which are constantly billed as the voice of the liberated
woman, telling it 'like it is', revealing all, are criticized by the authors of the
'Representation vs. Communication' extract for not being subversive enough.
Though large numbers of women read these books; though they feature on
women writers' courses and in women's study groups; though they present
their heroines 'for the first time as active, speaking subject'; nevertheless the
authors of this extract feel that the novels are in many ways closely tied to
conventional forms and aesthetic values. The use of a linear narrative, for
example, is common, charting the heroine's development from unhappy
conformity through adversity to autonomy; 'self-knowledge', 'experience',
'independence' emerge as keywords in the publishers' blurbs. Almost always
the heroine tells her own story, an autobiographical mode which can
encourage an identification between author, character, and reader that
belies the fictive nature of writing. Both the act of writing and the prevalent

theme of sexual fulfilment are offered as the problem of the individual woman trying to express her 'true self'. Furthermore, the authors propose that the interest in women's sexual pleasure in these novels functions not as a radical critique of a society that has no place for women's desire but, more often, as a confirmation of women's position as 'personal, ahistorical, sexual and non-political'.

Other critics have been less absolute about the individualism of the autobiographical voice. Rosalind Coward, for instance, suggests that it:

> often appeals to a collectivity. I am, but I am a representative of all women. The history of my oppression is the history of all women's oppression.[4]

A more general criticism of the extract is that the rather censorious tone of the writing leaves no space for women who do actually enjoy and value the novels. While teaching a women writer's class a few years ago I recall making some disparaging remarks about Marilyn French's *The Women's Room*. One of the students, a woman with a very conventional husband and several adult children, said that the book had been extremely important for her. As she struggled to find her feminism in an unsupportive environment, the novel had convinced her that the questions she was asking were legitimate and that she was not alone in asking them.

Romantic Fiction

A similar problem exists with popular romantic fiction. Until recently it would be difficult for a feminist to admit to an affection for this form of writing. The one-dimensional characters, the predictable plots, the purple prose ensured that all the books 'failed' on literary grounds. At the same time, the reactionary values — the double standard, passive heroines and masterful heroes, the triumph of heterosexual, marital bliss — made them politically unacceptable. A feminist might study them to expose their folly but never because she found them fun. Alison Light stresses that feminists should find a mode of criticism which can make the political points without dismissing the bulk of the readership as 'either masochistic or inherently stupid'. Over the last few years several developments in critical theory have allowed feminist readers of Mills and Boon to come out of the closet. Two factors are particularly important. Firstly, the emergence of a literary criticism that questions the division between 'Literature' and 'writing', 'high' and 'popular' culture, the 'classics' and the 'mass market', has permitted a less pejorative and patronizing reading of texts; it is no longer possible to say confidently that *Wuthering Heights* is suitable undergraduate material but Barbara Cartland is not. Secondly, the development of a feminist psychoanalytical theory which gives primacy of place to questions of female desire has encouraged a consideration of romantic writing and its compulsive and pleasurable qualities.

In the criticism of popular romantic fiction much interest has centred on the 'formula'. The characters, the relationships between them, the setting of the story, the narrative development, all fit into a standard pattern, closely

G. H. Lewes when surveying 'the lady novelists' in 1852. 'The domestic experiences which form the bulk of woman's knowledge finds an appropriate form in novels.'[82] With the connection between gender and genre posed in such condescending terms, spirited protests were called for, although few were as memorable as Olive Schreiner's mockery of the belief that 'there must be some inherent connection in the human brain between the ovarian sex function and the art of fiction'.[83]

NOTES

77   M—FLC, 'Women's writing', p. 31.
78   Blake, 'Pure Tess: Hardy on knowing a woman', *Studies in English literature*, 12 (1982), 700.
79   Buchan, *The ballad and the folk* (London, 1972), p. 64.
80   Eliot, 'Silly novels by lady novelists', p. 324.
81   Austen, *Northanger Abbey* (1818; Oxford, 1923), p. 38.
82   Lewes, 'The lady novelists [1852]', *Women's liberation and literature,* ed. Elaine Showalter (New York, 1971), p. 175.
83   Schreiner, *Woman and labour* (London, 1911), p. 158; Cynthia Ozick writes on 'the Ovarian Theory of Literature', in 'Women and creativity: the demise of the dancing dog [1969]', *Woman in sexist society*, ed. Gornick and Moran, pp. 309—10.

VIRGINIA WOOLF
A Room of One's Own

Here, then, one had reached the early nineteenth century. And here, for the first time, I found several shelves given up entirely to the works of women. But why, I could not help asking, as I ran my eyes over them, were they, with very few exceptions, all novels? The original impulse was to poetry. The 'supreme head of song' was a poetess. Both in France and in England the women poets precede the women novelists. Moreover, I thought, looking at the four famous names, what had George Eliot in common with Emily Brontë? Did not Charlotte Brontë fail entirely to understand Jane Austen? Save for the possibly relevant fact that not one of them had a child, four more incongruous characters could not have met together in a room — so much so that it is tempting to invent a meeting and a dialogue between them. Yet by some strange force they were all compelled, when they wrote, to write novels. Had it something to do with being born of the middle class, I asked; and with the fact, which Miss Emily Davies a little later was so strikingly to demonstrate, that the middle-class family in the early nineteenth century was possessed only of a single sitting-room between them? If a woman wrote, she would have to write in the common sitting-room. And, as Miss Nightingale was so vehemently to complain, — 'women never have an half hour . . . that they can call their own' — she was always interrupted. Still it would be easier to write prose and fiction there than to write poetry or a play. Less concentration is required. Jane Austen wrote like that to the end of her days. 'How she was able to effect all this,' her nephew writes in his Memoir, 'is surprising, for she had no separate study to repair to, and most of the work must have been done in the general sitting-room, subject to all kinds of casual interruptions. She was careful that her occupation should not be suspected by servants or visitors or any persons beyond her own family party.'[1] Jane Austen hid her manuscripts or covered them with a piece of blotting-paper. Then, again, all the literary training that a woman had in the early nineteenth century was training in the observation of character, in the analysis of emotion. Her sensibility had been educated for centuries by the influences of the common sitting-room. People's feelings were impressed on her; personal relations were always before her eyes. Therefore, when the middle-class woman took to writing, she naturally wrote novels, even though, as seems evident enough, two of the four famous women here named were not by nature novelists. Emily Brontë should have written poetic plays; the overflow of George Eliot's capacious mind should have spread itself when the creative impulse was spent upon history or biography. They wrote novels, however; one may even go further, I said, taking *Pride and Prejudice* from the shelf, and say that they wrote good novels. Without boasting or giving pain to the opposite sex, one may say that *Pride and Prejudice* is a good book. At any rate, one would not have been ashamed to have been caught in the act of writing *Pride and Prejudice.* Yet Jane Austen was glad that a hinge creaked, so that she might hide her manuscript before any one came in. To Jane Austen there was something discreditable in writing *Pride and Prejudice.* And, I wondered, would *Pride and Prejudice* have been a better novel if Jane Austen had not thought it necessary to hide her manuscript from visitors? I read a page or two to see; but I could not find any signs that her circumstances had harmed her work in the slightest. That, perhaps, was the chief miracle about it. Here was a woman about the year 1800 writing without hate, without bitterness, without fear, without protest, without preaching. That was how Shakespeare wrote, I thought, looking at *Antony and Cleopatra*; and when people compare Shakespeare and Jane Austen, they may mean that the minds of both had consumed all impediments; and for that reason we do not know Jane Austen and we do not know Shakespeare, and for that reason Jane Austen pervades every word that she wrote, and so does Shakespeare. If Jane Austen suffered in any way from her circumstances it was in the narrowness of life that was imposed upon her. It was impossible for a woman to go about alone. She never travelled; she never drove through London in an omnibus or had luncheon in a shop by herself. But perhaps it was the nature of Jane Austen not to want what she had not. Her gift and her circumstances matched each other completely. But I doubt whether that was true of Charlotte Brontë, I said, opening *Jane Eyre* and laying it beside *Pride and Prejudice.*

[. . .]

One could not but play for a moment with the thought of what might have

happened if Charlotte Brontë had possessed say three hundred a year — but
the foolish woman sold the copyright of her novels outright for fifteen
hundred pounds; had somehow possessed more knowledge of the busy
world, and towns and regions full of life; more practical experience, and
intercourse with her kind and acquaintance with a variety of character. In
those words she puts her finger exactly not only upon her own defects as a
novelist but upon those of her sex at that time. She knew, no one better, how
enormously her genius would have profited if it had not spent itself in
solitary visions over distant fields; if experience and intercourse and travel
had been granted her. But they were not granted; they were withheld; and
we must accept the fact that all those good novels, *Villette, Emma, Wuthering
Heights, Middlemarch*, were written by women without more experience of
life than could enter the house of a respectable clergyman; written too in the
common sitting-room of that respectable house and by women so poor that
they could not afford to buy more than a few quires of paper at a time upon
which to write *Wuthering Heights* or *Jane Eyre*.

NOTES

1   *Memoir of Jane Austen*, by her nephew, James Edward Austen-Leigh.

ELLEN MOERS
Literary Women

Fanny Burney, now Mme d'Arblay, became pregnant at forty-one and
ground out a novel — *Camilla* is her most lifeless production — to support
her family. For once in her life, she made the economics of publishing work
for her (they were just beginning to be organized to favor the independent
author) in the one way that mattered: the acquisition of enough money, all at
once, to pay for a house on a little piece of land in the country, which she
called Camilla Cottage.

The episode once again is instructive, and shows why novel-writing
became the profession of choice for literary women, and even for not
particularly literary women whose intelligence and talent might have led
them to different kinds of work. Only the novel offered the reward of capital
endowment, that lump of money without which middle-class women,
whatever their charms, would for long be virtually unmarriageable. Fanny
Burney's court post had paid her 200 pounds a year, a wretched sum as
Macaulay complained, but probably the highest salary a woman had ever
received for respectable work, or would receive for generations to come.
Camilla made her more than 2,000 pounds, or at least $50,000 in today's
money.

The career of journalism, while never so important to English literary
women as to French or American, began to open up to a few rare women in
England fairly early in the eighteenth century, perhaps because it was so ill

paid (almost as poorly paid as translating, which women of George Eliot's caliber would do for a pittance for generations to come). In the nineteenth century Harriet Martineau, for example, held an editorial post for which she received 15 pounds a year; but her first fiction, the *Political Economy* tales which took Martineau not much over two years to write, earned her more than 2,000 pounds.

Charlotte Brontë was dazzled by the first payment from her publishers for *Jane Eyre*: it was 100 pounds, the largest sum of money she had ever seen. There would be five such payments for the novel (probably an unfairly small slice of her publisher's profits) as opposed to the 20 pounds a year Brontë had been earning as a governess. ('My salary is not really more than £16 p.a.,' she wrote a friend in 1841, 'though it is nominally £20, but the expense of washing will be deducted therefrom.' Thus, to arrive at a sense of the real value of a governess' salary, we know that it was five times as much as the cost of laundering a governess' not very extensive wardrobe; we also know that it was about eleven times as much as the price of *Jane Eyre*. Governesses could not afford to buy three-volume novels, or almost anything else.)

The same 20 pounds, on the other hand, was the munificent sum Mrs. Gaskell was paid for a mere short story in 1850. 'I stared,' she wrote, 'and wondered if I was swindling them but I suppose I am not; and Wm has composedly buttoned it up in his pocket.' Through Mrs. Gaskell's letters can be traced the subtle and subtly changing attitudes of a successful literary woman to her husband's absolute control, in principle, over her earnings. Married life, however, as we all know, is a matter of practice as well as principle. By the late 1850s Mrs. Gaskell was paying for her own trips abroad out of the proceeds of her fiction, and in 1865 'I did a terribly grand thing! and a secret thing too!' she wrote Charles Eliot Norton. 'Only you are in America and can't tell. I bought a house . . . for Mr. Gaskell to retire and for a home for my unmarried daughters.' Including furnishings, the house would cost her 3,000 pounds or so, all to be paid for in the style of Camilla Cottage, by a literary woman's fiction.

The economic system that made novel-writing look particularly attractive to Fanny Burney was subscription publishing: that is, soliciting payment in advance of a guinea and a half direct from readers, whose names were printed at the head of the first edition. Among the three hundred subscribers to *Camilla* were some of the greatest names of the day. And there were three names on the list even better known to posterity than to Fanny Burney, for they were those of the leading women novelists, which is to say the leading novelists, of the next generation: Mrs. Radcliffe, Miss Edgeworth, and Miss Austen of Steventon.

Jane Austen was only twenty when she subscribed to *Camilla*, but then, she was also only twenty when she began 'First Impressions,' the first version of *Pride and Prejudice*, and she had already, in her teens, done a good deal of brilliant apprentice writing in imitation of or satirical reaction to the work of her female predecessors. When *Pride and Prejudice* finally appeared in 1813, women's literature came of age and with it the English novel, for in pure artistry no work in the form has ever surpassed it. It was a remarkable accomplishment of female professionalism, in the mere seventy years or so since *Pamela*, and the mere thirty years or so since *Evelina*.[1] Nor can the two phenomena be separated: the rise of the novel and the rise of women to professional literary status. And ever afterward the makeshift novel, last-born of literary genres, has dominated the literature of the world.

NOTE

1   Whose author was still alive, still writing fiction. Fanny Burney lived to almost ninety, and the posthumous publication of her diaries almost spanned the Victorian age; in the case of her longevity, her life was not characteristic of literary women after her. But her last exemplary act as a woman writer produced yet another manuscript treasure for the Berg Collection: a dozen densely written pages about the operation she underwent for breast cancer in 1811, before the invention of anesthetic.

IAN WATT
The Rise of the Novel

The distribution of leisure in the period supports and amplifies the picture already given of the composition of the reading public; and it also supplies the best evidence available to explain the increasing part in it played by women readers. For, while many of the nobility and gentry continued their cultural regress from the Elizabethan courtier to Arnold's 'Barbarians', there was a parallel tendency for literature to become a primarily feminine pursuit.

As so often, Addison is an early spokesman of a new trend. He wrote in the *Guardian* (1713): 'There are some reasons why learning is more adapted to the female world than to the male. As in the first place, because they have more spare time on their hands, and lead a more sedentary life . . . There is another reason why those especially who are women of quality, should apply themselves to letters, namely, because their husbands are generally strangers to them.'[1] For the most part quite unashamed strangers, if we can judge by Goldsmith's busy man of affairs, Mr Lofty, in *The Good Natur'd Man* (1768), who proclaims that 'poetry is a pretty thing enough for our wives and daughters; but not for us'.[2]

Women of the upper and middle classes could partake in few of the activities of their menfolk, whether of business or pleasure. It was not usual for them to engage in politics, business, or the administration of their estates, while the main masculine leisure pursuits such as hunting and drinking were also barred. Such women, therefore, had a great deal of leisure, and this leisure was often occupied by omnivorous reading.

Lady Mary Wortley Montagu, for example, was an avid novel reader, asking her daughter to send a list of novels copied down from newspaper advertisements, and adding: 'I doubt not that at least the greater part of these are trash, lumber, etc. However, they will serve to pass away the idle time . . .'[3] Later, and at a definitely lower social level, Mrs Thrale recounted that by her husband's orders she 'was not to *think of the kitchen*' and explained that it was as a result of this enforced leisure that she was 'driven . . . on literature as [her] sole resource'.[4]

Many of the less well-to-do women also had much more leisure than previously. B. L. de Muralt had already found in 1694 that 'even among the common people the husbands seldom make their wives work',[5] and another foreign visitor to England, César de Saussure, observed in 1727 that tradesmen's wives were 'rather lazy, and few do any needlework'.[6] These reports reflect the great increase in feminine leisure which had been made possible by an important economic change. The old household duties of spinning and weaving, making bread, beer, candles, and soap, and many others, were no longer necessary, since most necessities were now manufactured and could be bought at shops and markets. This connection between increased feminine leisure and the development of economic specialization was noted in 1748 by the Swedish traveller, Pehr Kalm, who was surprised to find that in England 'one hardly ever sees a woman here trouble herself in the least about outdoor duties'; even indoors, he discovered, 'weaving and spinning is also in most houses a rare thing, because their many manufacturers save them from the necessity of such'.[7]

Kalm probably conveys a somewhat exaggerated impression of the change, and he is in any case speaking only of the home counties. In rural areas further from London the economy changed much more slowly, and most women certainly continued to devote themselves almost entirely to the multifarious duties of a household that was still largely self-supporting. Nevertheless a great increase in feminine leisure certainly occurred in the early eighteenth century, although it was probably mainly restricted to London, its environs, and the larger provincial towns.

How much of this increased leisure was devoted to reading is difficult to determine. In the towns, and especially in London, innumerable competing entertainments offered themselves: during the season there were plays, operas, masquerades, ridottos, assemblies, drums, while the new watering-places and resort towns catered for the summer months of the idle fair. However, even the most ardent devotees of the pleasures of the town must have had some time left for reading; and the many women who did not wish to partake of them, or could not afford to, must have had much more. For those with puritan backgrounds, especially, reading would be a much more unobjectionable resource. Isaac Watts, a very influential early eighteenth-century Dissenter, dwelt luridly on 'all the painful and dismal consequences of lost and wasted time',[8] but he encouraged his charges, very largely feminine, to pass their leisure hours in reading and literary discussions.[9]

NOTE

1   No. 155.
2   Act II.
3   *Letters and Works*, ed. Thomas (London, 1861), I, p. 203; II, pp. 225 – 6, 305.
4   *A Sketch of Her Life . . .*, ed. Seeley (London, 1908), p. 22.

5 *Letters Describing the Character and Customs of the English and French Nations* (1726), p. 11.
6 *A Foreign View of England*, trans. Van Muyden (London, 1902), p. 206.
7 *Kalm's Account of His Visit to England . . .*, trans. Lucas (London, 1892), p. 326.
8 'The End of Time', *Life and Choice Works of Isaac Watts*, ed. Harsha (New York, 1857), p. 322.
9 *Improvement of the Mind* (New York, 1885), pp. 51, 82.

JULIET MITCHELL
'Femininity, Narrative and Psychoanalysis',
Women: The Longest Revolution

I want to look very briefly at one kind of history: that pre-eminent form of literary narrative, the novel. Roughly speaking, the novel starts with autobiographies written by women in the seventeenth century. There are several famous men novelists, but the vast majority of early novels were written by large numbers of women. These writers were trying to establish what critics today call the 'subject in process'. What they were trying to do was to create a history from a state of flux, a flux in which they were feeling themselves in the process of becoming women within a new bourgeois society. They wrote novels to describe that process — novels which said: 'Here we are: women. What are our lives to be about? Who are we? Domesticity, personal relations, personal intimacies, stories . . .' In the dominant social group, the bourgeoisie, that is essentially what a woman's life was to become under capitalism. The novel is that creation by the woman of the woman, or by the subject who is in the process of becoming woman, of woman under capitalism. Of course it's not a neat homogeneous construction: of course there are points of disruption within it; of course there are points of autocriticism within it. *Wuthering Heights*, for example, is a high point of autocriticism of the novel from within the novel. I shall discuss it soon in that light.

As any society changes its social structure, changes its economic base, artefacts are re-created within it. Literary forms arise as one of the ways in which changing subjects create themselves as subjects within a new social context. The novel is the prime example of the way women start to create themselves as social subjects under bourgeois capitalism — create themselves as a category: women. The novel remains a bourgeois form. Certainly there are also working-class novels, but the dominant form is that represented by the woman within the bourgeoisie. This means that when contemporary Anglo-Saxon feminist critics turn to women writers, resurrect the forgotten texts of these women novelists, they are, in one sense, being completely conformist to a bourgeois tradition. There is nothing wrong with that. It is an important and impressive tradition. We have to know where women are, why women have to write the novel, the story of their own domesticity, the story of their own seclusion within the home and the possibilities and impossibilities provided by that.

This tradition has been attacked by critics such as Julia Kristeva as 'the discourse of the hysteric'. I believe that it has to be the discourse of the hysteric. The woman novelist must be an hysteric. Hysteria is the woman's simultaneous acceptance and refusal of the organisation of sexuality under patriarchal capitalism. It is simultaneously what a woman can do both to be feminine and to refuse femininity, within patriarchal discourse. And I think that is exactly what the novel is; I do not believe there is such a thing as female writing, a 'woman's voice'. There is the hysteric's voice which is *the woman's masculine language* (one has to speak 'masculinely' in a phallocentric world) talking about feminine experience. It's both simultaneously the woman novelist's refusal of the woman's world — she is, after all, a novelist — and her construction from within a masculine world of that woman's world. It touches on both. It touches, therefore, on the importance of bisexuality.

I will say something very briefly about the psychoanalytical theories behind this position of the woman writer who must speak the discourse of the hysteric, who both refuses and is totally trapped within femininity. Then I'll lead on to some of the things that were said earlier about how to disrupt this.

There is much current interest in re-reading Freud in terms of the moment at which sexual division is produced within society: the moment of the castration complex, the moment when the heterogeneously sexual, poly-morphously perverse, carnivalesque child has imposed on it the divisions of 'the law'; the one law, the law of patriarchy, the mark of the phallus. At that moment two sexes are psychologically created as the masculine and the not-masculine. At the point in which the phallus is found to be missing in the mother, masculinity is set up as the norm, and femininity is set up as what masculinity is not. What is not there in the mother is what is relevant here; that is what provides the context for language. The expression which fills the gap is, perforce, phallocentric.

In Lacanian thinking this is called the moment of the symbolic. The symbolic is the point of organisation, the point where sexuality is constructed as meaning, where what was heterogeneous, what was not symbolised, becomes organised, becomes created round these two poles, masculine and not-masculine: feminine.

What has gone before can be called the pre-Oedipal, the semiotic, the carnivalesque, the disruptive. Now one can take two positions in relation to that. Either the pre-divided child, the heterogeneous child, the pre-Oedipal child, exists with its own organisation, an organisation of polyvalence, of polyphony. Or alternatively that very notion of heterogeneity, of bisexuality, of pre-Oedipality, of union in a dyadic possibility of child with mother, that image of oneness and heterogeneity as two sides of the same coin, is, in fact, provided by the law, by the symbolic law itself. The question to me has a political dimension to it. If you think that the heterogeneous pre-Oedipal polyvalent world is a separate structure in its own right, then the law is disruptable, the carnival can be held on the church steps. But if this is not the case, if the carnival and the church do not exist independently of each other, the pre-Oedipal and the Oedipal are not separate, discrete states — if, instead, the Oedipal with the castration complex is what defines the pre-Oedipal, then the only way you can challenge the church, challenge both the Oedipal and its pre-Oedipal, is from within an *alternative symbolic universe*. You cannot choose the imaginary, the semiotic, the carnival as an alternative to the symbolic, as an alternative to the law. It is set up by the law precisely as its own ludic space, its own area of imaginary alternative, but not as a symbolic alternative. So that politically speaking, it is only the symbolic, a new symbolism, a new law, that can challenge the dominant law.

Now this does have relevance for the two alternative types of feminist literary criticism which exist today. It was suggested in another paper at this conference that this area of the carnival can also be the area of the feminine. I don't think so. It is just what the patriarchal universe defines as the feminine, the intuitive, the religious, the mystical, the playful, all those things that have been assigned to women — the heterogeneous, the notion that women's sexuality is much more one of a whole body, not so genital, not so phallic. It is not that the carnival cannot be disruptive of the law; but it disrupts only within the terms of that law.

This suggests a criticism of the French school associated with Kristeva, and to me it explains why that school is essentially apolitical. One needs to ask why Kristeva and her colleagues, while producing very interesting ideas, choose exclusively masculine texts and quite often proto-fascist writings as well. Disruption itself can be radical from the right as easily as from the left. This type of disruption is contained within the patriarchal symbolic. To me this is the problem.

I shall just mention some things about *Wuthering Heights* here so that we can use it if we like as a text on which to hang some ideas. I do not want to offer a psychoanalytic reading of this novel; I want to use *Wuthering Heights* simply to illustrate some of the points that I have tried to make here.

Emily Brontë is not writing a carnivalesque query to the patriarchal order; she is clearly working within the terms of a language which has been defined as phallocentric. Yet she is, through a kind of irony, posing questions about patriarchal organisation, and I'll sketch in some of the questions that I think are asked by the novel. First, who tells the story? Emily Brontë's manuscript was stolen from her and presented to a publisher by her sister, Charlotte. It was eventually published under a male pseudonym: Ellis Bell. The author is a woman, writing a private novel; she is published as a man, and acquires some fame and notoriety. She uses two narrators — a man, Lockwood, and a woman, the nurse, Nelly Dean. The whole novel is structured through those two narrators. Lockwood is a parody of the romantic male lover. He is set up as a foppish gentleman from the town who thinks he loves all the things the romantic gentleman is supposed to love, such as solitude, or a heart of gold beneath a fierce exterior. These things are criticised from within the novel, particularly through the character of Isabella, who thinks that Heathcliff is a dark, romantic Gothic hero who will prove to be the true gentleman beneath all his cruelty.

The story of Catherine and Heathcliff is a story of bisexuality, the story of the hysteric. Catherine's father had promised he would bring her back a whip from his visit to Liverpool. Instead he picks up a gypsy child who is fatherless, who never has had and never will have a father's name, who is given just one name: Heathcliff, the name of a brother of Catherine's who had died in infancy. Catherine looks in her father's pocket, finds the whip broken; instead of this whip she gets a brother/lover: Heathcliff.

Heathcliff is what Cathy wants all the rest of her life. She, in fact, makes the conventional feminine choice and marries somebody with whom she cannot be fully united — Edgar Linton. Edgar provides only an illusion of complementarity. I do not mean that they do not have a sexual relation; they have a child whose birth in one sense — the most unimportant — causes Catherine's death. The person that Catherine wants to be 'one' with is Heathcliff. Breaking the incest taboo, she says, 'I *am* Heathcliff, he's more myself than I am.' And Heathcliff says the same of Catherine. Each is the bisexual possibility of the other one, evoking a notion of oneness which is the reverse side of the coin of diverse heterogeneity. This type of 'oneness' can only come with death. Catherine dies; she haunts Heathcliff for twenty years, which is the date when the novel opens: it opens with Lockwood, who is given Heathcliff's dream, thinking (because he is the parodic romantic figure) that he can also get oneness. Heathcliff himself waits the whole stretch of the novel to have his own dream, which is to get back to Catherine. He dies getting back to her. 'Oneness' is the symbolic notion of what happens before the symbolic; it is death and has to be death. The choices for the woman within the novel, within fiction, are either to survive by making the hysteric's ambiguous choice into a femininity which doesn't work (marrying Edgar) or to go for oneness and unity, by suffering death (walking the moors as a ghost with Heathcliff).

I want to end with my beginning, and with a question. I think the novel arose as the form in which women had to construct themselves as women within new social structures; the woman novelist is necessarily the hysteric wanting to repudiate the symbolic definition of sexual difference under patriarchal law, unable to do so because without madness we are all unable to do so. Writing from within that position can be conformist (Mills and Boon romantic novels) or it can be critical (*Wuthering Heights*). I think the novel starts at a point where society is in a state of flux, when the subject is in the process of becoming a woman (or man) as today we understand that identity. If we are today again talking about a type of literary criticism, about a type of text where the subject is not formed under a symbolic law, but within what is seen as a heterogeneous area of the subject-in-process, I would like to end with asking a question: *in the process of becoming what*? I do not think that we can live as human subjects without in some sense taking on a history; for us, it is mainly the history of being men or women under bourgeois capitalism. In deconstructing that history, we can only construct other histories. What are we in the process of becoming?

MICHELENE WANDOR
'The Impact of Feminism on the Theatre',
Feminist Review

New Women Playwrights and Problems of Patronage

In the British Alternative Theatre Directory[1] which lists anyone who sends
in information about themselves, only 15% of the playwrights are women.
However shocking this figure is — compared, for example, to the very large
number of women novelists — the situation in performance is even worse. A
recent survey shows that about 7% of all plays produced are by women, and
of these Agatha Christie accounts for nearly half.[2] Although there are all
kinds of constraints on women novelists, even the most misogynist of critics
at least acknowledges their importance in the development and achievement
of the novel. In theatre there are no female 'classics' to which to point, and
there is very little available in print which will testify to the fact that women
always have written plays.

There are a number of reasons for women's relative invisibility as
playwrights. The first is the perennial problem of publication. As a
production process, the core of theatre is its live performance. Commercial
success in performance is used as the yardstick by which to judge merit for
publication. Since relatively few plays achieve commercial success, relatively
few see the light of the printed page, and thus disappear from history.
Without a text, plays cannot continue to be produced; and the publication of
scripts by, for example Methuen, the largest drama publisher in this country,
depends largely on the approval of the theatres which have produced the
plays. Thus decisions about publication are essentially (if indirectly) made
by theatre directors. This militates against women playwrights' access to
print.

The second reason is ideologically more complex, though it is also to do
with the live nature of theatre performance, and is connected to the reason
why the anomaly of theatre censorship continued to exist for such a long
time. The public performance to a live audience is a collective act of
communication, akin to that of the public meeting. Theatrical performance
is indeed a powerful thing, but there are very few occasions when theatrical
performance has incited its audience to commit revolutionary acts en masse.
Nevertheless the sense of threat which hovers round the potential
subversiveness of theatre has remained with us. What is significant here is
the nature of the public and collective voice of theatre, and women have
rarely been seen overtly in charge of any kind of public voice. Of course, the
woman playwright does not personally stand up and make a speech in her
own voice, putting her own views and convictions, but she engages with
something which is unconsciously felt as a far greater threat: she provides a
text and meanings which others must follow. In her own voice, refracted
through the dialogue and structure of the play, she communicates to her

audience. She also controls the voices of others. She gives the performers the words which they must speak. Such control of a multiple set of voices, and the public control of an imaginative world (the action on a public stage) makes the woman playwright a far greater threat than the female novelist to the carefully maintained dominance of men as the custodians of public cultural creation. Women novelists still occupy that ambiguous area between private artistic acts (the individual writing in private, being read by another individual in private), and the public production and distribution of their work as commodities on the cultural market. Women playwrights may write in private, but both the collective rehearsal process and the street visibility of the playwright (on hoardings and in theatre advertisements) makes their presence more obvious. It is for this complex of reasons — as well as the male-gendered imaginative bias within plays themselves — that the theatre has been slower than the publishing industry to reflect the impact of feminism on writing.

From the slowly increasing number of women playwrights whose work is now being performed, it might appear that this is changing. Certainly as far as parity of employment goes, the more women playwrights there are, the better. Of course, not all women playwrights are necessarily feminists, and indeed some of the younger women playwrights think they are in a 'post-feminist' age, when all the essential struggles have been fought by their exhausted elder sisters. This is one of the hallmarks of bourgeois feminism.

There is a contradiction between the movement to achieve parity of employment, and the attitude towards the content of writing. Women playwrights who thus occupy a space within bourgeois feminism, or who are not feminists in their lives or work, are more easily taken up by the few liberal moves to increase the number of produced women playwrights. In the past couple of years the public face of women playwrights seems to be represented in two ways. Firstly, by the established, successful, older women playwrights — of whom really only Pam Gems and Caryl Churchill are at all widely known, and secondly, by what looks like a completely new generation (not always young) of women, many of whom are either undeveloped in the craft of writing, or simply throw off easy television-influenced sit-com type plays, or inadequately structured social realism.

In many ways the Royal Court theatre perfectly exemplifies this schizophrenia on the part of the theatre world towards writing by women. There is no problem about putting on plays by the already established; they do not need to be proven. It is easy to take a simple patronage attitude to the work of the new and untried, and by such patronage appear to be nobly encouraging the development of new writing (an absolutely essential thing) while at the same time implicitly suggesting that such 'primitive' work is part of allowing voices from a ghetto to speak to listeners from the same ghetto. Such patronage is only a problem because the Royal Court is one of the few theatres which has been consistent in encouraging work by women writers. But by veering between the established and the entirely new, they simply slide out of the responsibility of putting on plays by women who are in neither of these categories, but nevertheless are working playwrights.

When all theatres make sure that half the plays they put on are by women, the problem of patronage will be on its way out.

So the situation for women playwrights, while briefly improving, could be a matter of fashion. The playwrights currently being performed, if they are not part of a real effort to improve the position of women writers across the board, will merely be token presences of the moment, and perhaps disappear when the novelty of patronizing women's work has worn off. After all, there are already some historical precedents for this. It seems that women playwrights become prominent when there is some kind of fundamental social change which involves morality or sexual ideology: for example, during the Restoration;[3] at the turn of the century, coinciding with the movement for female suffrage;[4] and again in recent years, alongside the new feminism. As the political movements settle and lose their radical or revolutionary momentum, so women recede again from participation in the professional theatre as writers. There is a very real symbiotic relationship between the state of sexual mores, the presence of a feminist movement and the appearance of women playwrights; and the political struggle always comes first. Of course there are continuing flurries and resurgences of energy from women whose feminism or just sheer bloody mindedness makes them choose the theatre. Whether or not there continues to be a vigorous voice from women playwrights will depend to some degree on the state of feminism in a much broader sense. And after that question — of how theatre as an art form, a specific kind of cultural production, relates to politics — there are the vital questions of organization and power.

NOTES

1 Catherine Itzin, ed., *British Alternative Theatre Directory of Playwrights, Directors and Designers* (London, John Offord, 1983).
2 Conference of Women Theatre Directors and Administrators, *The Status of Women in the British Theatre 1982—1983* (London, WTDA, 1984).
3 Fidelis Morgan, ed., *The Female Wits* (London, Virago, 1981).
4 Jules Holledge, *Innocent Flowers: Women in Edwardian Theatre* (London, Virago, 1981).

SANDRA M. GILBERT and SUSAN GUBAR
Shakespeare's Sisters

Despite a proliferation of literary ancestresses, however, Elizabeth Barrett Browning commented mournfully in 1845 that 'England has had many learned women . . . and yet where are the poetesses? . . . I look everywhere for grandmothers, and see none.'[6] In 1862, moreover, Emily Dickinson, articulating in another way the same distinction between women's prose and women's verse, expressed similar bewilderment. Complaining that

> They shut me up in Prose —
> As when a little Girl
> They put me in the Closet —
> Because they liked me "still" — 7

she implied a recognition that poetry by women was in some sense inappropriate, unladylike, immodest. And in 1928, as if commenting on both Barrett Browning's comment and Dickinson's complaint, Woolf invented a tragic history for her 'Judith Shakespeare' because she so deeply believed that it is 'the poetry that is still denied outlet.'

Why did these three literary women consider poetry by women somehow forbidden or problematical? Woolf herself, after all, traced the careers of Anne Finch and Margaret Cavendish, admired the 'wild poetry' of the Brontës, noted that Barrett Browning's verse-novel *Aurora Leigh* had poetic virtues no prose work could rival, and spoke almost with awe of Christina Rossetti's 'complex song.'8 Why, then, did she feel that 'Judith Shakespeare' was 'caught and tangled,' 'denied,' suffocated, self-buried, or not yet born? We can begin to find answers to these questions by briefly reviewing some of the ways in which representative male readers and critics have reacted to poetry by representative women like Barrett Browning and Dickinson.

Introducing *The Selected Poems of Emily Dickinson* in 1959, James Reeves quoted 'a friend' as making a statement which expresses the predominant attitude of many male *literati* toward poetry by women even more succinctly than Woolf's story did: 'A friend who is also a literary critic has suggested, not perhaps quite seriously, that "woman poet" is a contradiction in terms.'9 In other words, from what Woolf would call the 'masculinist' point of view, the very nature of lyric poetry is inherently incompatible with the nature or essence of femaleness. Remarks by other 'masculinist' readers and critics elaborate on the point. In the midst of favorably reviewing the work of his friend Louise Bogan, for instance, Theodore Roethke detailed the various 'charges most frequently levelled against poetry by women.' Though his statement begins by pretending objectivity, it soon becomes clear that he himself is making such accusations.

> Two of the [most frequent] charges . . . are lack of range — in subject matter, in emotional tone — and lack of a sense of humor. And one could, in individual instances among writers of real talent, add other aesthetic and moral shortcomings: the spinning out; the embroidering of trivial themes; a concern with the mere surfaces of life — that special province of the feminine talent in prose — hiding from the real agonies of the spirit; refusing to face up to what existence is; lyric or religious posturing; running between the boudoir and the altar; stamping a tiny foot against God or lapsing into a sententiousness that implies the author has re-invented integrity; carrying on excessively about Fate, about time; lamenting the lot of the woman; caterwauling; writing the same poem about fifty times, and so on. . . .10

Even a cursory reading of this passage reveals its inconsistency: women are taxed for both triviality and sententiousness, for both silly superficiality and melodramatic 'carrying on' about profound subjects. More significant, however, is the fact that Roethke attacks female poets for doing just what male poets do — that is, for writing about God, fate, time, and integrity; for writing obsessively on the same themes or subjects, and so forth. But his language suggests that it is precisely the sex of these literary women that subverts their art. Shaking a Promethean male fist 'against God' is one perfectly reasonable aesthetic strategy, apparently, but stamping a 'tiny' feminine foot is quite another.

Along similar lines, John Crowe Ransom noted without disapproval in a 1956 essay about Emily Dickinson that 'it is common belief among readers (among men readers at least) that the woman poet as a type . . . makes flights into nature rather too easily and upon errands which do not have metaphysical importance enough to justify so radical a strategy.'[11] Elsewhere in the same essay, describing Dickinson as 'a little home-keeping person' he speculated that 'hardly . . . more' than 'one out of seventeen' of her 1,775 poems are destined to become 'public property,' and observed that her life 'was a humdrum affair of little distinction,' although 'in her Protestant community the gentle spinsters had their assured and useful place in the family circle, they had what was virtually a vocation.'[12] (But how, he seemed to wonder, could someone with so humdrum a social destiny have written great poetry?) Equally concerned with the problematical relationship between Dickinson's poetry and her femaleness — with, that is, what seemed to be an irreconcilable conflict between her 'gentle' spinsterhood and her fierce art — R. P. Blackmur decided in 1937 that 'she was neither a professional poet nor an amateur; she was a private poet who wrote indefatigably, as some women cook or knit. Her gift for words and the cultural predicament of her time drove her to poetry instead of antimacassars.'[13]

Even in 1971, male readers of Dickinson brooded upon this apparent dichotomy of poetry and femininity. John Cody's *After Great Pain* perceptively analyzes the suffering that many of Dickinson's critics and biographers have refused to acknowledge. But his conclusion emphasizes what he too sees as the incompatibility between womanly fulfillment and passionate art.

> Had Mrs. Dickinson been warm and affectionate, more intelligent, effective, and admirable, Emily Dickinson early in life would probably have identified with her, become domestic, and adopted the conventional woman's role. She would then have become a church member, been active in community affairs, married, and had children. The creative potentiality would of course still have been there, but would she have discovered it? What motivation to write could have replaced the incentive given by suffering and loneliness? If in spite of her wifely and motherly duties, she had still felt the need to express herself in verse, what would her subject matter have been? Would art have sprung from fulfillment, gratification, and completeness as abundantly as it did from longing, frustration, and deprivation?[14]

Interestingly, these questions restate an apparently very different position taken by Ransom fifteen years earlier: 'Most probably [Dickinson's] poems would not have amounted to much if the author had not finally had her own romance, enabling her to fulfill herself like any other woman.' Though Ransom speaks of the presence and 'fulfillment' of 'romance,' while Cody discusses its tormenting absence, neither imagines that poetry itself could possibly constitute a woman's fulfillment. On the contrary, both assume that the art of a woman poet must in some sense arise from 'romantic' feelings (in the popular, sentimental sense), arise either in response to a real romance or as compensation for a missing one.

In view of this critical obsession with womanly 'fulfillment' — clearly a nineteenth-century notion redefined by twentieth-century thinkers for their own purposes — it is not surprising to find out that when poetry by women *has* been praised it has usually been praised for being 'feminine,' just as it has been blamed for being deficient in 'femininity.' Elizabeth Barrett Browning, for instance, the most frequently analyzed, criticized, praised, and blamed woman poet of her day, was typically admired 'because of her understanding of the depth, tenderness, and humility of the love which is given by women,'[15] and because 'she was a poet in every fibre of her but adorably feminine. . . .'[16] As the 'Shakespeare of her sex,'[17] moreover, she was especially respected for being 'pure and lovely' in her 'private life,' since 'the lives of women of genius have been so frequently sullied by sin . . . that their intellectual gifts are [usually] a curse rather than a blessing.'[18] Significantly, however, when Barrett Browning attempted unromantic, 'unfeminine' political verse in *Poems Before Congress*, her collection of 1860, at least one critic decided that she had been 'seized with a . . . fit of insanity,' explaining that 'to bless and not to curse is a woman's function.. . .'[19]

As this capsule review of *ad feminam* criticism suggests, there is evidently something about lyric poetry by women that invites meditations on female fulfillment or, alternatively, on female insanity. In devising a story for 'Judith Shakespeare,' Woolf herself was after all driven to construct a violent plot that ends with her suicidal heroine's burial beneath a bus-stop near the Elephant and Castle. Symbolically speaking, Woolf suggests, modern London, with its technological fumes and its patriarchal roar, grows from the grim crossroads where this mythic woman poet lies dead. And as if to reinforce the morbid ferocity of such imagery, Woolf adds that whenever, reading history or listening to gossip, we hear of witches and magical wise women, 'I think we are on the track of . . . a suppressed poet . . . who dashed her brains out on the moor or mopped and mowed about the highways crazed with the torture that her gift had put her to.' For though 'the original [literary] impulse was to poetry,' and 'the "supreme head of song" was a poetess,' literary women in England and America have almost universally elected to write novels rather than poems for fear of precisely the madness Woolf attributes to Judith Shakespeare. 'Sure the poore woman is a little distracted,' she quotes a contemporary of Margaret Cavendish's as remarking: 'Shee could never be soe rediculous else as to venture at writeing books and in verse too, if I should not sleep this fortnight I should not come to that.'[20] In other words, while the woman novelist, safely shut in prose, may fantasize about freedom with a certain impunity (since she constructs purely fictional alternatives to the difficult reality she inhabits), it appears that the woman poet must in some sense become her own heroine, and that in enacting the diabolical role of witch or wise woman she literally or figuratively risks a melodramatic death at the crossroads of tradition and genre, society and art.

Without pretending to exhaust a profoundly controversial subject, we should note here that there are a number of generic differences between novel-writing and verse-writing which do support the kinds of distinctions Woolf's story implies. For one thing, as we noted earlier, novel-writing is a useful (because lucrative) occupation, while poetry, except perhaps for the narrative poetry of Byron and Scott, has traditionally had little monetary value. That novel-writing was and is conceivably an occupation to live by has always, however, caused it to seem less intellectually or spiritually valuable than verse-writing, of all possible literary occupations the one to which European culture has traditionally assigned the highest status. Certainly when Walter Pater in 1868 defined the disinterested ecstasy of art for his contemporaries by noting that 'art comes to you proposing frankly to give nothing but the highest quality to your moments as they pass, and simply for those moments' sake,' he was speaking of what he earlier called 'the poetic passion,' alluding to works like the Odes of Keats rather than the novels of Thackeray or George Eliot. Verse-writing — the product of mysterious 'inspiration,' divine afflatus, bardic ritual — has historically been a holy vocation.[21] Before the nineteenth century the poet had a nearly priestly role, and 'he' had a wholly priestly role after Romantic thinkers had appropriated the vocabulary of theology for the realm of aesthetics. But if in Western culture women cannot be priests, then how — since poets are priests — can they be poets? The question may sound sophistic, but there is a good deal of evidence that it was and has been consciously or unconsciously asked, by men and women alike, as often as women suffering from 'the poetic passion' have appeared in the antechambers of literature.

As Woolf shows, though, novel-writing is not just a 'lesser' and therefore more suitably female occupation because it is commercial rather than aesthetic, practical rather than priestly. Where novel-writing depends upon reportorial observation, verse-writing has traditionally required aristocratic education. 'Learn . . . for ancient rules a just esteem;/To copy Nature is to copy them,' Alexander Pope admonished aspiring critics and (by implication) poets in 1709, noting that 'Nature and Homer' are 'the same.'[22] As if dutifully acquiescing, even the fiery iconoclast Percy Bysshe Shelley assiduously translated Aeschylus and other Greek 'masters.' As Western society defines 'him,' the lyric poet must have aesthetic models, must in a sense speak the esoteric language of literary forms. She or he cannot simply record or describe the phenomena of nature and society, for literary theorists have long believed that, in poetry, nature must be mediated through tradition — that is, through an education in 'ancient rules.' But of course, as so many women writers learned with dismay, the traditional classics of Greek and Latin — meaning the distilled Platonic essence of Western literature, history, philosophy — constituted what George Eliot called 'spheres of masculine learning' inalterably closed to women except under the most extraordinary circumstances. Interestingly, only Barrett Browning, of all the major women poets, was enabled — by her invalid seclusion, her sacrifice of ordinary pleasures — seriously to study 'the ancients.' Like Shelley, she translated Aeschylus' *Prometheus Bound*, and she went even further, producing an unusually learned study of the little-known Greek Christian poets. What is most interesting about Barrett Browning's skill as a classicist, however, is the fact that it was barely noticed in her own day and has been almost completely forgotten in ours.

Suzanne Juhasz has recently and persuasively spoken of the 'double bind' of the woman poet,[23] but it seems almost as if there is a sort of triple bind here. On the one hand, the woman poet who learns a 'just esteem' for Homer is ignored or even mocked — as, say, the eighteenth-century 'Blue Stockings' were. On the other hand, the woman poet who does not (because she is not allowed to) study Homer is held in contempt. On the third hand, however, whatever alternative tradition the woman poet attempts to substitute for 'ancient rules' is subtly devalued. Ransom, for instance, asserts that Dickinson's meters, learned from 'her father's hymnbook,' are all based upon 'Folk Line, the popular form of verse and the oldest in our language,' adding that 'the great classics of this meter are the English ballads and Mother Goose.' Our instinctive sense that this is a backhanded compliment is confirmed when he remarks that 'Folk Line is disadvantageous . . . if it denies to the poet the use of English Pentameter,' which is 'the staple of what we may call the studied or "university" poetry, and . . . is capable of containing and formalizing many kinds of substantive content which would be too complex for Folk Line. Emily Dickinson appears never to have tried it.'[24] If we read 'pentameter' here as a substitute for 'ancient rules,' then we can see that once again 'woman' and 'poet' are being defined as contradictory terms.

Finally, and perhaps most crucially, where the novel allows — even encourages — just the self-effacing withdrawal society has traditionally fostered in women, the lyric poem is in some sense the utterance of a strong and assertive 'I.' Artists from Shakespeare to Dickinson, Yeats, and T. S. Eliot have of course qualified this 'I,' emphasizing, as Eliot does, the 'extinction of personality' involved in a poet's construction of an artful, masklike persona, or insisting, as Dickinson did, that the speaker of poems is a 'supposed person.'[25] But, nevertheless, the central self that speaks or sings a poem must be forcefully defined, whether 'she' 'he' is real or imaginary. If the novelist, therefore, inevitably sees herself from the *outside*, as an object, a character, a small figure in a large pattern, the lyric poet must be continually aware of herself from the *inside*, as a subject, a speaker: she must be, that is, assertive, authoritative, radiant with powerful feelings while at the same time absorbed in her own consciousness — and hence, by definition, profoundly 'unwomanly,' even freakish. For the woman poet, in other words, the contradictions between her vocation and her gender might well become insupportable, impelling her to deny one or the other, even (as in the case of 'Judith Shakespeare') driving her to suicide. For, as Woolf puts it, 'who shall measure the heat and violence of the poet's heart when caught and tangled in a woman's body?'

NOTES

6 *The Letters of Elizabeth Barrett Browning*, ed. Frederick G. Kenyon (2 vols. in 1, New York: Macmillan, 1899), I, 230—32. Compare Woolf's 'For we think back through our mothers if we are women. It is useless to go to the great men writers for help, however much one may go to them for pleasure' (*A Room*, p. 79).

7 Thomas Johnson, ed., *The Complete Poems of Emily Dickinson* (Boston: Little, Brown, 1960), #613.

8 See especially 'Aurora Leigh' and 'I am Christina Rossetti' in *The Second Common Reader* (New York: Harcourt Brace, 1932), pp. 182—92 and 214—21.

9 Reprinted in Richard B. Sewall, ed., *Emily Dickinson: A Collection of Critical Essays* (Englewood Cliffs, N.J.: Prentice-Hall, 1963), p. 120. In fairness to Reeves, we should note that he quotes this statement in order to dispute it.

10 Theodore Roethke, 'The Poetry of Louise Bogan,' *Selected Prose of Theodore Roethke*, ed. Ralph J. Mills, Jr. (Seattle: University of Washington Press, 1965), pp. 133—34.

11 'Emily Dickinson: A Poet Restored,' in Sewall, p. 92.

12 Ibid., p. 89.

13 Quoted in Reeves, p. 119.

14 John Cody, *After Great Pain: The Inner Life of Emily Dickinson* (Cambridge, Mass.: The Belknap Press of Harvard University Press, 1971), p. 495.

15 Gardner B. Taplin, *The Life of Elizabeth Barrett Browning* (New Haven: Yale University Press, 1957), p. 417.

16 *The Edinburgh Review*, vol. 189 (1899), 420—39.

17 Samuel B. Holcombe, 'Death of Mrs. Browning,' *The Southern Literary Messenger*, 33 (1861), 412—17.

18 *The Christian Examiner*, vol. 72 (1862), 65—88.

19 'Poetic Aberrations,' *Blackwood's*, vol. 87 (1860), 490—94.

20 *A Room*, p. 65.

21 See Pater, 'Conclusion' to *The Renaissance*, and, for a general discussion of the poet as priest, M. H. Abrams, *Natural Supernaturalism* (New York: Norton, 1971).

22 See Pope, 'An Essay on Criticism,' Part I, 11. 135—40.

23 Suzanne Juhasz, *Naked and Fiery Forms: Modern American Poetry by Women, A New Tradition* (New York: Harper & Row, 1976), 'The Double Bind of the Woman Poet,' pp. 1—6.

24 Ransom, ibid.; Sewall, pp. 99—100.

25 See T. S. Eliot, 'Tradition and the Individual Talent,' and Emily Dickinson, letter to T. W. Higginson, July 1892, in *The Letters of Emily Dickinson*, Thomas Johnson, ed. (Cambridge, Mass.: The Belknap Press of Harvard University Press, 1958), vol. II, p. 412.

CORA KAPLAN
Aurora Leigh and Other Poems

In the opening of Book V of *Aurora Leigh* there is a long discursive section on the poet's vocation where the author dismisses the lyric mode — ballad, pastoral and Barrett Browning's own favourite, the sonnet — as static forms: the poet 'can stand/Like Atlas in the sonnet and support/His own heavens pregnant with dynastic stars;/But then he must stand still, nor take a step.' The move into epic poetry chipped at her reputation in establishment circles, but enhanced her popularity. It was a venture into a male stronghold; epic and dramatic verse are associated with the Classicists and with Shakespeare, Milton, Shelley and Tennyson, and later, Browning. In 1893 the influential critic Edmund Gosse wrote that women have achieved nothing 'in the great solid branches of poetry in epic, in tragedy, in didactic and philosophical verse. . . . The reason is apparently that the artistic nature is not strongly developed in her.' This typical retrospective judgment may be a clue to *Aurora Leigh*'s modern oblivion, and one reason why such an important and diverse poet as Barrett Browning is now known almost exclusively as the author of *Sonnets from the Portuguese* (1850), her brilliant series of love lyrics to her husband. Twentieth-century male poet-critics echo Gosse's belief that women's voice in poetry, as in life, should be confined to the lyric. How can one account then for a sustained narrative poem that is both didactic and philosophical as well as passionate and female, an unmannerly intervention in the 'high' patriarchal discourse of bourgeois culture? *Aurora Leigh* makes few apologies for this rude eruption into the after-dinner subjects that go with the port and cigars. Barrett Browning knew less about 'this live throbbing age,/That brawls, cheats, maddens, calculates, aspires,' than Mrs Gaskell. But it is the latter, in *Mary Barton*, who intervenes with the authorial voice to offer a timid sop to male expertise: 'I am not sure if I can express myself in the technical terms of either masters or workmen. . . .'

The taboo, it is stronger than prejudice, against women's entry into public discourse as speakers or writers, was in grave danger of being definitively broken in the mid-nineteenth century as more and more educated, literate women entered the arena as imaginative writers, social critics and reformers. The oppression of women within the dominant class was in no way as materially brutal as the oppression of women of the working class, but it had its own rationale and articulation. The mid-century saw the development of a liberal 'separate but equal' argument which sometimes tangled with, sometimes included the definition of women's sphere and the development of the cult of true womanhood. The publicity given on the woman question hardly dented the continued elaboration of mores and manners which ensured that daughters were marriageable, i.e. virgins. Patriarchal dominance involved the suppression of women's speech outside the home and a rigorous censorship of what she could read or write. All the major women writers were both vulnerable to and sensitive about charges of 'coarseness'. The Brontë sisters, Sand and Barrett Browning were labelled coarse by their critics, and, occasionally, by other women. Sexual impurity, even in thought, was *the* unforgivable sin, the social lever through which Victorian culture controlled its females, and kept them from an alliance with their looser lived working-class sisters.

The debates on the woman question which took up so many pages of leading British periodicals between 1830 and 1860 should not be seen as marginal to a male-dominated ruling class, increasingly threatened from below by an organising proletariat. Caught between this and the need to accommodate a limited demand for equity from informed women of their own class, they were equally committed to the absolute necessity of maintaining social control over females, and its corollary, the sexual division of labour. To get a sense of the space and importance given to the issue, one only has to leaf through the major quarterlies for a given year. The winter 1857 issue of the *North British Review* had both a substantial review of *Aurora Leigh* and a long review article dealing with eight books, titled 'The Employment of Women', which ranges from an abrupt dismissal of Margaret Fuller's *Woman in the Nineteenth Century* for its romantic obscurity, to a serious discussion of Anna Jameson's *The Communion of Labour*, a work which argued that middle-class women should be 'employed' in ameliorating the condition of the female poor. In support of Mrs Jameson the article quotes both Tennyson's *The Princess* and *Aurora Leigh.*

The right to write was closely connected with every wider choice that women might wish to make. In an age characterised by the importance of the popular press as the place of ideological production and the spread of female literacy, it was of prime importance to warn women off questioning traditional sexual morality. Public writing and public speech, closely allied, were both real and symbolic acts of self-determination for women. Barrett Browning uses the phrase 'I write' four times in the first two stanzas of Book I, emphasising the connection between the first person narrative and the 'act' of women's speech; between the expression of woman's feelings and thoughts and the legitimate professional exercise of that expression. Barrett Browning makes the link between women's intervention into political debate and her role as imaginative writer quite clear in her defence of Harriet Beecher Stowe's *Uncle Tom's Cabin.* She rejoices in Stowe's success as 'a woman and a human being' and pushes the message home to her timid female correspondent:

> Oh, and is it possible that you think a woman has no business with questions like the question of slavery? Then she had better use a pen no more. She had better subside into slavery and concubinage herself I think as in the times of old, shut herself up with the Penelopes in the "women's apartment", and take no rank among thinkers and speakers.

Writing is a skilled task learnt at the expense of 'Long green days/Worn bare of grass and sunshine, — long calm nights/From which the silken sleeps were fretted out . . . with no amateur's/Irreverent haste and busy idleness/I set myself to art!' *Aurora Leigh* enters, however tentatively, into debates on *all* the forbidden subjects. In the first person epic voice of a major poet, it breaks a very specific silence, almost a gentlemen's agreement between women authors and the arbiters of high culture in Victorian England, that allowed women to write if only they would shut up about it.

ELLEN MOERS
Literary Women

Mary Shelley's *Frankenstein*, in 1818, made the Gothic novel over into what today we call science fiction. *Frankenstein* brought a new sophistication to literary terror, and it did so without a heroine, without even an important female victim. Paradoxically, however, no other Gothic work by a woman writer, perhaps no literary work of any kind by a woman, better repays examination in the light of the sex of its author. For *Frankenstein* is a birth myth, and one that was lodged in the novelist's imagination, I am convinced, by the fact that she was herself a mother.

Much in Mary Shelley's life was remarkable. She was the daughter of a brilliant mother (Mary Wollstonecraft) and father (William Godwin). She was the mistress and then wife of the poet Shelley. She read widely in five languages, including Latin and Greek. She had easy access to the writings and conversation of some of the most original minds of her age. But nothing so sets her apart from the generality of writers of her own time, and before, and for long afterward, than her early and chaotic experience, at the very time she became an author, with motherhood. Pregnant at sixteen, and almost constantly pregnant throughout the following five years; yet not a secure mother, for she lost most of her babies soon after they were born; and not a lawful mother, for she was not married — not at least when, at the age of eighteen, Mary Godwin began to write *Frankenstein*. So are monsters born.

[. . .]

Mary Shelley was a unique case, in literature as in life. She brought birth to fiction not as realism but as Gothic fantasy, and thus contributed to Romanticism a myth of geniune originality: the mad scientist who locks himself in his laboratory and secretly, guiltily works at creating human life, only to find that he has made a monster.

> It was on a dreary night of November, that I beheld the accomplishment of my toils. With an anxiety that almost amounted to agony, I collected the instruments of life around me, that I might infuse a spark of being into the lifeless thing that lay at my feet. . . . The rain pattered dismally against the panes, and my candle was nearly burnt out, when, by the glimmer of the half-extinguished light, I saw the dull yellow eye of the creature open; it breathed hard, and a convulsive motion agitated its limbs. . . . His yellow skin scarcely covered the work of muscles and arteries beneath; his hair was of a lustrous black, and flowing . . . but these luxuriances only formed a more horrid contrast with his watery eyes, that seemed almost of the same color as the dun white sockets in which they were set, his shrivelled complexion and straight black lips.

That is very good horror, but what follows is more horrid still: Frankenstein, the scientist, runs away and abandons the newborn monster, who is and remains nameless. Here, I think, is where Mary Shelley's book is most interesting, most powerful, and most feminine: in the motif of revulsion against newborn life, and the drama of guilt, dread, and flight surrounding birth and its consequences. Most of the novel, roughly two of its three volumes, can be said to deal with the retribution visited upon monster and creator for deficient infant care. *Frankenstein* seems to be distinctly a *woman's* mythmaking on the subject of birth precisely because its emphasis is not upon what precedes birth, not upon birth itself, but upon what follows birth: the trauma of the afterbirth.

[. . .]

Birth is a hideous thing in *Frankenstein*, even before there is a monster. For Frankenstein's procedure, once he has determined to create new life, is to frequent the vaults and charnel houses and study the human corpse in all its loathsome stages of decay and decomposition. 'To examine the causes of life,' he says, 'we must first have recourse to death.' His purpose is to 'bestow animation upon lifeless matter,' so that he might 'in the process of time renew life where death had apparently devoted the body to corruption.' Frankenstein collects bones and other human parts from the slaughterhouse and the dissecting room, and through long months of feverish and guilty activity sticks them together in a frame of gigantic size in what he calls 'my workshop of filthy creation.'

It is in her journal and her letters that Mary Shelley reveals the workshop of her own creation, where she pieced together the materials for a new species of romantic mythology. They record a horror story of maternity of the kind that literary biography does not provide again until Sylvia Plath.

As far as I can figure out, she was pregnant, barely pregnant but aware of the fact, when at the age of sixteen she ran off with Shelley in July 1814. Also pregnant at the same time was Shelley's legal wife Harriet, who gave birth in November 'to a son and possible heir,' as Mary noted in her journal. In February 1815 Mary gave birth to a daughter, illegitimate, premature, and sickly. There is nothing in the journal about domestic help or a nurse in attendance. Mary notes that she breast-fed the baby; that Fanny, her half sister, came to call; that Claire Clairmont, her stepsister, who had run off with Mary, kept Shelley amused. Bonaparte invaded France, the journal tells us, and Mary took up her incessant reading program: this time, Mme de Staël's *Corinne*. The baby died in March. 'Find my baby dead,' Mary wrote. 'A miserable day.'

In April 1815 she was pregnant again, about eight weeks after the birth of her first child. In January 1816 she gave birth to a son: more breastfeeding, more reading. In March, Claire Clairmont sought out Lord Byron and managed to get herself pregnant by him within a couple of weeks. This pregnancy would be a subject of embarrassment and strain to Mary and Shelley, and it immediately changed their lives, for Byron left England in April, and Claire, Shelley, Mary, and her infant pursued him to Switzerland in May. There is nothing yet in Mary's journal about a servant, but a good deal about mule travel in the mountains. In June they all settled near Byron on the shores of Lake Geneva.

In June 1816, also, Mary began *Frankenstein*. And during the year of its writing, the following events ran their swift and sinister course: in October Fanny Imlay, Mary's half sister, committed suicide after discovering that she was not Godwin's daughter but Mary Wollstonecraft's daughter by her American lover. (The suicide was not only a tragedy but an embarrassment to all. Godwin refused even to claim Fanny's body, which was thrown nameless into a pauper's grave.) In early December Mary was pregnant again, as she seems to have sensed almost the day it happened. (See her letter to Shelley of December 5, in which she also announced completion of Chapter 4 of her novel.) In mid-December Harriet Shelley drowned herself in the Serpentine; she was pregnant by someone other than Shelley. In late December Mary married Shelley. In January 1817 Mary wrote Byron that Claire had borne him a daughter. In May she finished *Frankenstein*, published the following year.

Death and birth were thus as hideously intermixed in the life of Mary Shelley as in Frankenstein's 'workshop of filthy creation.' Who can read without shuddering, and without remembering her myth of the birth of a nameless monster, Mary's journal entry of March 19, 1815, which records the trauma of her loss, when she was seventeen, of her first baby, the little girl who did not live long enough to be given a name. 'Dream that my little baby came to life again,' Mary wrote; 'that it had only been cold, and that we rubbed it before the fire, and it lived. Awake and find no baby. I think about the little thing all day. Not in good spirits.' ('*I thought, that if I could bestow animation upon lifeless matter, I might in process of time renew life where death had apparently devoted the body to corruption.*')

ROSEMARY JACKSON
Fantasy: The Literature of Subversion

Mary Shelley's other prolonged fantasy, *The Last Man*, is even more extreme as a text unable to imagine a resolution of social contradictions except through complete holocaust. Whereas *Frankenstein* depends upon *Political Justice, Caleb Williams*, various utopian fantasies, and Coleridge's *Ancient Mariner, The Last Man* depends upon a revolutionary political text, Volney's *Ruins of Empires*. This was an anti-despotic publication, brought over from France to be circulated amongst London's Jacobin circles during the 1790s. It celebrates the destruction of patriarchal empire through death's levelling, and many of its powerful, graphic images provide Mary Shelley with dramatic material: 'And now a mournful skeleton is all that subsists of this opulent city, and nothing remains of its powerful government but a vain and obscure remembrance.'[8]

From this revolutionary material, Mary Shelley constructs a remarkable fantasy of cultural annihilation. It is a long, slow-moving narrative, as it tells of a global plague which spreads gradually across the world. Its panorama of decay presents a complete erasure of the human species. Only Verney, the last man (like Frankenstein's creation of a parodic 'first' man, another inversion of Adam), remains to tell the tale of order lapsing into undifferentiation and decay: it is a vast fantasy of entropy. 'One by one we should dwindle into nothingness.' All civilized forms collapse with the plague's levelling: society becomes amorphous. 'I felt as if, from the order of the systematic world, I had plunged into chaos, obscure, contrary, unintelligible.' Through the plague, ordinary life is uncovered and metamorphosed into its opposite.[9]

Verney, as the last man, mourns for the death of culture, weeping over 'the ruins of the boundless continents of the east, and the desolation of the western world.' It is important to distinguish between his voice, as narrator, and Mary Shelley's position, as author. His human (male) lamentation is not hers. In 'dialogue' with his voice of distress is a huge silence: the plague itself, Mary Shelley's fantasy of annihilation of the human. Her writings open an alternative 'tradition', of 'female Gothic'.[10] They fantasize a violent attack upon the symbolic order and it is no accident that so many writers of a Gothic tradition are women: Charlotte and Emily Brontë, Elizabeth Gaskell, Christina Rossetti, Isak Dinesen, Carson McCullers, Sylvia Plath, Angela Carter, all of whom have all employed the fantastic to subvert *patriarchal* society — the symbolic order of modern culture.

A remarkable narrative feature of Mary Shelley's texts is their structural indeterminacy. *The Last Man* is a series of 'fragments', the end being left open. *Frankenstein* is similarly indefinite. Structured like a line of receding mirror images, it moves from the outer tale of Walton, to the inner tale of Frankenstein, to the tale-within-the-tale of the monster's confessions. The reader is progressively seduced from a straightforward epistolary 'realism' into the vortex at the centre where the monster is strangely present (i.e. absent), surrounded by the text's webs of language, 'embedded in the innermost circle . . . like the middle ring of a vast inferno'.[11] The three circles of narrative are not neatly re-situated within each other by the end, but collapse together, as Walton records the progressive vanishing of the monster, its end unknown. This open structure introduces a space within the initial 'closed' realistic form: through the monster, a 'place' has been given to non-human desires.

NOTES

8   Volney, *Ruins of Empires* (London, undated), p. 4.
9   This anticipates Artaud's metaphorical use of the plague in *The Theatre and its Double*: 'Society's barriers became fluid with the effects of the scourge. Order disappeared. He witnessed the subversion of all morality, the breakdown of all psychology.' (p. 7).
10 Ellen Moers, *Literary Women*, pp 90—110, identifies a tradition of 'female Gothic'. It is surely no coincidence that so many writers and theorists of fantasy as a countercultural form are women — Julia Kristeva, Irène Bessière, Hélène Cixous, Angela Carter. Non-realist narrative forms are increasingly important

in feminist writing: no breakthrough of cultural structure seems possible until linear narrative (realism, illusionism, transparent representation) is broken or dissolved.

11   M. A. Goldberg, 'Moral and Myth in Mrs Shelley's *Frankenstein*', *Keats-Shelley Journal*, 8 (1959), pp. 27–38.

MARY JACOBUS
'The Buried Letter: Feminism and Romanticism in Villette',
Women Writing and Writing About Women

Feminism and Romanticism: 'nothing but hunger, rebellion and rage . . . No fine writing can hide this thoroughly, and it will be fatal to her in the long run' — Arnold's prognosis was wrong (Charlotte Brontë died of pregnancy), but revealingly poses a split between rebellion and 'fine writing'. The divorce of the Romantic Imagination from its revolutionary impulse poses special problems for Victorian Romantics. Where vision had once meant a prophetic denunciation of the *status quo* and the imagining of radical alternatives, it comes to threaten madness or mob violence. Losing its socially transforming role, it can only turn inwards to self-destructive solipsism. Chalotte Brontë's own mistrust erupts in *Villette* with the fire that flames out during Vashti's performance or in the long-vacation nightmare which drives Lucy to the confessional; while the spectral nun (the Alastor of the Rue Fossette?) has to be laid in order to free Lucy from the burden of the autonomous imagination and allow her to become an economically independent headmistress. There are added complications for a woman writer. The drive to female emancipation, while fuelled by revolutionary energy, had an ultimately conservative aim — successful integration into existing social structures ('"I am a rising character: once an old lady's companion, then a nursery-governess, now a school-teacher"', Lucy tells Ginevra ironically (XXVII)). Moreover, while the novel's pervasive feminisation of the Romantic Imagination is a triumph, it runs the attendant risk of creating a female ghetto. The annexing of special powers of feeling and intuition to women and its consequences (their relegation to incompetent dependency) has an equally strong Romantic tradition; women, idiots and children, like the debased version of the Romantic poet, become at once privileged and (legally) irresponsible. The problem is illuminated by situating Charlotte Brontë's novels within a specifically feminist tradition. *Villette*'s crushing opposition between Reason and Imagination is also present in Mary Wollstonecraft's writing. *The Rights of Woman* (1791) — directed against the infantilising Rousseauist ideal of feminine 'sensibility' — not only advocates the advantages for women of a rational (rather than sentimental) education, but attempts to insert the author herself into the predominantly male discourse of Enlightenment Reason, or 'sense'. Yet, paradoxically, it is within this shaping Rousseauist sensibility that Mary Wollstonecraft operates as both woman and writer — creating in her two highly autobiographical novels, *Mary* (1788) and *The Wrongs of Woman* (1798), fictions which, even as they anatomise the constitution of femininity within the confines of 'sensibility', cannot escape its informing preoccupations and literary influence.[17] Though their concepts of Reason differ, the same split is felt by Charlotte Brontë. In *Villette*, Reason is the wicked and 'envenomed' step-mother as opposed to the succouring, nourishing, consoling 'daughter of heaven', Imagination (XXI). It is within this primal yet divisive relationship that the novelist herself is constituted as woman and writer — nurtured on Romanticism, fostered by uncongenial Reason. The duality haunts her novel, dividing it as Lucy is divided against herself.

NOTE

17   See Gary Kelly (ed.), *Mary, A Fiction and The Wrongs of Woman* (London, 1976), pp. vii—xxi, and Margaret Walters, 'The Rights and Wrongs of Women' in Juliet Mitchell and Ann Oakley (eds.), *The Rights and Wrongs of Women* (London, 1976), pp. 304—29.

CAROL FARLEY KESSLER
Daring to Dream

I   1836—1920

Of the 12 feminist Utopias published during this period but not included in this collection, two short stories — 'The Rappite's Economy'[1] and 'Transcendental Fruitlands'[2] — and one novel — *World War I Ourland*[3] — are satiric Utopias; a fourth — the African eutopia *Liberia*[4] — is the only work before 1900 to consider race. All of these reveal the hegemony of patriarchal ideology, particularly in the control of women's labor. Rebecca Harding Davis in 'The Harmonists' decries one man's power to maintain in a 'communist village' a 'utopia of prophets and poets,' who appear to a visitor as 'gross men' and 'poor withered women' with 'faded and tired' faces showing a 'curious vacancy'.[5] Louisa May Alcott in 'Transcendental Wild Oats' wryly describes 'the most ideal of all these castles in Spain,' where to the question posed by Mrs Lamb — 'are there any beasts of burden on the place?' — another — seeing how overworked she was — responded, 'Only one woman!' Fruitlands fails: 'The world was not ready for Utopia yet' and Mrs Lamb wonders to her disappointed husband, 'Don't you think Apple Slump would be a better name for it, dear?'[6] In each short story, women supply the labor to achieve a man's ideal and in both cases, the ideal fails to materialize as anticipated. (In two novels, Alcott shows women's co-operative ventures succeeding — four young women in *An Old-fashioned Girl* who share rooms, and the heterogeneous community of women concluding *Work*.)[7] Editor of *Godey's Lady's Book*, Sarah Josepha Hale in *Liberia; or Mr. Peyton's Experiments* provides yet another version of female labor in the service of male ideology. Black Keziah, indomitable manager of Mr Peyton's household, directs the labor of her husband Polydore in several of Mr Peyton's experiments to provide his 'servants' with an economic basis for living outside slavery. (Though racist by 1980s standards, for its time Hale's novel shows a measure of sympathy.) Hale, Davis, and Alcott all subscribe to the concept of women's moral guardianship of society. Gilman however, as noted above, saw women and men as both degenerate and remediable.

Several other works, while predominantly eutopian, use bad marriages to show how social regulation of woman's sexuality works to her disadvantage. First the marriage 'bargain' is shown corrupt: 'The man wants a housekeeper, the woman a home';[8] he married her to 'be stunning,' she him for money, called 'the god of civilization'.[9] Both exchange of services and exchange of objects — especially when one object is a person — do not work. Second, such corrupt marriages set eutopian sexual arrangements in relief: the freedom of exotic bronze-skinned women to select their sexual partners on a tropic island where mates 'strive to please each other' make a 'civilized' mate's demand to be pleased the more objectionable.[10] Third, the children resulting from such corrupt marriages receive inadequate financial support: a deserted mother of three small children tries taking in boarders as a livelihood, but crying infants drive boarders away. Then her husband abducts her son.[11]

To correct men's control of women's labour and sexuality, feminist eutopias of this period suggest several possibilities: paid work, education, suffrage, and co-operation. 'A New Society' envisioned by a Lowell 'mill girl' paid equal wages regardless of sex, limited the work day to eight hours, and required three hours daily of mental or manual labor, whichever was not a person's means of livelihood.[12] In general both women and men work with access to the full range of jobs.[13] A short story called 'Friend Island' boasts a sea-captain heroine: 'a true sea-woman of that elder time when woman's superiority to man had not been so long recognized'.[14] The story is her reminiscence of a sentient island, an early science-fiction tale that anticipates 1970s strategies for demonstrating interrelationships among human, animal, plant, and earth.

A second strategy for avoiding control is education — for daughters as well as sons,[15] especially to make 'an honorable living' instead of submitting to 'the best we can get' in a marriage.[16] And such self-sufficient women would of course keep their own names when they married.[17]

A third strategy, suffrage, is far more emphasized by subsequent histories of women than by Utopists: of the 59 Utopias appearing before 1920, only 14 or 24 per cent favor suffrage, though 10 more consider political issues, including general activity and office holding. Typical of a feminist viewpoint is a passage from Mary Theresa Shelhamer's *Life and Labor in the Spirit World* (1885):

> She should have a voice in the affairs of the country under whose laws she lives and educates her children. . . . Some people pretend to fear that when women vote they will have no time for domestic affairs, and the institution of

the home itself will be destroyed. . . . From the fuss made . . . one would think it took a week to put a small slip of paper into a medium-sized box. Why, we have known of men who could put in half a dozen in less than half that time, and no one suspects women to be less clever than men.[18]

The passage is interesting for its acknowledgment of popular fears that women would no longer perform traditional domestic roles once they were admitted to the political sphere reserved for men. Many accepted the view that women, family, and home were the calm center in a raging storm of social flux, that to permit change there would ensure complete social chaos. (One anti-feminist Utopia *Pantaletta* showed women's political control to be a comedy of error.[19] Shelhamer ridicules this popular fear at the same time that she assumes the sexes to be equally clever, such equality of intelligence more readily assumed however in Utopian fiction than by the public at large. Women Utopists ignore woman's traditional restriction to the home and thereby imply that integrating the public and private spheres for women will be no more disastrous than for men.[20]

More important than suffrage in feminist eutopias are co-operative or communitarian solutions to social control: some 54 per cent (32) for this period include such solutions. They take two forms — co-operative services or self-sufficient experimental communities. The earlier of two communitarian examples is *A New Aristocracy*, of 'brain and heart,' to be established in Idlewild, New York, upon a Parisian suburban model.[21] As in works by Howland and Graul (Selections 5 and 12), independent wealth makes possible the establishment of a factory, with workers' cottages and cultural buildings.[22] *Other Worlds* describes a society called 'The Colony,' to which members contribute an entry fee and work to support the Colony (compare Selection 8, Mason, 1889). Members own stock in their Colony, and enjoy its services. For example, a Nursery with a professionally trained staff cares for children, thus the single parent and a working couple are assured of responsible childrearing.[23] Such child care service is the major focus of *Reinstern* ('pure star'), 'a planet as yet undiscovered by your astronomers, who waste lifetimes searching with telescopes for what inner vision will readily disclose when you allow the real self to predominate'.[24] This eutopia presents an apprentice system to educate young adults for shared parenting, such training believed prerequisite to marriage.[25] Parents of each sex receive 'equal honors, salaries, and privileges,'[26] but biological parents are not solely responsible for children and systematically receive support appropriate to their children's ages. *Moving the Mountain*, another eutopia having co-operative services, also includes detailed nursery and child garden arrangements.[27] In addition by the 1940s apartment residences for self-supporting women had become common in the United States with facilities to provide food hygienically and knowledgeably! (Gilman was particularly outraged by 'the waste of private housekeeping' and devoted the novel *What Diantha Did* (1910) to demonstrating an alternative.)[28]

Two points emerging from this group of eutopias are especially salient for the concerns of Utopias during the 1970s. First, the observation that the 'nowhere' of Utopia can be the 'somewhere' of 'inner vision' marks the 1970s recognition of Utopia as a state of mind showing a spiritual or religious motive to underlie Utopia.[29] Some nineteenth-century Utopists called this visionary 'nowhere' by more theological names: 'heaven' (Selection 6, Phelps, 1883) or the 'spirit world'.[30] Several recent analysts of current Utopias by women consider these to be intrinsically spiritual.[31] In fact some would see women's liberation itself as a 'spiritual quest.'[32] Second, on a more mundane level, the domestic labor typically a concern of these communitarian eutopias before 1920 currently receives broadly based investigation in research, as well as visionary alternative solution in Utopia. Economists, historians, and anthropologists provide studies of women's triple labor loads: unpaid childcare and housekeeping work added to underpaid salaried work.[33] That 1970s eutopias completely restructure society to remove from women this triple burden should not surprise us. It is worth noting that the particular domestic solutions envisioned in Utopias before 1920 have not come to pass, but the domestic problems that we now seek to address were accurately forecast. Utopias, though not blueprints, can be harbingers.

NOTES

1   Rebecca Harding Davis, 'The Harmonists', *The Atlantic Monthly*, 17 (1866).
2   Louisa May Alcott, 'Transcendental Wild Oats: A Chapter from an Unwritten Romance', *The Independent*, 25 (1873).
3   Charlotte Perkins Gilman, 'With Her in Ourland', *The Forerunner*, 6 (1916).
4   Sarah Josepha Hale, *Liberia: or Mr Peyton's Experiments* (New York, Harpers and Brothers, 1853).
5   Davis, 'The Harmonists', pp. 531, 533, 535, 537.
6   Davis, 'The Harmonists', pp. 1570, 1571.
7   Louisa May Alcott, *An Old-Fashioned Girl* (Boston, Roberts, 1870), ch. 13: 'The Sunny Side'; *Work: A Story of Experience* (1873; rpt New York, Shocken, 1977), ch. 20.
8   Mary Theresa Shelhamer, *Life and Labor in the Spirit World. Being a Description of the Localities, Employments, Surroundings, and Conditions of the Spheres* (Boston: Colby & Rich, 1885), p. 12.
9   Mrs M. A. Weeks Pittock, *The God of Civilization: A Romance* (Chicago, Eureka, 1890), ch. 22.
10 Pittock, *The God of Civilization*, ch. 12, p. 60.
11 Lena Jane Fry, *Other Worlds: A Story Concerning the Wealth Earned by American Citizens and Showing How It Can Be Secured to Them Instead of to the Trusts* (Chicago: author, 1905), chs 12, 15.
12 Betsey Chamberlain (Tabitha pseud.), 'A New Society', *The Lowell Offering* I (1841).
13 Shelhamer, *Life and Labor*; Eloise O. Randall Richberg, *Reinstern* (Cincinnati, Editor Publishing, 1900); Fry, *Other Worlds*; Charlotte Perkins Gilman, *Moving the Mountain. The Forerunner*. 2, 1911; Charlotte Perkins Gilman, *Herland. The Forerunner*, 6 (1915).
14 Gertrude Barrows Bennett (Francis Stevens pseud.), 'Friend Island', *All-Story Weekly*, 7 September 1918, p. 126.
15 Chamberlain, 'A New Society'.
16 Shelhamer, *Life and Labor*.
17 Fry, *Other Worlds*, ch. 28; Gilman, *Herland*, pp. 118ff.

18 Shelhamer, *Life and Labor*, p. 13.
19 Mrs J. Wood, *Pantaletta: A Romance of Sheheland* (New York, American News Company, 1882).
20 For background, see Barbara Welter, 'Anti-Intellectualism and the American Woman, 1800—1860,' in *Dimity Convictions: The American Woman in the Nineteenth Century* (Athens, Ohio, Ohio University Press, 1976), pp. 71—82; Julia Ward Howe, ed., *Sex and Education* (1874; rpt New York, Arno, 1972), a collection of articles responding to Dr Edward H. Clarke, *Sex in Education* (1873).
21 Alice Elinor Bartlett (Arnold Birch pseud.), *A New Aristocracy* (New York, Bartlett, 1891).
22 Bartlett, *A New Aristocracy*, pp. 306—9.
23 Fry, *Other Worlds*.
24 Richberg, *Reinstern*, p. 10.
25 Richberg, *Reinstern*, pp. 19—20.
26 Richberg, *Reinstern*, pp. 23—4.
27 Gilman, *Moving The Mountain*, ch. 4.
28 Charlotte Perkins Gilman, 'The Waste of Private Housekeeping,' *Annals of the American Academy of Political and Social Science* (July 1913): 91—5; *What Diantha Did* (New York, Charlton, 1910).
29 Thea Alexander, *2150 AD* (Temple, Arizona, Macro Books, 1971); Dorothy Bryant, *The Comforter* (San Francisco, D. M. Bryant, 1971); Mary Staton, *From the Legend of Biel* (New York, Ace, 1975); Marge Piercy, *Woman on the Edge of Time* (New York, Knopf, 1976).
30 Shelhamer, *Life and Labor*.
31 See Lee Cullen Khanna, 'Women's Worlds: New Directions in Utopian Fiction,' *Alternative Futures*, 4 (2—3) 1981: 58—9; also Carol Pearson and Katherine Pope, *The Female Hero in American and British Literature* (New York: Bowker, 1981), pp. 260—5.
32 Carol P. Christ, *Diving Deep and Surfacing: Women Writers on Spiritual Quest* (Boston, Beacon Press, 1980), esp. pp. 1—12; Carol P. Christ and Judith Plaskow, eds, *Womanspirit Rising: A Feminist Reader in Religion* (San Francisco, Harper & Row, 1979), esp. pp. 1—17, 43—52, 217—19.
33 For examples, see John Kenneth Galbraith, 'The Economics of the American Housewife,' *Atlantic* 232 (August 1973): 78-83; Delores Hayden, *The Grand Domestic Revolution: A History of Feminist Designs for American Homes, Neighbourhoods and Cities* (Cambridge, Mass., MIT Press, 1981); Eleanor Leacock, 'History, Development, and the Division of Labor by Sex: Implications for Organization,' *Signs: Journal of Women in Culture and Society*, 7 (1981): 474—91; Bettina Berch, *The Endless Day: The Political Economy of Women and Work* (New York, Harcourt Brace Jovanovich, 1982); Susan Strasser, *Never Done: A History of American Housework* (New York: Pantheon, 1982).

CHRISTINE BERG and PHILIPPA BERRY

'"Spiritual Whoredom": An Essay on Female Prophets in the Seventeenth Century',

Literature and Power in the Seventeenth Century

The phenomenon of prophecy was of course not restricted to this historical time and place. Nor was prophesying during the revolutionary period the exclusive prerogative of women. Yet it is notable that prophecy in its most exaggerated form — that is, in the form in which it most clearly distinguishes itself from a rational discourse — has much in common with that phenomenon described by Luce Irigaray as 'the language of the feminine', and by Julia Kristeva as the semiotic; while its evident affinities with the discourse of hysteria have frequently been commented upon. We would stress that to confuse such a discourse with a female language, and to see it as articulated merely by women would be a mistake. Freud recognised early on in his career that the phenomenon of hysteria was not restricted exclusively to women. Likewise, a feminine language is one which both sexes may possess. But it does seem clear that the availability of this non-rationalist discursive mode made entry into the domain of politico-religious debate easier for a number of women, whether their contributions to public speech were made within the comparatively narrow confines of a single church or meeting house, or were available and proclaimed within a wider social spectrum. The prophetesses Eleanor Davies, Mary Cary and Anna Trapuel not only published or had their prophesies published by others, they also delivered oracular speeches in various places of public eminence like Parliament or Whitehall. The rough treatment received by many of the prophets of this period (both female and male) as the Revolution progressed — or sought to become more stable — is particularly striking. What emerges, in fact, is an enormous anxiety over the unique phenomenon of prophetic speech, and its refusal satisfactorily to be assimilated into a fixed symbolic order. Yet in what respect exactly did this kind of discourse constitute a threat? We believe that its threat lay precisely in its feminine character. By the sustaining of a multiplicity of various levels of speech and meaning, as well as by relinquishing the 'I' as the subjective centre of speech, the extremist forms of prophetic discourse constitute an extremely dangerous challenge to conventional modes of expression and control within seventeenth century patriarchal society.

[. . .]

Yet it seems clear that the female prophets of the period represented a threat that was in some respects more severe than that of any male prophetic figures of the day. This may in some respects be attributed to the more chaotic nature of many of their prophesyings; but we believe that the anxiety which these women promoted had rather deeper causes which related to the unique nature of the prophetic phenomenon, and to the scarcely admissible possibility that a woman could possess and transmit the word of God. The verbal transmission of the *logos* appears to have been threatening enough — the possibility of a physical *logos* being produced, in the shape of a new Messiah, induced even greater traumas. A number of women in this period proclaimed at different times that they were pregnant with the Christ, announcements which usually prompted rapid precautionary measures by the State. Probably the best known of these, a woman called Mary Adams, was immediately thrown into prison upon making the announcement. It was then proclaimed in a public statement (which suggests that popular interest in the matter had run high) that she had given birth to a monster and committed suicide. What really happened is anybody's guess, but the incident was certainly symptomatic of a deep anxiety about the possession of meaning.

The years between 1640 and 1660 might therefore be described as a period which opens with an excess of revolutionary activity on both the physical and verbal planes, a period characterised not only by Civil War but also by a fierce and bitter debate over the possession of meaning, of the logos. By 1660, however, the revolutionary struggle had failed on both these fronts. It is this tragic failure of course which constitutes the theme of Milton's *Paradise Lost.* In Milton's handling of the figures of Eve and Satan moreover, especially in the scene of temptation in the garden, the possibilities which the revolutionary period had opened up are quite explicitly surveyed. The enormous complexity of this scene seems symptomatic of Milton's own divided attitude to the revolution and its eventual failure. It has often been pointed out that Milton feels a great deal of sympathy for Satan as the failed revolutionary hero par excellence. We would argue that a fairly similar attitude can be traced in his treatment of the character of Eve, who is a figure of tremendous ambiguity within the poem.

Ultimately, however, Milton seems to have been unable to admit women to possession of the *logos*, and so to a specific relation with God. The Knowledge which the fruit of the tree offers Eve is the Knowledge of her body, of her own desire, but the speech which this produces is in the language of the court courtesan. The relationship of Adam and Eve at the end of the poem is hence fundamentally unchanged from that with which it began, as the female is returned to the control of her spouse:

'He for God only, she for God in him'.

What we have been trying to argue in relation to speech of the female prophets, therefore, is that these women and their prophetic activity represented a significant site of resistance in the revolutionary period — resistance against the acceptance of sexual difference and all that implied in the seventeenth century, this refusal of gender hinged upon the vital contemporary question of the possession of meaning or the *logos*. This challenge has of course been posed before, by various women writers and poets, but the threat which it represented became much more acute when the contest was over not only the actual word of God but over the public.

In these utterances, the assumption of gender and of sexual difference is implicitly refused, to be replaced by a peculiarly androgynous mode of speech which is tremendously threatening. When God delivers his word through or across the body of a woman, his masculine integrity and purity is evidently in danger of pollution. At best, the oracles of these women reinstate the feminine within these spheres of religious inspiration and political debate which had long since excluded it. At worst, their prophesying raises the awful, scarcely conceivable possibility that God might actually be a woman.

ELIZABETH COWIE et al.
'Representation vs. Communication', *No Turning Back*

The last decade has seen a revival of the women's novel as a first person realistic narrative, a form which is ideologically appropriate to feminism; authors see it as a way of telling women's story for the first time in an undisguised voice. The result has been an identification of author with protagonist, and of both with 'women', a result emphasised when commercial publishers use it as a marketing device, selling women's writing as subversive, sexual autobiography — the autobiography of a gender. The attempt has been to present women for the first time as active, speaking subject; the effect has been to obscure as well as mystify the activity of displacement present in all forms of imaginative writing, the distance between the author and his/her representation which can either be concealed or spoken by the literary text. Where it is spoken by women it always reveals how the meanings of the text are constructed (questions of ideology, realism etc) and also reveals the very specific problems of the history of woman as writers, or what it might mean for them to write at all.

Emotion and sexuality have traditionally dominated the content of women's poetry and fiction, more or less heavily censored (and self-censored) at different periods. A freely chosen sexuality as the symbol or apex of self-realisation is not a new radical demand but a demand as old as the novel (written by men *and* women), whose origin lay precisely in these questions of marriage and sexuality as free individual choice. What happens in this emphasis is that the rejection of woman as, simply, the object of desire in the text and her transformation into the subject of her sexuality, ignores the whole problem of her position as the subject of her own discourse; it assumes that the first resolves the second. The heroine gets what she thinks she wants, her man or her orgasm, and the author is assumed to have her unspoken demand for a voice fulfilled by writing about it. Furthermore, the celebration of a retrieved sexuality ironically confirms the assigning of women to a position as personal, ahistorical, sexual and non-political, therefore also concealing the question of her relationship to precise social and political demands.

Jong's *Fear of Flying* illustrates all that is worst in the 'new' literature, where the woman speaker, deliberately collapsed into the 'real' writer, is represented as an author with writer's block, seeking both sexual gratification and release into prose. A double triumph is equated with liberation. Neither writing nor sexual pleasure as valorised activities are queried in their relation to social and political meanings. Both are complacently offered as individual satisfactions, and silently substituted for a feminist politics.

JANICE A. RADWAY
'Women Read the Romance: The Interaction of
Text and Context', *Feminist Studies*

Dorothy Evans lives and works in the community of Smithton, as do most of
her regular customers. A city of about 112,000 inhabitants, Smithton is
located five miles due east of the state's second largest city, in a metropolitan
area with a total population of over 1 million. Dot was forty-eight years old
at the time of the survey, the wife of a journeyman plumber, and the mother
of three children in their twenties. She is extremely bright and articulate
and, while not a proclaimed feminist, holds some beliefs about women that
might be labeled as such. Although she did not work outside the home when
her children were young and does not now believe that a woman needs a
career to be fulfilled, she feels women should have the opportunity to work
and be paid equally with men. Dot also believes that women should have the
right to abortion, though she admits that her deep religious convictions
would prevent her from seeking one herself. She is not disturbed by the
Equal Rights Amendment and can and does converse eloquently about the
oppression women have endured for years at the hands of men. Despite her
opinions, however, she believes implicitly in the value of true romance and
thoroughly enjoys discovering again and again that women can find men
who will love them as they wish to be loved. Although most of her regular
customers are more conservative than Dot in the sense that they do not
advocate political measures to redress past grievances, they are quite aware
that men commonly think themselves superior to women and often mistreat
them as a result.

In general, Dot's customers are married, middle-class mothers with at
least a high school education.[11] More than 60 percent of the women were
between the ages of twenty-five and forty-four at the time of the study, a fact
that duplicates fairly closely Harlequin's finding that the majority of its
readers is between twenty-five and forty-nine.[12] Silhouette Books has also
recently reported that 65 percent of the romance market is below the age of
40.[13] Exactly 50 percent of the Smithton women have high school diplomas,
while 32 percent report completing at least some college work. Again, this
seems to suggest that the interview group is fairly representative, for
Silhouette also indicates that 45 percent of the romance market has attended
at least some college. The employment status and family income of Dot's
customers also seem to duplicate those of the audience mapped by the
publishing houses. Forty-two percent of the Smithton women, for instance,
work part-time outside the home. Harlequin claims that 49 percent of its
audience is similarly employed. The Smithton women report slightly higher

incomes than those of the average Harlequin reader (43 percent of the Smithton women have incomes of $15,000 to $24,999, 33 percent have incomes of $25,000 to $49,999 — the average income of the Harlequin reader is $15,000 to $20,000), but the difference is not enough to change the general sociological status of the group.

In one respect, however, Dot and her customers may be unusual, although it is difficult to say for sure because corroborative data from other sources are sadly lacking. Although almost 70 percent of the women claim to read books other than romances, 37 percent nonetheless report reading from five to nine romances each week. Even though more than one-half read less (from one to four romances a week), when the figures are converted to monthly totals they indicate that one-half the Smithton women read between four and sixteen romances a month, while 40 percent read more than twenty. This particular group is obviously obsessed with romantic fiction. The most recent comprehensive survey of American book readers and their habits has discovered that romance readers tend to read more books within their favorite category than do other category readers, but these readers apparently read substantially fewer than the Smithton group. Yankelovich, Skelly, and White found in their 1978 study that 21 percent of the total book reading public had read *at least* one gothic or romance in the last six months.[14] The average number of romantic novels read by this group in the last six months was only nine. Thus, while it is probably true that romance readers are repetitive consumers, most apparently do not read as consistently or as constantly as Dot and her customers. Romances undoubtedly play a more significant role, then, in the lives of the Smithton women than they do in those of occasional romance readers. Nevertheless, even this latter group appears to demonstrate a marked desire for, if not dependency upon, the fantasy they offer.

When asked why they read romances, the Smithton women overwhelmingly cite escape or relaxation as their goal. They use the word 'escape,' however, both literally and figuratively. On the one hand, they value their romances highly because the act of reading them literally draws the women away from their present surroundings. Because they must produce the meaning of the story by attending closely to the words on the page, they find that their attention is withdrawn from concerns that plague them in reality. One woman remarked with a note of triumph in her voice: 'My body may be in that room, but I'm not!' She and her sister readers see their romance reading as a legitimate way of denying a present reality that occasionally becomes too onerous to bear. This particular means of escape is better than television viewing for these women, because the cultural value attached to books permits them to overcome the guilt they feel about avoiding their responsibilities. They believe that reading of any kind is, by nature, educational.[15] They insist accordingly that they also read to learn.[16]

On the other hand, the Smithton readers are quite willing to acknowledge that the romances which so preoccupy them are little more than fantasies or fairy tales that always end happily. They readily admit in fact that the characters and events discovered in the pages of the typical romance do not resemble the people and occurrences they must deal with in their daily lives. On the basis of the following comments, made in response to a question about what romances 'do' better than other novels available today, one can conclude that it is precisely the unreal, fantastic shape of the story that makes their literal escape even more complete and gratifying. Although these are only a few of the remarks given in response to the undirected question, they are representative of the group's general sentiment.

> Romances hold my interest and do not leave me depressed or up in the air at the end like many modern day books tend to do. Romances also just make me feel good reading them as I identify with the heroines.

> The kind of books I mainly read are very different from everyday living. That's why I read them. Newspapers, etc., I find boring because all you read is sad news. I can get enough of that on TV news. I like stories that take your mind off everyday matters.

> Different than everyday life.

> Everyone is always under so much pressure. They like books that let them escape.

> Because it is an escape, and we can dream. And pretend that it is our life.

> I'm able to escape the harsh world a few hours a day.

> It is a way of escaping from everyday living.

> They always seem an escape and they usually turn out the way you wish life really was.

> I enjoy reading because it offers me a small vacation from everyday life and an interesting and amusing way to pass the time.

These few comments all hint at a certain sadness that many of the Smithton women seem to share because life has not given them all that it once promised. A deep-seated sense of betrayal also lurks behind their deceptively simple expressions of a need to believe in a fairy tale. Although they have not elaborated in these comments, many of the women explained in the interviews that despite their disappointments, they feel refreshed and strengthened by their vicarious participation in a fantasy relationship where the heroine is frequently treated as they themselves would most like to be loved.

[. . .]

In fact, the Smithton readers do not believe the books are identical, nor do they approve of all the romances they read. They have elaborated a complex distinction between 'good' and 'bad' romances and they have accordingly experimented with various techniques that they hoped would enable them to identify bad romances before they paid for a book that would only offend them. Some tried to decode titles and cover blurbs by looking for key words serving as clues to the book's tone; others refused to buy romances by authors they didn't recognize; still others read several pages *including the ending* before they bought the book. Now, however, most of the people in the Smithton group have been freed from the need to rely on these inexact predictions because Dot Evans shares their perceptions and evaluations of the category and can alert them to unusually successful romantic fantasies while steering them away from those they call 'disgusting perversions.'

When the Smithton readers' comments about good and bad romances are combined with the conclusions drawn from an analysis of twenty of their favorite books and an equal number of those they classify as particularly inadequate, an illuminating picture of the fantasy fueling the romance-reading experience develops.[21] To begin with, Dot and her readers will not tolerate any story in which the heroine is seriously abused by men. They find multiple rapes especially distressing and dislike books in which a woman is brutally hurt by a man only to fall desperately in love with him in the last four pages. The Smithton women are also offended by explicit sexual description and scrupulously avoid the work of authors like Rosemary Rogers and Judith Krantz who deal in what they call 'perversions' and 'promiscuity.' They also do not like romances that overtly perpetuate the double standard by excusing the hero's simultaneous involvement with several women. They insist, one reader commented, on 'one woman — one man.' They also seem to dislike any kind of detailed description of male genitalia, although the women enjoy suggestive descriptions of how the hero is emotionally aroused to an overpowering desire for the heroine. Their preferences seem to confirm Beatrice Faust's argument in *Women, Sex, and Pornography* that women are not interested in the visual display characteristic of male pornography, but prefer process-oriented materials detailing the development of deep emotional connection between two individuals.[22]

According to Dot and her customers, the quality of the *ideal* romantic fantasy is directly dependent on the character of the heroine and the manner in which the hero treats her. The plot, of course, must always focus on a series of obstacles to the final declaration of love between the two principals. However, a good romance involves an unusually bright and determined woman and a man who is spectacularly masculine, but at the same time capable of remarkable empathy and tenderness. Although they enjoy the usual chronicle of misunderstandings and mistakes which inevitably leads to the heroine's belief that the hero intends to harm her, the Smithton readers prefer stories that combine a much-understated version of this continuing antagonism with a picture of a gradually developing love. They most wish to participate in the slow process by which two people become acquainted, explore each other's foibles, wonder about the other's feelings, and eventually 'discover' that they are loved by the other.

11   Table 1.   Select Demographic Data: Customers of Dorothy Evans

Category	Responses	Number	%
Age	(42) Less than 25	2	5
	25 – 44	26	62
	45 – 54	12	28
	55 and older	2	5
Marital Status	(40) Single	3	8
	Married	33	82
	Widowed/separated	4	10
Parental Status	(40) Children	35	88
	No children	4	12
Age at Marriage	Mean – 19.9		
	Median – 19.2		
Educational Level	(40) High school diploma	21	53
	1 – 3 years of college	10	25
	College degree	8	20
Work Status	(40) Full or part time	18	45
	Child or home care	17	43
Family Income	(38) $14,999 or below	2	5
	15,000 – 24,999	18	47
	25,000 – 49,999	14	37
	50,000 +	4	11
Church Attendance	(40) Once or more a week	15	38
	1 – 3 times per month	8	20
	A few times per year	9	22
	Not in two (2) years	8	20

Note: (40) indicates the number of responses per questionnaire category. A total of 42 responses per category is the maximum possible. Percent calculations are all rounded to the nearest whole number.

12   Quoted by Barbara Brotman, 'Ah, Romance! Harlequin Has an Affair for Its Readers,' *Chicago Tribune*, 2 June 1980. All other details about the Harlequin audience have been taken from this article. Similar information was also given by Harlequin to Margaret Jensen, whose dissertation, 'Women and Romantic Fiction: A Case Study of Harlequin Enterprises, Romances, and Readers' (Ph.D. dissertation, McMaster University, Hamilton, Ontario, 1980), is the only other study I know of to attempt an investigation of romance readers. Because Jensen encountered the same problems in trying to assemble a representative sample, she relied on interviews with randomly selected readers at a used bookstore. However, the similarity of her findings to those in my study indicates that the lack of statistical representativeness in the case of real readers does not necessarily preclude applying those readers' attitudes and opinions more generally to a large portion of the audience for romantic fiction.

13   See Brotman. All other details about the Silhouette audience have been drawn from Brotman's article. The similarity of the Smithton readers to other segments of the romance audience is explored in greater depth in my book. However, the

only other available study of romance readers which includes some statistics, Peter H. Mann's *The Romantic Novel: A Survey of Reading Habits* (London: Mills & Boon, 1969), indicates that the British audience for such fiction has included in the past more older women as well as younger, unmarried readers than are represented in my sample. However, Mann's survey raises suspicions because it was sponsored by the company that markets the novels and because its findings are represented in such a polemical form. For an analysis of Mann's work, see Jensen, 389—92.

14   Yankelovich, Skelly and White, Inc., *The 1978 Consumer Research Study on Reading and Bookpurchasing*, prepared for the Book Industry Study Group, October 1978, 122. Unfortunately, it is impossible to determine from the Yankelovich study findings what proportion of the group of romance readers consumed a number similar to that read by the Smithton women. Also, because the interviewers distinguished between gothics and romances on the one hand and historicals on the other, the figures are probably not comparable. Indeed, the average of nine may be low since some of the regular 'historical' readers may actually be readers of romances.

15   The Smithton readers are not avid television watchers. Ten of the women, for instance, claimed to watch television less than three hours per week. Fourteen indicated that they watch four to seven hours a week, while eleven claimed eight to fourteen hours of weekly viewing. Only four said they watch an average of fifteen to twenty hours a week, while only one admitted viewing twenty-one or more hours a week. When asked how often they watch soap operas, twenty-four of the Smithton women checked 'never,' five selected 'rarely,' seven chose 'sometimes,' and four checked 'often.' Two refused to answer the question.

16   The Smithton readers' constant emphasis on the educational value of romances was one of the most interesting aspects of our conversations, and chapter 3 of *Reading the Romance* discusses it in depth. Although their citation of the instructional value of romances to a college professor interviewer may well be a form of self-justification, the women also provided ample evidence that they do in fact learn and remember facts about geography, historical customs, and dress from the books they read. Their emphasis on this aspect of their reading, I might add, seems to betoken a profound curiosity and longing to know more about the exciting world beyond their suburban homes.

[. . .]

21   Ten of the twenty books in the sample for the ideal romance were drawn from the Smithton group's answers to requests that they list their three favorite romances and authors. The following books received the highest number of individual citations: *The Flame and the Flower* (1972), *Shanna* (1977), *The Wolf and the Dove* (1974), and *Ashes in the Wind* (1979), all by Kathleen Woodiwiss; *The Proud Breed* (1978) by Celeste DeBlasis; *Moonstruck Madness* (1977) by Laurie McBain; *Visions of the Damned* (1979) by Jacqueline Marten; *Fires of Winter* (1980) by Joanna Lindsey; and *Ride the Thunder* (1980) by Janet Dailey. I also added *Summer of the Dragon* (1979) by Elizabeth Peters because she was heavily cited as a favorite author although none of her titles were specifically singled out. Three more titles were added because they were each voluntarily cited in the oral interviews more than five times. These included *The Black Lyon* (1980) by Jude Deveraux, *The Fulfillment* (1980) by LaVyrie Spencer, and *The Diplomatic Lover* (1971) by Elsie Lee. Because Dot gave very high ratings in her newsletter to the following, these last seven were

added: *Green Lady* (1981) by Leigh Ellis; *Dreamtide* (1981) by Katherine Kent; *Made For Each Other* (1981) by Parris Afton Bonds; *Miss Hungerford's Handsome Hero* (1981) by Noel Vreeland Carter; *The Sea Treasure* (1979) by Elisabeth Barr; *Moonlight Variations* (1981) by Florence Stevenson; and *Nightway* (1981) by Janet Dailey.

Because I did not include a formal query in the questionnaire about particularly bad romances, I drew the twenty titles from oral interviews and from Dot's newsletter reviews. All of the following were orally cited as 'terrible' books, labeled by Dot as part of 'the garbage dump,' or given less than her 'excellent' or 'better' ratings: *Alyx* (1977) by Lolah Burford; *Winter Dreams* by Brenda Trent; *A Second Chance at Love* (1981) by Margaret Ripy; *High Fashion* (1981) by Victoria Kelrich; *Captive Splendors* (1980) by Fern Michaels; *Bride of the Baja* (1980) by Jocelyn Wilde; *The Second Sunrise* (1981) by Francesca Greer; *Adora* (1980) by Bertrice Small; *Desire's Legacy* (1981) by Elizabeth Bright; *The Court of the Flowering Peach* (1981) by Janette Radcliffe; *Savannah* (1981) by Helen Jean Burn; *Passion's Blazing Triumph* (1980) by Melissa Hepburne; *Purity's Passion* (1977) by Janette Seymour; *The Wanton Fires* (1979) by Meriol Trevor; and *Bitter Eden* (1979) by Sharon Salvato. Four novels by Rosemary Rogers were included in the sample because her work was cited repeatedly by the Smithton women as the worst produced within the generic category. The titles were *Sweet Savage Love* (1974), *Dark Fires* (1975), *Wicked Loving Lies* (1976), and *The Insiders* (1979).

22   See Faust, passim.

ANN BARR SNITOW
'Mass Market Romance:
Pornography for Women is Different',
Radical History Review

III

Whar is the Harlequin romance formula? The novels have no plot in the usual sense. All tension and problems arise from the fact that the Harlequin world is inhabited by two species incapable of communicating with each other, male and female. In this sense these Pollyanna books have their own dream-like truth: our culture produces a pathological experience of sex difference. The sexes have different needs and interests, certainly different experiences. They find each other utterly mystifying.

Since all action in the novels is described from the female point of view, the reader identifies with the heroine's efforts to decode the erratic gesture of 'dark, tall and gravely handsome'[6] men, all mysterious strangers or powerful bosses. In a sense the usual relationship is reversed: woman is subject, man, object. There are more descriptions of his body than of hers ('Dark trousers fitted closely to lean hips and long muscular legs . . .') though her clothes are always minutely observed. He is the unknowable other, a sexual icon whose magic is maleness. The books are permeated by phallic worship. Male is good, male is exciting, without further points of reference. Cruelty, callousness, coldness, menace, are all equated with maleness and treated as a necessary part of the package: 'It was an arrogant remark, but Sara had long since admitted his arrogance as part of his attraction.'[7] She, on the other hand, is the subject, the one whose thoughts the reader knows, whose constant reevaluation of male moods and actions make up the story line.

The heroine is not involved in any overt adventure beyond trying to respond appropriately to male energy without losing her virginity. Virginity is a given here; sex means marriage and marriage, promised at the end, means, finally, there can be sex.

While the heroine waits for the hero's next move, her time is filled by tourism and by descriptions of consumer items: furniture, clothes, and gourmet foods. In *Writers Market* (1977) Harlequin Enterprises stipulates: 'Emphasis on travel.' (The exception is the occasional hospital novel. Like foreign places, hospitals offer removal from the household, heightened emotional states, and a supply of strangers.) Several of the books have passages that probably come straight out of guide books, but the *particular* setting is not the point, only that it is exotic, a place elsewhere.[8]

More space is filled by the question of what to wear. 'She rummaged in her cases, discarding item after item, and eventually brought out a pair of purple cotton jeans and a matching shift. They were not new. She had bought them a couple of years ago. But fortunately her figure had changed little, and apart from a slight shrinkage in the pants which made them rather tighter than she would have liked, they looked serviceable.'[9] Several things are going on here: the effort to find the right clothes for the occasion, the problem of staying thin, the problem of piecing together outfits from things that are not new. Finally, there is that shrinkage, a signal to the experienced Harlequin reader that the heroine, innocent as her intent may be in putting on jeans that are a little too tight, is wearing something revealing and will certainly be seen and noted by the hero in this vulnerable, passive act of self-exposure. (More about the pornographic aspects later. In any other titillating novel one would suspect a pun when tight pants are 'serviceable' but in the context of the absolutely flat Harlequin style one might well be wrong. More, too, about this style later on.)

Though clothes are the number one filler in Harlequins, food and furniture are also important and usually described in the language of women's magazines:[10] croissants are served hot and crispy and are 'crusty brown,'[11] while snapper is 'filleted, crumbed and fried in butter' and tomato soup is 'topped with grated cheese and parsley'[12] (this last a useful, practical suggestion anyone could try).

Harlequins revitalize daily routines by insisting that a woman combing her hair, a woman reaching up to put a plate on a high shelf (so that her knees show beneath the hem, if only there were a viewer), a woman doing what women do all day, is in a constant state of potential sexuality. You never can tell when you may be seen and being seen is a precious opportunity. Harlequin romances alternate between scenes of the hero and heroine together in which she does a lot of social lying to save face, pretending to be unaffected by the hero's presence while her body melts or shivers, and scenes in which the heroine is essentially alone, living in a cloud of absorption, preparing mentally and physically for the next contact.

The heroine is alone. Sometimes there is another woman, a competitor who is often more overtly aware of her sexuality than the heroine, but she is a shadow on the horizon. Sometimes there are potentially friendly females living in the next bungalow or working with the patient in the next bed, but they, too, are shadowy, not important to the real story, which consists entirely of an emotionally isolated woman trying to keep her virginity and her head when the only person she ever really talks to is the hero, whose motives and feelings are unclear: 'She saw his words as a warning and would have liked to know whether he meant [them] to be.'13

The heroine gets her man at the end, first, because she is an old-fashioned girl (this is a code for no premarital sex) and, second, because the hero gets ample opportunity to see her perform well in a number of female helping roles. In the course of a Harlequin romance, most heroines demonstrate passionate motherliness, good cooking, patience in adversity, efficient planning, and a good clothes sense, though these are skills and emotional capacities produced in emergencies, and are not, as in real life, a part of an invisible, glamorless work routine.

Though the heroines are pliable (they are rarely given particularized character traits; they are all Everywoman and can fit in comfortably with the life-style of the strong-willed heroes be they doctors, lawyers, or marine biologists doing experiments on tropical islands), it is still amazing that these novels end in marriage. After one hundred and fifty pages of mystification, unreadable looks, 'hints of cruelty'14 and wordless coldness, the thirty-page denouement is powerless to dispell the earlier impression of menace. Why should this heroine marry this man? And, one can ask with equal reason, why should this hero marry this woman? These endings do not ring true, but no doubt this is precisely their strength. A taste for psychological or social realism is unlikely to provide a Harlequin reader with a sustaining fantasy of rescue, of glamour, or of change. The Harlequin ending offers the impossible. It is pleasing to think that appearances are deceptive, that male coldness, absence, boredom, are not what they seem. The hero *seems* to be a horrible roué; he *seems* to be a hopeless, moody cripple; he *seems* to be cruel and unkind; or he *seems* to be indifferent to the heroine and interested only in his work; but always, at the end a rational explanation of all this appears. In spite of his coldness or preoccupation, the hero really loves the heroine and wants to marry her.

In fact, the Harlequin formula glorifies the distance between the sexes. Distance becomes titillating. The heroine's sexual inexperience adds to this excitement. What is this thing that awaits her on the other side of distance and mystery? Not knowing may be more sexy than finding out. Or perhaps the heroes are really fathers — obscure, forbidden objects of desire. Whatever they are, it is more exciting to wonder about them than to know them. In romanticized sexuality the pleasure lies in the distance itself. Waiting, anticipation, anxiety — these represent the high point of sexual experience.

Perhaps there is pleasure, too, in returning again and again to that breathless, ambivalent, nervous state *before* certainty or satiety. Insofar as women's great adventure, the one they are socially sanctioned to seek, is romance, adventurousness takes women always back to the first phase in love. Unlike work, which holds out the possible pleasures of development, of the exercise of faculties, sometimes even of advancement, the Harlequin form of romance depends on the heroine's being in a state of passivity, of not knowing. Once the heroine knows the hero loves her, the story is over. Nothing interesting remains. Harlequin statements in *Writers Market* stress 'upbeat ending essential here' (1977). Here at least is a reliable product that reproduces for women the most interesting phase in the love/marriage cycle and knows just when to stop.

IV

What is the world view implied by the Harlequin romance formula? What are its implicit values? The novels present no overt moral superstructure. Female virginity is certainly an ideal, but an ideal without a history, without parental figures to support it or religious convictions to give it a context. Nor can one say money is a value; rather it is a given, rarely mentioned. Travel and work, though glamorous, are not really goals for the heroine either. They are holding patterns while she awaits love.

Of course, the highest good is the couple. All outside events are subordinated to the psychodrama of its formation. But the heroine must struggle to form the couple without appearing to do so. Her most marketable virtue is her blandness. And she is always proud when she manages to keep a calm façade. She lies constantly to hide her desires, to protect her reputation. She tries to cover up all signs of sexual feeling, upset, any extreme of emotion. She values being an ordinary woman and acting like one. (Indeed, for women, being ordinary and being attractive are equated in these novels. Heroes are of course expected to have a little more dash and sometimes sport scars.) Finally, the heroine's value system includes the given that men are all right, that they will turn into husbands, despite appearances to the contrary.

The world of Harlequin novels has no past. (At most, occasionally the plot requires a flashback.) Old people hardly appear except as benevolent peripheral presences. Young women have no visible parents, no ties to a before. Everyone is young though the hero is always quite a bit older than the heroine. Is this why there are no parents, because the lover is really *in loco parentis*?

Harlequins make no reference to a specific ethnic group or religion. (In this they differ from a new popular mass form, the family saga, which is dense with ethnic detail, national identity, *roots*.) Harlequins are aggressively secular: Christmas is always the tinsel not the religious Christmas. One might expect to find romance linked, if only sentimentally, to nature, to universal categories, to first and last things. Harlequins assiduously avoid this particular shortcut to emotion (while of course exploiting others). They reduce awe of the unknown to a speculation on the intentions of the cold, mean stranger and generally strip romance of its spiritual, transcendent aspect.

At the other extreme from the transcendent, Harlequins also avoid all mention of local peculiarities beyond the merely scenic. They reduce the allure of difference, of travel, to a mere travelogue. The couple is alone. There is no society, no context, only surroundings. Is this what the nuclear family feels like to many women? Or is this, once again, a fantasy of safety and seclusion, while in actuality the family is being invaded continually and is under pressures it cannot control?

The denatured quality of Harlequins is convenient for building an audience: anyone can identify. Or, rather, anyone can identify with the fantasy that places all the characters in an upper-class, polite environment familiar not in experience but in the ladies' magazines and on television. The realities of class — workers in dull jobs, poverty, real productive relations, social divisions of labor — are all, of course, entirely foreign to the world of the Harlequin. There are servants in the novels lest the heroine, like the reader, be left to do all the housework, but they are always loyal and glad to help. Heroines have familiar service jobs — they are teachers, nurses, nursery-maids — but the formula finds a way around depicting the limitations of these jobs. The heroine can do the work ordinary women do while still seeming glamorous to the reader either because of *where* the heroine does her work or how she is rescued from doing it.

All fiction is a closed system in many respects, its language mainlining into areas of our conscious and subconscious selves by routes that by-pass many of the things we know or believe about the real world of our daily experience. This by-passing is a form of pleasure, one of art's pleasing tricks. As Fred Kerner, Harlequin's director of publishing, said when describing the formula to prospective authors in *The Writer*: 'The fantasy must have the same appeal that all of us discovered when we were first exposed to fairy tales as children.'[15] I do not wish to imply that I would like to remove a Harlequin romance from the hands of its readers to replace it with an improving novel that includes a realistically written catalogue of woman's griefs under capitalism and in the family. My purpose here is diagnostic. A description of the pared-down Harlequin formula raises the question: What is it about this *particular* formula that makes it so suggestive, so popular, with such a large female readership, all living under capitalism, most living — or yearning to live — in some form of the family?

Harlequins fill a vacuum created by social conditions. When women try to picture excitement, the society offers them one vision, romance. When women try to imagine companionship, the society offers them one vision, male, sexual companionship. When women try to fantasize about success, mastery, the society offers them one vision, the power to attract a man. When women try to fantasize about sex, the society offers them taboos on most of its imaginable expressions except those that deal directly with arousing and satisfying men. When women try to project a unique self, the society offers them very few attractive images. True completion for women is nearly always presented as social, domestic, sexual.

One of our culture's most intense myths, the ideal of an individual who is brave and complete in isolation, is for men only. Women are grounded, enmeshed in civilization, in social connection, in family and in love (a condition a feminist culture might well define as desirable) while all our culture's rich myths of individualism are essentially closed to them. Their one socially acceptable moment of transcendence is romance. This involves a constant return in imagination to those short moments in the female life cycle, courtship. With the exception of the occasional gourmet meal, which the heroine is often too nervous to eat, all other potential sources of pleasure are rigidly excluded from Harlequin romances. They reinforce the prevailing cultural code: pleasure for women is men. The ideal of romance presented in these books is a hungry monster that has gobbled up and digested all sorts of human pleasures.

There is another way in which Harlequin romances gloss over and obscure complex social relations: they are a static representation of a quickly changing situation — women's role in late capitalism. They offer a comfortably fixed image of the exchange between men and women at the very moment when the social actuality is confusing, shifting, frightening. The average American marriage now lasts about five years. A rape takes place every twelve minutes. While the social ferment of the sixties gave rise to the Gothic form in cheap fiction — family dramas that were claustrophic and anti-erotic compensations for an explosion of mobility and sexuality — in the seventies we have the blander Harlequins, novels that are picaresque and titillating, written for people who have so entirely suffered and absorbed the disappearance of the ideal of home that they don't want to hear about it any more. They want instead to read about premarital hopefulness.

Harlequin romances make bridges between contradictions; they soothe ambivalence. A brutal male sexuality is magically converted to romance; the war between men and women who cannot communicate ends in truce. Stereotyped female roles are charged with an unlikely glamour, and women's daily routines are revitalized by the pretense that they hide an ongoing sexual drama.

In a fine piece about modern Gothic romances, Joanna Russ points out that in these novels, '"Occupation: Housewife" is simultaneously avoided, glamorized, and vindicated.'[16] Female skills are exalted: it is good to nurture, good to observe every change in expression of the people around you, important to worry about how you look. As Russ says, the feminine mystique is defended and women are promised all sorts of psychological rewards for remaining loyal to it. Though in other respects, Gothics are very different from Harlequins, they are the same in this: both pretend that nothing has happened to unsettle the old, conventional bargain between the sexes. Small surface concessions are made to a new female independence (several researchers, misreading I believe, claim that the new heroines are brave and more interested in jobs than families[17]) but the novels mention the new female feistiness only to finally reassure readers that *plus ça change, plus c'est la même chose*. Independence is always presented as a mere counter in the sexual game, like a hairdo or any other flirtatious gesture;

sexual feeling utterly defeats its early stirrings.

In fact, in Harlequin romances, sexual feeling is probably the main point. Like sex itself, the novels are set in an eternal present in which the actual present, a time of disturbing disruptions between the sexes, is dissolved and only a comfortable timeless, universal battle remains. The hero wants sex; the heroine wants it, too, but can only enjoy it after the love promise has finally been made and the ring is on her finger.

NOTES

6   Rachel Lindsay, *Prescription for Love* (Toronto: Harlequin Books, 1977), p. 10.
7   Rebecca Stratton, *The Sign of the Ram* (Toronto: Harlequin Books, 1977), pp. 56, 147.
8   Here is an example of this sort of travelogue prose: 'There was something to appeal to all age groups in the thousand-acre park in the heart of the city — golf for the energetic, lawn bowling for the more sedate, a zoo for the children's pleasure, and even secluded walks through giant cedars for lovers — but Cori thought of none of these things as Greg drove to a parking place bordering the Inlet.' Graham, *Mason's Ridge*, p. 25.
9   Anne Mather, *Born Out of Love* (Toronto: Harlequin Books, 1977), p. 42.
10   See Joanna Russ, 'Somebody's Trying to Kill Me and I Think It's My Husband: The Modern Gothic,' *Journal of Popular Culture* 6, no. 4 (Spring 1973) 1:666—91.
11   Mather, *Born Out of Love*, p. 42.
12   Daphne Clair, *A Streak of Gold* (Toronto: Harlequin Books, 1978), p. 118.
13   Lindsay, *Prescription for Love*, p. 13.
14   Stratton, *The Sign of the Ram*, p. 66. The adjectives 'cruel' and 'satanic' are commonly used for heroes.
15   May 1977, p. 18.
16   Russ, 'Somebody's Trying to Kill Me,' p. 675.
17   See for example, Josephine A. Ruggiero and Louise C. Weston, 'Sex Role Characterizations of Women in Modern Gothic Novels,' *Pacific Sociological Review* 20, no. 2 (April 1977): 279—300.

ALISON LIGHT
'"Returning to Manderley" — Romance Fiction, Female Sexuality and Class', *Feminist Review*

In the aftermath of Charles and Di, a lot of critical attention has been turned toward romance and its fictions, from Mills and Boon to 'bodice rippers' and the latest high-gloss consumerist fantasies.[1] At the centre of the discussion has been the question of the possible political effects of reading romances — what, in other words, do they do to you? Romances have on the whole, been condemned by the critics on the Left (although Janet Batsleer's piece is a notable exception). They are seen as coercive and stereotyping narratives which invite the reader to identify with a passive heroine who only finds true happiness in submitting to a masterful male. What happens to women readers is then compared to certain Marxist descriptions of the positioning of all human subjects under capitalism.[2] Romance thus emerges as a form of oppressive ideology, which works to keep women in their socially and sexually subordinate place.

I want to begin by registering the political dangers of this approach to romance fiction and then to suggest that we should come at the question of its effects rather differently. David Margolies, for example, talks in highly dubious ways when he refers to women readers being 'encouraged to sink into feeling' and 'to feel without regard for the structure of the situation'.[3] 'Romance', he continues, 'is an opportunity for exercising frustrated sensitivity . . . inward-looking and intensely subjective', it is 'retrogressive' as a form of 'habitual reading for entertainment'. Such an analysis slides into a puritanical Left-wing moralism which denigrates readers. It also treats women yet again as the victims of, and irrational slaves to, their sensibilities. Feminists must baulk at any such conclusion which implies that the vast audience of romance readers (with the exception of a few up-front intellectuals) are either masochistic or inherently stupid. Both text and reader are more complicated than that. It is conceivable, say, that reading Barbara Cartland could turn you into a feminist. Reading is never simply a linear con-job but a process of interaction, and not just between text and reader, but between reader and reader, text and text. It is a process which helps to query as well as endorse social meanings and one which therefore remains dynamic and open to change.[4]

In other words, I think we need critical discussions that are not afraid of the fact that literature is a source of pleasure, passion *and* entertainment. This is not because pleasure can then explain away politics, as if it were a panacea existing outside of social and historical constraints. Rather it is precisely because pleasure is experienced by women and men within and despite those constraints. We need to balance an understanding of fictions as restatements (however mediated) of a social reality, with a closer examination of how literary texts might function in our lives as imaginative constructions and interpretations. It is this meshing of the questions of pleasure, fantasy and language which literary culture takes up so profoundly and which makes it so uniquely important to women. Subjectivity — the ways in which we come to express and define our concepts of our selves — then seems crucial to any analysis of the activity of reading. Far from being 'inward-looking' in the dismissive sense of being somehow separate from the realities of the state or the marketplace, subjectivity can be recognized as the place where the operations of power and the possibilities of resistance are also played out.

A re-emphasis on the imaginative dimensions of literary discourse may then suggest ways in which romance, as much because of its contradictory effects as despite them, has something positive to offer its audience, as readers and as *women* readers. It must at the very least prevent our 'cultural politics' becoming a book-burning legislature, a politics which is doomed to fail since it refuses ultimately to see women of all classes as capable of determining or transforming their own lives.

Romance fiction deals above all with the doubts and delights of heterosexuality, an institution which feminism has seen as problematic from the start. In thinking about this 'problem' I myself have found the psychoanalytic framework most useful since it suggests that the acquisition of gendered subjectivity is a process, a movement towards a social 'self', fraught with conflicts and never fully achieved. Moreover, psychoanalysis takes the question of pleasure seriously, both in its relation to gender and in its understanding of fictions as fantasies, as the explorations and productions of desires which may be in excess of the socially possible or acceptable. It gives us ways into the discussion of popular culture which can avoid the traps of moralism or dictatorship.

[. . .]

How then does *Rebecca* say anything at all about the formulaic fiction in which frail flower meets bronzed god? I would like to see *Rebecca* as the absent subtext of much romantic fiction, the crime behind the scenes of Mills and Boon. For it seems to me that perhaps what romance tries to offer us is a 'triumph' over the unconscious, over the 'resistance to identity which lies at the very heart of psychic life'.[5] *Rebecca* acts out the process of repression which these other texts avoid by assuming a fully-achievable, uncomplicated gendered subject whose sexual desire is not in question, not produced in struggle, but given. Above all, romantic fiction makes heterosexuality easy, by suspending history in its formulae (whether costume, hospital or Caribbean drama) and by offering women readers a resolution in which submission and repression are not just managed without pain or humiliation but managed at all.

Thus although women are undoubtedly represented as sexual objects, there might be a sense in which women are also offered unique opportunities for reader-power, for an imaginary control of the uncontrollable in the fiction of romance. Within that scenario of extreme heterosexism can be derived the pleasure of reconstructing any heterosexuality which is not 'difficult'. Romance offers us relations impossibly harmonized; it uses unequal heterosexuality as a dream of equality and gives women uncomplicated access to a subjectivity which is unified and coherent *and* still operating within the field of pleasure.

Perhaps then the enormous readership of romance fiction, the fact that so many women find it deeply pleasurable, can be registered in terms other than those of moralizing shock. Romance is read by over fifty per cent of all women, but it is no coincidence that the two largest audiences are those of young women in their teens and 'middle-aged housewives'.[6] I would suggest that these are both moments when the *impossibility* of being successfully feminine is felt, whether as a 'failure' ever to be feminine enough — like the girl's in *Rebecca* — or whether in terms of the gap between fulfilling social expectations (as wife and mother) and what those roles mean in reality. That women read romance fiction is, I think, as much a measure of their deep dissatisfaction with heterosexual options as of any desire to be fully identified with the submissive versions of femininity the texts endorse. Romance imagines peace, security and ease precisely because there is dissension, insecurity and difficulty. In the context of women's lives, romance reading might appear less a reactionary reflex or an indication of their victimization by the capitalist market, and more a sign of discontent and a technique for survival. All the more so because inside a boring or alienating marriage, or at the age of fifteen, romance may be the only popular discourse which speaks to the question of women's sexual pleasure. Women's magazines, for example, do at least prioritize women and their lives in a culture where they are usually absent or given second place.

Patterns of romance reading are also revealing. Readers often collect hundreds, which are shared and recycled amongst friends. Reading romance fiction means participating in a kind of subculture, one which underlines a collective identity as women around the issue of women's pleasure and which can be found outside a political movement. As Janet Batsleer has pointed out, romances are not valued because like 'Great Art' they purport to be unrepeatable stories of unique characters, they are valued precisely as ritual and as repetition. It is difficult then to assume that these narratives are read in terms of a linear identification — it is not real and rounded individuals who are being presented and the endings are known by *readers* to be a foregone conclusion. Romance offers instead of closure a postponement of fulfillment. They are addictive because the control they gesture toward is always illusory, always modified and contained by the heterosexuality which they seek to harmonize. In a sense the activity of reading repeats the compulsion of desire and testifies to the limiting regulation of female sexuality. Romances may pretend that the path to marriage is effortless (obstacles are there to be removed) but they have to cry off when the action really starts — after marriage. The reader is left in a permanent state of foreplay, but I would guess that for many women this is the best heterosexual sex they ever get.

I want to suggest then that we develop ways of analysing romances and their reception as 'symptomatic' rather than simply reflective. Romance reading then becomes less a political sin or moral betrayal than a kind of 'literary anorexia' which functions as a protest against, as well as a restatement of, oppression. Their compulsive reading makes visible an insistent search on the part of readers for more than what is on offer. This is not, of course, any kind of argument for romance fictions being somehow progressive. Within the realities of women's lives, however, they may well be *trans*gressive. Consumerist, yes; a hopeless rebellion, yes; but still, in our society, a forbidden pleasure — like cream cakes. Romance does write heterosexuality in capital letters but in so doing it is an embarrassment to the literary establishment since its writers are always asking to be taken seriously. Their activity highlights of course the heterosexism of much orthodox and important Literature. For, leaving aside the representation of femininity, what other models are available *anywhere* for alternative constructs of masculinity? Romance is not being wilfully different in its descriptions of virility as constituted around positions of authority, hierarchy and aggression. Male, left-wing critics might do well to address themselves to projects which set out to deconstruct 'normal' male heterosexuality — a phenomenon which does after all exist outside war-stories and cowboy books.

To say, as I have, that subjectivity is at stake in the practices of reading and writing is not to retreat into 'subjectivism'. It is to recognize that any feminist literary critical enterprise is asking questions about social and historical formations, not just as they operate 'out there', but as they inform and structure the material 'in there' — the identities through which we live, and which may allow us to become the agents of political change. Fiction is pleasurable at least in part because it plays with, displaces and resites these other fictions, and we need a language as critics of 'popular culture' which can politicize without abandoning the categories of entertainment. To say that everyone's art is somebody's escapism is not to underestimate the effects of a literary discourse, but to try to situate these effects across the vast spectrum of the production of meaning, of which literary texts are part. It would suggest too that it is not so much the abolition of certain literary forms which feminism necessitates as the changing of the conditions which produce them. I for one think that there will still be romance after the revolution.

If I have a soft spot for romance fiction then it is because nothing else speaks to me in the same way. It is up to us as feminists to develop a rigorous and compassionate understanding of how these fictions work in women's lives, keeping open the spaces for cultural and psychic pleasure whilst rechanneling the dissatisfactions upon which they depend. That then would seem to me to be the point of returning to Manderley.

NOTES

1   See, for example, Janet Batsleer, 'Pulp in the Pink', *Spare Rib*, No. 109 (1981); David Margolies, 'Mills and Boon — Guilt without Sex', *Red Letters*, No. 14 (1982); Sue Harper, 'History with Frills: Costume Fiction in World War II', *Red Letters*, No. 14 (1982).

2   I am referring here very briefly to the enormous body of theoretical arguments which have emerged largely from the work of the French Marxist Louis Althusser. For extended discussion of this work, and the different directions it has taken since the late 1960s see, for example, Rosalind Coward and John Ellis, *Language and Materialism* (London, Routledge & Kegan Paul, 1977); Michèle Barrett, *Women's Oppression Today* (London, Verso and NLB, 1980). For an analysis of the historical and political relations between Marxism, feminism and psychoanalysis, see Jacqueline Rose, 'Femininity and its Discontents', *Feminist Review*, 14 (1983).

3   Margolies, 'Mills and Boon', p. 9.

4   Michèle Barrett, in 'Feminism and the Definition of Cultural Politics', in Rosalind Brunt and Caroline Rowan, eds, *Feminism, Culture and Politics* (London, Lawrence and Wishart, 1982), takes up some of these points; but see also Rosalind Coward, 'Sexual Politics and Psychoanalysis: Some Notes on their Relation' in Brunt and Rowan, eds, *Feminism, Culture and Politics* and Rose,

'Femininity and its Discontents' for the importance of psychoanalysis as offering ways into the questions of subjectivity, representation and sexual politics.
5 Rose, 'Femininity and its Discontents', p. 9.
6 See Rachel Anderson, *The Purple Heart Throbs: The Sub-Literature of Love* (London, Hodder and Stoughton, 1974), for discussion of readership patterns and responses and Euromonitor Readership Surveys for more recent data.

ROSALIND COWARD
Female Desire: Women's Sexuality Today

In the adoration of the powerful male, we have the adoration of the father by the small child. This adoration is based on the father as all-powerful, before disillusionment and the struggle for autonomy set in. Sometimes the patriarchal nature of the fantasy becomes explicit:

> His words hit her physically, so forcibly did they remind her of her father: he had been the only person who had ever used that word to describe the colour of her hair. And now to hear Stephen do so — the man she loved, who could only see her as a machine — was more than she could bear. Eyes blinded by tears, she ran out.
>
> Roberta Leigh

The way in which these men are portrayed certainly involves a journey back to a world before any struggle for autonomy has occurred. It isn't even an adolescent fantasy; it's pre-adolescent, very nearly pre-conscious. As a fantasy, it represents the adoration of a person on whom your welfare depends, the exaggerated evaluation which children experience before the process of becoming a separate person begins. As the child beomes more independent there's invariably a re-estimation of the parent, perhaps even a disillusionment. The parent who is no longer omnipotent in the child's welfare is no longer seen as omnipotent in the world. The child begins the difficult process of recognizing social valuation as well as personal valuation of the parents. The struggle for autonomy also brings its problems. By adolescence, there's usually a full-scale struggle for independence. Power which might previously have been adored — after all, it ensured the welfare of a dependent child — becomes controlling and suffocating for a child struggling to become independent. The power of one person is seen as depriving another of autonomy. Especially for women, the relationship to patriarchal authority is bound to be hazardous. Men have power and authority only if women's equality is denied.

But in the fantasies represented by these novels, the power of men is adored. The qualities desired are age, power, detachment, the control of other people's welfare. And the novels never really admit any criticism of this power. Occasionally the heroines 'protest' their right to gainful employment, or rebel against the tyranny of the loved men. But in the end they succumb to that form of power. And what attracted them in the first place were precisely all the attributes of the unreconstructed patriarch. The qualities which make these men so desirable are, actually, the qualities which feminists have chosen to ridicule: power (the desire to dominate others); privilege (the exploitation of others); emotional distance (the inability to communicate); and singular love for the heroine (the inability to relate to anyone other than the sexual partner).

It is interesting to realize that obstacles do exist in the way of the heroine's adoration of her man. But the obstacles are never the criticisms or ambiguity which a woman might really feel towards that kind of man. The obstacles come from the outside, from material circumstances or misunderstandings. The work of the narrative is to remove these misunderstandings and obstacles, one by one. Instead of contradictory feelings towards such men, or feelings of suffocation, we have a number of frustrating circumstances which are finally cleared away to allow for the heroine safely to feel her respect and love for the man. In other words, these fantasies admit a belief that everything would be all right between the sexes were it not for a series of foolish misperceptions and misunderstandings.

There are a number of other factors which indicate a powerful infantile fantasy at work. For instance, there's the jealousy to which the heroine is invariably exposed. A rival for the hero's affections is almost obligatory, and the rival is usually better suited by class or by temperament. The crunch point in the narrative often comes when the heroine sees the hero and the other woman embracing, or meets the other two together. When the narrative is resolved, we discover that the hero was thinking about our heroine all along. He was either seeking consolation in another's arms, or was taken in by some scheming type. A satisfactory resolution of this obstacle is the discovery that the hero was after all loyal to the heroine, at least with the emotions if not the body.

The obliteration of a rival is another standard component of an infantile fantasy. The sight of the hero in another's arms is reminiscent of Freud's accounts of one of the forms taken by infantile jealousy provoked by the sight of the parents embracing. The child sees this and is jealous, seeking in fantasy to obliterate the intruding parent. Common childhood fantasies are of obliterating that parent and taking her/his place, becoming the rightful and only recipient of the other parent's love. In pulp romance, the disappointments based on discovering that others have claims on the loved one's attention are obliterated. There aren't really obstacles to total monomaniacal love, only temporary frustrations which the narrative then removes.

There is another significant way in which these narrative fantasies are regressive. It is the way in which sexual desire is portrayed. The hero's power is not only reminiscent of the father's perfection before the fall, so to speak; the power also works to absolve the women from any responsibility for the sexual engagement. Heroes are usually established as either sexually active (lots of girlfriends) or as almost untouchable. In the first case, the heroes are the objects of intense sexual interest, and have active sexual lives but refuse to settle down. In the end it is the overwhelming nature of their

special desire for the heroine which is eventually secured. She alone has
kindled the overwhelming desire that is going to end in marriage. The
'untouchable' syndrome is really very similar. In these cases, the hero is
remote, too good for sexual intrigue, better still a priest — someone, in short,
who ought not to feel sexual passion. The heroine alone awakens his desire.
The desire he feels for her is so great that he has to come off his pedestal,
gather her in his arms and crush her to his chest.

All the frustrations and delays integral to a good romance only heighten
this outcome, where the hero's desire is made suddenly explicit. The hero's
desire is so great that it borders on the uncontrollable. One journalist called
it the 'bruised lips' syndrome, and it is certainly the case that the
uncontrollable desire has close resemblances with descriptions of rape. The
heroine keeps her blouse buttoned up only with the greatest difficulty until
they can breathlessly mutter the marriage vows at each other and bring the
novel to a satisfactory close: '"Please put your dress on," he murmured
huskily, "so we can go talk to your parents about our wedding"' (Janet
Dailey).

This fantasy is the ultimate expression of passive sexuality. The heroine
may well be 'in love' with the hero. She may well adore him and admire him.
But her *desire* is only ever triggered as a response, crushed out of her, as it
were, as a series of low moans. Again psychoanalytic writing is illuminating
about this kind of fantasy. It represents the projection of active desires by
yourself on to another person, who then becomes responsible for that desire.

[. . .]

One thing about these fantasies, though, is that however passive the
female, she is not actually powerless. The conclusion of marriage isn't
necessary so much for reasons of morality, but because these fantasies are
very obviously about a certain transfer of power, from the man to the
woman. The woman is not annihilated by her subordination to the patriarch;
she also assumes some power over him since his great power is finally
harnessed to one woman — the heroine. Indeed, there are often other
elements in romantic novels where the men are rendered helpless and
dependent, like children. There's often a scene where the hero falls ill,
suffers from hallucinations in the desert, or is even injured:

> The human frailty of Stephen Brandon's sickness — even though momentary
> — robbed Julia of her awesome fear with which she had regarded him. One
> could not see a man prostrate and not feel sorry for him; and sympathy —
> however fleeting — left change in its wake.
>
> Roberta Leigh

Rendering the hero ill, dependent, or injured is a narrative device which
crops up all over the place. There's a common theme in fiction and films of
women being attracted to cripples, or having fantasies about nursing men
through illness during which the man suddenly realizes that 'what he's been
feeling is love'. Dick Francis's racing thrillers, which are extremely popular

with women, have this theme of male mutilation down to a fine art. We can be sure that if the hero isn't brutalized within the first few pages, he'll certainly get shot, beaten up or fall off his horse pretty soon. Now, all this is extremely interesting; it points to a push for power in female fantasy.

In romantic fiction, the hero is made dependent only 'fleetingly', as Roberta Leigh would undoubtedly have it. But this momentary impotence allows the woman to acquire power, the power of a mother caring for a child. And the concluding marriage is the symbol of the woman achieving power. The men are castrated and then restored. The power which the heroine achieves is the power of the mother; the daughter has taken the mother's place.

4

Towards Definitions of Feminist Writing

INTRODUCTION

Defining Feminist Imaginative Writing

How would a reader recognize an example of feminist imaginative writing? Are there certain definable characteristics that mark 'x' as a feminist and 'y' as a non-feminist text? Leaving aside for a moment all the problems around the word 'tradition', can we say that a tradition of women's writing is one of *feminist* writing? Or if this seems too all-embracing a definition, can we at least establish that the writing of declared feminists must be feminist? In short, is authorial intention everything? On the other hand, does the feminism lie in interpretation; could feminists agree on a definitive list of books that are more open than others to a feminist reading? Perhaps the nature of the readership is the key. Are the women-centred novels Rosalind Coward mentions to be categorized as 'feminist' because lots of feminists read them? Or does the problem ultimately resolve itself as one of content? Does the placing of women's experience, ideas, visions, achievements at the centre of a piece of writing, or, as in Michèle Barrett's example, an art exhibition, make that work feminist?

The extracts from Coward and Barrett prove that these problems are not open to easy solutions. Both agree that we cannot take 'women's' writing to be a synonym for 'feminist' writing: feminism is 'an alignment of political interests' (Barrett), which some women writers may adopt and others not. But Coward claims further that:

> Feminism can never be the product of the identity of women's experiences and interests — there is no such unity.

While Barrett agrees than an emphasis on female experience does not *necessarily* make the work feminist she is uneasy about Coward's sweeping rejection:

> it is not possible to conceive of a feminist art that could be detached from a shared experience of oppression.

Equally, an examination of authorial intention raises more questions than answers. Books conceived with the most laudable political motives can prove, on reading, to be lame and unconvincing. Conversely, books from authors with no particular sympathy for feminism are widely read by feminists and provide a rich vein for feminist criticism; much of Doris Lessing's work would illustrate this point. Readers too are unreliable guides. Coward makes clear that women-centred novels do not become feminist simply because feminists read them. On the other hand, Barrett believes that it was precisely the audience's reading of *The Dinner Party* that made the event, rather than the specific work, feminist:

> In this sense, although I disputed the claims of *The Dinner Party* to be an *intrinsically* feminist work I would not dispute that it is a feminist event. But this is because its meaning has been constructed, collectively, as such.[1]

The problems of definition are tangibly illustrated in the difficulties which face feminist and left-wing bookshops in arranging their stock. Should they adopt a separatist policy and have a special section for women's writing? Should there be sub-sections for the work of lesbians and women of colour? Are all the books in a women's section feminist? Are the excluded books by male authors all closed to a feminist interpretation? The apparently innocuous task of putting books on shelves is curiously transformed into a political dilemma. And this is but one visible example from a production process — financing, publishing, marketing, distribution — that is charged with contradictions. Feminists weigh the conflicting appeals of an all-women minority press, politically committed but publishing on a very small scale, and a mainstream company for which feminism is ultimately a marketable commodity but which has a wide distribution network; they ponder the gap between the desire for radical change and the necessary involvement of feminist publishing houses in capitalism; they query the intensive, populist and — at times — sensationalist marketing of some women's writing; is this a sign of being incorporated or a sign of a widening feminist interest?[2]

Defining Feminist Literary Criticism

A similar set of questions has been put concerning feminist literary criticism. What makes it distinctive from other forms of criticism? Should it have defined aims? How should it relate to non-feminist criticism or the practice of imaginative writing? Should feminist critics have a common political position and critical method? Deborah McDowell's introductory paragraph again shows the impossibility of precise definition, but strangely, she does not seem to see this looseness of terminology as indicating any theoretical problems.

Prescriptive Criticism. Cheri Register's response, to establish a 'prescriptive' feminist criticism, has been a common one, though not all have been as programmatic. Register starts from a position with which no feminist would disagree. She recognizes the political nature of writing; she wants to link feminist criticism with the women's movement; and she is equally wary of 'ivory tower academism' and political ranting. There is an energy and enthusiasm in the writing, an eagerness to raise issues and a healthy disregard for 'objective' judgements. But what she proposes is a highly dogmatic form of criticism, couched in authoritarian language — we keep being told what we should do, what is correct, or what is not permissible — and offering a very reductive analysis of the relationship between writing and politics. 'To earn feminist approval, literature must perform one or more of the following functions', illustrates the approach. At the same time, what is interesting about Register's essay is that she is tentatively aware of some of the dangers in what she advocates and frequently qualifies her demands, but she is unable finally to resolve the contradictions inherent in her argument. For example, she asserts that feminist writing should 'express female experience authentically', but also that 'authors should not feel obligated to offer an exact representation of their own lives'; she quotes, approvingly, Wendy Martin's suggestion that literature should provide role-models who are 'self-actualizing, whose identities are not dependent on men', but then stresses that 'characters should not be idealised beyond plausibility'; she suggests that 'concrete political issues' have a place in 'feminist-approved literature', but immediately adds that that place 'must be consistent with the demands for authenticity and subjectivity . . .'.

These brief quotations indicate that a crucial concept in prescriptive criticism is the belief in 'authenticity' and in the revelation of a 'true' female identity. Indeed a whole series of terms — 'experience', 'truth', 'authentic', 'identity', 'realistic' — operates as either connecting or interchangeable buzz-words in the debate. The author herself must be 'authentic', telling the entire and unvarnished truth about her experiences and perceptions: Register quotes Erica Jong's condemnation of a poet who 'has not really looked into herself and told it true'. Secondly, the text should express a 'representative' female experience which we, the readers, can accept as an 'authentic reflection' of our lives. And each individual woman should be struggling to find her own 'true' identity, for which task strong, independent female characters may provide inspiring role-models. The intimation is that, hitherto, we have been presented with 'false' realities, 'false' images, 'unrepresentative' models, and that these, like dead skins, should be shed to find the 'true' reality and the 'authentic' selves at the core of our beings.

Elizabeth Baines's extract indicates how unhelpful prescriptive criticism can be to the practising imaginative writer, constraining rather than enabling her, and mystifying the process of writing rather than illuminating it. Far from imaginative writing being conscious, coherent and fully controllable, many writers testify that they do not know where their writing comes from, or, when they start their work, where their writing is going to lead them, or what form it is going to take along the way. This is not to argue that writing is the product of some inexplicable inspiration that cannot be theorised; nor is it to deny that writing is painstakingly and consciously crafted by the writer. Rather, my claim is that writing is a highly complex process, which can be neither explained nor facilitated merely by reference to political goals.

The reductive nature of prescriptive criticism lies partly in its seeing literature as 'a straight reflection of ideology' with the feminist writer simply replacing 'an incorrect patriarchal reading with one "more" correct and equally prescriptive' (Light), or, as Baines expresses it, 'women's fiction must set the record straight'. Writers critical of prescriptive criticism contend that there is no 'true' reality waiting to be revealed and, thus, fiction cannot offer that to the reader. Alison Light looks to texts not for coherence but for the contradictions and ambiguities that allow us a 'plurality of readings'.[3] Nor is there a simple and direct channel of communication from author to text to reader. Even if the authorial intention was to present a feminist message, there is no guarantee that the reader would receive the text in that way. Furthermore, as Cora Kaplan and Elizabeth Wilson argue, the search for a hidden, true, autonomous and unified identity is alluring but futile. They see identity as unresolved and contradictory, what Kaplan calls 'the inherently unstable and split character of all human subjectivity'. Thus to look, in either life or literature, for strong women as role-models is far from satisfactory. The image of the strong woman is too simple, too resolved and one-dimensional; it 'allows for no moment of weakness, and cannot reflect the diversity and complexity of our desires' (Wilson). Instead of being inspired by such images women can feel inadequate in comparison. In these triumphant, achieving, heroic characterizations, where is there any place for all my inadequacies, failings, and impure motives?

Playful Pluralism. At the opposite extreme to prescriptive criticism is Annette Kolodny's 'playful pluralism'. Concerned about both reductive readings and the wholesale rejection of non-feminist criticism, Kolodny suggests that feminist criticism should be viewed as *one* reading among many, taking part in an 'ongoing dialogue of competing potential possibilities'. She sees feminist criticism as useful 'in recognizing the particular achievements of woman-as-author' and 'in conscientiously decoding woman-as-sign'. This pluralism will not lead to chaos, Kolodny argues, but instead will prevent critics from claiming that their work is 'either exhaustive or definitive'. And it will not simply reproduce the *bourgeois* appeal to pluralism because this version will stress, rather than deny, 'the power of ideology'. However, Toril Moi worries whether Kolodny's brand of feminist criticism is not 'throwing the baby out with the bathwater'. If we accept an endless plurality of readings will we, in so doing, endorse the existence of 'the most "masculinist" of criticism'? For instance, would Kolodny look upon my fourth-form English language text book, which explained rhythm as 'the pulsating sounds that incite natives to kill', as simply an aspect of the plurality of interpretation? Moi is not looking for a prescriptive criticism, but she does see the need for a more analytical and evaluative approach than the one Kolodny suggests, and that means closely scrutinizing critical theory to ensure that the methods and tools we use genuinely aid the development of a feminist politics.

Gynocritics. Elaine Showalter has looked at critical theory and seen in it — even in feminist literary theory — an alarming attachment to the 'male theoretician' and to 'male texts or films'. The names she finds suspect — Althusser, Barthes, Macherey and Lacan — are, presumably, the very ones

ʾound most useful when she writes of her interest in
st appropriations of psychoanalytic and structuralist
rasting responses clearly expose the problematic
st literary criticism to other critical theories. Are the
ʾl to be rejected as irrevocably androcentric and male-
e transformed and used for the benefit of feminism?
distinction, can we say that *some* male-centred
nism while others are not? Showalter sees no place
models and theories' or, indeed, for 'the angry or
ature'. She proposes instead 'gynocritics' which
ework for the analysis of women's literature'
d on the study of female experience'. There is
alter's proposition, particularly in her search
diacy and relevance for women and which,
the centre of the debate. Her concern that
they may, unconsciously, still delight in
g masters are warnings that need heeding.

of Theory

n over-emphasis on theory can lead
sive knowledge of women's texts' is
oi, the opposition between 'theory'
owledge" is ever uninformed by
itics such as Moi and the Marxist-
fem   e no choice as to whether or not
to t   d unavoidable aspect of their
critic   dge' that does not need to be
unders   ale experience' that does not
have to   ognize that the production of
theory   t look upon theorizing as
essential   ale-dominated theories —
Marxism,   sis — as malleable and
helpful to fe   process is 'a revisionism
which becor   t-feminists or feminists
working in th   engaging in a principled
critical dialog   r views their work as,
at times, dange   nen-centred.

In their turn,   ists have complained
that a lack of t   inist criticism has,
unwittingly, draw   at do no service to
the feminist cause   nstance, reads in
many ways like a fe   nstead of writing
placing itself at the s   ow at the service
of feminist liberation,   y, writing now
promotes sisterhood; in   racters, writing
should 'serve as a forum   al role-models

and writing with the specific intention of raising consciousness are stressed. For Cora Kaplan and Elizabeth Wilson it is the continuing influence in feminist criticism of Romantic aesthetic theory that is questionable. Kaplan feels that the Romantic view of writers as 'the conscious, constant and triumphant sources of the meanings they produce' is still prevalent in feminism; Wilson views the 'longing for utopias and reconstructed selves' as a sign of feminism's failure to analyse 'political romanticism'. Finally, Moi takes issue with what she sees as Showalter's uncritical acceptance of humanism and empiricism. Showalter's rejection of 'male' theory is, ultimately, a rejection of only some 'male' theories and an unperceived acquiescence with others; the charge of complicity is returned.

Should feminism look to socialist realism or Romanticism or humanism to help establish its theoretical position? Should it look to Marxism or structuralism or psychoanalysis? For feminists — as for everyone else — there seems to be no escape from theoretical debates and the need to constantly define and refine our responses. As Toril Moi comments most tellingly, unless we continue to theorize we may, unawares, drift 'perilously close to the male critical hierarchy whose patriarchal values (we) oppose'.

NOTES

1 Michèle Barrett, 'Feminism and the Definition of Cultural Politics', in *Feminism, Culture and Politics* eds. Rosalind Brunt and Caroline Rowan (London, Lawrence and Wishart, 1982), p. 57.
2 A very useful introduction to some of the problems of feminist publishing is Eileen Cadman, Gail Chester, Agnes Pivot, *Rolling Our Own: Women as Printers, Publishers and Distributors* (London, Minority Press Group, 1981).
3 An earlier and more extensive exploration of this idea, as Light indicates, is to be found in Cora Kaplan, 'Radical Feminism and Literature: Rethinking Millett's *Sexual Politics*', anthologized in *The Woman Question: Readings on the Subordination of Women* ed. Mary Evans (London, Fontana, 1982).
4 Elaine Showalter, 'Feminist Criticism in the Wilderness', in *Critical Inquiry*, vol. 8, no. 2 (Winter, 1981), p. 205. This article is discussed by Toril Moi in *Sexual/Textual Politics: Feminist Literary Theory* (London, Methuen, 1985), p. 77 from which Moi's comment is taken.
5 Ibid., p. 183.

ROSALIND COWARD

'"This Novel Changes Lives": Are Women's Novels Feminist Novels? A Response to Rebecca O'Rourke's Article "Summer Reading"', *Feminist Review*

Women-centred Writing

It is just not possible to say that women-centred writings have any necessary relationship to feminism. Women-centred novels are by no means a new phenomenon. The Mills and Boon romantic novels are written by, read by, marketed for and are all about women. Yet nothing could be further from the aims of feminism than these fantasies based on the sexual, racial and class submission which so frequently characterise these novels. The plots and elements of these novels are frequently so predictable that cynics have suggested that Mills and Boon's treasured authors might well be computers. Yet the extraordinary rigidity of the formula of the novels, where the heroine invariably finds material success through sexual submission and marriage, does not prevent these publishers having a larger sales than Pan and Penguin. The average print run for each novel is 115,000. While Mills and Boon may have a highly individual market, their formulae are not so radically different from romance fiction in general. Such immensely popular writers as Mary Stewart and Georgette Heyer invariably have the experience of the heroine at the centre, and concentrate on the vagaries of her emotions as the principal substance of the novel. In the cinema, the equivalent of the romantic novel is melodrama, and melodrama is often promoted as 'women's pictures', suggesting that they are directed towards women as well as being about women. Indeed it would not be stretching credibility too far to suggest that the consciousness of the individual heroine has been a principal narrative device of the English novel in the last century, a fact which may well have contributed to the relative presence of women writers in this field.

While this all shows how misguided it would be to mark a book of interest to feminism because of the centrality it attributes to women's experiences, it could be argued that what we loosely call feminist novels are qualitatively different. But to make such a claim it would be necessary to specify in what way 'women-centred' writing, allying itself with feminist politics, did mark itself out as different. Some of the so-called feminist novels like *The Women's Room* and *A Piece of the Night* do make explicit their allegiance to the women's liberation movement. However, many of the others in roughly the same genre do not. *Fear of Flying, Kinflicks* and *Loose Change* all fall into this category. Yet the encounter with the milieu and aspirations of feminism often forms a central element in the narrative of these novels. And, the practice of consciousness raising — the reconstruction of personal histories within a group of women — sometimes forms the structure of the novel. Then there is a further category. Here we find novels like Kate Millett's *Sita* whose feminist commitment is guaranteed not so much by the content of the book as by the other theoretical and political writings of the author. And finally there is a whole host of novels which are adopted as honorary 'feminist novels', taking in such different writers as Doris Lessing, Fay Weldon and Alison Lurie. Their writings deal not so much with the milieu of contemporary feminism as with charting the experience of women's oppression.

Now, there is a certain convention within all these novels which does clearly mark them off from the romance genre for example. One striking feature is the frequency with which we meet with the quasi-autobiographical structure. *The Women's Room, Fear of Flying, Kinflicks, Sita* all foreground the writer, struggling to turn her experience into literature, even if this figure loiters in the background in god-like omnipotence as in *The Women's Room.* Moreover the 'voice' of the central protagonist, if not presenting itself directly as the author's voice, frequently offers itself as 'representative' of women in general, firstly claiming sexual experience as a vital terrain of all women's experience, sometimes also making generalities as to the oppressive nature of that experience. The distinctiveness of the genre has attracted attention; a Sunday Times colour supplement heading shows one response to the self-consciously 'representative' nature of these novels:

> Liberating the Libido. Getting sex straight was an essential first step along the noisy road to liberation; writing about it could be the next leap forward. Books by women surveying sex, and novels by women whose heroines savour sex are selling like hotdogs in America — beating men into second place and turning the authoresses into millionairesses at the drop of a hard sell dust-jacket.

I have raised this here in order to show that we do have a recognizable group of novels whose roots are, in a variety of ways, in the women's liberation movement but that their relation to feminism is not the necessary outcome of taking women's experience as central. But other questions arise in relation to this statement, questions as to whether the 'representativeness' which these novels claim is simply a reflection of 'feminist consciousness', or a propaganda device towards such a consciousness, or whether we have to be more cautious in analysing their structure and effects.

The Commercial Success of the Novels that Change Lives

Rebecca seems to imply that the widespread success of these novels can be attributed to a widespread diffusion of 'feminist consciousness'. In fact the disparity between the print runs of these novels and political texts gives rise to the exactly opposite suspicion in more cynical minds. Perhaps the kind of writing involved in *Kinflicks* or *The Women's Room* corresponds more closely to the structures of popular fiction rather than satisfying the incipient feminism of the population. The fact is that the space occupied by these novels is not so radically different from the conventional structures which make up the 'novelistic'. In other words that space of themes, modes of writing, hierarchies of appropriate statements which constitute these 'feminist novels' is not so utterly unlike those of popular fiction in general. We can isolate several aspects of this correspondence.

A dominant element in contemporary fiction has been that of the 'confessional' novel — the structuring of the novel, and the significant events of the narrative, around the voice of a principal protagonist describing her/his life. Novels like J. D. Salinger's *Catcher in the Rye* or *Lucky Jim* by Kingsley Amis bear an exceptionally strong resemblance to feminist works such as Alice Monroe's *Lives of Girls and Women* in this respect. But the similarity does not end here. For this structure has increasingly been characterized by the absolute centrality given to the experience of adolescence and young adulthood. In particular the experiences of this period have come to be almost synonymous with sexual experience. In drawing attention to the reception of feminist writers by the bourgeois press, I have already hinted how this preoccupation with the confession of sexual experience is one of the most characteristic features of contemporary feminist writings. Like the confessional novel in general, the novels by feminists also present the experience of sexuality as the significant experience of the novel. Whereas in romantic fiction (and indeed quite often in 'the classics') it was the events leading to marriage, or events disrupting love, which occupied the position of significant events, increasingly sexual experience is becoming sufficient.

Certain points can be made about the confessional form of these novels and their preoccupation with sexuality. An obvious point is that speaking about sexuality, and a preoccupation with sexuality, is not in and of itself progressive. Feminists have been involved for too long now in the analysis of images and ideologies to be conned into thinking that accounts of sexuality are progressive just because they take women's sexuality as their central concern. Criticism of pornography, which frequently highlights the sexual experiences of women, is just one example of representations of sexuality which feminists have actually contested.

It has been suggested that the centrality which the confession of sexuality has assumed and which is now an integral part of our culture does not in fact represent a radical break with the past. Michel Foucault (1978) for example has suggested that it represents a continuation of certain practices of dealing with sexuality which have been part of western culture for several centuries. He argues that sexuality has never been 'repressed' as such but has been the object of a variety of discourses for several centuries. In the past these discourses were frequently directed towards a control or negation of certain sexual practices, as with the medical and educational discourses of the Victorian period: they nevertheless had sexuality as their object. In Catholic countries, he suggests that the practice of the church confessional was taken over into scientific and social discourses, where once again sexuality became an object to be interrogated, spoken about, controlled. Again and again however, whatever the explicit aim of the discourses, sexuality was taken to be the element which revealed the 'true' and 'essential' nature of people. Foucault sees within this concern with sexuality the workings of power; the identity of the subject is found through discourses which multiply areas of pleasure and attention only to control, classify, subject. To deny a sudden rupture in the history of sexuality — from repression to liberation — does not mean that we have to go along with Foucault in suggesting that there have not been radical changes in the representations of sexuality themselves. For women, discourses on sexuality have changed importantly. The equation of female sexuality with the illicit and disgusting is no longer a dominant representation, and the possibilities of sexual enjoyment no longer focussed on motherhood, are changes for which feminism has fought.

Nevertheless these ideas are useful in this context. They indicate how the centrality which sexuality has assumed in the novel, either coyly in romantic preoccupations or explicitly in the confession of sexual experiences, has definite correspondences with other social practices. Within the novel, the 'confession' has appeared, structured by traditions, specific to the novel. In particular it has been influenced by the importance of narrative, which organizes a series of events or experiences as significant and progressing towards a meaningful conclusion. This space of time, or narrative, is one in which the central character or characters undergo an experience or series of experiences which radically affect their lives or transform their attitudes. The effect of this structure is to create a distinct ideology of knowledge and indeed life — that experience brings knowledge and possibly wisdom. But where women have been, and are, the central focus of the novel, a variation occurs. That variation is that the only space where knowledge or understanding for women is produced is across sexual experience — love, marriage, divorce or just sex. In romance for example, the significant space is that of encounter, love, (possibly) a hindrance and marriage; understanding is finding the proper mate. It is rare to find a novel such as Jane Austen's *Emma* where the sentimental lesson is combined with an intellectual lesson, that of discretion. An examination of novelistic practices — customs of the single central character, 'realistic' writing, the delineation of time as progressive and significant — would require a lengthy article but it is sufficient to bring them forward here to indicate that women-centred novels are *not* the product of a feminist audience. Nor can we say that the structures of the realist novel are neutral and that they can just be filled with a feminist content. Indeed, it could be argued that the emergence of this particular form of 'women's writing' with its emphasis on sexual experience as the source of significant experience, might have the effect of confirming women as bearers of sentiment, experience and romance (albeit disillusioned).

It is quite clear that there are compelling similarities between 'novels that change lives' and contemporary fictional conventions, which should warn us against any simple designation of these novels as feminist. This does not mean that we cannot say anything about the emergence of this group of novels in their specificity, nor does it mean that there is nothing progressive about these novels. First of all, it is clear that female sexuality (as distinct from just female emotions) is becoming more and more an object to be interrogated, in a variety of social practices — film, sociological, psychological and 'sexological' studies. The novel's own history — its confessional form, and its highlighting of sexual events as significant time — make it particularly responsive to this preoccupation. And this preoccupation undoubtedly at a certain level represents a response to a problem: what is female sexual pleasure? Thus, though feminist writing may well be compromised by its uncritical use of the conventional forms of the novel, it is also an important presence in a popular form of fiction.

But it would also be limited to suggest that all the novels which we loosely designate feminist never escape beyond defining women entirely by their sexuality. Occasionally some go beyond the limits of the conventional novelistic forms and preoccupations. Doris Lessing and Fay Weldon, for example, both occasionally disrupt the conventions of the central narrative voice or character, and their writings suddenly become a myriad of historical, social and sexual concerns which do not 'belong' to an individual subjectivity. Where sexuality is treated as political this is occasionally the outcome and is one of the most interesting aspects of novels like these.

It is by paying attention to practices of writing, conventions of genre and their relation to other forms of writing, that we can differentiate between novels and assess their political effects. And it is only in conjunction with an analysis of the conventions internal to the text that we can understand marketing strategies.

Publishing Practices and Women-centred Novels

Rebecca O'Rourke suggests that commercial publishers are cashing in on feminism. I have already suggested that we cannot designate many of the novels she discusses as feminist in any simple sense. And a cursory glance at the marketing of these 'women-centred' novels by commercial publishers confirms my view that they are often directed towards the popular fiction market. Look at the difference between the 'sensationalist' cover of *Kinflicks* (a cover which many found incongruous with the content of the book) and the restful paintings which characterize the publications of the feminist publishing groups — paintings which lay claim for the novels as 'classics'.

There are undoubtedly important considerations in the relationship between commercial publishing groups and political movements, both socialist and feminist. You would have to be blind not to notice how the publication by commercial publishing houses of 'women's studies' texts has proliferated. These sections clearly have a commercial viability but their existence is no less the product of hard fought battles of feminists within more conventional publishing groups. The kinds of numbers printed of 'academic' feminist books are minimal compared with say *Kinflicks*, (about 4,000 versus 50,000), but the issue seems to be similar. It is just not enough to regret the profits of commercial firms. In fact such profits should be welcomed if they encourage groups with a mass market to invest in other such books. The question is much rather what is the relationship of the practice of reading, both of fiction and non-fiction, with political movements, in what way are texts effective, and, most importantly, which ones are. The passive relation which Rebecca assumes (that is, that these novels simply provide pleasure for the already converted) would surely be a cause for pessimism.

MICHELE BARRETT
'Feminism and the Definition of Cultural Politics',
Feminism, Culture and Politics

II. When Is Women's Art Feminist Art?

This leads to a second problem. This is the question asked by Rosalind Coward in her article 'Are Women's Novels Feminist Novels?'.[1] Although Coward's piece is directed towards one particular review article on feminist fiction, her argument is in fact a generalized critique of a major (if not the main) tendency in feminist literary criticism. She argues that feminists have emphasized the unity and continuity of women's creative work and have tended to confuse feminist art with, simply, women's art. Coward rejects this conflation of the two, and she suggests that the current popularity of 'women's fiction' is not necessarily feminist at all. Feminism, she argues, is an alignment of political interests and not a shared female experience; hence a tradition of women's art is of no particular importance.

This goes right to the nub of a number of controversial questions about feminism and culture. Is the recovery of women's artistic work of the past an integral part of our developing feminist project, or merely a sentimental resuscitation of marginalia better left in the obscurity to which establishment criticism has consigned it? What do we gain by elevating traditional crafts such as embroidery and knitting to the status of art objects and hanging them in galleries? What is the meaning of an art exhibition where the objects displayed are kitchen utensils or the careful record of a child's upbringing? How should we react to art that claims to be based on a 'female language' or on an artistic rendering of the female body and genitalia? In what sense might these various imaginative comments on women's experience be seen as 'feminist' art? Is a work of art feminist because the artist says it is, or the collective who produced it announce their feminist principles of work?

These questions were crystallized for me in a thought-provoking way by Judy Chicago's exhibition *The Dinner Party*, and although this has not yet been shown in Britain I want to use it to illustrate some points. The leaflet accompanying the show states that '. . . the goal of *The Dinner Party* is to ensure that women's achievements become a permanent part of our culture', and the scale of the exhibition matches this monumental aspiration.

The central conception is a triangular dining-table, along the sides of which are placed symbolic representations of thirty-nine women: pre-Christian goddesses; historical figures such as Sappho and Boadaceia; women like the suffragist Susan B. Anthony and the artist Georgia O'Keefe. (This dining-table echoes the 'last supper' so significant to our male-dominated Christian culture.) Each of the figures at the table has a place setting of a runner, cutlery, goblet and plate, whose different designs evoke her particular character. From these thirty-nine women the names of 999 less resoundingly famous, but still reasonably well-known, women radiate in inscriptions on the 'heritage floor'. Surrounding this central focus of the exhibition are banners designed for the entrance, documentation of the five year's work by Judy Chicago and her team of helpers, an exhibition of china-painting, and a display of congratulatory telegrams from feminist artists all over the world.

The size of the exhibition — completely devoted to women's achievements — is, literally, spectacular. When I saw it an entire floor of the San Francisco Museum of Modern Art had been given over to it. The dining-table itself totals nearly 150 feet in length, each woman's place setting using about three and a half feet of space. The combination of this impressive scale and the lavish, beautiful, solid, ceramics and embroidery made the experience of being there an obviously moving one for many women. Never before, it seemed, had women taken over the cultural arena in such a flamboyant and confident way. The atmosphere, too, was wonderful — bringing back all the most positive and sisterly dimensions of a large women's liberation conference since there were so many feminists there.

The experience of being there was for me a striking one and I warmed immediately to the project. It conveyed a real sense of women's achievements and perhaps we too frequently refuse to take pride in them. The feeling of straightforward gender-congratulation was a new and welcome one. Yet in other respects the exhibition was extremely disturbing.

First, it was clear from the documentation that Judy Chicago had not only conceived the project but had directed the work of her many assistants with a positively dictatorial zeal. The principles of collective work vaunted here were not so much the ones I might recognize as feminist but an attempt to recreate the 'school' or studio of an 'Artistic Genius' like Michelangelo. Although hundreds of people gave much time and work to the project it is Judy Chicago personally who has, apparently not unwillingly, made an international reputation from it.

Second, we have to question whether it is necessarily progress to retrieve embroidery and china-painting from the inglorious role of women's drudgery (or at best 'craft') and re-allocate them to the realm of 'high art'. This is undoubtedly the aim of the show, and it one that is fraught with problems. What has happened to previous radical artists who attempted to challenge prevailing definitions of the 'appropriate' contents of art galleries? This is not a reactionary question, for the answer is that by and large their iconoclasm has been effectively dampened by a versatile establishment and so their challenge to the institution has been converted into artistic novelty. To sail into the establishment without seeing this as a problem is to beg the question of what 'art' is and how it differs from other forms of work. It is not enough simply to get what women do recognized as 'art'.

Third, I found the uncritical exercise of ranking 'great women' rather disturbing. There is something rather crude in deeming (to take some British examples of the figures used) the composer Ethel Smythe and the writer Virginia Woolf as worthy of individual places at the dining-table, while Jane Austen and Dorothy Wordsworth merit only an inscription on the floor. The heroines of feminism are here graded, ranked according to a set of criteria that are highly subjective. (On what grounds was it decided that Eleanor of Acquitaine made a greater contribution to feminism than the Virgin Mary? Is there not something bizarre in ranking Emily Dickinson with the Primordial Goddess?) The list of names in the catalogue is studded with epithets like 'pioneer', 'prizewinning', 'cultural leader' and 'eminent intellectual' — all of them terms of evaluation which we have developed a critical stance towards. The search for heroines and role models, for the great women of history, is one which raises a number of difficulties.

Finally, there are the problems surrounding how these women are represented in the exhibition. It is, perhaps, unsurprising and even appropriate that mythological goddesses are symbolized through renderings of clitoral and vaginal imagery. We have little to know them by. But for other women, of whose lives and beliefs we know far more (since they are historical rather than mythological figures), the inevitable vaginal imagery is less appropriate. Less appropriate! I was in fact horrified to see a 'Virginia Woolf' whose image to me represented a reading of her life and work which contradicted all she had ever stood for. There she sits: a genital sculpture in deep relief (about four inches high) resting on a runner of pale lemon gauze with the odd blue wave embroidered on it. Gone is Woolf's theory of androgyny and love of gender ambiguity; gone the polemical public voice; gone the complex symbolic abstractions of her writing. I found this exclusive emphasis on genitalia, and the sentimentality of the trappings, a complete betrayal — as was the 'Emily Dickinson' whose vagina is trimmed with a white lace effect over the palest pink. Very few of our celebrated sisters manage to escape this dreadful posthumous fate. Ethel Smythe appears here as a rather fine grand piano on a background of grey pin-stripe, but this, one fears, is attributable to Chicago's perceptions of her as a dyke. It is in fact typical of Chicago's somewhat biologistic approach to feminism that various of her protagonists are credited for creating a 'female form' of art or literature — in itself a controversial achievement since the possible existence of 'female' forms of art has yet to be established. The notion that some forms of art are intrinsically female (or male) is a dubious one.

All these reservations about *The Dinner Party* have a bearing on the problem of what can be said to be feminist art. This particular case is of interest in that Chicago's claims for the exhibition — that it serves her project of securing artistic recognition for women's achievements — crystallize one specific approach to feminist cultural politics. Her argument that women's art is systematically excluded from the artistic establishment is demonstrated by the fact that after an immensely popular American tour the show went into storage rather than on to Europe.

But problems still remain in (i) the difficulty of arriving at a consensus among feminists as to what constitutes 'feminist' art and (ii) the fact that the use of women's lives, histories and experience does not necessarily ensure the coherent, feminist, reading of Chicago's work that the artist appears to desire. In this sense the case of *The Dinner Party* does seem to me to illustrate the truth of Rosalind Coward's warning that women's art is not necessarily feminist art. Feminist art is not the same as any art which emphasizes women's experience.

We cannot, however, completely separate feminist art from women's experience and hence I would not go so far as Rosalind Coward when she writes:

> Feminism can never be the product of the identity of women's experiences and interests — there is no such unity. Feminism must always be the alignment of women in a political movement with particular political aims and objectives. It is a grouping unified by its *political interests*, not by its common experiences.[2]

Whatever the problems of basing feminism on the experience shared by women, far greater problems arise in attempting completely to divorce feminism (as a political project) from women's experience. This leads to the position that women's shared experience of oppression plays no significant part in the construction of a feminist cultural politics, which in turn must lead to the conclusion that feminist art could equally well be developed by (for instance) a man. Although an emphasis on women's experience, or the fact of female authorship, or indeed a concern with the female body, is not enough to make a work of art feminist I do not see how feminism can ever take women to be a dispensable category. So although I agree than an emphasis on women is not a sufficient condition to make cultural production feminist it must at least be a *necessary* condition. Put another way, feminist art could be seen as a category *within* a tradition of women's art but I fail to see how it could be generated outside it. It may be that in general women's art is only indirectly useful or inspiring to feminism, but it is not possible to conceive of a feminist art that could be detached from a shared experience of oppression.

NOTES

1   Rosalind Coward, '"This Novel Changes Lives": Are Women's Novels Feminist Novels? A Response to Rebecca O'Rourke's Article "Summer Reading"', *Feminist Review*, 5 (1980).
2   Coward, '"This Novel Changes Lives"', p. 63.

DEBORAH E. McDOWELL
'New Directions for Black Feminist Criticism',
Black American Literature Forum

Despite the shortcomings of Smith's article, she raises critical issues on which Black feminist critics can build. There are many tasks ahead of these critics, not the least of which is to attempt to formulate some clear definitions of what Black feminist criticism is. I use the term in this paper simply to refer to Black female critics who analyze the works of Black female writers from a feminist or political perspective. But the term can also apply to any criticism written by a Black woman regardless of her subject or perspective — a book written by a male from a feminist or political perspective, a book written by a Black woman or about Black women authors in general, or any writings by women.[23]

In addition to defining the methodology, Black feminist critics need to determine the extent to which their criticism intersects with that of white feminist critics. Barbara Smith and others have rightfully challenged white women scholars to become more accountable to Black and Third World women writers, but will that require white women to use a different set of critical tools when studying Black woman writers? Are white women's theories predicated upon culturally-specific values and assumptions? Andrea Benton Rushing has attempted to answer these questions in her series of articles on images of Black women in literature. She maintains, for example, that critical categories of women, based on analyses of white women characters, are Euro-American in derivation and hence inappropriate to a consideration of Black women characters.[24] Such distinctions are necessary and, if held uniformly, can materially alter the shape of Black feminist scholarship.

Regardless of which theoretical framework Black feminist critics choose, they must have an informed handle on Black literature and Black culture in general. Such a grounding can give this scholarship more texture and completeness and perhaps prevent some of the problems that have had a vitiating effect on the criticism.

This footing in Black history and culture serves as a basis for the study of the literature. Termed 'contextual,' by theoreticians, this approach is often frowned upon if not dismissed entirely by critics who insist exclusively upon textual and linguistic analysis. Its limitations notwithstanding, I firmly believe that the contextual approach to Black women's literature exposes the conditions under which literature is produced, published, and reviewed. This approach is not only useful but necessary to Black feminist critics.

To those working with Black women writers prior to 1940, the contextual approach is especially useful. In researching Jessie Fauset, Nella Larsen, and Zora Neale Hurston, for example, it is useful to determine what the prevalent attitudes about Black women were during the time that they wrote. There is much information in the Black 'little' magazines published during the Harlem Renaissance. An examination of *The Messenger*, for instance, reveals that the dominant social attitudes about Black women were strikingly consistent with traditional middle class expectations of women. *The Messenger* ran a monthly symposium for some time entitled 'Negro Womanhood's Greatest Needs.' While a few female contributors stressed the importance of women being equal to men socially, professionally, and economically, the majority emphasized that a woman's place was in the home. It was her duty 'to cling to the home [since] great men and women evolve from the environment of the hearthstone.'[25]

One of the most startling entries came from a woman who wrote:

the New Negro Woman, with her head erect and spirit undaunted is resolutely marching forward, ever conscious of her historic and noble mission of doing her bit toward the liberation of her people in particular and the human race in general. Upon her shoulders rests the big task to create and keep alive, in the breast of black men, a holy and consuming passion to break with the slave traditions of the past; to spurn and overcome the fatal, insidious inferiority complex of the present, which . . . bobs up ever and anon, to arrest the progress of the New Negro Manhood Movement; and to fight with increasing vigor, with dauntless courage, unrelenting zeal and intelligent vision for the attainment of the stature of a full man, a free race and a new world.[26]

Not only does the contributor charge Black women with a formidable task, but she also sees her solely in relation to Black men.

This information enhances our understanding of what Fauset, Larsen, and Hurston confronted in attempting to offer alternative images of Black women. Moreover, it helps to clarify certain textual problems and ambiguities of their work. Though Fauset and Hurston, for example, explored feminist concerns, they leaned toward ambivalence. Fauset is especially alternately forthright and cagey, radical and traditional, on issues which confront women. Her first novel, *There Is Confusion* (1924), is flawed by an unanticipated and abrupt reversal in characterization that brings the central female character more in line with a feminine norm. Similarly, in her last novel, *Seraph on the Swanee* (1948), Zora Neale Hurston depicts a female character who shows promise for growth and change, for a departure from the conventional expectations of womanhood, but who, in the end, apotheosizes marriage, motherhood, and domestic servitude.

These two examples alone clearly capture the tension between social pressure and artistic integrity which is felt, to some extent, by all women writers. As Tillie Olsen points out, the fear of reprisal from the publishing and critical arenas is a looming obstacle to the woman writer's coming into her own authentic voice. 'Fear — the need to please, to be safe — in the literary realm too. Founded fear. Power is still in the hands of men. Power of validation, publication, approval, reputation. . . .'[27]

While insisting on the validity, usefulness, and necessity of contextual approaches to Black women's literature, the Black feminist critic must not ignore the importance of rigorous textual analysis. I am aware of many feminist critics' stubborn resistance to the critical methodology handed down by white men. Although the resistance is certainly politically consistent and logical, I agree with Annette Kolodny that feminist criticism would be 'shortsighted if it summarily rejected all the inherited tools of critical analysis simply because they are male and western.' We should, rather, salvage what we find useful in past methodologies, reject what we do not, and, where necessary, move toward 'inventing new methods of analysis.'[28] Particularly useful is Lillian Robinson's suggestion that 'A radical kind of textual criticism . . . could usefully study the way the texture of sentences, choice of metaphors, patterns of exposition and narrative relate to [feminist] ideology.'[29]

This rigorous textual analysis involves, as Barbara Smith recommends, isolating as many thematic, stylistic, and linguistic commonalities among Black women writers as possible. Among contemporary Black female novelists, the thematic parallels are legion. In Alice Walker and Toni Morrison, for example, the theme of the thwarted female artist figures prominently.[30] Pauline Breedlove in Morrison's *The Bluest Eye*, for example, is obsessed with ordering things:

> Jars on shelves at canning, peach pits on the step, sticks, stones, leaves. . . . Whatever portable plurality she found, she organized into neat lines, according to their size, shape or gradations of color. . . . She missed without knowing what she missed — paints and crayons.[31]

Similarly, Eva Peace in *Sula* is forever ordering the pleats in her dress. And Sula's strange and destructive behavior is explained as 'the consequence of an idle imagination.'

> Had she paints, clay, or knew the discipline of the dance, or strings; had she anything to engage her tremendous curiosity and her gift for metaphor, she might have exchanged the restlessness and preoccupation with whim for an activity that provided her with all she yearned for. And like any artist with no form, she became dangerous.[32]

Likewise, Meridian's mother in Alice Walker's novel, *Meridian*, makes artificial flowers and prayer pillows too small for kneeling.

The use of 'clothing as iconography'[33] is central to writings by Black women. For example, in one of Jessie Fauset's early short stories, 'The Sleeper Wakes' (1920), Amy, the protagonist, is associated with pink clothing (suggesting innocence and immaturity) while she is blinded by fairy-tale notions of love and marriage. However, after she declares her independence from her racist and sexist husband, Amy no longer wears pink. The imagery of clothing is abundant in Zora Neale Hurston's *Their Eyes Were Watching God* (1937). Janie's apron, her silks and satins, her head scarves, and finally her overalls all symbolize various stages of her journey from captivity to liberation. Finally, in Alice Walker's *Meridian*, Meridian's railroad cap and dungarees are emblems of her rejection of conventional images and expectations of womanhood.

A final theme that recurs in the novels of Black women writers is the motif of the journey. Though one can also find this same motif in the works of Black male writers, they do not use it in the same way as do Black female writers.[34] For example, the journey of the Black male character in works by Black men takes him underground. It is a 'descent into the underworld,'[35] and is primarily political and social in its implications. Ralph Ellison's *Invisible Man*, Imamu Amiri Baraka's *The System of Dante's Hell*, and Richard Wright's 'The Man Who Lived Underground' exemplify this quest. The Black female's journey, on the other hand, though at times touching the political and social, is basically a personal and psychological journey. The female character in the works of Black women is in a state of becoming 'part of an evolutionary spiral, moving from victimization to consciousness.'[36] The heroines in Zora Neale Hurston's *Their Eyes Were Watching God*, in

Alice Walker's *Meridian*, and in Toni Cade Bambara's *The Salt Eaters* are emblematic of this distinction.

Even though isolating such thematic and imagistic commonalities should continue to be one of the Black feminist critic's most urgent tasks, she should beware of generalizing on the basis of too few examples. If one argues authoritatively for the existence of a Black female 'consciousness' or 'vision' or 'literary tradition,' one must be sure that the parallels found recur with enough consistency to support these generalizations. Further, Black feminist critics should not become obsessed in searching for common themes and images in Black women's works. As I pointed out earlier, investigating the question of 'female' language is critical and may well be among the most challenging jobs awaiting the Black feminist critic. The growing body of research on gender-specific uses of language might aid these critics. In fact wherever possible, feminist critics should draw on the scholarship of feminists in other disciplines.

An equally challenging and necessary task ahead of the Black feminist critic is a thoroughgoing examination of the works of Black male writers. In her introduction to *Midnight Birds*, Mary Helen Washington argues for the importance of giving Black women writers their due first. She writes:

> Black women are searching for a specific language, specific symbols, specific images with which to record their lives, and, even though they can claim a rightful place in the Afro-American tradition and the feminist tradition of women writers, it is also clear that, for purposes of liberation, black women writers will first insist on their own name, their own space.[37]

I likewise believe that the immediate concern of Black feminist critics must be to develop a fuller understanding of Black women writers who have not received the critical attention Black male writers have. Yet, I cannot advocate indefinitely such a separatist position, for the countless thematic, stylistic and imagistic parallels between Black male and female writers must be examined. Black feminist critics should explore these parallels in an effort to determine the ways in which these commonalities are manifested differently in Black women's writing and the ways in which they coincide with writings by Black men.

Of course, there are feminist critics who are already examining Black male writers, but much of the scholarship has been limited to discussions of the negative images of Black women found in the works of these authors.[38] Although this scholarship served an important function in pioneering Black feminist critics, it has virtually run its course. Feminist critics run the risk of plunging their work into cliche and triviality if they continue merely to focus on how Black men treat Black women in literature. Hortense Spillers offers a more sophisticated approach to this issue in her discussion of the power of language and myth in female relations in James Baldwin's *If Beale Street Could Talk*. One of Spillers's most cogent points is that 'woman-freedom or its negation, is tied to the assertions of myth, or ways of saying things.'[39]

Black feminist criticism is a knotty issue, and while I have attempted to describe it, to call for clearer definition of its methodology, to offer warnings of its limitations, I await the day when Black feminist criticism will expand to embrace other modes of critical inquiry. In other words, I am philosophically opposed to what Annis Pratt calls 'methodolatry.' Wole Soyinka has offered one of the most cogent defenses against critical absolutism. He explains:

> The danger which a literary ideology poses is the act of consecration — and of course excommunication. Thanks to the tendency of the modern consumer-mind to facilitate digestion by putting in strict categories what are essentially fluid operations of the creative mind upon social and natural phenomena, the formulation of a literary ideology tends to congeal sooner or later into instant capsules which, administered also to the writer, may end by asphyxiating the creative process.[40]

Whether or not Black feminist criticism will or should remain a separatist enterprise is a debatable point. Black feminist critics ought to move from this issue to consider the specific language of Black women's literature, to describe the ways Black women writers employ literary devices in a distinct way, and to compare the way Black women writers create their own mythic structures. If they focus on these and other pertinent issues, Black feminist critics will have laid the cornerstone for a sound, thorough articulation of the Black feminist aesthetic.

NOTES

23   I am borrowing here from Kolodny who makes similar statements in 'Some Notes Defining a "Feminist Literary Criticism,"' p. 75.

24   Andrea Benton Rushing, 'Images of Black Women in Afro-American Poetry,' in *The Afro-American Woman: Struggles and Images*, ed. Sharon Harley and Rosalyn Terborg-Penn (Port Washington, NY: Kennikat Press, 1978), pp. 74 – 84. She argues that few of the stereotypic traits which Mary Ellmann describes in *Thinking About Women* 'seem appropriate to Afro-American images of black women.' See also her 'Images of Black Women in Modern African Poetry: An Overview,' in *Sturdy Black Bridges: Visions of Black Women in Literature* (New York: Anchor Press-Doubleday, 1979), pp. 18 – 24. Rushing argues similarly that Mary Ann Ferguson's categories of women (the submissive wife, the mother angel or 'mom,' the woman on a pedestal, for example) cannot be applied to Black women characters whose cultural imperatives are different from white women's.

25   *The Messenger*, 9 (April 1927), 109.

26   *The Messenger*, 5 (July 1923), 757.

27   Tillie Olsen, *Silences* (New York: Delacorte Press, 1978), p. 257.

28   Kolodny, 'Some Notes,' p. 89.

29   Robinson, 'Dwelling in Decencies: Radical Criticism and the Feminist Perspectives,' in *Feminist Criticism*, ed. Cheryl Brown and Karen Olson (New Jersey: The Scarecrow Press, 1978), p. 34.

30   For a discussion of Toni Morrison's frustrated female artists see Renita Weems, 'Artists Without Art Form: A Look at One Black Woman's World of Unrevered Black Women,' *Conditions: Five*, 2 (Autumn 1979), 48 – 58. See also Alice Walker's classic essay, 'In Search of Our Mothers' Gardens,' *Ms.*, May 1974, for a discussion of Black women's creativity in general.

31   Toni Morrison, *The Bluest Eye* (New York: Pocket Books—Simon and Schuster, 1970), pp. 88—89.
32   Toni Morrison, *Sula* (New York: Bantam Books, 1980), p. 105.
33   Kolodny, 'Some Notes on Defining a "Feminist Literary Criticism,"' p. 86.
34   In an NEH Summer Seminar at Yale University, Summer 1980, Carolyn Naylor of Santa Clara University suggested this to me.
35   For a discussion of this idea see Michael G. Cooke, 'The Descent into the Underworld and Modern Black Fiction,' *Iowa Review*, 5 (Fall 1974), 72—90.
36   Mary Helen Washington, *Midnight Birds* (Garden City, NY: Anchor Press-Doubleday, 1980), p. 43.
37   Washington, p. xvii.
38   See Saundra Towns, 'The Black Woman as Whore: Genesis of the Myth,' *The Black Position*, 3 (1974), 39—59, and Sylvia Keady, 'Richard Wright's Women Characters and Inequality,' *Black American Literature Forum*, 10 (1976), 124—128, for example.
39   'The Politics of Intimacy: A Discussion,' in *Sturdy Black Bridges*, p. 88.
40   Wole Soyinka, *Myth, Literature and the African World* (London: Cambridge University Press, 1976), p. 61.

CHERI REGISTER
'American Feminist Literary Criticism:
A Bibliographical Introduction', *Feminist Literary Criticism*

Can feminists establish themselves as objective literary critics, given their political orientation?

The opponents of Phallic Criticism doubt whether any form of criticism can be truly objective; methods that appear to be non-ideological are actually supporting the status quo.[57] Nancy Hoffman thinks it not only impossible, but even undesirable, to create a feminist criticism that is totally objective. Her classroom method integrates objective distance and emotional involvement.[58] Feminist critics recognize that theirs is a specialized, highly political type of analysis, only one of many to which literature might be subjected. There are, however, varying opinions about feminist criticism's place in the spectrum that ranges between ivory tower academism and political activism. Lillian Robinson speaks from the political end:

> Some people are trying to make an honest woman out of the feminist critic, to claim that every "worthwhile" department should stock one. I am not terribly interested in whether feminism becomes a respectable part of academic criticism; I am very much concerned that feminist critics become a useful part of the women's movement.[59]

Because of its origin in the women's liberation movement, feminist criticism values literature that is of some use to the movement. Prescriptive Criticism, then, is best defined in terms of the ways in which literature can serve the cause of liberation. To earn feminist approval, literature must perform one or more of the following functions: (1) serve as a forum for women; (2) help to achieve cultural androgyny; (3) provide role-models; (4) promote sisterhood; and (5) augment consciousness-raising. I would like to discuss these functions one by one.

In order to be useful as a *forum*, literature must allow forthright and honest self-expression, writing which is not constrained by pre-existing standards that may be alien to female culture. Virginia Woolf's first directive to female writers was: 'Above all, you must illumine your own soul with its profundities and its shallows, and its vanities and its generosities, and say what your beauty means to you or your plainness.' She regretted that the female author of the nineteenth century wrote with 'a mind which was slightly pulled from the straight, and made to alter its clear vision in deference to external authority.'[60] Ellen Morgan renews Woolf's advice: 'Feminist criticism should, I believe, encourage an art true to women's experience and not filtered through a male perspective or constricted to fit male standards.'[61] On the other hand, authors should not feel obligated to offer an exact representation of their own lives, but rather 'the fictional myths *growing out of their lives* and told by themselves for themselves.'[62] The arts must help people understand what female experience is, 'what it's like, what you think, how it operates. What it feels like to be us.'[63] Before literature can begin to perform the other functions, however, it must express female experience authentically, in all its variety. The emphasis on variety is apparent in the course syllabi in the *Female Studies* series. The works selected represent various ages, classes, and races of women. Tillie Olsen's 'Women: A List Out of Which to Read,' which appears in cumulative fashion in the *Women's Studies Newsletter* (Old Westbury, New York: The Feminist Press), is an example of a growing tendency on the part of feminist critics and teachers to seek out materials that will compass the totality of the female life experience.

Once literature begins to serve as a forum, illuminating female experience, it can assist in humanizing and equilibrating the culture's value system, which has historically served predominantly male interests. That is, it can help to bring about *cultural androgyny*. Carolyn Heilbrun has reintroduced Woolf's 'androgyny' into the vocabulary of literary criticism in her book *Toward a Recognition of Androgyny* (New York: Alfred A. Knopf, 1973).[64] Other feminist critics agree that a 'female impulse' in literature is necessary for the achievement of cultural androgyny. Firestone expresses it succinctly: The 'development of "female" art . . . is progressive: an exploration of strictly female reality is a necessary step to correct the warp in a sexually biased culture. It is only after we have integrated the dark side of the moon into our world view that we can begin to talk seriously of universal culture.'[65] Of course, a pluralistic society like the one that exists in the United States must also draw on the experiences of its ethnic and regional groups if it is to be truly balanced.

Feminists often emphasize that they are not simply seeking more room for women in the present social order. They want a new social order founded on 'humanistic' values, some of which are traditionally 'female' and not respected in contemporary society. Those traditionally 'male' values that feminists believe harmful to the common good — excessive competition, for example — would be de-emphasized. Therefore, a female literary personage with 'masculine' characteristics does not necessarily meet with feminist approval. Ellen Harold, writing about Emma Peel, the heroine of 'The Avengers,' a British television series shown in the United States, comments: 'What is truly sad is that, though she is equal to a man and superior to most men, the measure of her competence is a strictly *macho* one — her capacity for violence. As an attempt at an emancipated woman she leaves something to be desired, for both men and women need new standards against which to measure themselves.'[66]

A literary work should provide *role-models*, instill a positive sense of feminine identity by portraying women who are 'self-actualizing, whose identities are not dependent on men.'[67] This function is particularly crucial in children's literature. In *Dick and Jane as Victims*, Women on Words and Images find fault with elementary school readers for reserving active mastery skills for boys — that is, creativity, ingenuity, adventurousness, curiosity, perseverance, bravery, autonomy — and describing girls as passive, docile, dependent, incompetent, and self-effacing. Adult women who are re-examining their lives may also depend on literature to introduce new possibilities and to help them evaluate the alternatives open to them. 'We cannot live in a certain way, we cannot see ourselves as the people we wish to be, until we perceive the wished-for life and self in our imaginations.'[68] To compensate for the dearth of satisfactory fictional role-models, feminist teachers are enlarging the definition of literature to include biography, autobiography, and memoirs. The syllabus for the Women's Biography Course offered at California State University in Sonoma illustrates the urgency of the search for role-models.[69]

It is important to note here that although female readers need literary models to emulate, characters should not be idealized beyond plausibility. The demand for authenticity supercedes all other requirements. Mary Anne Ferguson assigns works like Tillie Olsen's *Tell Me a Riddle* and Willa Cather's *My Antonia* to help her students 'realize that liberation involves hard choices; that it begins and ends with the self; that self-knowledge depends upon contact with the real world.'[70]

Literature should show women involved in activities that are not traditionally 'feminine,' to speed the dissolution of rigid sex roles. It is not enough, however, to simply place a female character in a new occupation, with no corresponding change in her personality and behavior. Marion Meade describes the effects of the women's liberation movement on television heroines: although a few series feature female doctors or lawyers or television producers, the women's behavior and their relationships with men follow the familiar stereotyped pattern. They are caricatures, not realistic women, she says.[71]

The feminist movement in America is seeking to create a feeling of *sisterhood*, a new sense of community among women, in order to overcome group self-hatred, the animosity that many women feel for others of their sex as a result of isolation, competition for male attention, and belief in female inferiority. Virginia Woolf noticed the dearth of gratifying woman-to-woman relationships in literature:

> "Chloe liked Olivia," I read. And then it struck me how immense a change was there. Chloe liked Olivia perhaps for the first time in literature. Cleopatra did not like Octavia. And how completely *Antony and Cleopatra* would have been altered had she done so! . . . All these relationships between women, I thought, rapidly recalling the splendid gallery of fictitious women, are too simple. So much has been left out, unattempted.[72]

In addition to testing new female-female (and female-male) relationships, a literary work can serve the cause of sisterhood by recounting experiences that the reader can identify as her own, experiences that are, perhaps, shared by many women. She will feel a common bond with the author and other readers who have similar reactions to the book. This is vital for adolescent readers, says Susan Koppelman Cornillon:

> We are all aware of the agony of adolescence in our culture, the evasive fumblings as we attempt to communicate about our fears and our needs and our anxieties without actually ever mentioning to anyone what they really are: the creation of elaborate private symbologies that enable us to grieve about our pimples, our sexual fantasies, our masturbation, the strange changes happening to our bodies. But boys outgrow this secretiveness soon — because there is a vast wealth of literature for them to stumble on, both great and popular, classical and contemporary, pious and lewd, that assures them that, indeed, they are normal. Or even better, their suffering is portrayed as a prerequisite for maturity, if not a prelude to greatness.[73]

Literature might also enable a reader to empathize with women whose subjective accounts of female reality differ from her own.

> Loving someone is wanting to know them. Insofar as we are able to learn and know of each other, we can acknowledge, and even in part assimilate into our own imaginative life, the thousand differences that have always been used as wedges to drive us apart. So that the experience of all women everywhere becomes, in a sense, our communal property, a heritage we bestow upon each other, the knowledge of what it has meant to be female, a woman in this man's world.[74]

In order to augment *consciousness-raising*, literature should provide realistic insights into female personality development, self-perception, interpersonal relationships, and other 'private' or 'internal' consequences of sexism. The reader can then note recurring problems and generalize from them with the aid of factual information about the status of women from other sources.[75] Feminist critics are far more concerned with exposing these private effects than with raising concrete issues, such as job discrimination and lack of child care facilities. In this age of mass communications, public forums, and official investigative committees, fiction is no longer the most effective means of arousing concern about measurable social problems. That is not to say that concrete political issues have no place in feminist-approved literature. But their presence must be consistent with the demands for authenticity and subjectivity prerequisite to an effective integration of the personal and the political. In disparaging didactic feminist poetry, Erica Jong noted, 'We all claim to believe that political oppression and personal feelings are related, and yet a great deal of the self-consciously polemical poetry that has come out of the Women's Movement reads like a generalized rant and it lacks any sort of psychological grounding. The poet has not really looked into herself and told it true. She has been content to echo simplistic slogans.'[76] Likewise, a fictional account of job discrimination that covers only the material consequences will not suffice. If the protagonist is, indeed, fully characterized, we will also see the private or psychic effects of discrimination. Ellen Morgan values a subtle rendering of both types of problems in which 'neo-feminist consciousness informs the novel as light informs a painting, rather than appearing as subject matter.'[77]

There is a precedent for this sort of personalized polemic in black literature. James Baldwin's novels are not single-issue tracts, but rather in-depth studies of individual examples of black humanity. Ralph Ellison's *Invisible Man* was successful not because it exposed conditions that were completely foreign to whites in America, but because it appealed to common, multiracial feelings of insignificance and alienation, showing how much more intense they are when institutionalized. Perhaps the difference between this and the muckraking and Socialist literatures of the early twentieth century is due to the fact that the victims have become the authors.[78]

Factual information about discrimination should be carefully integrated into a story with a larger focus, so that its presence seems natural. Joyce Nower warns, however, against condemning the author who merely translates position papers into fiction: 'A woman artist who writes a lousy story on a woman active in the Movement, or involved in getting an abortion, should be accorded the respect of critical appraisal: a lousy writer but important in that she is trying to use new materials.'[79] Ellen Morgan concurs: 'The capacity to teach and to delight which some of this work has would suggest that critical standards which deny literary legitimacy and value to [propagandistic] writing may be inadequate tools for [its] evaluation.'[80]

No feminist critic insists that a fictional work include political analysis.[81] The author need only describe the problems and offer some solutions, if the character herself can find them. The remaining tasks involved in consciousness-raising are left to the reader: to compare the problems encountered by female literary characters with her own, to explain similarities in terms of causes, and to decide on appropriate political action. Literature can thus augment the face-to-face consciousness-raising that is fundamental to the American women's liberation movement.

There is a potential conflict between the consciousness-raising function and the role-model function. A work that offers a thorough literary description of women's oppression may also feature a 'heroine' who is thoroughly oppressed and therefore unlikely to be emulated by female readers. Erica Jong, for one, is dissatisfied with 'all those so-called feminist novels in which women are depicted as helpless victims.'[82] The ideal feminist fictional work is one that fulfills all five functions in equilibrium. Rather than being driven to mental breakdown or suicide or immobility, the heroines of new feminist fiction will somehow manage to resist destruction, perhaps with the support and confidence of other women. Their outlook and behavior will presage a new social order that integrates the best aspects of 'female culture' with selected 'male' values.

NOTES

57 Lillian Robinson and Lise Vogel, 'Modernism and History,' *Images of Women in Fiction*, ed. Koppelman Cornillon, pp. 278—305; and Fraya Katz-Stoker, 'The Other Criticism: Feminism vs. Formalism,' ibid., pp. 313—25.

58 Hoffman, 'A Class of Our Own,' pp. 14—27.

59 Robinson, 'Dwelling in Decencies,' p. 889.

60 Woolf, *A Room of One's Own*, pp. 93, 77.

61 Ellen Morgan to author, February 13, 1972.

62 Russ, 'What Can a Heroine Do?' p. 19.

63 Millett, 'Notes on the Making of *Three Lives*,' p. 2.

64 See also Carolyn Heilbrun, 'The Masculine Wilderness of the American Novel,' *Saturday Review*, January 29, 1972, pp. 41—44.

65 Firestone, *Dialectic of Sex*, p. 167.

66 Harold, 'A Look at Some Old Favorites,' pp. 44—45.

67 Martin, 'The Feminine Mystique in American Fiction,' p. 33.

68 Michele Murray, 'Introduction' to *A House of Good Proportion, Images of Women in Literature*, ed. Murray (New York: Simon and Schuster, 1973), p. 19.

69 *Female Studies VII*, ed. Rosenfelt, pp. 82—85.

70 Quoted in Showalter, 'Introduction: Teaching about Women, 1971,' p. x.

71 Marion Meade, 'On the Trail of the Liberated TV Heroine,' *Aphra* 2 (Spring 1971): 30—34.

72 Woolf, *A Room of One's Own*, p. 86.

73 Susan Koppelman Cornillon, 'The Fiction of Fiction,' *Images of Women in Fiction*, ed. Koppelman Cornillon, p. 115.

74 Millett, 'Introduction' to 'Prostitution: A Quartet,' p. 23. See also Hoffman, 'A Class of Our Own.'

75 See Morgan's critique of Alix Kates Schulman, *Memoirs of an Ex-Prom Queen* (New York: Alfred A. Knopf, 1972) in 'Humanbecoming,' pp. 197—204.

76 Erica Jong, 'Visionary Anger' (a review of Adrienne Rich, *Diving Into the Wreck*) *Ms*, July 1973, p. 31.

77 Morgan, 'Humanbecoming,' p. 197.

78 For a discussion of this earlier literature see Walter B. Rideout, *The Radical Novel in the United States, 1900—1954: Some Interrelations of Literature and Society* (Cambridge: Harvard University Press, 1956).

79 Joyce Nower to author, March 7, 1972.

80 Morgan, 'Humanbecoming,' p. 187.

81 With the possible exception of Kate Millett. In *Sexual Politics*, p. 139, she criticizes Virginia Woolf for not explaining the causes of Rhoda's suicidal misery in *The Waves*, but in 'Notes on the Making of *Three Lives*,' written two years later, she says that she would now rather *express* female experience than analyze it.

82 Jong, 'Visionary Anger,' p. 34.

ELIZABETH BAINES
'Naming the Fictions'

Suddenly a new alter-ego entered my life: The Feminist Writer.

She had this thing about Truth: Since men's fiction had belied women's experience, then women's fiction must set the record straight.

Now indeed for me the whole point of making fictions — right back to my childhood imaginary friend — had been to counter social 'reality', to expose it as a construct, at best another fiction, at worst a downright lie. But could it be that the Feminist Writer was taking Fiction itself as a record of social reality?

I protested: The truth that Fiction seeks is *emotional* truth; Fiction is intuition, Fiction is dreams!

She countered: Look at that 'intuitive' first published story of yours, colonised by sexism: some dream!

The Left still mistrusts the unconscious, and it's not hard to see why. So the Feminist Writer valued writing that was *conscious*: we women should write consciously out of our gender; Virginia Woolf's notion of androgyny masks colonisation.

I had to agree. Male writers too, I thought, should acknowledge the limitations of their gender.

Ah, but the Feminist Writer wasn't interested in men. She held that, given that fundamentally we can write only out of our own experience, then in the name of honesty we have no business, any of us, representing the experience of the sex that isn't our own. She went further, she put it this way: we women must free ourselves of our traditional concern for the viewpoint of men; men have no *right* to concern themselves in literature with the viewpoint of women.

Well, now I was uneasy. I was beginning to understand about the need for women's space away from men who'd automatically dominate, but wasn't there a philosophical tangle somewhere here? Wasn't it men's ability to disregard the viewpoint of women that was what the patriarchal mess was all about anyway? Didn't this preclude two of the most important elements of Fiction — and indeed the most socially useful — imagination and empathy?

And here again was this concept of Fiction as testimony, confession or reportage. Being honest about who you are intellectually and emotionally had slipped over somehow into proving your credentials, proving your life matched up to your art (and I *thought* we'd all agreed how deceptive our real-life roles can be!).

But she insisted: Art doesn't exist outside life or society. She went on: We Feminist Writers are engaged *with others* in a process of social change. And then she breathed the magic phrase: *Collective Creativity.*

I was enchanted. The notion of a pooling of all our individual consciousnesses and unconsciousnesses, a democratic cross-fertilisation of visions and ideas — well, *that* would surely be a force for social change!

But as it turned out she didn't mean quite that, or only in theory. The Left, after all, finds it hard to trust the Fiction-writer. Such an embarrassingly private enterprise, shutting oneself up in a room, sometimes for six months to a year, without (or so it seems from the outside) reference or deference to anyone else! (As if the writer of fiction were not affected by collective creativity long before she puts pen to paper!) So self-centred, so ivory-tower-ish! Such crass arrogance to commit one's idiosyncratic subjectivity to paper for the rest of the world! It would be no surprise, would it, if the writer of fiction were at best colonised by imperialist and phallocentric thinking, or at worst actually the Enemy Within? So the writer's fiction must be carefully monitored, and if necessary brought into line with agreed reality.

Well, I had to consider this seriously. Of course I'd be glad to have my pernicious tendencies knocked out of me. Of course I'd have been glad not to have made the mistakes of that early story.

But I said, Hang on, writing for me has always been a *rebellion*, this feels too much like conforming. It denies me the fictional authority which has always for me been the whole point of writing!

She didn't like the word *authority*, associated as it was with the patriarch and the imperialist. In a word I'd condemned myself.

She said, Are you sure that what you've been striving for isn't a *phallus*?

Well, I felt dreadful. Really ashamed. Though I managed to whine: But it's all a matter of confidence. If you question my fictions, you damage my confidence, as the patriarchy once did, and I can't write at all without lots of confidence!

And I said, Isn't there also in what you're advocating a dangerous notion of a truer truth, a more objective reality? And isn't 'objectivity' the fallacy of the patriarch and the dictator? Isn't it *you*, after all, who are trading in the notion of a greater authority (than personal subjectivity)?

But she wasn't listening, she was describing ways in which we might improve our work to serve society. She said, Can't you do something about your literary *forms*? We need forms that are more recognisable; this job's too urgent for eccentricity or frills, we must get the message over in the simplest way possible.

I cried: But the form *is* the meaning! Remember, the accessible forms were the ones that couldn't say what we wanted to?

She said, No point in being radical if no-one understands you.

She went on to her next point: We need to create Positive Images.

Which was when I perked up and cried: Ah! So *you too* have dreams?

Well, she tried to deny it. She said she'd rather define it as seeing the need to show how we should live.

I said, *What*? You think that, having spent my whole writing life trying to escape other people's prescriptions for how I should behave, I'd now write conduct books for others?

She shifted her ground. She said, Well, we want to show that, in spite of what has been believed, women *are* positive.

But in fact I'd got her cornered. Within the terms of her own argument she was being inconsistent. She couldn't have it both ways — Fiction as record, *and* Fiction as vision. Not, that is, unless she recognised that the relation between Fiction and social reality is far more complex than she'd so far acknowledged.

ALISON LIGHT
'Feminism and the Literary Critic',
LTP: Journal of Literature, Teaching, Politics

Kate Millett's *Sexual Politics* (1970) was for me in many ways the starting point from which to move toward a feminist literary criticism. Crucially, Millett chose to use literary texts as the key source of illustrations for her arguments as to the dominant political organisation of all social formations, as casebook evidence, that is, for the development of a radical feminist theory of patriarchy. This theory in turn depended upon a particular notion of ideology and of the relation between literature and politics which has been extremely influential and has informed many other aspects of feminist discussion ever since.[1]

Sexual Politics attempts a far-reaching analysis of patriarchy, traced across cultures and history as the primary political institution, the expression of the distribution of political power according to an original sexual division of labour. Patriarchy is thus envisaged as the hierarchical institutionalisation of the unequal roles and status given to the two biological genders — 'the birthright priority whereby male rules females' (Millett, 1972 edition, p. 25). Ideology then is posited as the system of ideas and values which works to maintain the psychological, emotional, and social consent of the State's subjects to such a form of government. It is a kind of conditioning agent which, like the family in Millett's analysis, 'mediating between the individual and the social structure' (p. 33), is both a mirror and a restatement of the ways in which patriarchy functions to degrade and subordinate the female. Patriarchal ideology ensures the socialisation of individuals according to already given and thus 'stereotyped lines of sex category' (p. 26). It promotes, and elsewhere in Millett's text often *is*, the false consciousness which works continually to misrepresent women and their lives.

Consequently for Millett, literature, together with all other cultural products of this patriarchal consciousness, is proposed as ideological because it teaches, amongst other things, the acceptance of those sex roles. Male writers, by virtue of their gender, must reproduce the sexual politics of the real world in the little worlds of their fiction. Thus, in her section 'The Literary Reflection', Millett takes four twentieth century authors: Lawrence, Miller, Mailer, and Genet to provide her with 'instances of sexual description' (p. 23) which she sees as merely reproducing the normative values of a patriarchal sexual politics.

The task of the feminist critic becomes, as Millett demonstrates with her full scholarly apparatus, a matter of the exposure of that 'sexism' which will have been expressed with different amounts of force in every literary text. The acts of reading and criticising are seen in terms either of a succumbing to or a resisting of the ideological onslaughts of the text; the feminist literary critic, as cultural revolutionary, then, works to free the text from its ideological burden, leaving both the work and the author liberated, able at last to be properly acclaimed as examples of 'distinguished moral and intellectual integrity' (p. xii).

But Millett's polemic begs many questions, questions which I was beginning to ask myself, in a fairly untheorised way, when I started my postgraduate course. What for example would happen if different authors were chosen, those for whom, like Joyce and Forster, an exploration of female consciousness was central to their narratives? Where is history in Millett's account — either in relation to the ideas of sexuality she sees expressed in a text, or in terms of the developing literary genre itself? How indeed, since Millett only looks at novels, would other genres be accessible to this analysis, especially those which don't produce a coherent narrative at all? And what about the meaning of sexuality in different texts by the same authors? Of course Millett's choice of authors was a particularly loaded one, but even so wasn't it possible to produce different readings of the same novels she discusses?

In fact my first reading of *Sexual Politics* was not as a feminist, but as a budding (and suitably pompous) literary critic in the sixth form. I used Millett as another, decidedly eccentric, authority on *Sons and Lovers*, my A level text. Against her insistence on seeing the novel as Lawrence's autobiography, and the arrogant Paul Morel as simply his mouthpiece, I had scrawled exasperated comments in the margin — 'But we see this!' and 'Lawrence shows us!' In my own reading at seventeen I identified desperately with Miriam, and contrived to reject Paul even though I was well aware that I was often reading against the grain. My objections, however, point to my recognition that if Lawrence *is* Paul, he is also Paul's mother and girl-friends, and if, as Millett does, we take their part, we haven't somehow escaped Lawrence but exposed the way in which novels, as constructs of the imagination, might be attempts at 'ungendering', and, however unsuccessful, at dispersing or even at transgressing the gendered experience of an author and its usual restraints. I suspected that it was these displacements, contradictions, and tensions which I enjoyed in following a narrative — but in any case Millett's analysis brought me no nearer to understanding where the pleasure, which I took to be the main motivation in reading, lay.

Further, in seeing each text as autobiography, Millett of course needs the authoritative narrative voice which she finds in her narrowly-selected authors. Ironically Millett is here aligned with much traditional literary criticism, and she leaves the literary establishment free to continue to scapegoat such authors as fanatical exceptions to the rule of 'objective' genius, without having to examine its own practice.

Millett's position, with its stress on literature as a straight reflection of ideology, it appeared, necessarily left little room for the specifically literary at all. There is no discussion of what the demands of writing may be, of how one text is read and written through another, or of how reading, writing, and criticising, as different activities, are situated in history and — as Millett's own feminism suggests — engaged with differently by different individuals or groups. For Millett finally resists the logic of her own intervention, and, in exposing the false consensus of earlier readings, wants not a plurality of readings but to replace an incorrect patriarchal reading with one 'more' correct and equally prescriptive. Far from her readings opening out and liberating the reader, criticism operates as a mode of gaining access and control, an appropriation of an incontrovertible, but this time 'feminist', truth.

The dissatisfaction I felt with a feminist literary criticism which focused on an exposure of sexist ideology as content involved, at least in part, a sense of the dependence of Millett's radical feminist politics upon those very established values and categories — whether sexual, social, or literary — which it was attempting to subvert. Millett's emphasis on an unmediated ideology functioning as a reflex of State power, her slippage towards biologistic definitions of gender positions, her refusal of the literary where it might engage with a notion of the unconscious, were not simply produced by a radical feminist politics, but were — and still are — necessary and mutually supportive parts of the whole package.

Feminism to me, and especially my experience of consciousness-raising, meant precisely that socialisation, whether into femininity or masculinity, was never successfully achieved, and it was this possibility of unconscious resistance which gave room for political mobilisation. Women's (and men's) relation to any ideology was lived in the midst of contradictions — ideology was not a blanket of ignorance thrown over the heads of fully conscious and grown human beings.

Millett's cultural politics, on the other hand, seemed to me to keep both culture and politics the property of the enlightened few. For if the text is ideology's dupe, and the feminist critic its only hope, where does that leave the rest of us ordinary women in the struggle for a cultural politics? In Millett's programme we can only go back to 'the limited role allotted to the female' which 'tends to arrest her at the level of biological experience' (p. 26). Not surprisingly then there are few women's voices in Kate Millett's *Sexual Politics*, except, of course, her own.

It's only fair to say that my re-reading of Millett last year left me feeling pained and confused, since however unsatisfactory I felt her textual analyses to be, they were in a crucial way infinitely preferable to all those of traditional literary criticism: they validated my anger as a feminist, they recognised that as a woman I had been relegated, misrepresented, and often excluded by 'culture', and that some kind of struggle around the practices of art and literary criticism was possible. And it needs to be remembered that this culture and its dominant values were being forcefully asserted elsewhere in the university. Indeed, if I found the prospect of three years spent league-tabling authors a profoundly depressing one, that had as much to do with my own attachment to the concepts of Art and Genius, to the universalizing values of literary criticism, as with a dislike of the feminist strategy itself. I was afraid to take on my 'cultural heritage'. As a feminist my pleasure in these authors could never be the same again, but I had no way of using that sense of alienation, no way of making it productive, trapped as I was inside the standards of a literary criticism which made me feel at best 'original' and at worst highly 'subjective'.

NOTE

1   For an extended discussion of this see Cora Kaplan, 'Radical Feminism and Literature: Rethinking Millett's *Sexual Politics*', *Red Letters*, No. 9 (1979).

CORA KAPLAN
'Speaking/Writing/Feminism', *On Gender and Writing*

In the early stages of thinking about women and writing I had, in common with other feminists, talked mostly about the ways in which women were denied access to something I have called 'full' subjectivity. While any term so abstract evokes more meaning than it can possibly contain in a given context, what I was working towards was a description of a position within culture where women could, without impediment, exist as speaking subjects. I now think that this way of posing the question of writing/speaking and subjectivity is misleading. It assumes, for instance, that *men* write from a realised and realisable autonomy in which they are, in fact, not fantasy, the conscious, constant and triumphant sources of the meanings they produce. This assumption is part of an unreconstructed romantic definition of the poet as it was most eloquently expressed in Wordsworth's 1800 introduction to *Lyrical Balllads.* Here the poet has a universalised access to experience of all kinds, feels things more deeply, and expresses those feelings 'recollected in tranquillity' for all men. It did not take much thought to point out how difficult it was for women to appropriate this romantic definition of genius and transcendence, given the contemporary restraints on their experience and the contempt in which their gender-specific feelings were held. A more interesting question was about the status of the definition itself which even today has enormous currency within traditional literary criticism. How far was it an ideological fiction? In what sense could any writing or writer — widen the thing defined, the romantics did — any *actor* in history *be* that romantic subject? For if one were to accept a modern re-working of the romantic definition of the creative process, then as a feminist 'full subjectivity' would become a political goal for feminism, as well as a precondition for all acts of struggle and intervention, writing included.

   In the last few years I have come round to a very different perspective on the problem, drawn from Marxist and feminist appropriations of psycho-analytic and structuralist theories, but confirmed, I think, by my own and other women's fragmented experience of writing and identity. Rather than approach women's difficulty in positioning themselves as writers as a question of barred access to some durable psychic state to which all humans should and can aspire, we might instead see their experience as foregrounding the inherently unstable and split character of all human subjectivity. Within contemporary western culture the act of writing and the romantic ideologies of individual agency and power are tightly bound together, although that which is written frequently resists and exposes this unity of the self as ideology. At both the psychic and social level, always intertwined, women's subordinate place within culture makes them less able to embrace or be held by romantic individualism with all its pleasures and dangers. The instability of 'femininity' as female identity is a specific instability, an eccentric relation to the construction of sexual difference, but it also points to the fractured and fluctuant condition of all consciously held identity, the impossibility of a will-full, unified and cohered subject.

Romantic ideologies of the subject suppress this crucial and potentially hopeful incoherence, or make its absence a sign of weakness and thus an occasion for mourning or reparation. Feminism has been caught up far too often in this elegiac mood, even when on other fronts it has mounted an impressive critique of Western rationalism as a phallocratic discourse of power. One option within feminism to combat the seeming weakness which inheres in women's split subjectivity has been to reassert an economy of control, to deny the constant effect of unconscious processes in utterance and practice, and to pose an unproblematic rationalism for women themselves, a feminist psyche in control of femininity. For myself, this avenue is closed, if only because it makes me feel so demoralised, a not-good-enough feminist as I was a not-good-enough daughter. I would rather see subjectivity as always in process and contradiction, even female subjectivity, structured, divided and denigrated through the matrices of sexual difference. I see this understanding as part of a more optimistic political scenario than the ones I have been part of, one that can and ought to lead to a politics which will no longer overvalue control, rationality and individual power, and which, instead, tries to understand human desire, struggle and agency as they are mobilised through a more complicated, less finished and less heroic psychic schema.

ELIZABETH WILSON
Mirror Writing: An Autobiography

I did not enter the women's movement in search of an identity. Political activity simply presented itself to me as an imperative and as an escape, a liberation from the privatised obsessions of the search for identity.

The radical movements of the late sixties and of the seventies did, though, raise the question of personal identity in a way no political movement had raised it before. Earlier socialists may have tried to raise questions of the personal life, but only now was a culture already saturated with the individualism of popularised psychotherapies awaiting the revolution of everyday life. Changed consciousness had become a necessary part of revolutionary change.

Yet this heightened and fractured sense of individual identity — a key feature of modern Western culture — which charged the radical movements with power, has also acted as a brake upon them. For it has become ever more chancy for revolutionaries to rely on the once powerful appeal of solidarity with a class or group. We failed to develop a collective subjectivity.

Feminists found this too. At first it seemed enough for women to speak out. If they did this, they would find themselves, and find themselves together. Many of the journals and books of the movement have names that suggest this, for instance *Women's Voice — Another Voice — Call to Women*, and if there is a typical literary form of feminism it is the fragmented, intimate form of confessional, personal testimony, autobiography, the diary, 'telling it like it was'.

The idea that women need only throw off their oppression for a 'real' self to appear is, nonetheless, oversimplified. Can we really say that our socially constructed 'feminine' identity is merely a husk to be discarded as we bite into the kernel, or a chrysalis the butterfly breaks out of? Women have spoken out, have given testimony as if the 'truth' of their experiences were transparent and straightforward. But — is it?

Feminists have turned to testimonies written by women who were not or could not be part of any movement. In many such testimonies a woman's identity is built, initially at least, out of pain and suffering, out of false experience. We thrill, as if someone had drawn the edge of a razor across our flesh, to the way in which Jean Rhys tears off a layer of skin to reveal her raw experience as victim of male cruelty and indifference. We sink towards madness with Doris Lessing at the pain of that same cruelty turned on women who dare to be 'free'. Kate Millett tells of the same pain, which she hoped to escape in the women's movement, but which returned to torment her from within feminism itself.

Some women speak of the moment of optimism when at last they have thrown off the role of victim and martyr. Some go further still in finding a new identity in the women's movement.

Yet women are offered only a collective identity 'in the movement'. A new identity is assumed but remains amorphously within 'sisterhood'. The 'movement' is a vague, formless conception of the celebration of womenness, an essence of womanhood; sometimes it is described as an endless dance in which women-loving-women sing as they circle in the weaving hand-in-hand of an embrace of all by all in which all individuality, all difference — all identity — is dissolved. Anja Meulenbelt writes of this moment:

> I dance in the crowd to the witch music . . . Or just look, at women whom I have begun to find so beautiful, who dance close together in couples, who dance in groups, with swinging hair and shining eyes, proud of what they are. Grown-up and now stronger than those people who had no need to fight oppression. I am in love, I think, with a species . . . I dance with old friends and new ones, my body supple . . . I feel beautiful among women, am beautiful . . . It is as if I have come home . . . Back in mother's arms . . .[8]

Thus have women tried to construct a collective identity out of a shared experience of collective oppression. For many women, the moment of commitment to the women's movement must also have seemed like the birth of a new *individual* identity: 'I am a feminist.' Yet an emphasis on the moment of collective identification, although necessary, is not enough. It can become static. It does not develop the idea of identity as process, and it also in a curious way is blind to what each of us *as an individual* brings with us into the movement. For all its emphasis on the truth of experience, it ignores — although perhaps necessarily in seeking a basis for solidarity and sisterhood — our sense of individuality and of an unique past, an unique self.

Yet we carry this unique identity forward with us in the movement, after the moment of collective identification. What comes after the moment when we say: 'I am a feminist'? How do we develop a collective subjectivity that allows for difference and diversity?

Feminists have written an enormous amount about stereotypic constructions of 'femininity'. There has also been a popular stereotypic construction of 'feminist' (dungarees — no make-up — hates men — angry). But what do those feminists do who reject equally both these images from the dominant culture? Perhaps, instead of dwelling so obsessively on how femininity gets inside our heads, feminists should have thought more about how to construct a plurality of positive images of women. As it is, women have fallen back on to the notion of the 'strong woman'. But however good it is to be strong, we feel ambivalent about the strong, powerful woman, since this too is an image that allows for no moment of weakness, and cannot reflect the diversity and complexity of our desires. Women who have sought to identify with 'strong women' in the movement have sometimes been so disappointed when these turned out not to be super-human after all that they have even turned against feminism itself.

This is a form of romanticism. The contemporary radical sexual liberation movements were supposed to be grounded in a rejection of romanticism. Yet the rejection of romanticism at the individual level, at the level of personalised romantic love, was over-emphasised at the expense of any real examination of political romanticism — the longing for utopias and reconstructed selves, and the longing for the pure, revolutionary moment. That political romanticism can easily give way to a 'left wing melancholy' which stresses the inescapable awfulness of the 'society of the spectacle', our destiny as victims, the impossibility of escape.

Even more dangerously, in hard times we seek out 'my identity' not in the clamour of revolutionary affirmation on the streets, but in the cover of small, enclosed spaces. We seek it, if we are lucky, in the haunts of the new hedonism, in the hushed hour of the analytic couch, in the jacuzzi baths, in the cult of the body beautiful, in the discos and restaurants of the glittering metropolis — Manhattan heaven. If we are less privileged we may seek it in the harsh consolation of cult churches or even in the rhetoric of fascism with its deliberate, seductive elevation of the irrational, its call to the unconscious. Socialist and revolutionary movements seem somehow to have lost their ability to give the individual an enhanced identity within the powerful safety of the movement. They have come to be seen, all too often, as a submission to conformity, which is the opposite of what they were intended to be.

Feminists and radicals need some powerful sense of identity as both collective and individualised. There is not one tyrannical identity to which all must approximate, but a group insistence on the value of difference. The testimony of consciousness raising, and of those 'women's' literary forms of diary, autobiography and confession, do not suggest an identical experience of the world, although the testimony has made possible the identification of points of similarity which have formed the basis for collective politics.

NOTE

8   Meulenbelt, Anja (1980) *The Shame is Over* (London: The Women's Press).

ANNETTE KOLODNY
'Dancing Through the Minefield: Some Observations on the Theory, Practice and Politics of a Feminist Literary Criticism', *Feminist Studies*

What distinguishes our work from those similarly oriented 'social conscious-ness' critiques, it is said, is its lack of systematic coherence. Pitted against, for example, psychoanalytic or Marxist readings, which owe a decisive share of their persuasiveness to their apparent internal consistency as a system, the aggregate of feminist literary criticism appears woefully deficient in system, and painfully lacking in program. It is, in fact, from all quarters, the most telling defect alleged against us, the most explosive threat in the minefield. And my own earlier observation that, as of 1976, feminist literary criticism appeared 'more like a set of interchangeable strategies than any coherent school or shared goal orientation,' has been taken by some as an indictment, by others as a statement of impatience. Neither was intended. I felt then, as I do now, that this would 'prove both its strength *and* its weakness,'[48] in the sense that the apparent disarray would leave us vulnerable to the kind of objection I've just alluded to; while the fact of our diversity would finally place us securely where, all along, we should have been: camped out, on the far side of the minefield, with the other pluralists and pluralisms.

In our heart of hearts, of course, most critics are really structuralists (whether or not they accept the label) because what we are seeking are patterns (or structures) that can order and explain the otherwise inchoate; thus, we invent, or believe we discover, relational patternings in the texts we read which promise transcendence from difficulty and perplexity to clarity and coherence. But, as I've tried to argue in these pages, to the imputed 'truth' or 'accuracy' of these findings, the feminist must oppose the painfully obvious truism that what is attended to in a literary work, and hence what is reported about it, is often determined not so much by the work itself as by the critical technique or aesthetic criteria through which it is filtered or, rather, read and decoded. All the feminist is asserting, then, is her own equivalent right to liberate new (and perhaps different) significances from these same texts; and, at the same time, her right to choose which features of a text she takes as relevant because she is, after all, asking new and different questions of it. In the process, she claims neither definitiveness nor structural completeness for her different readings and reading systems, but only their usefulness in recognizing the particular achievements of woman-as-author and their applicability in conscientiously decoding woman-as-sign.

That these alternate foci of critical attentiveness will render alternate readings or interpretations of the same text — even among feminists — should be no cause for alarm. Such developments illustrate only the pluralist contention that, 'in approaching a text of any complexity . . . the reader must choose to emphasize certain aspects which seem to him crucial' and that, 'in fact, the variety of readings which we have for many works is a function of the selection of crucial aspects made by a variety of readers.' Robert Scholes, from whom I've been quoting, goes so far as to assert that 'there is no single "right" reading for any complex literary work,' and, following the Russian formalist school, he observes that 'we do not speak of readings that are simply true or false, but of readings that are more or less rich, strategies that are more or less appropriate.'[49] Because those who share the term 'feminist' nonetheless practice a diversity of critical strategies, leading, in some cases, to quite different readings, we must acknowledge among ourselves that sister critics, 'having chosen to tell a different story, may in their interpretation identify different aspects of the meanings conveyed by the same passage.'[50]

Adopting a 'pluralist' label does not mean, however, that we cease to disagree; it means only that we entertain the possibility that different readings, even of the same text, may be differently useful, even illuminating, within different contexts of inquiry. It means, in effect, that we enter a dialectical process of examining, testing, even trying out the contexts — be they prior critical assumptions or explicitly stated ideological stances (or some combination of the two) — that led to the disparate readings. Not all will be equally acceptable to every one of us, of course, and even those prior assumptions or ideologies that are acceptable may call for further refinement and/or clarification. But, at the very least, because we will have grappled with the assumptions that led to it, we will be better able to articulate *why* we find a particular reading or interpretation adequate or inadequate. This kind of dialectical process, moreover, not only makes us more fully aware of what criticism is, and how it functions; it also gives us access to its future possibilities, making us conscious, as R. P. Blackmur put it, 'of what we have done,' 'of what can be done next, or done again,'[51] or, I would add, of what can be done differently. To put it still another way: just because we will no longer tolerate the specifically sexist omissions and oversights of earlier critical schools and methods does not mean that, in their stead, we must establish our own 'party line.'

In my view, our purpose is not and should not be the formulation of any single reading method or potentially procrustean set of critical procedures nor, even less, the generation of prescriptive categories for some dreamed-of nonsexist literary canon.[52] Instead, as I see it, our task is to initiate nothing less than a playful pluralism, responsive to the possibilities of multiple critical schools and methods, but captive of none, recognizing that the many tools needed for our analysis will necessarily be largely inherited and only partly of our own making. Only by employing a plurality of methods will we protect ourselves from the temptation of so oversimplifying any text — and especially those particularly offensive to us — that we render ourselves unresponsive to what Scholes has called 'its various systems of meaning and their interaction.'[53] Any text we deem worthy of our critical attention is usually, after all, a locus of many and varied kinds of (personal, thematic, stylistic, structural, rhetorical, etc.) relationships. So, whether we tend to treat a text as a *mimesis*, in which words are taken to be recreating or representing viable worlds; or whether we prefer to treat a text as a kind of equation of communication, in which decipherable messages are passed from writers to readers; and whether we locate meaning as inherent in the text, the act of reading, or in some collaboration between reader and text — whatever our predilection, let us not generate from it a straitjacket that limits the scope of possible analysis. Rather, let us generate an ongoing dialogue of competing potential possibilities — among feminists and, as well, between feminist and nonfeminist critics.

The difficulty of what I describe does not escape me. The very idea of pluralism seems to threaten a kind of chaos for the future of literary inquiry while, at the same time, it seems to deny the hope of establishing some basic conceptual model which can organize all data — the hope which always begins any analytical exercise. My effort here, however, has been to demonstrate the essential delusions that inform such objections: If literary inquiry has historically escaped chaos by establishing canons, then it has only substituted one mode of arbitrary action for another — and, in this case, at the expense of half the population. And if feminists openly acknowledge ourselves as pluralists, then we do not give up the search for patterns of opposition and connection — probably the basis of thinking itself; what we give up is simply the arrogance of claiming that our work is either exhaustive or definitive. (It is, after all, the identical arrogance we are asking our nonfeminist colleagues to abandon.) If this kind of pluralism appears to threaten both the present coherence of and the inherited aesthetic criteria for a canon of 'greats,' then, as I have earlier argued, it is precisely that threat which, alone, can free us from the prejudices, the strictures, and the blind spots of the past. In feminist hands, I would add, it is less a threat than a promise.

What unites and repeatedly invigorates feminist literary criticism, then, is neither dogma nor method, but, as I have indicated earlier, an acute and impassioned *attentiveness* to the ways in which primarily male structures of power are inscribed (or encoded) within our literary inheritance; the consequences of that encoding for women — as characters, as readers, and as writers; and, with that, a shared analytic *concern* for the implications of that encoding not only for a better understanding of the past, but also for an improved reordering of the present and future as well. If that *concern* identifies feminist literary criticism as one of the many academic arms of the larger women's movement, then that *attentiveness*, within the halls of academe, poses no less a challenge for change, generating, as it does, the three propositions explored here. The critical pluralism that inevitably follows upon those three propositions, however, bears little resemblance to what Robinson has called 'the greatest bourgeois theme of all, the myth of pluralism, with its consequent rejection of ideological commitment as "too simple" to embrace the (necessarily complex) truth.'[54] Only ideological commitment could have gotten us to enter the minefield, putting in jeopardy our careers and our livelihood. Only the power of ideology to transform our conceptual worlds, and the inspiration of that ideology to liberate long-suppressed energies and emotions, can account for our willingness to take on critical tasks that, in an earlier decade, would have been 'abandoned in despair or apathy.'[55] The fact of differences among us proves only that, despite our shared commitments, we have nonetheless refused to shy away from complexity, preferring rather to openly disagree than to give up either intellectual honesty or hard-won insights.

Finally, I would argue, pluralism informs feminist literary inquiry not simply as a description of what already exists but, more importantly, as the only critical stance consistent with the current status of the larger women's movement. Segmented and variously focused, the different women's organizations neither espouse any single system of analysis nor, as a result, express any wholly shared, consistently articulated ideology. The ensuing loss in effective organization and political clout is a serious one, but it has not been paralyzing; in spite of our differences, we have united to *act* in areas of clear mutual concern (the push for the Equal Rights Amendment is probably the most obvious example). The trade-off, as I see it, has made possible an ongoing and educative dialectic of analysis and proferred solutions, protecting us thereby from the inviting traps of reductionism and dogma. And so long as this dialogue remains active, both our politics and our criticism will be free of dogma — but never, I hope, of feminist ideology, in all its variety. For, 'whatever else ideologies may be — projections of unacknowledged fears, disguises for ulterior motives, phatic expressions of group solidarity' (and the women's movement, to date, has certainly been all of these, and more) — whatever ideologies express, they are, as Geertz astutely observes, 'most distinctively, maps of problematic social reality and matrices for the creation of collective conscience.' And despite the fact that 'ideological advocates . . . tend as much to obscure as to clarify the true nature of the problems involved,' as Geertz notes, 'they at least call attention to their existence and, by polarizing issues, make continued neglect more difficult. Without Marxist attack, there would have been no labor reform; without Black Nationalists, no deliberate speed.'[56] Without Seneca Falls, I would add, no enfranchisement of women, and without 'consciousness raising,' no feminist literary criticism nor, even less, women's studies.

NOTES

48 Annette Kolodny, 'Literary Criticism,' Review Essay in *Signs 2*, no. 2 (Winter 1976): 420.
49 Scholes, *Structuralism in Literature*, p. 144—45. These comments appear within his explication of Tzvetan Todorov's theory of reading.
50 I borrow this concise phrasing of pluralistic modesty from M. H. Abrams's 'The Deconstructive Angel,' *Critical Inquiry* 3, no. 3 (Spring 1977): 427. Indications of the pluralism that was to mark feminist inquiry were to be found in the diversity of essays collected by Susan Koppelman Cornillon for her early and ground-breaking anthology, *Images of Women in Fiction: Feminist Perspectives* (Bowling Green, Ohio: Bowling Green University Popular Press, 1972).
51 R. P. Blackmur, 'A Burden for Critics,' *The Hudson Review* 1 (1948): 171. Blackmur, of course, was referring to the way in which criticism makes us unconscious of how art functions; I use his wording here because I am arguing that that same awareness must also be focused on the critical act itself. 'Consciousness,' he avers, 'is the way we feel the critic's burden.'
52 I have earlier elaborated my objection to prescriptive categories for literature in 'The Feminist as Literary Critic,' Critical Response in *Critical Inquiry* 2, no. 4 (Summer 1976): 827—28.
53 Scholes, *Structuralism in Literature*, pp. 151—52.
54 Lillian Robinson, 'Dwelling in Decencies: Radical Criticism and the Feminist Perspective,' *College English* 32, no. 8 (May 1971); reprinted in *Sex, Class, and Culture*, p. 11.
55 'Ideology bridges the emotional gap between things as they are and as one would have them be, thus insuring the performance of roles that might otherwise be abandoned in despair or apathy,' comments Geertz in 'Ideology as a Cultural System,' p. 205.
56 Ibid., p. 205, 220.

ELAINE SHOWALTER
'Towards a Feminist Poetics',
Women Writing and Writing About Women

The Feminist Critique: Hardy

Let us take briefly as an example of the way a feminist critique might proceed, Thomas Hardy's *The Mayor of Casterbridge*, which begins with the famous scene of the drunken Michael Henchard selling his wife and infant daughter for five guineas at a country fair. In his study of Hardy, Irving Howe has praised the brilliance and power of this opening scene:

> To shake loose from one's wife; to discard that drooping rag of a woman, with her mute complaints and maddening passivity; to escape not by a slinking abandonment but through the public sale of her body to a stranger, as horses are sold at a fair; and thus to wrest, through sheer amoral wilfulness, a second

chance out of life — it is with this stroke, so insidiously attractive to male fantasy, that *The Mayor of Casterbridge* begins.[8]

It is obvious that a woman, unless she has been indoctrinated into being very deeply identified indeed with male culture, will have a different experience of this scene. I quote Howe first to indicate how the fantasies of the male critic distort the text; for Hardy tells us very little about the relationship of Michael and Susan Henchard, and what we see in the early scenes does not suggest that she is drooping, complaining or passive. Her role, however, is a passive one; severely constrained by her womanhood, and further burdened by her child, there is no way that *she* can wrest a second chance out of life. She cannot master events, but only accommodate herself to them.

What Howe, like other male critics of Hardy, conveniently overlooks about the novel is that Henchard sells not only his wife but his child, a child who can only be female. Patriarchal societies do not readily sell their sons, but their daughters are all for sale sooner or later. Hardy wished to make the sale of the daughter emphatic and central; in early drafts of the novel Henchard has two daughters and sells only one, but Hardy revised to make it clearer that Henchard is symbolically selling his entire share in the world of women. Having severed his bonds with this female community of love and loyalty, Henchard has chosen to live in the male community, to define his human relationships by the male code of paternity, money and legal contract. His tragedy lies in realising the inadequacy of this system, and in his inability to repossess the loving bonds he comes desperately to need.

The emotional centre of *The Mayor of Casterbridge* is neither Henchard's relationship to his wife, nor his superficial romance with Lucetta Templeman, but his slow appreciation of the strength and dignity of his wife's daughter, Elizabeth-Jane. Like the other women in the book, she is governed by her own heart — man-made laws are not important to her until she is taught by Henchard himself to value legality, paternity, external definitions, and thus in the end to reject him. A self-proclaimed 'woman-hater', a man who has felt at best a 'supercilious pity' for womankind, Henchard is humbled and 'unmanned' by the collapse of his own virile façade, the loss of his mayor's chain, his master's authority, his father's rights. But in Henchard's alleged weakness and 'womanishness', breaking through in moments of tenderness, Hardy is really showing us the man at his best. Thus Hardy's female characters in *The Mayor of Casterbridge*, as in his other novels, are somewhat idealised and melancholy projections of a repressed male self.

As we see in this analysis, one of the problems of the feminist critique is that it is male-oriented. If we study stereotypes of women, the sexism of male critics, and the limited roles women play in literary history, we are not learning what women have felt and experienced, but only what men have thought women should be. In some fields of specialisation, this may require a long apprenticeship to the male theoretician, whether he be Althusser, Barthes, Macherey or Lacan; and then an application of the theory of signs or myths or the unconscious to male texts or films. The temporal and intellectual investment one makes in such a process increases resistance to questioning it, and to seeing its historical and ideological boundaries. The critique also has a tendency to naturalise women's victimisation, by making it the inevitable and obsessive topic of discussion. One sees, moreover, in works like Elizabeth Hardwick's *Seduction and Betrayal*, the bittersweet moral distinctions the critic makes between women merely betrayed by men, like Hetty in *Adam Bede*, and the heroines who make careers out of betrayal, like Hester Prynne in *The Scarlet Letter*. This comes dangerously close to a celebration of the opportunities of victimisation, the seduction *of* betrayal.[9]

Gynocritics and Female Culture

In contrast to this angry or loving fixation on male literature, the programme of gynocritics is to construct a female framework for the analysis of women's literature, to develop new models based on the study of female experience, rather than to adapt male models and theories. Gynocritics begins at the point when we free ourselves from the linear absolutes of male literary history, stop trying to fit women between the lines of the male tradition, and focus instead on the newly visible world of female culture. This is comparable to the ethnographer's effort to render the experience of the 'muted' female half of a society, which is described in Shirley Ardener's collection, *Perceiving Women*.[10] Gynocritics is related to feminist research in history, anthropology, psychology and sociology, all of which have developed hypotheses of a female subculture including not only the ascribed status, and the internalised constructs of femininity, but also the occupations, interactions and consciousness of women. Anthropologists study the female subculture in the relationships between women, as mothers, daughters, sisters and friends; in sexuality, reproduction and ideas about the body; and in rites of initiation and passage, purification ceremonies, myths and taboos. Michelle Rosaldo writes in *Woman, Culture, and Society*,

> the very symbolic and social conceptions that appear to set women apart and to circumscribe their activities may be used by women as a basis for female solidarity and worth. When men live apart from women, they in fact cannot control them, and unwittingly they may provide them with the symbols and social resources on which to build a society of their own.[11]

Thus in some women's literature, feminine values penetrate and undermine the masculine systems which contain them; and women have imaginatively engaged the myths of the Amazons, and the fantasies of a separate female society, in genres from Victorian poetry to contemporary science fiction.

In the past two years, pioneering work by four young American feminist scholars has given us some new ways to interpret the culture of nineteenth-century American women, and the literature which was its primary expressive form. Carroll Smith-Rosenberg's essay 'The Female World of Love and Ritual' examines several archives of letters between women, and outlines the homosocial emotional world of the nineteenth century. Nancy Cott's *The Bonds of Womanhood: Woman's Sphere in New England*

1780—1835 explores the paradox of a cultural bondage, a legacy of pain and submission, which none the less generates a sisterly solidarity, a bond of shared experience, loyalty and compassion. Ann Douglas's ambitious book, *The Feminization of American Culture*, boldly locates the genesis of American mass culture in the sentimental literature of women and clergymen, two allied and 'disestablished' post-industrial groups. These three are social historians; but Nina Auerbach's *Communities of Women: An Idea in Fiction* seeks the bonds of womanhood in women's literature, ranging from the matriarchal households of Louisa May Alcott and Mrs Gaskell to the women's schools and colleges of Dorothy Sayers, Sylvia Plath and Muriel Spark. Historical and literary studies like these, based on English women, are badly needed; and the manuscript and archival sources for them are both abundant and untouched.[12]

NOTES

8 Irving Howe, *Thomas Hardy* (London, 1968), p. 84. For a more detailed discussion of this problem, see my essay 'The Unmanning of the Mayor of Casterbridge' in Dale Kramer (ed.), *Critical Approaches to Hardy* (London, 1979).

9 Elizabeth Hardwick, *Seduction and Betrayal* (New York, 1974).

10 Shirley Ardener (ed.), *Perceiving Women* (London, 1975).

11 'Women, Culture, and Society: A Theoretical Overview' in Louise Lamphere and Michelle Rosaldo (eds.), *Women, Culture and Society* (Stanford, 1974), p. 39.

12 Carroll Smith-Rosenberg, 'The Female World of Love and Ritual: Relations Between Women in Nineteenth-Century America', *Signs: Journal of Women in Culture and Society*, vol. 1 (Autumn 1975), pp. 1—30; Nancy Cott, *The Bonds of Womanhood* (New Haven, 1977); Ann Douglas, *The Feminization of American Culture* (New York, 1977); Nina Auerbach, *Communities of Women* (Cambridge, Mass., 1978).

TORIL MOI

Sexual/Textual Politics: Feminist Literary Theory

Arguing that feminist criticism is a fundamentally 'suspicious' approach to literature, Kolodny sees the principal task of the feminist critic as that of examining the validity of our aesthetic judgments: 'What ends do those judgments serve, the feminist asks; and what conceptions of the world or ideological stances do they (even if unwittingly) help to perpetuate?' (15). This is surely one of her most valuable insights.

The problem arises when she proceeds from this to a wholesale recommendation of *pluralism* as the appropriate feminist stance. Feminist criticism lacks systematic coherence, she argues, and this fact ('the fact of our diversity'), should 'place us securely where, all along, we should have been: camped out, on the far side of the minefield, with the other pluralists and pluralisms' (17). Feminists cannot and indeed should not provide that 'internal consistency as a system' that Kolodny ascribes to psychoanalysis and Marxism. In her discourse, these two theoretical formations come to figure as monolithically oppressive blocks towering over the diversified, anti-authoritarian feminist field. But it is not only untrue that Marxism and psychoanalysis offer such a unified theoretical field; it is also surely doubtful that feminist criticism is *that* diversified.[2] Kolodny acknowledges that feminist politics is the basis for feminist criticism; so that though we may argue over what constitutes proper feminist politics and theory, that debate nevertheless takes place within a feminist political framework, much like debates within contemporary Marxism. Without common political ground, there can simply be no recognizable *feminist* criticism. In this context, Kolodny's 'pluralist' approach risks throwing the baby out with the bathwater:

> Adopting a "pluralist" label does not mean, however, that we cease to disagree; it means only that we entertain the possibility that different readings, even of the same text, may be differently useful, even illuminating, within different contexts of inquiry.
>
> (18)

But if we wax pluralistic enough to acknowledge the feminist position as just one among many 'useful' approaches, we also implicitly grant the most 'masculinist' of criticism the right of existence: it just *might* be 'useful' in a very different context from ours.

Kolodny's intervention in the theoretical debate pays too little attention to the role of politics in critical theory. When she states, correctly, that 'If feminist criticism calls anything into question, it must be that dog-eared myth of intellectual neutrality' (21), she still seems not to recognize that even critical theory carries with it its own political implications. Feminist criticism cannot just

> initiate nothing less than a playful pluralism, responsive to the possibilities of multiple critical schools and methods, but captive of none, recognizing that the many tools needed for our analysis will necessarily be largely inherited and only partly of our own making.
>
> (19)

Feminists must surely also conduct a political and theoretical evaluation of the various methods and tools on offer, to make sure that they don't backfire on us.

[. . .]

In the first article, Showalter distinguishes between two forms of feminist criticism. The first type is concerned with woman as reader, which Showalter labels 'feminist critique'. The second type deals with woman as writer, and Showalter calls this 'gynocritics'. 'Feminist critique' deals with works by male authors, and Showalter tells us that this form of criticism is a 'historically grounded inquiry which probes the ideological assumptions of literary phenomena' (25). This sort of 'suspicious' approach to the literary text seems however to be largely absent from Showalter's second category, since among the primary concerns of 'gynocritics' we find 'the history, themes, genres and structures of literature by women' as well as the 'psychodynamics of female creativity' and 'studies of particular writers and works' (25). There is no indication here that the feminist critic concerned with women as writers should bring other than sympathetic, identity seeking approaches to bear on works written by women. The 'hermeneutics of suspicion', which assumes that the text is not, or not only, what it pretends to be, and therefore searches for underlying contradictions and conflicts as well as absences and silences in the text, seems to be reserved for texts written by men. The feminist critic, in other words, must realize that the woman-produced text will occupy a totally different status from the 'male' text.

Showalter writes:

> One of the problems of the feminist critique is that it is male-oriented. If we study stereotypes of women, the sexism of male critics, and the limited roles women play in literary history, we are not learning what women have felt and experienced, but only what men have thought women should be.
>
> (27)

The implication is not only that the feminist critic should turn to 'gynocritics', the study of women's writings, precisely in order to learn 'what women have felt and experienced', but also that this experience is directly available in the texts written by women. The text, in other words, has disappeared, or become the transparent medium through which 'experience' can be seized. This view of texts as transmitting authentic 'human' experience is, as we have seen, a traditional emphasis of Western patriarchal humanism. In Showalter's case, this humanist position is also tinged by a good portion of empiricism. She rejects theory as a male invention that apparently can only be used on men's texts (27−8). 'Gynocritics' frees itself from pandering to male values and seeks to 'focus . . . on the newly visible world of female culture' (28). This search for the 'muted' female culture can best be carried out by applying anthropological theories to the female author and her work: 'Gynocritics is related to feminist research in history, anthropology, psychology and sociology, all of which have developed hypotheses of a female subculture' (28). The feminist critic, in other words, should attend to historical, anthropological, psychological and sociological aspects of the 'female' text; in short, it would seem, to everything but the text as a signifying process. The only influences Showalter appears to recognize as constitutive of the text are of an empirical, extra-literary sort. This attitude, coupled with her fear of 'male' theory and general appeal to 'human' experience, has the unfortunate effect of drawing her perilously close to the male critical hierarchy whose patriarchal values she opposes.

NOTE

2 Lukács, Brecht, Stalin, Trotsky, Benjamin, Gramsci and Althusser are all considered Marxists, and psychoanalysis comprises names as divergent as Freud, Adler, Jung, Reich, Horney, Fromm, Klein and Lacan.

MARXIST-FEMINIST LITERATURE COLLECTIVE
'Women's Writing: "Jane Eyre", "Shirley", "Villette", "Aurora Leigh"', 1848: The Sociology of Literature

Who Are We?

This paper arises from the work of a group which has been meeting in London for one and a half years (though some of its members joined more recently). It was presented at the Conference by the whole Collective, whose members at the time were Cheris Kramer, Cora Kaplan, Helen Taylor, Jean Radford, Jennifer Joseph, Margaret Williamson, Maud Ellmann, Mary Jacobus, Michèle Barrett and Rebecca O'Rourke.

The cumbersome title — Marxist-feminist Literature Collective — covers (or perhaps conceals), on one side of the hyphen — in the adjective 'Marxist' — a diversity of positions in relation to Marxism. On the other side of the hyphen, the adjective 'feminist' points, among other things, to an important aspect of our practice. A major contribution of the women's movement has been the organisational principle of collective work; for all of us, the method of work within the group has been a departure from and a challenge to the isolated, individualistic ways in which we operate in academic spheres. Our paper, in its polylogic structure and presentation, draws on the continuing play of ideas and debate from within which we speak, and challenges the monologic discourse of patriarchal literary criticism.

Theoretical Introduction

A Marxist-feminist critical practice proposes to account for the inadequacies of a standard Marxist approach to literature and ultimately to transform this approach. In this paper we discuss the articulation of class and gender in terms both of the historical conjuncture of 1848 and of the problems of a Marxist-feminist method in theorising literature. Literary texts are assumed to be ideological in the sense that they cannot give us a knowledge of the social formation; but they do give us something of equal importance in analysing culture, an imaginary representation of real relations.

A Marxist-feminist approach, by focussing on gender as a crucial determinant of literary production, can provide a better understanding of literature as a gender differentiated signifying practice. This is not to privilege gender over class, but to challenge the tradition in which women's writing has often been hived off from the mainstream of male writing and criticism.

Both Marxism and feminism have rightly taken considerable interests recently in the possibility of an integration between Marxist and psycho-analytic thought. Both Marxism and psychoanalysis propose their methods as exhaustive; but we argue that it is only through a synthesis of these two, problematic though that is, that we can unfold the crucial inter-dependence between class structure and patriarchy.

Lukacs argued that coherent literary works could only be produced by a unified, ascending social class, and in this context he stressed 1848 as the date at which the bourgeoisie as a class and realism as a literary form began to decline. The limitations of this approach are notorious, and too numerous to list here. What we shall do is not only, using the ideas of Jacques Lacan, Pierre Macherey and others, analyse the incoherences and contradictions in the texts we discuss, but also relate these precisely to the marginal position of female literary practice in this period.

Central to our analysis of these texts is a recognition of the marginality of their authors to the public discourse of mid-nineteenth century society. The partial exclusion of women from the public literary world is one aspect of the general marginality of women in this period, as instanced by their exclusion from the exercise of political power and their separation from production. This congruence between the marginality of women writers and the general position of women in society is represented in the situation of many female characters in the texts.

The period of protest which culminated in the political events of the 1840s marked the transition from a manufacturing economy to the industrial capitalist mode of production — developments which had serious consequences for women and the family. Working-class women were drafted into production as a source of cheap labour; bourgeois women remained in the home and were separated from production. In both cases women were excluded from ownership of the means of production, distribution and exchange.

However, the inadequacy of a solely economic mode of analysis is shown by Engels' optimistic claim in 1884, that because of working-class women's entry into the industrial labour process, '. . . the last remnants of male domination in the proletarian home have lost all foundation'.[1] It is clearly necessary also to analyse the contemporary ideological formation in terms of the hegemony of patriarchal attitudes. Such attitudes are represented for example in the double standard of sexual morality, whereby women were either madonnas or whores, and middle-class women in particular were subject to the constraints of the ideology of domesticity and the angel in the house. The ideology of romantic love, while masking the economic basis of bourgeois marriage in this period as the exchange of women, shows by its persistence that it exists autonomously, independent of its specific economic functions in a given historical conjuncture.

The four texts under consideration foreground these questions. *Jane Eyre* (1847), *Shirley* (1849), *Villette* (1853), and *Aurora Leigh* (1857), can be read as a discussion of gender definition, kinship structures, and to some extent the relation between these and social class. The texts of Charlotte Brontë and Elizabeth Barrett Browning refuse to reproduce contemporary economic and ideological determinations; instead they represent a systematic 'evasion' or interrogation of the 'Law' of these determinations. Althusser has stressed its inescapability: 'The Law cannot be "ignored" by anyone, least of all by those ignorant of it, but may be evaded or violated by everyone. . .'.[2]

We argue that this 'evasion' of the law occurs in the texts in the inter-related areas of social class, kinship and Oedipal socialisation. The necessary connections between these three areas are represented in the texts' presentation of two key points of articulation — the institution of marriage and the role of the *pater familias.*

All the major female characters of the texts have an extremely marginal and unstable class position, and all display an obvious discrepancy between their class position and their alleged rightful status; their status is bourgeois, but they are all orphans and most of them are without financial independence. Comparing these texts with those of Jane Austen, the lack of determinacy of class background is striking.

The bourgeois kinship structure of the period, predicated on the exchange of women, is similarly evaded. None of the heroines have fathers present to give them away in marriage. More importantly, we can analyse marriage itself as the crucial point of articulation between class and kinship structures. This can be seen in two ways: on one hand, the only women in the texts who are free to exercise choice in marrying — Jane Eyre, Aurora Leigh, Shirley and Polly de Bassompierre — have, or miraculously acquire, some degree of financial independence. On the other hand, the example of Caroline Helstone demonstrates with great force the law which Charlotte Brontë otherwise evades, in that her marriage to Robert Moore can only take place when the repeal of the Orders in Council has enabled him to be a successful capitalist. Without this repeal, he would have emigrated to Canada and she would have been an Old Maid!

The evasion of Oedipal determination, so crucial to gender definition in this period, will be discussed in more detail in its most striking manifestation, in *Aurora Leigh.* But in all these texts the devised absence of the father represents a triple evasion of all the areas we have so far mentioned — class structure, kinship structure and Oedipal socialisation. Its consequences are that there is no father from whom the bourgeois woman can inherit property, no father to exchange her in marriage, and no father to create the condition for typical Oedipal socialisation.

The subversiveness of this evasion was recognised by contemporary reviewers, for in 1848 Lady Eastlake wrote in the *Quarterly Review*:

> We do not hesitate to say that the tone of mind and thought which has overthrown authority and violated every code human and divine abroad, and festered chartism and rebellion at home, is the same which has also written *Jane Eyre.*[3]

In discussing literary texts, it is important to look at the way women's access to language is ideologically determined. One of the effects of the lack of access to education of which women writers complain is to exclude them from the discourses of institutions such as universities, law, politics and finance which structure their oppression. Women, who are speaking subjects but partially excluded from culture, find modes of expression which the hegemonic discourse cannot integrate. Whereas the eruptive word cannot make the culturally inaccessible accessible, it can surely speak its absence. Kristeva has classified these modes of expression as 'semiotic' as opposed to 'symbolic'.

Inevitably, the work of Kristeva has been considered for its obvious bearing on our analysis. Her notion of the semiotic comprised the repressed, pre-linguistic elements which are located in the tonal, rhythmic, expressive and gestural qualities of poetic discourse. In our view, her association of these qualities with the feminine is fallacious; she has used a cultural ascription of femininity to describe pre-linguistic elements which are in fact universal, and she thus risks privileging and feminising the irrational. But as we all know, intuition is still the short-change given women by the patriarchy. Not only are there limitations from a feminist perspective, but by culling the feminine, or the semiotic, subversive, she formulates an anarchic revolutionary poetics which is politically unsatisfactory. Her argument, seductive as it is, idealises and romanticises the discursive ruptures of the avant-garde. Her failure to locate these notions historically also tends to eternalise the social exaggerations of biological difference. Nevertheless, her suggestive writings have polyphonic resonances in our work, which alludes to, sometimes even dwells on, the explosive and temporarily liberating dissonances within the texts.

NOTES

1   F. Engels, *The Origins of the Family, Private Property and the State* Pathfinder, New York, 1972, p. 80.
2   L. Althusser, 'Freud and Lacan' in *Lenin and Philosophy and Other Essays* New Left Books, London, 1975, p. 195.
3   Lady Eastlake, review of *Jane Eyre, Quarterly Review*, Vol LXXXIV, December 1848, p. 174. Quoted in J. Stern, 'Women and the Novel' in *Women's Liberation Review*, No. 1, October 1972.

TORIL MOI
'Sexual/Textual Politics', *The Politics of Theory*

From this short account of feminist theory, one can draw one important conclusion: there is no specific feminist literary criticism if by this one understands some sort of method or approach which should be inherently and exclusively feminist. There is no method or theoretical approach used in feminist criticism which is not also used or usable by non-feminist critics. The problem for feminist critics is to find out which theories and methods are compatible with a feminist stance and which are not, and as we have seen I believe that for instance the humanist empiricism examined in the first part of this paper is an example of such incompatibility.

The aims of feminist criticism are or should be revolutionary. It is politics, the opposition to patriarchy and sexism in all its forms, which gives feminist criticism its specificity. This feminist commitment necessarily also entails the opposition to the exploitative, hierarchical and authoritarian structures of capitalism, and this is why feminist criticism is and must be a revolutionary form of criticism. It is because Kristeva tries to theorize the revolutionary potential of women and not because she is a semiotician that she can be considered a feminist critic. The problem for the Anglo-American feminist critic resides in the contradiction between their strong political position and the inherently reactionary literary theory they also practise and defend.

A further example of the reactionary consequences of the identity-seeking humanist reading is to be found in the absence of any challenge to the concept of literature in the Anglo-American tradition. Where the French have substituted texts or 'writing' for literature and are sceptical about the ideological implications of the word 'literature', the Anglo-American feminists do not seem to preceive this as a problem. This is all the more grievous since the general conventions for deciding what is literary have always excluded women's writings as best they could — as they have excluded working-class writers. Nursery rhymes, fairy tales, children's books, popular romantic literature — the majority of such texts have been written by women and none has been found worthy of full 'literary' status.

Feminist theory and practice have, as we have seen, deconstructed the opposition between literature and non-literature, between canon and non-canon, but even this is not enough. It is also necessary to deconstruct the hierarchical opposition between author and reader and between text and reader. This has long been seen as an important practical task in the women's movement. Though feminist criticism has its background and its main source of inspiration in the women's movement, it has not always followed up the lead given by the movement on this point. The women's movement has always seen cultural oppression as an important part of patriarchal oppression as a whole, and through many practical activities it has challenged established notions of what culture is and how it is produced: writers' workshops, street theatre, collective art-work and exhibitions have questioned the whole established dichotomy between active producer and passive consumer of texts and other cultural products. Anglo-American feminist criticism has on the whole decided not to notice this development and has therefore lost out on the possibility of participating in and influencing feminist cultural practice. The French feminists have not only encouraged feminist creative practices (through for instance the magazine *des femmes en mouvements* published by *des femmes*), but they have also taken advantage of existing textual theory to deconstruct the opposition between producer and consumer of texts and other cultural practices. They have extended the notion of text to cover all signifying practices from political theatre to the representation of women in advertisements and the language of fashion. Literature is only one category in this spectrum, and as we have seen, not even necessarily the best defined and the most privileged one.

In textual terms both Kristeva, Cixous and others (like for instance Roland Barthes) have stressed the importance of the concept of *jouissance*. For Kristeva and Cixous *jouissance* is what happens when writing becomes pulsional pleasure linked to the presence of the *chora* (Kristeva) or the mother's body (Cixous). And for Barthes, *jouissance* is what the *reader* experiences when producing or possibly re-producing precisely the kind of text which suspends the bland certainties of the ego dominated by the symbolic order. And so in the last instance it is impossible to distinguish between the productive *jouissance* of the writer, the *jouissance* of the text and the productive *jouissance* of the reader: the hierarchy between these terms has been broken down.

The situation, then, is this: On the one hand we have in France an active and energetic development of feminist theory concerned with female creativity and textual production. On the other hand we have the strong, politically committed institutional critique developed in the Anglo-American tradition. The French often seem to forget about the historical and social aspects of women's oppression, whereas the Anglo-Americans cling in the main to a reactionary humanist empiricism and refuse to see problems of textual theory as relevant for feminist criticism. The French have done very little work in the field of literary criticism and cultural studies, while the Anglo-Americans have flooded the academic market with empirical and empiricist literary studies. It is our task now to take feminist criticism one step further and transform it into the politically committed and the theoretically highly developed criticism it clearly has the potential to become.

5

Do Women Write Differently?

INTRODUCTION

Three American Responses

The first three extracts in this chapter — all by American women — illustrate three classic positions in the debate about whether women write differently from men. Joyce Carol Oates appeals for an individual style, for a sexless writing, beyond definitions of 'male' and 'female'. To have a 'male' or 'female' style is 'symptomatic of inferior art' where the female style might degenerate into mere propaganda on women's issues. Against this Oates offers what is, at root, an idealist view of literature as the expression of an individual authorial voice which 'transcends' the material and the political, 'even while being fueled by them'. At the same time she realizes, with resignation, that a 'sex-determined voice' is probably the best that criticism will offer the woman writer.

Ellen Moers, looking at the use of bird metaphors in women's writing, concludes that there *is* something distinctive in the way women writers have used certain images. The tendency in Moers's argument is to see a link between particular metaphors and the social and historical position of women writers and women characters: so, given what we know of the restricted life-style of middle-class women in the nineteenth century, the caged bird metaphor in *Jane Eyre* is appropriate — almost predictable. But what is confusing in Moers's writing is the interchangeable use she makes of the terms 'feminine' and 'female'. The recurrent references in women's writing to 'the little hard nut, the living stone' constitute 'a feminine metaphor'; the caged bird metaphor 'truly deserves the adjective female'.[1] The convention in feminist writing has been to use 'feminine' to refer to the cultural construction of women and 'female' to refer to biology. So, while women have no choice but to be female, they do not have to be feminine. Though it generally appears that Moers is talking about culture rather than biology, there are occasions when her use of 'female' instead of 'feminine' suggests that she is attributing to women some innate propensity to certain images or forms of language. This confusion of terminology poses a particular problem in understanding French feminist writing since the adjective *féminin* can mean both 'female' and 'feminine'.[2]

Moers's method of textual analysis, searching for distinctive imagery, tones or stylistic devices, has been a common one in American criticism. Feminists involved in this work do not feel that they are in pursuit of 'inferior art' (Oates). On the contrary, they look upon the search for a female style as a further stage in uncovering a female tradition, in exploring the interconnections between women writers, and in establishing the methodology which Elaine Showalter terms 'gynocritics'. They are eager to find conclusive similarities in women's writing but reluctant to make extravagant claims; their work often contends that we need more stylistic analysis to really substantiate any proposition.[3] But there is no indication that criticism will ever discern a definitive female style. The differences between women writers always seem to outnumber the similarities. Moreover, there is no way of knowing whether the common factors are due to the writers' sex, their shared class or racial background, the demands of the literary form they all employ, or to any one of a dozen other factors. As Annette Kolodny warns, the thesis can operate as a self-fulfilling prophecy. If the explicit aim is to find stylistic similarities in women's writing, it is not surprising if, in that mass of material, some similarities are actually discovered.[4]

Mary Ellmann offers a different approach. She does not write of 'male' and 'female' but of 'masculine' and 'feminine' modes of writing, characterizing the 'masculine' in terms of an authority apparently absent in the so-called 'feminine'. Crucially, she presents this masculine voice as not necessarily the prerogative of the male writer, nor is the feminine voice possible only for women. Thus, in Simone de Beauvoir she discovers an adherence to the tone of authority, which disappoints her, but in Norman Mailer, a delightful exhilarating abuse of it. It is in the writing which expresses the 'disruption of authority' or the 'disruption of the rational' that Ellmann finds the characteristics of 'what were previously considered feminine habits of thought'; there is an advantage, therefore, in the woman writer allying herself with 'a literature at odds with authority'. Rashness, daring, mockery, 'sudden alternations of the reckless and the sly, the wildly voluble and the laconic' are the stylistic qualities that can undercut the 'established masculine mode' — and are, of course, precisely the qualities which Ellmann's own writing embodies.

The Semiotic and the Avant-garde

In several ways Ellmann's remarks foreshadow contemporary French feminist theory. Her interest in 'the "sex" of the writing', as Toril Moi expresses it, rather than the sex of the author, would accord with Terry Eagleton's comments on the work of Julia Kristeva and her concept of the 'semiotic'. 'The semiotic is thus closely connected with femininity: but it is by no means a language exclusive to women. . . .'. Similarly, the feminine is 'a mode of being and discourse not necessarily identical with women'. Mary Jacobus asserts that feminists should not advocate 'a return to a specifically feminine linguistic domain which in fact marks the place of women's oppression and confinement'. Hélène Cixous, quoted by Moi, rejects the very term 'feminine writing'. Finally, Stephen Heath firmly declares:

> There is no essential male or female language, immediate and inevitable, determined by the sex.[5]

Yet, at the same time, these critics believe that feminine writing — that is, writing 'attempting to break the dominance of the inscription of . . . male positions' (Heath) — is more likely to come from women. Cixous points to 'historico-cultural reasons'; Heath claims that 'the force of their experience' will provoke such writing; Eagleton speaks of 'complex psychoanalytical reasons', while Kristeva privileges the link between the semiotic and the close contact between the child and the mother's body.

Secondly, Ellmann's interest in the feminine as a playfulness, an irony or an excess which displaces authority and the rational, echoes the description of the semiotic as 'a means of undermining the symbolic order' (Eagleton), and as the 'pleasurable and rupturing aspects of language' which can become part of a subversive political challenge (Jacobus). In this connection the French theorists have looked to avant-garde writers whose work illustrates a decentring and questioning of fixed meanings; most of the writers they have considered, however, are male. They offer their analysis not as a turning away from women but as a route to women; Kristeva, for instance, writes that the 'modern breaks with tradition and the development of new forms of discourse are harmonious with the women's cause'.[6] Not all feminists would agree. The movement of the theory from a denial of women's distinctive language, to the claim that they are more likely than men to write in a feminine style, to textual examples of femininity that largely focus on male writers has evoked suspicion from some critics. Once again, it seems, women have disappeared from the centre of attention to be replaced by the male author. Elaine Showalter laments the loss of 'the experience of women' and specifically states that seeking women 'in history, in anthropology, in psychology, and in ourselves' must precede any attempt to locate 'the feminine not-said, in the manner of Pierre Macherey, by probing the fissures of the female text'[7] — a position which Kristeva dismisses as 'if not sentimentalism, at least romanticism'.[8]

Furthermore, there is no reason to think that the unsettling of meaning is necessarily going to promote a feminist future. 'It is quite possible for a text to do this in the name of some right-wing irrationalism, or to do it in the name of nothing much at all' (Eagleton). Juliet Mitchell asks why Kristeva and her colleagues 'choose exclusively masculine texts and quite often proto-fascist writings as well';[9] and Gayatri Chakravorty Spivak, confirming another of Eagleton's points, remarks that 'even if one knows how to undo identities, one does not necessarily escape the historical determination of sexism'.[10] On the other hand, if we do accept a link between a disruptive movement in books we read and a revolutionary disruption in the whole social order, we need to understand the relationship between those two elements. How do we move from one to the other and how does the struggle of some women with language connect with the struggle of other women in their work place or against domestic violence?

The Case of Virginia Woolf

The English-speaking woman writer who is most frequently discussed with reference to sexual difference in writing is Virginia Woolf, though anyone looking to her work for some decisive answer will be disappointed. At one moment she tells us that 'it is fatal for anyone who writes to think of their sex', and criticizes Charlotte Brontë for so emphatically expressing personal needs and grievances in her writing, while praising Shakespeare for his mind which is 'incandescent, unimpeded'.[11] With her next breath, however, she commends Jane Austen and Emily Brontë for writing 'as women write, not as men write',[12] makes reference to 'a woman's sentence' and 'the psychological sentence of the feminine gender', and asserts that the sex of the author is transparent in 'the first words in which either a man or a woman is described'. Thus her first set of comments accords with Joyce Carol Oates's views; there is the same wish to avoid propagandizing, to establish writing as a genderless art rather than a partial and spurious special pleading. Yet the second set of comments indicates that Woolf sees a marked sexual difference in writing, and is willing to discuss the stylistic differences between male and female writers and the particular awareness and perceptions of the woman writer.

Michèle Barrett is wary that Woolf's appeal to difference could lead to essentialism, to the opinion that there are 'intrinsic differences between the male and the female author in terms of the language they use'. Barrett wants to see Woolf's position as 'a social rather than a biological or psychological one'. But, in so doing, she glides over the contradictions in Woolf's writing, making it appear more consistent than it actually is. Barrett interprets Woolf's references to difference as solely about subject-matter, and related to 'the different social experience of women'. Yet the quotation Barrett uses — from Woolf's review of a book on women novelists — does more to disprove her case than support it. Even in the section Barrett quotes it is not clear that Woolf *is* talking about subject-matter; the fact that men may write about war and women about childbirth is swiftly dismissed. Moreover, what Barrett does not quote is the end of Woolf's paragraph where she mentions as needing consideration a series of other differences — 'the difference between the man's and the woman's view of what constitutes the importance of any subject', 'marked differences of plot and incident', and 'infinite differences in selection, method and style'.[13]

Neither Stephen Heath nor Mary Jacobus attempts to resolve the contradictions in Woolf's writing; for them it is precisely the points of inconsistency or tension that they find most illuminating. Despite all Woolf's assertions to the contrary, Heath believes her language unconsciously betrays 'the meshes of sex'. In the passage he analyses, Woolf writes from a male-defined position, 'caught up in a web of words and images and ways of writing that bring with them a position, a sexual stance, a certain representation'. Conversely, what provokes Jacobus is the 'recuperation of feminist energy' in another passage from *A Room of One's Own*. Woolf in her critique of the 'excesses' of Charlotte Brontë brings into her own book 'a point of instability which unsettles her own urbane and polished decorum'. Female desire, female anger, what cannot and should not be said suddenly surfaces, at once questioning the nature of fiction and authorial control, and exhibiting the power of writing to destabilize.

The Problems of Difference

When Virginia Woolf refers to Dorothy Richardson's sentence as 'of a more elastic fibre than the old, capable of stretching to the extreme, of suspending the frailest particles, of enveloping the vaguest shapes', her aim is to valorize the difference she perceives. As noted above, Barrett has indicated the dangers of essentialism in this viewpoint. Heath suggests another problem:

> To lay the emphasis on difference and the specificity of women (as of men) in the paradigm male/female is a gesture within the terms of the existing system, for which, precisely, women are different *from* men.

In extolling the female, the woman writer does not break the pattern of patriarchal binary though whereby the female is defined in relation to the male. According to binary thinking the male constitutes the norm, the positive, and the superior; the female is the aberration, the negative, the inferior. Her difference, as Mary Jacobus comments, is 'defined as lack', the difference of not being male. Even to praise the female is still 'a gesture within the terms of the existing system'.

Difference as binary opposition is largely acceptable to the dominant order. Indeed, there is a long tradition of reactionary argument which enthusiastically discusses sexual difference in language. At its best, this tradition will label women's language as subjective, emotional or impressionistic; at its worst, as bitchy or gossip, marked by the inconsequential. The implicit rider to this definition is that 'male' language is authoritative, rational, appropriate for serious public platforms, and that if women wish to improve their position, then they must become adept in the use of this language. Yet despite this, Heath does see the potential for a progressive politics in 'the appeal to difference'. In certain specific situations, it 'can be a powerful and necessary mode of struggle and action, can take the force of an alternative representation', and 'can clearly become important as a basis for movement and challenge and transformation'.

Mary Jacobus is concerned with another meaning of difference — female difference not as lack but as 'Otherness'. Femininity is 'the repressed term by which discourse is made possible', what Julia Kristeva refers to as the semiotic. Difference in this sense is not restricted to the opposition of male and female; it is 'not bonded by any system or any structure' but is 'an authentic difference set outside of the established system'.[14] It seeks to subvert fixed, unitary meanings in favour of plurality and diversity, 'the

multiplicity, joyousness and heterogeneity which is that of textuality itself'
(Jacobus).

The passage from Hélène Cixous — and Toril Moi's commentary on her
work — illustrates such an approach to difference. As Moi demonstrates,
Cixous's concepts of 'feminine writing', 'writing as différance', and the 'other
bisexuality', all interrelate: feminine texts 'work on the difference', the other
bisexuality 'doesn't annul differences, but stirs them up, pursues them,
increases them', while writing is 'infinitely dynamized by an incessant
process of exchange from one subject to another'. Cixous stresses the notion
of movement, abundance and openness. There is an expansive, jubilant
creativity when she speaks of 'infinite richness' or the 'inexhaustible' or
'luminous torrents'. Far from the feminine being defined in relation to the
masculine, it is, in Cixous's terms, that which escapes being 'theorized,
enclosed, coded'.

Writing the Body

What is also clear in Cixous's passage is the connection she draws between,
on the one hand, the feminine practice of writing and, on the other, the
female body and desire. 'Write! Writing is for you, you are for you; your
body is yours, take it.' The variety, the exuberance, the plenitude of writing,
links with the multiplicity, the orgasmic overflowing of female pleasure,
'jouissance'. Because female desire, what women want, is so repressed or so
misrepresented in a phallocentric society, its expression becomes a key
location for deconstructing that control. Beverley Brown and Parveen Adams
have illustrated the ambiguity on which this theory is founded. The body 'as
representative of the feminine condition' is 'thwarted and manipulated,
unrecognised', but, at the same time, it 'manages to retain intact its own
integrity and authenticity which allow it to utter an effective political
critique. . . .'.[15] The body is thus placed outside history, culture and social
interaction, an eternal source of meaning and social change.

Ann Rosalind Jones argues that French feminists make the female body
'too unproblematically pleasurable and totalized an entity'. Do all women
find pleasure in their bodies? Do all women — lesbian and heterosexual,
women of different races or different classes — find pleasure in the same
way? Is this pleasure necessarily politically progressive? Are women directly
in touch with their bodies or is that contact socially mediated? Moreover, if
the woman writer does wish to 'write the body', what is the connection
between her pleasure and the words on the page? Cixous's comments seem
to go little further than suggesting some 'spontaneous outpouring' (Jones).
Generalized references to the 'imbecilic capitalist machinery' and 'smug-faced
readers, managing editors, and big bosses' are the nearest she gets to a
criticism of the institutions of literary production. The concern of the Anglo-
American critics with the social position of the woman writer — whether she
has a room of her own, whether her work will be restricted by pregnancies
— finds much less emphasis in the work of French feminists.

Jones believes that this theory of the female body is insufficiently materialist and historical, a view supported by the editorial collective of *Quéstions féministes.* It disputes both the claim that 'women's language is closer to the body' and the suggestion that 'this closeness to the body and to nature would be subversive'. But the theory of 'writing the body' is not without its defendants, who would point to an unacceptable 'literalism' in certain readings of this work. Gisela Ecker, for example, while admitting that some passages in Cixous's writing reduce 'femininity to biological functions', stresses that generally the female body 'stands for instinctual drives and desire emerging from the unconscious, both of which are inserted into writing'.[16] Others have commented that the female body is used as a symbol or as an analogy. Though the warning against being over-literal is needed, there is no solution in viewing the female body as 'simply' a symbol. As Heath's analysis suggests, symbols are not neutral; they come to us with a history of cultural associations, a whole 'sexual fix'.

Conclusion

Domna Stanton's reference in her title to the 'Franco-American Dis-Connection' indicates what, at some stage or other, every American or English article on French feminist theory has to face — namely its strangeness and difficulty for an Anglo-American audience. Stanton is surely right to point out that much of this criticism is dependent on a convenient blindness to our own position. Anglo-American criticism is also theoretically based, reliant on a history of *master* practitioners, and feminist scholarship, in England and America as much as in France, is 'intellectual and privileged'. Yet, on the other hand, to dismiss the anxiety about intellectualism and elitism as 'facile', as Stanton does in her opening sentence, and then to admit that a study of French feminism 'requires a knowledge of philosophy, linguistics, and psychoanalytic theory', a willingness to 'decipher dense texts replete with plays on words and devoid of normal syntactical constructions', and, one could add, a fluency in French, is hardly addressing the problem.

The cultural gap between the French and Anglo-American approaches is wide. Alice Jardine has summarized some of the oppositions.[17] The Anglo-Americans emphasize 'oppression', the French 'repression'; the Anglo-Americans wish to raise consciousness, the French explores the unconscious; the Anglo-Americans discuss power, the French pleasure; the Anglo-Americans are governed by humanism and empiricism while the French have developed an elaborate debate on textual theory. But Jardine ends with a hope for contact between the Anglo-American 'prescription for action' and the French preoccupation with the 'human subject's inscription in culture through language'. Her way forward looks to a cautious and critical marriage between the two positions.

NOTES

1　Ellen Moers, *Literary Women* (London, Women's Press, 1978), p. 244.

2 Toril Moi makes this point in *Sexual/Textual Politics: Feminist Literary Theory* (London, Methuen, 1985), p. 97.
3 See, for example, the extract from Deborah McDowell in Ch. 4. See also Josephine Donovan, 'Feminist Style Criticism', in *Images of Women in Fiction, Feminist Perspectives*, ed. Susan Koppleman Cornillon (Bowling Green, Ohio, Bowling Green University Popular Press, 1972), and Annette Kolodny, 'Some Notes on Defining a "Feminist Literary Criticism"', in *Critical Inquiry*, Volume 2, No. 1 (Autumn, 1975).
4 Kolodny (1975), p. 78.
5 This and the following comment by Heath are from *The Sexual Fix* (London, Macmillan, 1982), pp. 120 and 121.
6 Quoted by Elaine Marks, 'Women and Literature in France', in *Signs: Journal of Women in Culture and Society*, vol. 3, no. 4 (1978), p. 837.
7 Elaine Showalter, 'Towards a Feminist Poetics', in *Women Writing and Writing About Women*, ed. Mary Jacobus (London, Croom Helm, 1979), p. 39.
8 Quoted by Elaine Marks, op. cit., (1978), p. 837.
9 This quotation is taken from Juliet Mitchell's extract in Ch. 3, p. 100.
10 Gayatri Chakravorty Spivak, 'French Feminism in an International Frame', in *Yale French Studies*, 62 (1981), p. 169.
11 Virginia Woolf, *A Room of One's Own* (New York, Harcourt Brace Jovanovich, 1963), p. 59.
12 Ibid., p. 78.
13 Virginia Woolf, Review of R. Brimley Johnson's *The Women Novelists*, in *Virginia Woolf: Women and Writing*, ed. and intro. Michèle Barrett (London, Harcourt Brace Jovanovich, 1979), p. 71.
14 Josette Féral, 'The Powers of Difference', in *The Future of Difference*, eds. Hester Eisenstein and Alice Jardine (Boston, Mass., G. K. Hall, 1980), pp. 91 and 89.
15 Beverley Brown and Parveen Adams, 'The Feminine Body and Feminist Politics', in *m/f*, 3, p. 35.
16 Gisela Ecker, 'Introduction', in *Feminist Aesthetics*, ed. Gisela Ecker (London, Women's Press, 1985), p. 18.
17 Alice Jardine, 'Prelude: The Future of Difference', in *The Future of Difference*, eds. Hester Eisenstein and Alice Jardine (Boston, Mass., G. K. Hall, 1980), p. xxvi.

JOYCE CAROL OATES
'Is There a Female Voice? Joyce Carol Oates Replies',
Gender and Literary Voice

If there is a distinctly 'female' voice — if there is a distinctly 'male' voice — surely this is symptomatic of inferior art?

For a practicing writer, for a practicing artist of any kind, 'sociology,' 'politics,' and even 'biology' are subordinate to matters of personal vision, and even to matters of craftsmanship. Content cannot make serious art. Good intentions cannot make serious art. 'Characters with whom women identify' don't make serious art. No one would confuse propaganda with art, nor should one confuse — however generously, however charitably — propagandistic impulses with the impulses of art. To me, the concepts embodied in the title of your journal simply don't have the same weight. 'Women' refers to a sociological, political, and biological phenomenon (or class, or function, or stereotype); 'literature' refers to something that always transcends these categories *even while being fueled by them.* A feminist 'theme' doesn't make a sentimental, weak, cliché-ridden work valuable; a non- or even anti-feminist 'theme' doesn't make a serious work valueless, even for women. Unfair, perhaps, unjust — but inevitable. Content is simply raw material. Women's problems — women's insights — women's very special adventures: these are material: and what matters in serious art is ultimately the skill of execution and the uniqueness of vision. My personal and political sympathy for feminist literature keeps me silent (I mean in my role as a reviewer of new books) when confronted with amateurish and stereotypical works by women. Having little to say that would be welcomed (to put it mildly) I think it is most prudent to say nothing at all, or discuss a work's interesting and valuable *content.* As if fiction were a matter of content and not of language.

Then again — how am I to feel when discussed in the *Harvard Guide to Contemporary American Literature* under the great lump 'Women Writers,' the only works of mine analyzed being those that deal explicitly with *women's problems* — the rest of my books (in fact, the great majority of my books) ignored, as if they had never been written? What should a serious woman writer feel? Insult . . . hurt . . . anger . . . frustration . . . indifference . . . amusement? Or gratitude for having been recognized at all, even if it is only as a 'woman writer' (and I stress the *only*, though not with much reproach). Attempting to rise out of categories (and there are many besides that of 'women'), the writer is thrown back, by critics frequently as well-intentioned as not. No response is adequate, or feels genuine. Of course the serious artistic voice is one of individual *style*, and it is sexless; but perhaps to have a sex-determined voice, or to be believed to have one, is, after all, better than to have no voice at all.

ELLEN MOERS
Literary Women

Is the bird merely a species of the littleness metaphor? Or are birds chosen
because they are tortured, as little girls are tortured, by boys like John Reed,
who 'twisted the necks of the pigeons, killed the little peachicks. . . .'? Or
because bird-victims can be ministered to by girl-victims — as in the scene
where Jane, a prisoner in the nursery, tugs at the window sash to put out a
few crumbs from her meager breakfast for the benefit of 'a little hungry
robin, which came and chirruped on the twigs of the leafless cherry-tree
nailed against the wall near the casement' — a metaphor which draws as
much on the crucifixion as on country winters. Or is it because birds are
beautiful and exotic creatures, symbols of half-promised, half-forbidden
sensual delights, like the bird of paradise painted 'nestling in a wreath of
convolvuli and rosebuds' on the china teaplate which Jane begs to take in her
hands and examine closely, but is 'deemed unworthy of such a privilege'?

Because birds are soft and round and sensuous, because they palpitate
and flutter when held in the hands, and especially because they sing, birds
are universal emblems of love.

> My heart is like a singing bird
> Whose nest is in a watered shoot:

proclaims Christina Rossetti in her best-known poem, because 'the birthday
of my life/Is come, my love is come to me.' Indeed, without birds, those
patterns of animal monogamy, the Jane Eyre/Rochester love affair could not
advance from romantic beginning to marital consummation. They meet on
an icy moonlit road: Rochester, fierce and virile on a black horse, but lamed;
and Jane — '"Childish and slender creature! It seemed as if a linnet had
hopped to my foot and proposed to bear me on its tiny wing."' She peers at
him through wide, inquisitive eyes 'like an eager bird'; she struggles in his
arms 'like a wild frantic bird'; and when at last they are united, Rochester in
his maimed blindness is like 'a royal eagle, chained to a perch, . . . forced to
entreat a sparrow to become its purveyor.'

[. . .]

Of all creatures, birds alone can fly all the way to heaven — yet they are
caged. Birds alone can sing more beautifully than human voices — yet they
are unheeded, or silenced. It is only when we hear the woman as well as the
poet in Christina Rossetti that we sense the full force of her metaphor in 'A
Royal Princess':

> Me, poor dove that must not coo —
> eagle that must not soar.

It is only when we explore the agonizing splits in the meaning to a girl of the bird itself — freedom against sexual fulfillment, love that also means murder by the hunter — that we can respond fully to 'A White Heron,' the poignant tale by Sarah Orne Jewett.

Whenever a girl stands at a window, as Jane Eyre does, and looks toward the winding white road that vanishes over the horizon, she yearns for the wings of liberty: 'for liberty I gasped; for liberty I uttered a prayer; it seemed scattered on the wind then faintly blowing.' Boys too gasp for liberty, but boys do not receive, they only send such valentines to young ladies as Mary Russell Mitford describes in *Our Village* as a sample of the newest in London taste: 'a raised group of roses and heartsease, executed on a kind of paper cut-work, which, on being lifted up, turned into a cage enclosing a dove — tender emblem!'

From Mary Wollstonecraft's *Maria* — to Brontë's *Jane Eyre* — to Anne Frank's *Diary of a Young Girl* — I find that the caged bird makes a metaphor that truly deserves the adjective female. And I am not at all surprised by George Eliot's and Virginia Woolf's delight in Mrs. Browning's version of the caged bird metaphor in *Aurora Leigh*. The heroine's spinster aunt, that pattern of English propriety, had lived, Aurora says,

> A sort of cage-bird life, born in a cage,
> Accounting that to leap from perch to perch
> Was act and joy enough for any bird.
> Dear heaven, how silly are the things that live
> In thickets, and eat berries!
> I alas,
> A wild bird scarcely fledged, was brought to her cage,
> And she was there to meet me. Very kind.
> Bring the clean water, give out the fresh seed.

So in *Jane Eyre*, when Rochester proposes an illicit sexual union, Jane fights to get free of the man she loves, but will not have on the wrong terms. '"Jane, be still,"' he says, '"don't struggle so, like a wild, frantic bird. . . ."' Her reply is touched with Brontë pomposity, but there is also Brontë wit in her use of a metaphor hallowed with female associations: '"I am no bird; and no net ensnares me; I am a free human being with an independent will, which I now exert to leave you."' In Brontë's work, both aspirations — to female freedom and moral freedom — are served by the bird metaphor, free flying.

MARY ELLMANN
Thinking About Women

(1)

A generalization is in order at this point. Perhaps a third of future humanity will at some time during the course of their lives need an organ transplant. Terminal patients, victims of fatal accidents, condemned criminals who might be persuaded to will their healthy organs to society, and suicides, who number 22,000 a year in the United States, all die anyway. It will be a tragic waste if their organs are not made available to patients whose lives could be prolonged. With certain obvious qualifications, obtaining these organs involves questions of legal and social machinery rather than basic morality. We have not yet run quite full tilt into the moral dilemma.[1]

(2)

I know nothing of the circumstances surrounding Herbert Blau's resignation from the Lincoln Center Repertory Company, but it is a melancholy decision for which we all bear some measure of reponsibility. Blau's tenure with the company was far from distinguished; it is hard to think of a single play produced by him at the Vivian Beaumont that stimulated any real excitement, expectation, or sense of adventure. But given the quality of the man himself and of his past work, we must surely look to other causes than artistic inadequacy for some clue to his failure.[2]

(3)

Whether the 'newer kind of shorter fiction' — be it a stylized snapshot as in Robbe-Grillet's 'The Secret Room' or a 'near-novel' as in Flannery O'Connor's 'Wise Blood' — marks a genuine departure is a moot point. The stories gathered by Mr. Marcus may represent a rear-guard action, an after-life of the novel and the long tales of Conrad or Henry James. It is too early to tell. My own hunch is that the future of imaginative form lies elsewhere, in works part philosophic, part poetic, part autobiographical. It is, I think, the writings of Blake, of Nietzsche, of such solitary masters as Elias Canetti and Ernst Bloch, that contain the seeds of the next major literary genre. If the act of fiction is to reassert its claims on the adult mind, it will have to embody more knowledge, more intensity of thought and an awareness of language more in tune with that of Wittgenstein and Lévi-Strauss. What is, just now, more old-fashioned than a novel?[3]

The first statement sets off with an exemplary firmness, which opens the door for a bold prediction in turn. This prediction hurries past its own *perhaps* to appal the reader: must *a third* of all his descendants undergo this surgery? But to frighten is a subordinate effect of authority. Its chief effect is rather one of confidence, reason, adjustment and efficacy. These appear in the third sentence and come to an incomparable climax in the words *all die anyway.* How calmly the dead are found dead here! But no, there is regret — men may hang themselves anyway, but to bury their kidneys with them is a 'tragic waste.' In fact, the statement alienates the reader from the (defensible) goal of organ transplantation: why go to such lengths to keep bodies alive in a society habituated to accident, crime, capital punishment and despair?

But this is admittedly an extreme instance of the idiom. The topic, surgery, is in itself extreme. Only an exceptional self-confidence and aggressive purpose enable the surgeon to invade the body, which has for civilized laymen (except in moments of rage or hatred) a profound sanctity. One has to think of surgery as a virtuous barbarity, and expect barbaric terms to intrude upon explanations of its legitimate point of view. The second and third statements are more representative, however, in that they apply themselves to matters of no practical or physical urgency, and yet advance themselves along the same rhetorical route of authority as does the first statement. What unites the second and third is again the sensation of firmness, directness, confidence. They seem to me fair examples of critical prose now in this country, of an established masculine mode of speaking competently on esthetic issues. Particularly in the second passage, the decision with which even dull phrases are delivered makes them work. This decision dwindles somewhat in the third (where the *moot point* and the *hunch* are drains upon it), but here too the certainty with which even a predictable point is made establishes the effect of validity. 'What is, just now, more old-fashioned than a novel?' For a moment, while he bears the weight of this question, the reader is subdued, and cannot at once remember that in fact nothing is, just now, more old-fashioned than the question itself.

[. . .]

Unexpectedly, as though one found that some frivolous expenditure was practical after all, in this new idiom women writers move about with an ease they could not feel before. Again, I am not speaking of those who relentlessly prolong our evening with Elizabeth Barrett Browning (they will *not* get up and say, 'Enough of this lucrative distress. Call me a cab.'). Instead, I hope to define the way in which it is now possible for women to write well. Quite simply, having not had physical or intellectual authority before, they have no reason to resist a literature at odds with authority. There are, of course, those who prefer instead to wear hand-me-downs, to borrow now the certitude of the nineteenth century. One might say that the defect of Simone de Beauvoir is the authority of her prose: the absence of hesitation in hesitant times amounts to a presence, a tangible deficiency, a sense of obtuseness.

In better work by women now, while sentiment is avoided as stigmatic (as the inimical mark of their sex in others' minds), authority too is skirted — again, as in Mailer and Svevo, by deliberate rashness or by ironic constraint. The tenor of Mary McCarthy's remarks on *Macbeth* is rather different from that of E. E. Stoll's:

> He is a general and has just won a battle; he enters the scene making a remark about the weather. "So fair and foul a day I have not seen." On this flat note Macbeth's character tone is set. "Terrible weather we're having." "The sun can't seem to make up its mind." "Is it hot/cold/wet enough for you?" A commonplace man who talks in commonplaces, a golfer, one might guess, on the Scottish fairways, Macbeth is the only Shakespeare hero who corresponds to a bourgeois type: a murderous Babbitt, let us say.
>
> Macbeth has absolutely no feeling for others except envy, a common middle-class trait. He *envies* the murdered Duncan his rest, which is a strange way of looking at your victim.[4]

At once a comical and a suicidal wit: the intention of wit exceeds that of justice or plausibility. What is said is said more naturally and more quickly than what Stoll says, and the opinion of Macbeth is engaging. But wrong. One doesn't for a minute *accept* Macbeth as the general, the golfer, the Eisenhower. And the Babbitt reference is quite dead, like a hemline of the late thirties. The point of view is feminine, in the pejorative sense, not only in its wifely depreciation of Macbeth (Lady Macbeth's 'good sense' is later preferred to Macbeth's 'simple panic'), but also in its social narrowness. In its determination to make Macbeth middle-class, the criticism is middle-class itself. It is hard to imagine a more philistine conception of envy than that 'common middle-class trait.' But it is the rashness of the judgment which redeems it, its daring, its mocking diminution of a subject which God knows had taken on an institutionalized grandeur.[5] The rashness links Mary McCarthy, for all their disagreements, with Norman Mailer; the diminution with Svevo, and with now.

NOTES

1   Roy L. Walford, M.D., 'A Matter of Life and Death,' *Atlantic*, August 1967, p. 70.
2   Robert Brustein, 'Saturn Eats His Children,' *New Republic*, January 28, 1967, p. 34.
3   George Steiner, 'The Search for New Genres,' *Book Week*, December 11, 1966, p. 16.
4   Mary McCarthy, 'General Macbeth,' *Harper's*, June 1962, pp. 35 and 37.
5   It is perhaps necessary to distinguish between varieties of rashness. The rashness of Mary McCarthy, which ousts conventional attitudes, is not the rashness, say, of Rebecca West: 'We were not alone. The house was packed with little girls, aged from twelve to sixteen, in the care of two or three nuns. They were, like any gathering of their kind in any part of the world, more comfortable to look at than an English girls' school. They were apparently waiting quite calmly to grow up. They expected it, and so did the people looking after them. There was no panic on anybody's part. There were none of the unhappy results which follow the English attempt to make all children look insipid and docile, and show no signs whatsoever that they will ever develop into adults. There were no little girls with poked chins and straight hair, aggressively proud of being plain, nor were there pretty girls making a desperate precocious proclamation of their femininity. But, of course, in a country where there is very little homosexuality, it is easy for girls to grow up into womanhood.' (*Black Lamb and Grey Falcon*, Vol. I, p. 163.)
       The final generalization is the clue: a person is obviously rash to allow herself to say anything so simple-silly. But the rashness is placid and auntlike. In the end, it reiterates an old point of view rather than risking a new one.

TERRY EAGLETON
Literary Theory: An Introduction

We can find another meeting-point of political and psychoanalytical theories in the work of the feminist philosopher Julia Kristeva. Kristeva's thinking is much influenced by Lacan; yet for any feminist such influence clearly poses a problem. For the symbolic order of which Lacan writes is in reality the patriarchal sexual and social order of modern class-society, structured around the 'transcendental signifier' of the phallus, dominated by the Law which the father embodies. There is no way, then, in which a feminist or pro-feminist may uncritically celebrate the symbolic order at the expense of the imaginary: on the contrary, the oppressiveness of the actual social and sexual relations of such a system is precisely the target of the feminist critique. In her book *La Révolution du langage poétique* (1974), Kristeva therefore opposes to the symbolic not so much the imaginary, as what she terms the 'semiotic'. She means by this a pattern or play of forces which we can detect inside language, and which represents a sort of residue of the pre-Oedipal phase. The child in the pre-Oedipal phase does not yet have access to language ('infant' means 'speechless'), but we can imagine its body as criss-crossed by a flow of 'pulsions' or drives which are at this point relatively unorganized. This rhythmic pattern can be seen as a form of language, though it is not yet meaningful. For language as such to happen, this heterogeneous flow must be as it were chopped up, articulated into stable terms, so that in entering the symbolic order this 'semiotic' process is repressed. The repression, however, is not total: for the semiotic can still be discerned as a kind of pulsional pressure within language itself, in tone, rhythm, the bodily and material qualities of language, but also in contradiction, meaninglessness, disruption, silence and absence. The semiotic is the 'other' of language which is nonetheless intimately entwined with it. Because it stems from the pre-Oedipal phase, it is bound up with the child's contact with the mother's body, whereas the symbolic, as we have seen, is associated with the Law of the father. The semiotic is thus closely connected with femininity: but is by no means a language exclusive to women, for it arises from a pre-Oedipal period which recognizes no distinctions of gender.

Kristeva looks to this 'language' of the semiotic as a means of undermining the symbolic order. In the writings of some of the French Symbolist poets and other avant-garde authors, the relatively secure meanings of 'ordinary' language are harassed and disrupted by this flow of signification, which presses the linguistic sign to its extreme limit, values its tonal, rhythmic and material properties, and sets up a play of unconscious drives in the text which threatens to split apart received social meanings. The semiotic is fluid and plural, a kind of pleasurable creative excess over precise meaning, and it takes sadistic delight in destroying or negating such signs. It is opposed to all fixed, transcendental significations; and since the ideologies of modern male-dominated class-society rely on such fixed signs for their power (God, father, state, order, property and so on), such literature becomes a kind of equivalent in the realm of language to revolution in the sphere of politics. The reader of such texts is equally disrupted or 'decentred' by this linguistic force, thrown into contradiction, unable to take up any one, simple 'subject-position' in relation to these polymorphous works. The semiotic throws into confusion all tight divisions between masculine and feminine — it is a 'bisexual' form of writing — and offers to deconstruct all the scrupulous binary oppositions — proper/improper, norm/deviation, sane/mad, mine/ yours, authority/obedience — by which societies such as ours survive.

The English-language writer who perhaps most strikingly exemplifies Kristeva's theories is James Joyce.[9] But aspects of it are also evident in the writings of Virginia Woolf, whose fluid, diffuse, sensuous style offers a resistance to the kind of male metaphysical world symbolized by the philosopher Mr Ramsay in *To the Lighthouse*. Ramsay's world works by abstract truths, sharp divisions and fixed essences: it is a patriarchal world, for the phallus is the symbol of sure, self-identical truth and is not to be challenged. Modern society, as the post-structuralists would say, is 'phallocentric'; it is also, as we have seen, 'logocentric', believing that its discourses can yield us immediate access to the full truth and presence of things. Jacques Derrida has conflated these two terms to the compound 'phallogocentric', which we might roughly translate as 'cocksure'. It is this cocksureness, by which those who wield sexual and social power maintain their grip, that Woolf's 'semiotic' fiction could be seen as challenging.

This raises the vexed question, much debated in feminist literary theory, as to whether there is a specifically feminine mode of writing. Kristeva's 'semiotic' is not, as we have seen, *inherently* feminine: indeed most of the 'revolutionary' writers she discusses are male. But because it is closely related to the mother's body, and because there are complex psychoanalytical reasons for holding that women retain a closer relationship to that body than men do, one might expect such writing to be on the whole more typical of women. Some feminists have sharply rejected this theory, fearing that it simply reinvents some 'female essence' of a non-cultural kind, and perhaps also suspecting that it may be no more than a high-falutin version of the sexist view that women babble. Neither of these beliefs is in my view necessarily implied by Kristeva's theory. It is important to see that the semiotic is not an *alternative* to the symbolic order, a language one could speak instead of 'normal' discourse: it is rather a process *within* our conventional sign systems, which questions and transgresses their limits. In Lacanian theory, anyone who is unable to enter the symbolic order at all, to symbolize their experience through language, would become psychotic. One might see the semiotic as a kind of internal limit or borderline of the symbolic order; and in this sense the 'feminine' could equally be seen as existing on such a border. For the feminine is at once constructed within the symbolic order, like any gender, and yet is relegated to its margins, judged inferior to masculine power. The woman is both 'inside' and 'outside' male society, both a romantically idealized member of it and a victimized outcast. She is sometimes what stands between man and chaos, and sometimes the embodiment of chaos itself. This is why she troubles the neat categories of such a regime, blurring its well-defined boundaries. Women are represented within male-governed society, fixed by sign, image, meaning, yet because they are also the 'negative' of that social order there is always in them something which is left over, superfluous, unrepresentable, which refuses to be figured there.

On this view, the feminine — which is a mode of being and discourse not necessarily identical with women — signifies a force within society which opposes it. And this has its obvious political implications in the form of the women's movement. The political correlative of Kristeva's own theories — of a semiotic force which disrupts all stable meanings and institutions — would appear to be some kind of anarchism. If such an unending overthrow of all fixed structure is an inadequate response in the political realm, so too in the theoretical sphere is the assumption that a literary text which undermines meaning is *ipso facto* 'revolutionary'. It is quite possible for a text to do this in the name of some right-wing irrationalism, or to do it in the name of nothing much at all. Kristeva's argument is dangerously formalistic and easily caricaturable: will reading Mallarmé bring down the bourgeois state? She does not, of course, claim that it will; but she pays too little attention to the political *content* of a text, the historical conditions in which its overturning of the signified is carried out, and the historical conditions in which all of this is interpreted and used. Nor is the dismantling of the unified subject a revolutionary gesture in itself. Kristeva rightly perceives that bourgeois individualism thrives on such a fetish, but her work tends to halt at the point where the subject has been fractured and thrown into contradiction. For Brecht, by contrast, the dismantling of our given identities through art is inseparable from the practice of producing a new kind of human subject altogether, which would need to know not only internal fragmentation but social solidarity, which would experience not only the gratifications of libidinal language but the fulfilments of fighting political injustice. The implicit anarchism or libertarianism of Kristeva's suggestive theories is not the only kind of politics which follows from her recognition that women, and certain 'revolutionary' literary works, pose a radical question to existing society precisely because they mark out the frontier beyond which it dare not venture.

NOTE

9   See Colin MacCabe, *James Joyce and the Revolution of the Word* (London, 1978).

MARY JACOBUS
'The Difference of View',
Women Writing and Writing About Women

Contemporary feminist criticism is more likely to stress pleasure than suffering — the freeing of repressed female desire; *jouissance* and '*la mère qui jouit*' (no longer barred from sexual pleasure) as against the burden of womanhood. Recent French writing about women and literature, marked as it is by the conjunction of neo-Freudian psychoanalysis and structuralism, has particularly tended to diagnose the repression of women's desire by representation itself, and by the order of language as instated by the Law of the Father: the Symbolic order, predicated on lack and castration.³ In this theoretical scheme, femininity itself — hereogeneity, Otherness — becomes the repressed term by which discourse is made possible. The feminine takes its place with the absence, silence, or incoherence that discourse represses; in what Julia Kristeva would call the *semiotic*, the pre-Oedipal phase of rhythmic, onomatopoeic babble which precedes the Symbolic but remains inscribed in those pleasurable and rupturing aspects of language identified particularly with *avant-garde* literary practice. But here again, there's a problem for feminist criticism. Women's access to discourse involves submission to phallocentricity, to the masculine and the Symbolic: refusal, on the other hand, risks re-inscribing the feminine as a yet more marginal madness or nonsense. When we speak (as feminist writers and theorists often do) of the need for a special language for women, what then do we mean?

Not, surely, a refusal of language itself; nor a return to a specifically feminine linguistic domain which in fact marks the place of women's oppression and confinement. Rather, a process that is played out within language, across boundaries. The dream of a language freed from the Freudian notion of castration, by which female difference is defined as lack rather than Otherness, is at first sight essentially theoretical, millennial and Utopian. Its usefulness lies in allying feminism and the *avant-garde* in a common political challenge to the very discourse which makes them possible; the terms of language itself, as well as the terms of psychoanalysis and of literary criticism, are called in question — subverted from within. Woman and artist, the feminine and the *avant-garde*, are elided in the privileged zone of contemporary intellectual and aesthetic concern: writing. Such a move has the advantage of freeing off the 'feminine' from the religion-bound, ultimately conservative and doom-ridden concept of difference-as-opposition which underlies Virginia Woolf's reading of the 'case' of George Eliot. *Difference* is redefined, not as male *versus* female — not as biologically constituted — but as a multiplicity, joyousness and heterogeneity which is that of textuality itself. Writing, the production of meaning, becomes the site both of challenge and Otherness; rather than (as in more traditional approaches) simply yielding the themes and representation of female oppression. *Difference*, in fact, becomes a traversal of the boundaries inscribed in Virginia Woolf's terms, but a traversal that exposes these very boundaries for what they are — the product of phallocentric discourse and of women's relation to patriarchal culture. Though necessarily working within 'male' discourse, women's writing (in this scheme) would work ceaselessly to deconstruct it: to write what cannot be written.

[. . .]

'Thus thought Maria' — the container overflowed by authorial Enthusiasm — has its analogue in a famous 'awkward break' noticed by Virginia Woolf. Her example is Charlotte Brontë's intrusion into *Jane Eyre* with what *A*

Room of One's Own rightly identifies as a protest against the confinement of the nineteenth-century woman writer:

> It is in vain to say human beings ought to be satisfied with tranquillity: they must have action; and they will make it if they cannot find it . . . Women are supposed to be very calm generally: but women feel just as men feel; they need exercise for their faculties, and a field for their efforts as much as their brothers do; they suffer from too rigid a restraint, too absolute a stagnation, precisely as men would suffer . . . It is thoughtless to condemn them, or laugh at them, if they seek to do more or learn more than custom has pronounced necessary for their sex.
> *When thus alone, I not unfrequently heard Grace Poole's laugh . . .*[6]

('That is an awkward break, I thought', comments Virginia Woolf.) The author herself has burst the bounds of 'too rigid a restraint' — making action if she cannot find it. By a breach of fictional decorum, writing enacts protest as well as articulating it. It is not simply that the excess of energy disrupts the text; it is that the disruption reveals what the novel cannot say within its legitimate confines, and hence reveals its fictionality. The unacceptable text gets the blue pencil from Virginia Woolf ('the woman who wrote those pages . . . will write in a rage where she should write calmly . . . She will write of herself where she should write of her characters. She is at war with her lot'); but it also opens up a rift in her own seamless web. What she herself cannot say without loss of calmness (rage has been banned in the interests of literature) is uttered instead by another woman writer. The overflow in *Jane Eyre* washes into *A Room of One's Own*. This oblique recuperation of feminist energy has implications for feminist criticism as well as for fiction; might, in fact, be said to characterise the practice of the feminist critic, for whom the relation between author and text (her own text) is equally charged. Editing into her writing the outburst edited out of Charlotte Brontë's, Virginia Woolf creates a point of instability which unsettles her own urbane and polished decorum. The rift exposes the fiction of authorial control and objectivity, revealing other possible fictions, other kinds of writing; exposes, for a moment, its own terms.

NOTES

3   See Elaine Marks, 'Women and Literature in France', *Signs: Journal of Women in Culture and Society*, vol. iii (1978), pp. 833—42 for a discussion of the work of recent French feminist literary and psychoanalytic theorists, especially Hélène Cixous, *La Jeune Née* (Paris, 1975) and 'Le Rire da la Méduse', translated as 'The Laugh of the Medusa' by Keith and Paula Cohen, *Signs:*, vol. i (1976), pp. 875—93; Luce Irigaray, *Speculum de l'autre femme* (Paris, 1974) and *Ce Sexe qui n'en est pas un* (Paris, 1977); Julia Kristeva, *La Révolution du langage poétique* (Paris, 1974), *Polylogue* (Paris, 1977) and, from *La Révolution du langage poétique,* 'Phonétique, phonologie et bases pulsionelles', translated as 'Phonetics, Phonology and Impulsional Bases' by Caren Greenberg, *Diacritics*, vol. iv (Fall 1974), pp. 33—7. See also Michèle Montrelay, 'Inquiry into Femininity', translated by Parveen Adams, *m/f*, vol. i (1978), pp. 83—101, from *L'Ombre et le nom: sur la féminité* (Paris, 1977). The work of Luce Irigaray and

Julia Kristeva is reviewed and compared by Josette Feral, 'Antigone or *The Irony of the Tribe*', *Diacritics*, vol. viii (Fall 1978), pp. 2—14. See also Stephen Heath, 'Difference', *Screen*, vol. xix (1978), pp. 51—112, esp. pp. 78—83 for a discussion of the theoretical implications raised by these writers.

6   *A Room of One's Own* (London, 1929), p. 104 (*Jane Eyre*, XII); my italics.

STEPHEN HEATH
The Sexual Fix

There is a passage towards the end of *A Room of One's Own* in which Virginia Woolf sums up something of her thinking as regards the introduction of determinations of sex into writing:

> Even so, the very first sentence that I would write here, I said, crossing over to the writing-table and taking up the page headed Women and Fiction, is that it is fatal for anyone who writes to think of their sex. It is fatal to be a man or woman pure and simple; one must be woman-manly or man-womanly. It is fatal for a woman to lay the least stress on any grievance; to plead even with justice any cause; in any way to speak consciously as a woman. And fatal is no figure of speech; for anything written with that conscious bias is doomed to death. It ceases to be fertilized. Brilliant and effective, powerful and masterly, as it may appear for a day or two, it must wither at nightfall; it cannot grow in the minds of others. Some collaboration has to take place in the mind between the woman and the man before the art of creation can be accomplished. Some marriage of opposites has to be consummated. The whole of the mind must lie wide open if we are to get the sense that the writer is communicating his experience with perfect fullness. There must be freedom and there must be peace. Not a wheel must grate, not a light glimmer. The curtains must be close drawn. The writer, I thought, once his experience is over, must lie back and let his mind celebrate its nuptials in darkness. He must not look or question what is being done. Rather, he must pluck the petals from a rose or watch the swans float calmly down the river.[1]

'It is fatal for anyone who writes to think of their sex.' That proposition reverses Cixous's emphasis on the need specifically to pose sex, woman, her wants, female pleasure, writing that. Suppose in turn we re-reverse it: it is fatal for anyone who writes — reads, speaks, takes up language — not to think of their sex, not to bring into reflection their sexual positioning and its effects in language, speech, discourse, writing.

Reading the Woolf passage, we can grasp something of the difficulties, the meshes of sex in language. The thesis is clear — it is fatal for anyone who writes to think of their sex, one must be woman-manly or man-womanly — but it is not clear that we are not given a quite different position in the writing itself. 'Some marriage of opposites has to be consummated', for example. 'Consummated' is already a whole sexual history: 'consummate', 'to complete marriage by sexual intercourse', as the OED defines it, giving 1540 as the date for its first appearance; a legality, the law of marriage, a male scenario. How is consummation defined? The legal procedures for the invalidation of marriages from the seventeenth century on are explicit: by penetration and emission (in France there existed an extraordinary and extreme procedure known as *'congrès'* under which judges could order trial consummations before witnesses, the husband or wife against whom the demand for annulment was made having to defend themselves by demonstrating that they could actually manage intercourse). Woolf is writing discursively here in a male-defined position; the 'marriage of opposites' is one-sided in its representation — creation as consummation, a finality, an end, penetration and climax, male climax. After which, 'when his experience is over', the writer 'must lie back and let his mind celebrate its nuptials in darkness'. Perhaps it might be said that here exactly Woolf does bring in the balance, shifts to different terms, elements of a potentially female position, lying back, as earlier, more evidently, she has stressed that 'the mind must lie wide open'. But this 'female position' is equally male, part of the same scenario: the penetrating active man, the receptive passive woman. The marriage in the writing is one single order with its two given sides, its two specified positions. The very notion of 'opposites' is from within that order: man and woman, male and female, complement one another, with the latter derived as the difference from the former, so many essential female qualities in counterpart to his essential and defining maleness. Working with marriage, consummation, opposites, man and woman added together, Woolf is returned, even against the possibilities of her thesis, to what is a representation that assigns women to a certain place as woman, in relation to a certain domination and evaluation from men, the place of man.

[. . .]

It is fatal for anyone who writes to think of their sex but, even as she sets out that thesis, Woolf is caught up in a web of words and images and ways of writing that brings with them a position, a sexual stance, a certain representation. Cixous's question, how is female pleasure to be written? Or, how is the fatality — the historical fatality, the fix — of this position of 'sexuality', male and female, the man and the woman, the one and the other, the difference, to be broken, written away from?

This is an important area of theoretical discussion and literary practice today, most notably from the perspective of feminism and in terms of the possibility of the development of a specifically woman's language. 'Woman's desire would not speak the same language as man's'[2] (this and following quotations are from French feminist writers, Cixous herself, Michèle Montrelay and, as here, Luce Irigaray); the point now is to achieve an authentic language of that desire — and thus to write thinking of one's sex.

In this context, a number of theses and arguments are advanced and made as regards the relation of woman and language:

— The woman is more naturally a writer, since close to the mother tongue, close to creation: 'it is the woman who is more the writer, by the very fact that she creates an idiom; and the poet well knows that it is the mother tongue he speaks and no other';[3] woman's pleasure being in excess and at the expense of the phallus, the phallic order of the signifier, it is like a process of writing (understanding the latter as a play in language, the disturbance of fixed meanings): 'female pleasure can be seen as *writing* . . . this pleasure and the literary text (which is also written like an orgasm produced from within discourse) are the effect of the same murder of the signifier'.[4]

— The woman is close to the body, the source of writing: 'it is obvious that a woman does not write like a man, because she speaks with the body, writing is from the body'.[5] Writing resembles the body and the sexual division of male and female is expressed in the difference of women's writing: 'a feminine textual body can be recognized by the fact that it is always without end, has no finish, which moreover is what makes the feminine text very often difficult to read'.[6] Against 'the "I" of phallocratic language'[7] (this formulation in fact taken from an American feminist, Mary Daly), erect and single, the 'two lips' of the female sex in a female language, constantly moving and plural.

— A woman's writing is anti-theory, has no metalanguage ('cannot describe itself from outside or in formal terms'[8]), it has no place for 'the concept as such', is 'fluid' in style, breaking syntax and developing towards a new syntax of 'auto affection'[9] (the 'two lips' of the female sex are perpetually joining in embrace), with 'neither subject nor object'.[10]

Clearly what these theses and arguments do is to assert a very powerful sexual determination in language and language use, and in particular to valorize sexual difference as male/female, female versus male, by an appeal to signs and correspondences of a femininity, a femaleness — flow, liquid, lips, holes — as well as to specifically women's experiences — menstruation, pregnancy, and so on. All of which, of course, bears first on literary production, women writing, but equally on literary reception, women reading and their literary criticism. Thus an English critic, Gillian Beer, follows the idea of the feminine textual body as being without end exactly when she talks in connection with Virginia Woolf of how 'the eschewing of plot is an aspect of her feminism. The avoidance of narrative climax is a way of getting outside the fixing properties of event';[11] and Woolf herself, despite her fatal-to-think-of-one's-sex stress, could praise her contemporary fellow-novelist Dorothy Richardson for her invention of 'a woman's sentence', 'the psychological sentence of the feminine gender' — 'of a more elastic fibre than the old, capable of stretching to the extreme, of suspending the frailest particles, of enveloping the vaguest shapes'.[12]

Problems quickly emerge however. To lay the emphasis on difference and the specificity of women (as of men) in the paradigm male/female is a gesture within the terms of the existing system, for which, precisely, women are different *from* men. Patriarchy, men in its order, has never said anything but that women are — the woman, the female, is — different: they are not men. Lawrence's novels, for instance, are full of 'pure man'/'pure woman', 'male soul'/'female soul', the antithesis derived from and justifying the reign of the phallus. Different as female to male, women are readily pinned to and identified with their sex, their bodies, a biology (the poet Ezra Pound: 'the female/Is an element, the female/Is a chaos/An octopus/A biological process'[13]): woman as the female animal, as sexuality, in every sense a sex object. The signs and correspondences claimed are none other than those of the system itself: women as fluid, flowing (Lawrence, regretting the rise of 'the modern woman': 'But women used to know better . . . Women used to see themselves as a softly flowing stream of attraction and desire and beauty, soft quiet rivers of energy and peace'[14]); women as maternity (Lawrence again can argue *for* matriarchy, meaning by the latter 'full self-responsibility as mothers and heads of the family',[15] leaving men alone to get on with 'the life of society').

And so the litany of difference has gone on and continues, attributing ('recognizing', as it would say) 'qualities' (often defects as far as its view of women—woman is concerned). 'If the male orgasm is in some sort "consonantic", is not the female orgasm "vocalic"?'[16] At school, as we were guided through Palgrave's *Golden Treasury of English Poetry*, we were much taken with liquid vowels and hard consonants but were not quite together enough to make the obvious connections which only a French psychoanalyst today could so felicitously spell out for us (and doubtless tomorrow we will be reminded that men are active and women passive verbs — or is it transitive and intransitive?). 'Feminine in its lack of restraint, its wordiness, and the utter absence of feeling for form',[17] wrote Arnold Bennett of George Eliot's style; 'feminine forgetfulness of one's self',[18] added his contemporary Walter Pater writing generally; while David Holbrook sums up the tradition within which such remarks are automatically made with his recent unsparing praise for 'the female elements of intuition, creativity, and sympathy'.[19] A pat on the back from the solid men and women can be sent happily clucking back to the farmyard, to what Lawrence calls 'the lovely henny surety, the hensureness which is the real bliss of every female'.[20]

Difference, that is, is difficult, speedily comes round to an essence of woman and man, male and female, a kind of anthropologico-biological nature. But men and women are not simply given biologically; they are given in history and culture, in a social practice and representation that includes biological determinations, shaping and defining them in its process. The appeal to an 'undeniable' biological reality as essential definition is always itself a form of social representation, within a particular structure of assumption and argument. It is this appeal indeed that is made by the existing system and its 'sexuality', which holds to the clear identity — determined and fixed, rooted in nature — of the man and the woman, with the latter the difference, and runs over from there into an elaborate account of 'masculine' and 'feminine' modes of behaviour, characteristics, styles — the whole gamut of 'qualities' that the theses and arguments on the relations of woman and language uncannily reproduce (compare the idea of a breakdown of syntax, a writing with 'neither subject nor object', never-ending, an 'elastic' sentence 'enveloping the vaguest shapes', with Bennett's 'feminine in its lack of restraint, its wordiness, and the utter absence of feeling for form'; the whole idea of resemblance to the body is that of the system: women are like — *are* — their bodies which then specify their nature, define them essentially, their condition for ever).

This is difficult again, however, in that in a given situation the appeal to difference can be a powerful and necessary mode of struggle and action, can take the force of an alternative representation, turning difference against the order of the same that it is used to support (the single identity of man and woman from him); thus, for example, the reappropriation of the question of 'what does a woman want?', at once a question in the system *and* a moment of trouble that can be brought round against it, as its contradiction. The attempt to distinguish specifically feminine elements of writing, to develop a specifically female language, can clearly become important as a basis for movement and challenge and transformation. Virginia Woolf can perfectly well lay down that it is fatal to think of one's sex (as though there were one sex that one was, an absolute identity of sex) and at the same time praise Richardson's 'woman's sentence', this having a precise radical value, 'only in the sense that it is used to describe a woman's mind by a writer who is neither proud nor afraid of anything that she may discover in the psychology of her sex'. A critic such as Gillian Beer can perfectly well reverse Arnold Bennett's commonplace about the feminine inability to manage form into a feminist valuation of Woolf's eschewing of plot and narrative climax, inasmuch as in the context in which Woolf writes the latter are exactly strategies of the system, part of its novelistic resolution.

NOTES

1 Virginia Woolf, *A Room of One's Own* (1929) (St Albans and London: Granada, 1977), p. 99.
2 Luce Irigaray, *Ce Sexe qui n'en est pas un* (Paris: Seuil, 1977) p. 25.
3 Eugénie Lemoine-Luccioni, 'Ecrire', *Sorcières* no. 7, p. 14.
4 Michèle Montrelay, *L'Ombre et le nom*, pp. 80—1.
5 Hélène Cixous, 'Quelques questions à Hélène Cixous', *Les Cahiers du GRIF* no. 13 (October 1976), p. 20.
6 H. Cixous, 'Le sexe ou la tête', *Les Cahiers du GRIF* no. 13 (October 1976), p. 14.
7 Mary Daly, *Gyn/Ecology* (London: The Women's Press, 1979), p. 327.
8 Luce Irigaray, 'Woman's Exile', *Ideology and Consciousness* no. 1 (May 1977), p. 65.
9 Irigaray, *Ce Sexe*, p. 130 ('I'm trying to say that the female sex would be, above all, made up of "*two lips*" . . . these "*two lips*" *are always joined in an embrace*' 'Woman's Exile', pp. 64—5).
10 ibid. p. 132. Translations of French feminist texts, including one or two pieces by Irigaray, can be found in *New French Feminisms* ed. Elaine Marks and Isabelle de Courtivron (Amherst: University of Massachusetts Press, 1980).
11 Gillian Beer, 'Beyond Determinism: George Eliot and Virginia Woolf', in *Women Writing and Writing About Women* (London: Croom Helm, 1979), p. 95.
12 Virginia Woolf, 'Romance and the Heart' (1923), *Contemporary Writers* (London: Hogarth, 1965), pp. 124—5.
13 Ezra Pound, Canto xxix, *The Cantos of Ezra Pound* (London: Faber & Faber, 1968), p. 149.

14   D. H. Lawrence, 'Do Women Change?' (1929), *Phoenix* II, p. 541.
15   D. H. Lawrence, 'Matriarchy' (1928), *Phoenix* II, p. 552.
16   Jean-Louis Tristani, *Le Stade du respir* (Paris: Minuit, 1978), p. 36.
17   Arnold Bennett, *The Journals of Arnold Bennett* ed. Newman Flower (London: Cassell, 1932), vol. 1, p. 6.
18   Walter Pater, *Plato and Platonism* (1893) (London: Macmillan, 1920), p. 281.
19   Holbrook, *The Masks of Hate*, p. 237.
20   D. H. Lawrence, 'Cocksure Women and Hensure Men' (1929), *Phoenix* II, p. 555.

MICHELE BARRETT
Virginia Woolf: Women and Writing

Virginia Woolf on the female literary tradition

It is symptomatic of Virginia Woolf's relevance to contemporary feminism that one of the questions considered in her work on women and fiction — the existence of an intrinsically feminine literary style — is at present highly controversial. The argument that women not only write about different things from men, but that they write about them in a different way, often lies behind feminist literary criticism, and may also underlie the interest in re-examining various female authors of the past. In addition to this some feminists have argued that since men and women are differently constructed as individuals through the learning of language, the relationship of men and women to language is necessarily different. With growing criticism by feminists of the dominance of men in the literary tradition, there has also grown a concern with differences between men and women writers, not only in the images which are used in literature, but in the actual use of language itself. There are times when Virginia Woolf might be thought to subscribe to this view; in her discussion of Jane Austen, in *A Room of One's Own*, she comments on how Austen rejected the classic form of the sentence and created one more suitable for her own use.

> The sentence that was current at the beginning of the nineteenth century ran something like this perhaps:
> "The grandeur of their works was an argument with them, not to stop short, but to proceed. . . ." That is a man's sentence; behind it one can see Johnson, Gibbon, and the rest. It was a sentence that was unsuited to a woman's use. . . . Jane Austen looked at it and laughed at it and devised a perfectly natural, shapely sentence proper for her own use and never departed from it.

Yet this description does not really imply any notion that this use of language is anything other than fully conscious and deliberate; it does not appeal to intrinsic differences between the male and the female author in terms of the language they use. Virginia Woolf's argument is a social, rather than a biological or psychological, one, as is made clearer when she continues:

> There is no reason to think that the form of the epic or of the poetic play suits a

woman any more than the sentence suits her. But all the older forms of literature were hardened and set by the time she became a writer. The novel alone was young enough to be soft in her hands — another reason, perhaps, why she wrote novels.

Woolf's position is made even clearer in reviews of Dorothy Richardson's work, a writer who herself claimed in the Foreword to her first book to have created a new, female type of sentence. Virginia Woolf writes

> She has invented, or if she has not invented, developed and applied to her own uses, a sentence which we might call the psychological sentence of the feminine gender. It is of a more elastic fibre than the old, capable of stretching to the extreme, of suspending the frailest particles, of enveloping the vaguest shapes.

The central point which Woolf makes in her review of Dorothy Richardson's novel is that this sentence is not intrinsically a woman's sentence, it is so only by virtue of its subject matter, and the different social experience of women. She continues:

> Other writers of the opposite sex have used sentences of this description and stretched them to the extreme. But there is a difference. Miss Richardson has fashioned her sentence consciously, in order that it may descend to the depths and investigate the crannies of Miriam Henderson's consciousness. It is a woman's sentence, but only in the sense that it is used to describe a woman's mind by a writer who is neither proud nor afraid of anything that she may discover in the psychology of her sex.

In her review of a book on women novelists, Virginia Woolf stresses that it is the subject matter of women's novels which is different from that of men's.

> . . . no one will admit that he can possibly mistake a novel written by a man for a novel written by a woman. There is the obvious and enormous difference of experience in the first place; but the essential difference lies in the fact not that men describe battles and women the birth of children, but that each sex describes itself. The first words in which either a man or a woman is described are generally enough to determine the sex of the writer . . .

HELENE CIXOUS
'The Laugh of the Medusa', *New French Feminisms*

I shall speak about women's writing: about *what it will do*. Woman must write her self: must write about women and bring women to writing, from which they have been driven away as violently as from their bodies — for the same reasons, by the same law, with the same fatal goal. Woman must put herself into the text — as into the world and into history — by her own movement.

The future must no longer be determined by the past. I do not deny that the effects of the past are still with us. But I refuse to strengthen them by repeating them, to confer upon them an irremovability the equivalent of destiny, to confuse the biological and the cultural. Anticipation is imperative.

Since these reflections are taking shape in an area just on the point of being discovered, they necessarily bear the mark of our time — a time during which the new breaks away from the old, and, more precisely, the (feminine) new from the old (*la nouvelle de l'ancien*). Thus, as there are no grounds for establishing a discourse, but rather an arid millennial ground to break, what I say has at least two sides and two aims: to break up, to destroy; and to foresee the unforeseeable, to project.

I write this as a woman, toward women. When I say 'woman,' I'm speaking of woman in her inevitable struggle against conventional man; and of a universal woman subject who must bring women to their senses and to their meaning in history. But first it must be said that in spite of the enormity of the repression that has kept them in the 'dark' — that dark which people have been trying to make them accept as their attribute — there is, at this time, no general woman, no one typical woman. What they have *in common* I will say. But what strikes me is the infinite richness of their individual constitutions: you can't talk about *a* female sexuality, uniform, homogeneous, classifiable into codes — any more than you can talk about one unconscious resembling another. Women's imaginary is inexhaustible, like music, painting, writing: their stream of phantasms is incredible.

I have been amazed more than once by a description a woman gave me of a world all her own which she had been secretly haunting since early childhood. A world of searching, the elaboration of a knowledge, on the basis of a systematic experimentation with the bodily functions, a passionate and precise interrogation of her erotogeneity. This practice, extraordinarily rich and inventive, in particular as concerns masturbation, is prolonged or accompanied by a production of forms, a veritable aesthetic activity, each stage of rapture inscribing a resonant vision, a composition, something beautiful. Beauty will no longer be forbidden.

I wished that that woman would write and proclaim this unique empire so that other women, other unacknowledged sovereigns, might exclaim: I, too, overflow; my desires have invented new desires, my body knows unheard-of songs. Time and again I, too, have felt so full of luminous torrents that I could burst — burst with forms much more beautiful than those which are put up in frames and sold for a stinking fortune. And I, too, said nothing, showed nothing; I didn't open my mouth, I didn't repaint my half of the world. I was ashamed. I was afraid, and I swallowed my shame and my fear. I said to myself: You are mad! What's the meaning of these waves, these floods, these outbursts? Where is the ebullient, infinite woman who, immersed as she was in her naiveté, kept in the dark about herself, led into self-disdain by the great arm of parental-conjugal phallocentrism, hasn't been ashamed of her strength? Who, surprised and horrified by the fantastic tumult of her drives (for she was made to believe that a well-adjusted normal woman has a . . . divine composure), hasn't accused herself of being a monster? Who, feeling a funny desire stirring inside her (to sing, to write, to dare to speak, in short, to bring out something new), hasn't thought she was sick? Well, her shameful sickness is that she resists death, that she makes trouble.

And why don't you write? Write! Writing is for you, you are for you; your body is yours, take it. I know why you haven't written. (And why I didn't write before the age of twenty-seven.) Because writing is at once too high, too great for you, it's reserved for the great — that is for 'great men'; and it's 'silly.' Besides, you've written a little, but in secret. And it wasn't good, because it was in secret, and because you punished yourself for writing, because you didn't go all the way, or because you wrote, irresistibly, as when we would masturbate in secret, not to go further, but to attenuate the tension a bit, just enough to take the edge off. And then as soon as we come, we go and make ourselves feel guilty — so as to be forgiven; or to forget, to bury it until the next time.

Write, let no one hold you back, let nothing stop you: not man; not the imbecilic capitalist machinery, in which publishing houses are the crafty, obsequious relayers of imperatives handed down by an economy that works against us and off our backs; and not *yourself*. Smug-faced readers, managing editors, and big bosses don't like the true texts of women — female-sexed texts. That kind scares them.

I write woman: woman must write woman. And man, man. So only an oblique consideration will be found here of man; it's up to him to say where his masculinity and femininity are at: this will concern us once men have opened their eyes and seen themselves clearly.[1]

Now women return from afar, from always: from 'without,' from the heath where witches are kept alive; from below, from beyond 'culture'; from their childhood which men have been trying desperately to make them forget, condemning it to 'eternal rest.' The little girls and their 'ill-mannered' bodies immured, well-preserved, intact unto themselves, in the mirror. Frigidified. But are they ever seething underneath! What an effort it takes — there's no end to it — for the sex cops to bar their threatening return. Such a display of forces on both sides that the struggle has for centuries been immobilized in the trembling equilibrium of a deadlock.

Translated by Keith Cohen and Paula Cohen

NOTE

1 Men still have everything to say about their sexuality, and everything to write. For what they have said so far, for the most part, stems from the opposition activity/passivity from the power relation between a fantasized obligatory virility meant to invade, to colonize, and the consequential phantasm of woman as a 'dark continent' to penetrate and to 'pacify.' (We know what 'pacify' means in terms of scotomizing the other and misrecognizing the self.) Conquering her, they've made haste to depart from her borders, to get out of sight, out of body. The way man has of getting out of himself and into her whom he takes not for the other but for his own, deprives him, he knows, of his own bodily territory. One can understand how man, confusing himself with his penis and rushing in for the attack, might feel resentment and fear of being 'taken' by the woman, of being lost in her, absorbed or alone.

RACHEL BLAU DuPLESSIS and MEMBERS OF WORKSHOP 9
'For the Etruscans: Sexual Difference and Artistic Production — The Debate over a Female Aesthetic',
The Future of Difference

April 28

The Body, and its language, which is of course, all language. These notions of writing from the neck up. All that fear, almost terror, of the women at Barnard, of being caught in the old stereotype — woman/body, mother/ nature, an inferior kind of mind, and flee it sisters deny it don't be trapped by our own feminism.

But that male body, how IT dominates the culture, the environment, the language. Since 3,000 B.C. in Sumeria, Tiamat's monsters again and again, and every myth an effort to keep the sun rising. Save the sun, everybody, from the watery deeps, the dark underneath it must go — Into — Every night into such dangers, such soft inchoate darkness, what will become of it, will it rise again will it will it rise again? The language of criticism: 'lean, dry, terse, powerful, strong, spare, linear, focused, explosive' — god forbid it should be 'limp'!! But — 'soft, moist, blurred, padded, irregular, going around in circles,' and other descriptions of *our* bodies — the very *abyss* of aesthetic judgment, danger, the wasteland for artists! That limp dick — an entire civilization based on it, help the sun rise, watch out for the dark underground, focus focus focus, keep it high, let it soar, let it transcend, let it aspire to Godhead — — — —

Frances Jaffer

ANN ROSALIND JONES
'Writing the Body: Toward An Understanding of L'Ecriture Féminine', *Feminist Studies*

Can the body be the source of a new discourse? Is it possible, assuming an unmediated and *jouissant* (or, more likely, a positively reconstructed) sense of one's body, to move from that state of unconscious excitation directly to a written female text?

Madeleine Gagnon says yes, in *La Venue à l'écriture*, written with Cixous in 1977. Her view is that women, free from the self-limiting economy of male libido ('I will come once and once only, through one organ alone; once it's up and over, that's it; so I must beware, save up, avoid premature overflow'), have a greater spontaneity and abundance in body and language both:

> We have never been the masters of others or of ourselves. We don't have to confront ourselves in order to free ourselves. We don't have to keep watch on ourselves, or to set up some other erected self in order to understand ourselves.

All we have to do is let the body flow, from the inside; all we have to do is erase
. . . whatever may hinder or harm the new forms of writing; we retain whatever
fits, whatever suits us. Whereas man confronts himself constantly. He pits
himself against and stumbles over his erected self.[25]

But psychoanalytic theory and social experience both suggest that the leap
from body to language is especially difficult for women.[26] Lacanian theory
holds that a girl's introduction into language (the symbolic order represented
by the father and built on phallic/non-phallic oppositions) is complex,
because she cannot identify directly with the positive poles of that order.
And in many preliterate and postliterate cultures, taboos against female
speech are enforced: injunctions to silence, mockery of women's chatter or
'women's books' abound. The turn taking in early consciousness-raising
groups in the United States was meant precisely to overcome the verbal
hesitancy induced in women by a society in which men have had the first
and the last word. Moreover, for women with jobs, husbands or lovers,
children, activist political commitments, finding the time and justification to
write at all presents an enormous practical and ideological problem.[27] We
are more likely to write, and to read each other's writing, if we begin by
working against the concrete difficulties and the prejudices surrounding
women's writing than if we simplify and idealize the process by locating
writing as a spontaneous outpouring from the body.

Calls for a verbal return to nature seem especially surprising coming from
women who are otherwise (and rightly!) suspicious of language as penetrated
by phallocentric dogma. True, conventional narrative techniques, as well as
grammar and syntax, imply the unified viewpoint and mastery of outer
reality that men have claimed for themselves. But literary modes and
language itself cannot be the only targets for transformation; the *context* for
women's discourses needs to be thought through and broadened out. A
woman may experience *jouissance* in a private relationship to her own body,
but she writes for others. Who writes? Who reads? Who makes women's
texts available to women? What do women want to read about other
women's experience? To take a stance as a woman poet or novelist is to enter
into a role criss-crossed with questions of authority, of audience, of the
modes of publication and distribution. I believe that we are more indebted to
the 'body' of earlier women writers and to feminist publishers and booksellers
than to any woman writer's libidinal/body flow. The novelist Christiane
Rochefort sums up with amusing directness the conflicting public forces
and voices that create the dilemma of the French woman who wants to
write:

Well. So here you are now, sitting at your writing table, alone, not allowing
anybody anymore to interfere. Are you free?

First, after this long quest, you are swimming in a terrible soup of values —
for, to be safe, you had to refuse the so-called female values, which are not
female but a social scheme, and to identify with male values, which are not
male but an appropriation by men — or an attribution to men — of all human
values, mixed up with the anti-values of domination-violence-oppression and
the like. In this mixture, where is your real identity?

Second, you are supposed to write in certain forms, preferably: I mean you feel that in certain forms you are not too much seen as a usurper. Novels. Minor poetry, in which case you will be stigmatized in French by the name of "poetesse": not everybody can afford it. . . .

You are supposed, too, to write *about* certain things: house, children, love. Until recently there was in France a so-called *littérature féminine*.

Maybe you don't want to write *about*, but to write, period. And of course, you don't want to obey this social order. So, you tend to react against it. It is not easy to be genuine.[28]

Whatever the difficulties, women are inventing new kinds of writing. But as Irigaray's erudition and plays with the speaking voice show (as do Cixous's mischievous puns and citations of languages from Greek through German to Portuguese, and Wittig's fantastic neologisms and revision of conventional genres), they are doing so deliberately, on a level of feminist theory and literary self-consciousness that goes far beyond the body and the unconscious. That is also how they need to be read. It takes a thoroughgoing familiarity with *male* figureheads of Western culture to recognize the intertextual games played by all these writers; their work shows that a resistance to culture is always built, at first, of bits and pieces of that culture, however they are disassembled, criticized, and transcended. Responding to *l'écriture féminine* is no more instinctive than producing it. Women's writing will be more accessible to writers and readers alike if we recognize it as a conscious response to socioliterary realities, rather than accept it as an overflow of one woman's unmediated communication with her body. Eventually, certainly, the practice of women writers will transform what we can see and understand in a literary text; but even a woman setting out to write about her body will do so against and through her socioliterary mothers, midwives, and sisters. We need to recognize, too, that there is nothing universal about French versions of *écriture féminine*. The speaking, singing, tale telling, and writing of women in cultures besides that of the Ile de France need to be looked at and understood in their social context if we are to fill in an adequate and genuinely empowering picture of women's creativity.

But I risk, after all this, overstating the case against *féminité* and *l'écriture féminine*, and that would mean a real loss. American feminists can appropriate two important elements, at least, from the French position: the critique of phallocentrism in all the material and ideological forms it has taken, and the call for new representations of women's consciousness. It is not enough to uncover old heroines or to imagine new ones. Like the French, we need to examine the words, the syntax, the genres, the archaic and elitist attitudes toward language and representation that have limited women's self-knowledge and expression during the long centuries of patriarchy. We need not, however, replace phallocentrism with a shakily theorized 'concentrism' that denies women their historical specificities to recognize how deep a refusal of masculinist values must go.[29] If we remember that what women really share is an oppression on all levels, although it affects us each in different ways — if we can translate *féminité* into a concerted attack not only on language, but also directly upon the sociosexual arrangements that keep us from our own potentials and from each other — then we are on our way to becoming 'les jeunes nées' envisioned by French feminisms at their best.

NOTES

25 Madeleine Gagnon, 'Corps I,' *New French Feminisms*, p. 180. See Chantal Chawaf for a similar statement, in 'La Chair linguistique,' *New French Feminisms*, pp. 177–78.
26 Cora Kaplan combines psychoanalytic and anthropological accounts of women's hesitations to speak, in 'Language and Gender,' *Papers on Patriarchy* (Brighton, England: Women's Publishing Collective, 1976). Similarly, Sandra M. Gilbert and Susan Gubar demonstrate how socially derived ambivalence toward the role of writer has acted upon women's writing in English, in *The Madwoman in the Attic: The Woman Writer and the Nineteenth-Century Literary Imagination* (New Haven: Yale University Press, 1979).
27 See Tillie Olsen's *Silences* (New York: Delacorte, 1979) for a discussion of the practical demands and self-doubts that have hindered women's writing, especially 'The Writer Woman: One out of Twelve,' pp. 177–258.
28 Christiane Rochefort, 'Are Women Writers Still Monsters?' a speech given at the University of Wisconsin, Madison, Wis., February 1975, translated in *New French Feminisms*, pp. 185–86.
29 'Concentrism' is Elaine Showalter's term, used in a speech, 'Feminist Literary Theory and Other Impossibilities,' given at the Smith College Conference on Feminist Literary Criticism, Northampton, Mass., October 25, 1980.

TORIL MOI

Sexual/Textual Politics: Feminist Literary Theory

Ecriture féminine   1) masculinity, femininity, bisexuality

Cixous's concept of *feminine writing* is crucially related to Derrida's analysis of writing as *différance*. For Cixous, feminine texts are texts that 'work on the difference', as she once put it (RSH, 480), strive in the direction of difference, struggle to undermine the dominant phallogocentric logic, split open the closure of the binary opposition and revel in the pleasures of open-ended textuality.

However, Cixous is adamant that even the term *écriture féminine* or 'feminine writing' is abhorrent to her, since terms like 'masculine' and 'feminine' themselves imprison us within a binary logic, within the 'classical vision of sexual opposition between men and women'.[1] She has therefore chosen to speak either of a 'writing said to be feminine' (or masculine) or, more recently, of a 'decipherable libidinal femininity which can be read in writing produced by a male or a female' (Conley, 129). It is not, apparently, the empirical sex of the author that matters, but the kind of writing at stake.

She thus warns against the dangers of confusing the sex of the author with the 'sex' of the writing he or she produces:

> Most women are like this: they do someone else's — man's — writing, and in their innocence sustain it and give it voice, and end up producing writing that's in effect masculine. Great care must be taken in working on feminine writing not to get trapped by names: to be signed with a woman's name doesn't necessarily make a piece of writing feminine. It could quite well be masculine writing, and conversely, the fact that a piece of writing is signed with a man's name does not in itself exclude femininity. It's rare, but you can sometimes find femininity in writings signed by men: it does happen.
>
> ('Castration', 52)

Indeed one of the reasons why Cixous is so keen to get rid of the old opposition between masculine and feminine, and even of terms like male or female, is her strong belief in the inherently *bisexual* nature of all human beings. In 'The laugh of the Medusa' (and also in *La Jeune Née* — some of the passages dealing with these themes are reproduced in both texts) she first attacks the 'classic conception of bisexuality', which is 'squashed under the emblem of castration fear and along with the fantasy of a 'total' being (though composed of two halves), would do away with the difference' ('Medusa', 254/46, JN, 155). This homogeneous conception of bisexuality is designed to cater for the male fear of the Other (woman) in so far as it allows him to fantasize away the ineluctable signs of sexual difference. Opposing this view, Cixous produces what she calls the *other bisexuality*, which is multiple, variable and ever-changing, consisting as it does of the 'non-exclusion either of the difference or of one sex'. Among its characteristics is the 'multiplication of the effects of the inscription of desire, over all parts of my body and the other body, indeed, this *other bisexuality* doesn't annul differences, but stirs them up, pursues them, increases them' ('Medusa', 254/46, JN, 155).

Today, according to Cixous, it is 'for historico-cultural reasons . . . *women* who are opening up to and benefiting from this vatic bisexuality', or as she puts it: 'In a certain way, "woman" is bisexual; man — it's a secret to no one — being poised to keep glorious phallic monosexuality in view' ('Medusa', 254/46, JN, 156−7). She denies the possibility of ever *defining* a feminist practice of writing:

> For this practice can never be theorized, enclosed, coded — which doesn't mean that it doesn't exist. But it will always surpass the discourse that regulates the phallocentric system; it does and will take place in areas other than those subordinated to philosophico-theoretical domination.
>
> ('Medusa', 253/45)

She does, however, supply a definition that not only echoes Derrida's concept of *écriture*, but also seems to be identical with her own concept of the 'other bisexuality':

> To admit that writing is precisely working (in) the in-between, inspecting the process of the same and of the other without which nothing can live, undoing the work of death — to admit this is first to want the two, as well as both, the

ensemble of one and the other, not fixed in sequence of struggle and expulsion or some other form of death but infinitely dynamized by an incessant process of exchange from one subject to another.

('Medusa', 254/46)

Here it would seem that for Cixous writing *as such* is bisexual. However, she also argues that, at least at present, *women* (which clearly indicates biological females as opposed to males) are much more likely to be bisexual in this sense than men. *Bisexual* writing is therefore overwhelmingly likely to be *women's* writing, though some exceptional men may in certain cases manage to break with their 'glorious monosexuality' and achieve bisexuality as well. This position is clearly logical enough. In keeping with this anti-essentialist vein, Cixous, in 'The laugh of the Medusa', argues that in France only Colette, Marguerite Duras and Jean Genet really qualify as feminine (or bisexual) writers. In *La Jeune Née* she also points to Shakespeare's Cleopatra and Kleist's Penthesilea as powerful representations of the feminine libidinal economy.

NOTE

1   Vera Andermatt Conley, *Hélène Cixous: Writing the Feminine* (Lincoln and London, University of Nebraska Press, 1984). Includes the appendix 'An exchange with Hélène Cixous', pp. 129–61.

EDITORIAL COLLECTIVE OF QUESTIONS FEMINISTES
'Variations on Common Themes', *New French Feminisms*

Otherness and the Identity-Body

Some women declare that 'language must be shattered,' because language is supposed to be male as it is a conveyor of, among other things, male chauvinism. They claim for themselves 'another' language, that, in its new form, would be closer to woman's lived experience, a lived experience in the center of which the Body is frequently placed. Hence the watchwords: 'liberate-the-body' and 'speak-the-body.' It is legitimate to expose the oppression, the mutilation, the 'functionalization' and the 'objectivation'[2] of the female body, but it is also dangerous to place the body at the center of a search for female identity. Furthermore, the themes of Otherness and of the Body merge together, because the most visible difference between men and women, and the only one that we know for sure to be permanent (barring mutations) is indeed the difference in body. This difference has been used as a pretext to 'justify' full power of one sex over the other.

When a group is in power it propagates the reigning ideology, it imposes categories. The group in power, which always needs to justify its domination, condemns those that it oppresses to being different: he or she cannot be treated equally because — Therefore colonized people are generally 'lazy' and 'incapable' of producing anything from their head themselves, etc. Such 'differences' are not explained by specific historical circumstances because history evolves and can bring about resolutions. For the oppressor, it is safer to speak of natural differences that are invariable by definition. That is the basis of racist and sexist ideologies. And thus a status of inferiority is inextricably bound to a status of difference.

Now, after centuries of men constantly repeating that *we* were different, here are women screaming, as if they were afraid of not being heard and as if it were an exciting discovery: 'We are different!' Are you going fishing? No, I am going fishing.

The very theme of difference, whatever the differences are represented to be, is useful to the oppressing group: as long as such a group holds power, any difference established between itself and other groups validates the only difference of importance, namely, having power while others do not. The fact that blacks have 'a sense of rhythm' while whites do not is irrelevant and does not change the balance of power. On the contrary, any allegedly natural feature attributed to an oppressed group is used to imprison this group within the boundaries of a Nature which, since the group is oppressed, ideological confusion labels 'nature of oppressed person.' In the present context, since oppression is not over, to demand the right to Difference without analyzing its social character is to give back to the enemy an effective weapon.

To advocate a 'woman's language' and a means of expression that would be specifically feminine seems to us equally illusory. First, the so-called explored language extolled by some women writers seems to be linked, if not in its content at least by its style, to a trend propagated by literary schools governed by male masters. This language is therefore as academic and as 'masculine' as other languages. Secondly, it is at times said that woman's language is closer to the body, to sexual pleasure, to direct sensations, and so on, which means that the body could express itself directly without social mediation and that, moreover, this closeness to the body and to nature would be subversive. In our opinion, there is no such thing as a direct relation to the body. To advocate a direct relation to the body is therefore not subversive because it is equivalent to denying the reality and the strength of social mediations, the very same ones that oppress us in our bodies. At most, one would advocate a different socialization of the body, but without searching for a true and eternal nature, for this search takes us away from the most effective struggle against the socio-historical contexts in which human beings are and will always be trapped. If there is one natural characteristic of human beings, it is that human beings are by nature social beings.

Translated by Yvonne Rochette-Ozzello

NOTE

2   The tendency to 'nominalize' is characteristic of contemporary theoretical discourse in France and corresponds to the preoccupation with process. — Tr.

CATHERINE CLEMENT
'Enslaved Enclave', *New French Feminisms*

'*Bravo, sir.*' A woman, among the others, sends forth this salutation from the balcony. It tumbles, falls. To speak, then, and still worse, to put oneself in a public position of theoretical premeditation, is to assume the position of 'the man.' That explains the shouts, mimicking, gestures, and, soon, the piercing cries of 'Hey, hey'; though theory and articulated speech are inadmissible, shouted speech is allowed. In other words, more seriously and irremediably: that would mean that dialectics, for example — but there is nothing else — would be inaccessible to women, and it then becomes impossible to understand all contradiction and hence, all struggle. That would mean that by their nature — innate or acquired in oppression — women could not use thought to help free themselves; that the only scansion of violence permitted them is obtuse, unthinking in its expression. That would mean that language is always masculine, that it is determined according to sex, and that discursiveness is not an integral part of feminine discourse. Even if somewhere it is true that rhetoric and vocabulary are formed by centuries of male cultural domination, to renounce the exercise of thought, to give it to them, is *to perpetuate*, as always when it is a matter of 'not being part of the system.' 'Be a feminist and shout'; an unchanged variant of 'Be beautiful and keep your tongue.'

Translated by Marilyn R. Schuster

DOMNA C. STANTON
'Language and Revolution: The Franco-American Dis-Connection', *The Future of Difference*

No less disturbing is the facile rejection of *écriture féminine* as too intellectual and elitist to be feminist. Admittedly, our understanding of Cixous, Kristeva, Irigaray, and others requires knowledge of philosophy, linguistics, and psychoanalytic theory. Even more, one must be willing to decipher dense texts replete with plays on words and devoid of normal syntactical constructions. Through their very mode of writing, however, these texts are striving to practice what they preach by subverting the syntax, the semantics, and even the Cartesian logic of the Logos. As Kristeva has written, '. . . playful language ergo disrupted law, violated, pluralized, maintained solely to allow a poly-valent, poly-logic game which leads to a conflagration of the essence of the Law. . . .'[35] We American feminists tend to consider such wordplay virtuosic and exhibitionistic. We ignore the paradoxical disjunction between *what* we say and *how* we say it, and thus we continue to speak *about* subverting the patriarchal order in pellucid rationalistic discourse. Indeed, the charge of intellectualism and elitism directed at *écriture féminine*

is connected to a serious lack of awareness about the nature of our own
critical practice that verges on bad faith. Viewed within their specific
contexts, Anglo-American feminist empiricism is certainly not any less
intellectual than *écriture féminine*. The opposite could in fact be argued: for
écriture féminine not only combines theory with a subjectivism that
confounds the protocols of scholarly discourse, it also strives to break the
phallologic boundaries between critical analysis, essay, fiction, and poetry.
Moreover, those who maintain that *écriture féminine* is not feminist because
it appropriates concepts from such 'seminal' thinkers as Saussure, Freud,
Lacan, and Derrida choose to forget that it was not feminists but Anglo-
American patriarchs who founded, and trained us in, the biographical,
thematic, stylistic, sociohistorical, or Marxist literary criticism that we
unquestioningly practice. Instead of blinding ourselves to the academic
origins and present boundaries of our critical discourse, we should
acknowledge that, when compared to the work of other women in our
society, feminist scholarship is fundamentally both intellectual and
privileged. That admission, however, should not be the cause for futile self-
flagellation. Nor should it compound the existing, nefarious tendency to
assign intellectuality, the capacity for abstraction and speculation, and the
use of rigorous modes of analysis to the male, and intuitiveness, sensibility,
and emotionality to the female — a type of thinking which validates
traditional stereotypes, reinforces the tyranny of the binary, and thus
strengthens the phallologocentric order. Rather, we should celebrate our
own and all women's heterogeneous contributions to the demolition of the
old and the building of a new order of thought and being.

   This is not to suggest, however, that the presuppositions and goals of
écriture féminine should be espoused without serious examination. American
and French women should interrogate the premise that the global subversion
of the Logos can be achieved through language, and we should question the
proposition that there *can* exist a locus outside of the symbolic order from
which woman might speak her difference. In *Les Guérillères* (1969), for
example, Monique Wittig endorsed the notion that there is no reality outside
the symbolic.[36] But whereas in that epic work she argued 'that in the first
place the vocabulary of every language is to be examined, modified, turned
upside down, that every word must be screened,'[37] in her recent paper 'The
Straight Mind,' Wittig insists that emphasis on language has made French
women writers lose sight of material reality[38] — a view which many
American feminists might echo. We should also point out that French
theorizing on the subversion of the Logos has tended to replace, and not
merely to supplement, the kind of political activism which Americans
consider crucial to their self-definition as feminists. Last, and as some recent
French texts seem to confirm, a dis-connection with the *real* can lead to a
regressive mystification of the 'feminine' and may yield nothing more than a
new 'lingo,' a code doomed to repetition and extinction.[39]

NOTES

35 Kristeva, 'Un Nouveau type d'intellectuel: Le Dissident,' *Tel Quel* 74 ['Recherches féminines'] (Winter 1977): 5. '. . . Langue enjouée donc loi bouleversée, violée, pluralisée, maintenue uniquement pour permettre un jeu polyvalent, polylogique, qui conduit à l'embrasement de l'être de la loi. . . .'

36 Monique Wittig, *Les Guérillères* (New York: Avon Books, 1973), trans. David Le Vay, p. 134.

37 Ibid.

38 See 'The Straight Mind,' *Questions féministes* 7 (December 1979); and *Feminist Issues* 1, 1 (Summer 1980).

39 In my view, this danger is immanent in the recurring identification of the female in *écriture féminine* with madness, antireason, primitive darkness, mystery, self-diffusion, and self-irridiation, traits which represent a revalorization of traditional 'feminine' stereotypes. I discuss this problem briefly in 'Parole et écriture: Women's Studies, USA,' *Tel Quel* 71—73 (Autumn 1977): 126. Françoise Colin, an editor of *Les Cahiers du GRIF*, has noted the danger signals of a new female 'lingo' and stressed the need for multiplicity and heterogeneity in 'polyglo(u)ssons' in *Les Cahiers du GRIF* 12 ['Parlez-vous française?: femmes et langages I'] (June 1976): 3—9.